GENES, MEMES AND HUMAN HISTORY

Stephen Shennan

GENES, MEMES AND HUMAN HISTORY

DARWINIAN ARCHAEOLOGY
AND CULTURAL EVOLUTION

with 47 illustrations

For Sophie and Henry

First published in hardcover in the United States of America
in 2003 by Thames & Hudson Inc., 500 Fifth Avenue,
New York, New York 10110

thamesandhudsonusa.com

Library of Congress Catalog Card Number 2002102984
ISBN 0-500-05118-6

Printed and bound in Slovenia by Mladinska Knjiga

CONTENTS

PREFACE

THIS BOOK IS THE PRODUCT of a long gestation. In fact, I can remember precisely how my initial interest in evolutionary ideas was aroused. It was by reading Richard Dawkins' *The Selfish Gene* in the late 1970s. The sheer excitement of that experience has remained with me. The lucidity of the writing and the power and elegance of the ideas were exhilarating. The idea that animal social behaviour could be explained in terms of the evolutionary interests of their genes was something totally novel to someone whose background was in archaeology and anthropology, but its potential implications for the study of human societies and their history were very obvious. Dawkins went on to propose that the human case was not quite the same. He speculatively suggested that just as genes were passed on from generation to generation by biological reproduction, so there were discrete elements of culture, for which he coined the term 'meme', which could be passed on from one person to another and could lead to individuals acting in ways that benefited their memes rather than their genes.

At the time I couldn't see any way of doing anything with the meme idea in archaeology, despite what I felt to be its attractiveness, but I sought out the early attempts by anthropologists such as William Irons to understand human behaviour in terms of its implications for people's reproductive success and began to use some of these ideas in my teaching in the Department of Archaeology at the University of Southampton.

The next step came in 1986, when, on a visit to Cambridge, I found on the shelves of Heffers' bookshop a book called *Culture and the Evolutionary Process* by Robert Boyd and Peter Richerson. Like *The Selfish Gene*, although not as accessible, it proved to be a revelation. It showed how human culture could be considered as an inheritance system, analogous to the genetic one but working in a different way, and used mathematical models to work out the concrete implications of cultural inheritance processes and how they would interact with genetic ones. In doing so it demonstrated that one did not have to make a prior commitment to cultural or biological explanations of human cultures and societies but that the aim should be to come up with concrete accounts of the factors operating in particular cases. These ideas too I gradually absorbed and they began to form part of my courses and, in a very tentative way, my publications.

However, most of my energies at this time were absorbed with carrying out and publishing fieldwork related to an earlier research agenda on the role of metallurgy in the origins of the social hierarchies of the European Bronze Age and I was only able really to turn my attention to evolutionary matters in the mid-1990s, when I moved from the Department of Archaeology at Southampton to the Institute of Archaeology at University College London. A couple of years later I was discussing with the Brazilian archaeologist, Eduardo Neves, the possibility of giving some lectures at the University of Sao Paulo, on a visit to Brazil, and suggested doing something on evolutionary approaches in archaeology. In the event the course never happened but the germ of an idea was formed, which turned eventually into this book.

The title deserves some explanation. The book contains very little about the specifics of human genes and in Chapter 3 I express considerable reservations about the role and reality of memes in the strict sense, conceived as specific, discrete cultural elements copied from one person to another. Nevertheless, genes and memes, considered in a broad sense, encapsulate the two ideas which are central to the book. First, many of the main patterns in human history can be understood in the light of the fact that humans, like other animals, are the outcome of a long history of natural selection based on differential reproductive success. Second, this is not the whole story. Dawkins was right in proposing that cultural inheritance – the meme idea in its broad sense – does make a difference. Precisely what that difference is we are only just beginning to explore. The Darwinian theory of memes is a long way behind its genetic equivalent. This book is an attempt to think through the implications of a biological and cultural evolutionary framework for archaeology and to see what archaeology has to contribute to the development of the framework itself.

INTRODUCTION:
WHY DARWINIAN ARCHAEOLOGY?

FOR A DISCIPLINE SUPPOSEDLY CONCERNED with the past, archaeology today is more than ever subject to the tyranny of the present. Its ideas are reduced to their sources in contemporary or recent society and subject to retrospective disapproval. With the rise of the cultural heritage movement, key debates about interpretations have increasingly become centred on who owns them, rather than on their validity as representations of some aspect of past reality. Furthermore, the focus of interpretation in archaeology today is increasingly on those aspects of the past which place archaeologists in the role of ethnographers of a lost 'ethnographic present', struggling hopelessly to overcome the problems posed by the fact that the people they would like to talk to are long dead and most of the residues of their lives long decayed. One example of this is the current preoccupation with how prehistoric people might have perceived and experienced past landscapes. Such studies generally leave it very unclear whether the perceptions and experiences proposed are those of the investigator or the past people whose lives are supposedly being studied. Finally, archaeologists' desire to see people in the past as the active knowledgeable agents we naïvely believe ourselves to be, has meant that they want to see all change as the outcome of the conscious choices of individuals with existentialist mentalities walking clear-sightedly into the future.[1]

In contrast, the starting assumption of this book is that the main aim of archaeology is to obtain valid knowledge about the past. In a world increasingly dominated by images and brands, rather than material commodities, studies of how images and ideas from the past are used for political and economic advantage are going to become ever more important. Nevertheless, this does not mean that the growth of such 'cultural heritage' studies, important though they are, should be allowed to displace an archaeology concerned with finding out about the past. This book tries to show that archaeologists do not need to be failed ethnographers, forever regretting the demise of the people they would like to talk to. It argues that there are patterns in the past which we can discern retrospectively, but of which people at the time would have been only dimly and partially aware at best. These patterns can only be described and explained from the point of view of the present-day archaeologist, using appropriate theoretical tools. This does not mean that archaeology is condemned to produce accounts of 'progress' leading up to the present. Rather, it means that archaeology should investigate the past in a way that plays to archaeologists' strengths. These undoubtedly lie in the characterization of long-term patterning in past societies and their material products. This takes us away from dubious attempts to write prehistory as a tabloid human-interest story about people's supposed 'lived experience', but that is not a loss. Making sense of patterns and processes in world prehistory is both a lot more interesting and a lot more important.[2]

To a considerable extent, archaeology has abdicated its responsibility in this respect as a result of the rise of post-modernism, which has largely killed off grand narratives across the social and historical disciplines. The great materialist stories, whether the rise of civilization or the rise of class exploitation and capitalism, have come to be seen as Eurocentric origin myths. It is suggested that there are no empirical foundations to knowledge, only a constant play of verbal difference, in which arguments are endlessly undermined and exposed as situated in relation to particular contexts and interests. In archaeology the impact of these ideas has been heralded, with some justification, as a much-needed loss of innocence,[3] but it has also led to a loss of nerve[4] and a loss of direction. If the archaeology of Eurocentric origin myths has been exposed for what it is, what sort of framework for the identification and explanation of long-term patterns is there, in Europe or anywhere else?

The object of this book is to propose that recent developments in the application of Darwinian evolutionary ideas to the study of human behaviour can provide such a framework. More than that, archaeology can actually contribute to the development of the ideas, because it is the *only* subject that can tell us what past behaviour was like in the vast majority of past societies that were non-literate. The attraction of such ideas is not simply that they represent the opposite pole of the contemporary *Zeitgeist* to post-modernism, nor that they give direction to a discipline now badly in need of one. On the contrary, as I will try to show, it arises from the fact that they make greater sense of a lot of the things that archaeologists have always done, but often in a rather unreflecting kind of way and without a clear understanding of why they apparently work. Nevertheless, for many archaeologists the claim that Darwinian ideas have a contribution to make is a controversial one, for reasons that pertain within most domains of social and cultural studies, and others that are specific to archaeology.

The general reasons are well known. When it is applied to humanity, Darwinism is seen by many as a philosophy of biological determinism that has had catastrophic effects on human history. Darwinian ideas were first a focus of general interest outside of biology in the social and historical disciplines over 100 years ago, following on the publication of *On the Origin of Species* (1859) and *The Descent of Man* (1871), when social Darwinism was seen as providing a 'scientific' justification for late-19th-century racism and imperialism, which in turn provided the foundation for the racist biological determinism of the Nazis. In the late 20th century the beginning of the appearance of Darwinian ideas on the public stage may be identified with the publication of E. O. Wilson's *Sociobiology: A New Synthesis* (1975) and Richard Dawkins' *The Selfish Gene* (1976).

Wilson's book was not a technical scientific treatise but a large-format book for the general reader. It presented the argument that patterns of animal social behaviour were explicable in terms of the operation of processes of natural selection, and the argument was supported by detailed case studies, especially of the social insects on which Wilson was an expert. However, what attracted the public attention was Wilson's suggestion that the same principles could be applied to the study of human social behaviour, and that one day, when benighted social scientists either saw the light or had died out, the human social sciences would become a branch of evolutionary biology.

Dawkins presented broadly the same stock of recently developed ideas in evolutionary biology to the general public in *The Selfish Gene*. With clarity and brilliance, he developed the argument that animal social behaviour in general, and altruism in particular, were controlled by the selfish 'interests' of the animals' genes, dictated by natural selection. Individual creatures were no more than vehicles driven by their genes; they would die but successful genes would be transmitted through the generations. Although, like Wilson's, the book concerned animal behaviour in general, the anthropomorphic language made it difficult to avoid the implication that what was being said applied just as much to humans as to other animals. At the end of the book Dawkins addressed this issue by trying to provide humanity with a get-out clause: humans do not just have genes, they have culture. Just as genes are passed on and provide the basis for biological inheritance, so a process of cultural inheritance operates through the passing on of 'memes', units of cultural information. Because these are passed on by very different mecha-

nisms from genes, they provide a basis for humanity to accept and spread
ideas which can overcome 'the tyranny of the genes'. The success of the
meme concept in at least one sense is not in doubt: it has become so widely
used that it is now in the *Oxford English Dictionary*. But to many, especially in
the social sciences, even memes seemed like just another form of determinism: if individuals were not driven by their genes it was because their minds
were being parasitized by memes. Either way, they did not have much autonomy or control over their own destiny. Unsurprisingly, the ideas generated
both wide interest and great hostility.

Apart from what was seen as the imperialistic hubris of biologists
wanting to take over the social sciences – actually, not necessarily an unpopu-
lar cause with the public at large – the sociobiologists, as they came to be
known, were seen as providing an ideological justification for right-wing
political positions, in the same way as social Darwinism had done a century
earlier. Biology was destiny and people's fates lay not in their actions but in
their genes. This was the time of the beginning of the Reagan-Thatcher
political ascendancy in the Anglo-American world and the ideas seemed to fit
in a number of ways. For example, at a time when feminists were arguing that
societies needed to change to overcome the oppression of half the human
race, sociobiology seemed to be suggesting that the different roles of males
and females in society arose as a result of their different biological attributes,
so that nothing could or should be done about it: the inference seemed to be
that women were naturally drawn to the kitchen sink and did not need to be
chained to it. At the same time, by suggesting that altruism was simply the
outcome of selfish individualistic interests when the calculations were done
in the right way, it appeared to provide a basis for attacking social welfare
programmes and for suggesting that the core social and economic processes
involve competitive interactions between individuals; in Margaret
Thatcher's words, 'there is no such thing as society'. If the implications
really were as they were claimed, then to anyone but right-wing ideologues
there were excellent reasons to have nothing to do with evolutionary biological explanations. Anything other than total rejection was easily seen as
'supping with the devil', and no spoon could be long enough for this.[5]

However, Darwinian ideas have also impinged recently on the world at
large for a more specific reason: the rise of molecular genetics. The Human
Genome Project, the flagship scientific project of the late 20th century, has
been given huge publicity. It recently completed the first stage of its goal of
mapping the full list of human genes, an event which was headline news. It is

now widely known that certain diseases are genetic in origin, and that even where they are not, there are major differences in individual susceptibility to specific diseases as a result of genetic differences between them. Newspapers have discussed not just genetically modified food or animal cloning but the (widely misunderstood) concept of 'mitochondrial Eve' as the origin of the human race.[6] The extraction of ancient DNA from the skeleton of a Neanderthal human,[7] and its evolutionary implications, attracted worldwide interest. Small wonder then that many people have become prepared to entertain the possibility that our genes have a greater role in our lives than was previously thought and, since the key to understanding genetic evolution is modern Darwinian theory, to accept that the latter is relevant to us as well. In this sense, sociobiology and molecular genetics seem to some to converge on a revised biological determinism, potentially as open to abuse as its social Darwinist predecessor and equally negative in its implications for the social sciences. That is not the case. However, it is not the task of this book to address general misconceptions about the application of evolutionary concepts to the study of human societies. This has already been done well by others.[8] The aim here is to explore their implications for archaeology.

The general point about the role of molecular genetics in altering public perceptions leads on to a quite specific reason why archaeologists have become concerned about such developments. Geneticists have begun to use their growing knowledge of human genetic variation to rewrite human prehistory; in other words, to usurp the role of archaeologists as some would see it. To name just a few examples, patterns of present-day genetic variation have been used to suggest that modern humans originated in Africa between 200,000 and 100,000 years ago,[9] to chart the colonization of Polynesia,[10] and to suggest that the spread of agriculture into Europe 9,000–7,000 years ago involved a significant expansion or movement of population from the Near East, as well as to suggest that it didn't![11] Moreover, this work has attracted a great deal of media interest. Archaeologists, on the other hand, and the historical linguists who are also involved in some of the debates, rightly accuse geneticists of often being very naïve in the way they interpret their results.[12] The links between gene patterns in present-day samples and the past history which geneticists often claim they relate to are by no means straightforward. In one sense, however, archaeologists only have themselves to blame. If the 'loss of nerve' leads to failure to address big questions which are of real interest to people, is it any wonder that someone else comes along and fills the gap, especially if they apparently have a new and powerful method for doing so?

In the light of all the dubious baggage described above, it may seem at best misguided to advocate that archaeology should have an agenda in any way related to Darwinian ideas or biological evolution. Even if it wants to, though, archaeology cannot escape so easily. Some branches of the subject are actually concerned with the history of human biological evolution, from the first appearance of stone tools 2.5 million years ago, associated with early forms of hominins (the term now used to describe our early ancestors), at least to the appearance of modern humans 200,000–100,000 years ago, if not to around 25,000 years ago, when Neanderthal humans had finally become extinct[13] and what we recognize as 'modern human culture' was well established.

The transition from the archaeology of human evolution to the archaeology of modern humans has always posed problems for archaeologists. Even those archaeologists sceptical of evolutionary ideas will normally allow that the archaeological study of human biological evolution has to be seen in an evolutionary biological context. In fact, that context is often extended to include all societies that gain(ed) a living from hunting and gathering. Societies that had an agricultural subsistence base, on the other hand, were always looked at from a different, more socially oriented, theoretical perspective. One of the reasons the distinction has been such a strong one is that the boundary between foraging and agricultural societies has long been the basis of a division of labour among academic archaeologists, one group specializing in farmers, the other in foragers. However, a number of archaeologists have pointed out the problematical nature of this distinction, best encapsulated by Richard Bradley's comment that Neolithic farmers had social relations with one another, while their Mesolithic forager predecessors had ecological relations with hazel nuts!

Bradley wanted to extend Neolithic social archaeology backwards into the earlier past and show that social relations were important to foragers too.[14] The aim of this book is to take evolutionary archaeology forwards, but also to show that it is about much more than relations with hazel nuts. In the course of doing this I hope that two things will become clear: the power of the approach in explaining many of the patterns we observe in the past, and the fact that Darwinian approaches do not necessarily have the dubious implications that many, if not most, archaeologists believe; in particular they are much more about the importance of historical trajectories, situationally appropriate strategies and differences in interests than differences in human capacities.

DARWINIAN ARCHAEOLOGY: AN INTRODUCTION

Like most such labels, Darwinian archaeology covers an enormous range of different, often mutually antagonistic views. The unifying element is that all of these views draw on aspects of the modern neo-Darwinian evolutionary synthesis in biology in attempting to explain patterns of cultural stability and change. What they do with it though is very different. In later chapters we will look at all these differences in detail, but it is important to sketch the map of the territory at the beginning and outline what Eric Alden Smith[15] has recently called 'three styles in the evolutionary analysis of human behaviour'. All of them are currently in use in archaeology.

Evolutionary psychology takes the view that the make-up of the modern human mind can only be understood in the light of its evolutionary history and the forces that have acted on it. One of its key assumptions is that the human mind is modular, made up of a linked set of special-purpose modules which perform particular tasks. The selective pressures that shaped these mechanisms acted over the millions of years of human evolution after we separated from other primate lineages, in the so-called 'environment of evolutionary adaptedness' (or EEA for short). In principle this approach directs attention to the behavioural evolution of modern humans and their ancestors over the long term and should therefore assign a prominent role to archaeology. In practice, evolutionary psychologists tend to make generic assumptions about factors relevant to the behaviour of Pleistocene hunter-gatherers, for example that they would have lived in small groups and depended heavily on reciprocity, and do not take too much interest in what archaeology might be able to tell them about what people actually did. It follows from the evolutionary psychology approach that what people do in the present, or did in the recent past, cannot be assumed to be adaptive to present circumstances, because the psychological mechanisms leading to action were created in the distant past. For example, the adaptive desire of our ancestors for fruit that was sweet and therefore ripe leads to bad dietary habits and obesity in modern, urban societies.

Steven Mithen's book, *The Prehistory of the Mind* (1996), is the best example of an archaeological approach to evolutionary psychology, and specifically addresses the need for evolutionary psychology to deal with the evidence for prehistoric behaviour, rather than just assumptions about it.

The second style represents what we might call the classical Darwinian view, drawing its inspiration from the assumption that in evolutionary terms humans are little different from any other animal, simply another unique species. Accordingly, we can assume that, since humans are the outcome of a long history of natural selection – a long line of reproductively successful ancestors – they have a propensity to take decisions, consciously or unconsciously, in the light of the costs and benefits of the consequences of those decisions for their future reproductive success. What explains diversity in behaviour in the present and recent past is the different pay-offs for different courses of action in different environments. Humans can weigh up these and respond to them thanks to the flexibility of their behaviour. It is generally assumed that culture does not make much difference in this process because any cultural behaviour which leads to deviation from the best outcome in terms of the reproductive cost-benefit calculus will not last very long.[16] The best-known substantive approach based on these assumptions is optimal foraging theory, which will be described in a later chapter. It generates predictions about the subsistence strategies which will give people the best cost-benefit outcome in any given set of circumstances and compares them with actual subsistence strategies, or, in the case of archaeology, compares their predicted residues with those found in the archaeological record. The evolutionary study of behaviour in this way is known as *behavioural ecology*.

The third of Smith's styles represents the view that variation in human behaviour cannot be explained solely in terms of criteria linked to reproductive success. Humans have a second inheritance system, culture, in addition to their genes. Cultural traditions are handed down from one generation, and indeed from one day, to the next, by specifically cultural mechanisms.[17] Since cultural inheritance operates in different ways from genetic inheritance, its dynamics can lead to outcomes that are different from those predicted by the requirements of reproductive success, including outcomes that are actually maladaptive from the reproductive point of view. However, the fact that humans have this second inheritance system is not a reason to reject the idea that evolutionary theory is relevant to people. Rather, we can explore the properties of the cultural inheritance system and how they relate to those of the biological inheritance system – the genes. The attraction of doing this is that the processes of biological evolution and genetic transmission, and the factors affecting them from one generation to the next, are much better understood than cultural transmission, so there may be much to be learned from exploring both the positive and negative analogies between the systems and the way they operate. This may lead to the development of useful theory that helps us to understand particular cases of cultural stability and change. The approach is generally known as dual inheritance theory and is particularly associated with Robert Boyd and Peter Richerson (1985).

The three different styles are summarized in the table below, taken from Smith's article. They are often seen as being in conflict with one another,[18] but as the table suggests they may be in some respects complementary, for example in terms of the time-scales at which they are relevant and the topics they address. Nevertheless, there are certainly situations, and we will see some of them later, where the different approaches have different explanatory implications. So long as we have methodologies for distinguishing between their implications this is a source of strength rather than weakness because we can play off the different approaches against one another and gain knowledge in this way.

This book will have very little to say about evolutionary psychology, but the behavioural-ecology and dual-inheritance-theory styles of evolutionary analysis, and the tensions between them, will be evident throughout. In fact, they relate closely to a long-standing debate in archaeology about the relative importance of adaptation and history in accounting for the patterns we find in the archaeological record.

Three Styles of Evolutionary Explanation

	Evolutionary psychology	Behavioural ecology	Dual inheritance theory
What is being explained:	Psychological mechanisms	Behavioural strategies	Cultural evolution
Key constraints:	Cognitive, genetic	Ecological, material	Structural, information
Temporal scale of adaptive change:	Long-term (genetic)	Short-term (phenotypic)	Medium-term (cultural)
Expected current adaptiveness:	Lowest	Highest	Intermediate
Hypothesis generation:	Informal inference	Optimality models	Population-level models
Hypothesis-testing methods:	Survey, lab experiment	Quantitative ethnographic observation	Mathematical modelling and simulation
Favoured topics:	Mating, parenting, sex differences	Subsistence, reproductive strategies	Large-scale cooperation, maladaptation

What is interesting though about Smith's table is that it does not mention archaeology at all as a relevant methodology for testing evolutionary hypotheses, when in fact it is crucial to all three of his approaches. Thus, a key implication of dual inheritance theory is that the specific features of people's cultural histories matter for what they do and the decisions they make at any given point in time. These things are not predictable simply from an analysis of the environmental context. Although attempts are now being made to infer the form and content of such traditions through the comparative analysis of present-day ethnographic data,[19] the archaeological record is the only source of direct evidence about them. Similarly, ethnographically based behavioural ecology cannot follow through the long-term implications of the cost-benefit decisions people make, for example over-exploitation leading to declines in favoured resources. Only the archaeological study of long-term change in subsistence patterns can do this. In short, archaeology has a vital contribution to make to the evolutionary analysis of human behaviour, so long as archaeologists can develop methods for putting the ideas into operation. As we will see, they have already been quite successful. Equally, the application of evolutionary ideas to archaeology can be a powerful means of explaining the patterns observed in the archaeological record.

THE ORGANIZATION OF THIS BOOK

In the light of this introduction the next two chapters develop and justify the framework of evolutionary theory which has been briefly outlined. Chapter 2 outlines the theoretical basis for the evolutionary study of animal behaviour, in terms of the implications of behaviour for the goal of maximizing reproductive success. This inevitably leads on to the key question of the extent to which behaviour is genetically determined. Genetic interests turn out to be quite complex, in that individuals can achieve reproductive success not just through themselves alone but through the efforts of their close relations that share genes in common. Nevertheless, despite the complexities, the key point about the theory of behavioural ecology is that it provides a basis for making predictions about how animals should behave in specific circumstances. These predictions can be compared with the results of observations of animal behaviour in a non-circular fashion to see if they are met.

Chapter 3 considers the argument that culture can be regarded as humanity's second inheritance system, in addition to the genes, and suggests that this perspective gives new insight into the nature of cultural dynamics of great importance for archaeologists. It examines the various routes along which cultural information is transmitted and the mechanisms by which transmission occurs. It also looks at the extent to which the processes of biological evolution – natural selection, mutation and drift – affect cultural traditions, as well as the implications of processes that are specific to cultural evolution. Lastly, it addresses the question of whether the cultural inheritance system can run counter to the genetic one in leading to human behaviour which is maladaptive from the biological reproductive success point of view but leads to greater cultural success.

With this theoretical framework established, we can turn to the specific issues where the application of evolutionary ideas to archaeology stands or falls in terms of the insight they provide. It follows from the importance of cultural inheritance that a key task for archaeology is the identification and characterization of cultural traditions and population histories. These represent the record of descent with modification. It is on these traditions and histories that evolutionary processes operate. Without a knowledge of them it is difficult if not impossible to explain the past. Studies of present-day gene distributions and historical linguistics are increasingly being used to infer such histories, but archaeology is the only discipline that provides direct information about them, in the form of variation in material culture objects and their distribution in time and space. This sort of study of cultural traditions goes right back to the beginning of archaeology as a discipline, under the name of culture history, but went out of fashion, at least in Anglo-American archaeology, 30–40 years ago. The object of Chapter 4 is to explore the issues it raises and to examine the extent to which an evolutionary approach provides a basis for reviving culture history in a new and more powerful guise, of central importance to understanding the past and also to the development and application of dual inheritance theory.

If Chapter 4 is concerned with documenting specific histories and traditions, the remaining ones are much more concerned with the processes affecting them. Chapter 5 deals with population, whose role in the explanation of culture change has long been a subject of inconclusive archaeological debate. It contends that the reason for the inconclusiveness is that archaeologists have looked at population in the wrong way, by imagining that it was something that people in the past tried to regulate at a group level. The Darwinian approach to demography looks at population patterns as the outcome of 'decisions' people make in the light of the costs and benefits of particular courses of action as they attempt to maximize their reproductive success. The pattern of costs and benefits varies in relation to such factors as the individual's age and the availability of resources at a particular place and time. This is the realm of life history theory. The chapter shows the way in which the theory makes sense of the large-scale population patterns which archaeologists can identify and explores some of the implications of population patterns for culture histories, not least the fact that the sizes of regional populations must have fluctuated considerably.

Chapter 6 deals with one of the areas of archaeology where evolutionary approaches are most developed: how and why people get their living in the way that they do. These questions are the subject of optimal foraging theory, which generates expectations and predictions on the basis of the evolutionary assumptions already described. Such approaches are most often applied to the anthropological and archaeological study of the foraging decisions of hunter-gatherers, and are the basis for the jibe about foragers having ecological relations with hazel nuts mentioned earlier. In fact, as we shall see, optimal foraging theory can illuminate the study of any economic system, including production for exchange. Furthermore, it provides a basis for understanding patterns of change which archaeologists have long observed and partially explained, but without being able to place their explanations in a coherent framework. More importantly, though, when the archaeology of subsistence is looked at from an optimal foraging perspective, it provides crucial evidence for current debates about human exploitation of the world's resources. Finally, no consideration of human subsistence systems would be complete without considering the role of technology in affecting patterns of costs and benefits.

The aim of Chapter 7 is to present an evolutionary approach to the archaeological study of male-female relations, based on the theory of sexual selection. Given the history of debate on this issue, it is perhaps the most controversial of all the different topics with which this book is concerned. It is proposed that the evolutionary approach leads to productive programmes of archaeological research and makes male-female relations central to the archaeological study of past societies, rather than placing it in some sort of special-interest 'ghetto', where it has tended to remain until now, despite the best efforts of its advocates. Without such a theoretical basis, archaeological case studies of male-female relations will never amount to much more than a series of disconnected observations and reconstructions, limited in their scope because of the shortcomings of the archaeological record.

One of the features to emerge from Chapter 7 is that variation in sex and gender relations can only be understood in a broader social context, and it is this broader context that is the subject of chapters 8 and 9. Chapter 8 begins with a discussion of the shortcomings of traditional archaeological approaches to the reconstruction and explanation of past societies based on the idea of progressive 'social evolution'. Darwinian approaches based on evolutionary game theory offer a different perspective on these issues, which leads to different research agendas. For example, with their insistence on starting at the level of the individual, they do not assume that societies will exist as functioning entities but raise the question of how any sort of social order can come into existence and be maintained. Social institutions represent widespread patterns of expected behaviour that give good pay-offs to those who use them when they interact with others. The chapter goes on to examine the role and significance of different sources of social inequality. In particular, it argues that the appearance of the private ownership of enduring resources makes a major difference to subsequent forms of social order. This is because, through such social institutions as inheritance, storage and market-type exchange, the value of controlling increasing quantities of resources can go on increasing: the rich can get richer.

Chapter 9, in contrast, explores inter- rather than intra-group relations. It shows that group selection, the overriding of individual benefits by group benefits, can emerge as a result of inter-group competition, especially if this involves warfare. On the other hand, patterns of inter-group cooperation can also arise which provide benefits at the individual level to those involved. Using archaeological evidence it is possible to trace trajectories through time from cooperative to hostile inter-group relations and back again. The higher levels of organization that emerge from group selection and analogous processes have some of the features of 'superorganisms', reviving the 19th-century organic analogy for society.

The concluding chapter brings the various threads of the book together and sketches out some directions for future work, re-emphasizing the particular contribution that archaeology has to offer to evolutionary studies of human behaviour, as well as the light evolutionary ideas throw on the patterning we find in the archaeological record.

-2-

BEHAVIOURAL ECOLOGY:
THE EVOLUTIONARY STUDY OF BEHAVIOUR

SO LONG AS STUDIES of biological evolution focused on the morphology of animals, they were in some respects relatively uncontroversial once the initial mid-19th-century shock of removing God from a role in creation had passed. However, after World War II, some biologists turned to the evolutionary study of animal behaviour. This involved looking at behaviour in terms of selection; that is to say, looking at how variations in behaviour relate to variations in survival, in reproduction and in the rearing of offspring. It assumes, therefore, that behaviour is to some extent at least genetically determined. This is quite easy for us to imagine in the case of organisms such as insects, but at first sight it is harder to conceive in relation to more complex animals, which have a capacity for learning that can give them considerable behavioural flexibility. Nevertheless, while the extent of genetic determination is open to argument,[1] its existence is not in doubt. For example, a selective breeding experiment on a species of birds called blackcaps started off with a population which was three-quarters migratory and one-quarter resident. By breeding separately from migratory and non-migratory parents it was possible to produce varieties of blackcap which were either all migratory or all non-migratory, in three and six generations respectively.[2]

The claim that there is a link between behavioural differences among individuals and genetic differences does not necessarily imply that the version of the gene in one individual programmes one kind of behaviour and the version of the gene in the other programmes a different kind. What it does imply is that if we look at, for example, the feeding behaviour of a random sample of animals with the first version of the gene and compare it with the feeding behaviour of a random sample of animals with the second version, then there will be a difference of some kind in the average behaviour of the types, despite all the other factors which will obviously affect that feeding behaviour as well. Furthermore, if the difference has some effect on the survival and reproductive success of the individuals concerned, then the variation in the character, in this case feeding behaviour, will be under selection. Therefore, over the generations the more successful feeding behaviour will spread through the population. This will be so even if the difference is only slight and even if, as will inevitably be the case, many other factors also affect feeding success. We may not have much idea about the nature of the link between variation in the gene and variation in the behaviour, but this does not alter the fact that we can talk about genetic variation affecting behavioural variation in the situation just described, with the implication that in some respects at least the behaviour is under genetic control.[3]

Some authors express this situation by saying that there is a 'gene for' the behaviour concerned, but in my view this kind of statement has led to a great deal of the misunderstanding that makes many people so antagonistic to the idea that behaviour in complex animals is affected by their genes. Talking about average behavioural differences between samples of individuals with specific genetic differences is a lot less dramatic than talking about a 'gene for feeding behaviour' but a lot clearer.

In fact, the link may be even more indirect. It may be that there is no link of this kind between genes and a specific behaviour. The behaviour pattern, and the appropriate circumstances to use it, may simply be learned, either individually or from others. Nevertheless, if individuals vary for genetic reasons in their sensitivity to the environmental cues that indicate the appropriateness of particular forms of behaviour, there is still a gene-behaviour link.

A further alternative possibility is that individuals may simply have very general naturally selected psychological propensities, which vary in their strength between the members of a population and which again produce appropriate behaviour in specific circumstances as a result of learning. One example might be a propensity to avoid what is perceived to be unnecessary effort.

In fact, with few exceptions, little is known about the way in which specific behaviours are influenced by genes, because there are likely to be many genes involved and the interactions between them and the environments in which they are expressed are complex. For this reason behavioural ecologists ignore the details of the inheritance process and look at behaviour on the working assumption that it represents an adaptation produced by 'decision-rules' which are under selection. This approach is sometimes known as the 'phenotypic gambit',[4] and we will see plenty of examples of its use in later chapters. One of the most powerful ways of putting it into action is the comparative approach. This involves comparing the way a particular aspect of behaviour varies among a group of related species and assessing the extent to which the differences relate to differences in ecology.

Peter Jarman[5] carried out a study of African ungulate species such as dikdik and eland to discover the nature of the link there appeared to be between the different kinds of plant material they ate and differences in their movements, their social organization and the way they reacted to predators. He found that because of their higher metabolic rate the smaller species such as dikdik required higher-quality food, which tended to be found in the forest and to be scattered rather than concentrated, so it could not support large groups of animals. The result of this situation is that animals are dispersed and the best way of avoiding predators is to hide. In these circumstances pairs of males and females tend to occupy a territory together. Large species such as eland or buffalo, on the other hand, can eat poor-quality plant material which is available in large quantities on the plains, which can therefore support large groups. It is not necessary to defend a territory and it is also not possible to escape predators by hiding. Either fleeing or using the herd as a safety or defence mechanism are the only options. A further feature of herd-living is the potential it offers for the strongest males to control a number of females.

Clearly, there is no reason in principle for humans to be excluded from such cross-species comparisons or equally why the different units in the analysis should not be species but individual human societies whose similarities and differences we wish to explain.

OPTIMIZATION

The key principle behind behavioural ecology analyses of animal behaviour is the principle of optimization, which assumes that individuals will relate to their environments in ways which maximize their reproductive success. It is important to understand that its advocates are not claiming this as a valid empirical generalization about the state of the world. In fact, it is a framework for generating hypotheses[6]. If we can characterize the factors relevant to some aspect of the process of attaining reproductive success for a particular species in a particular environment, then we can ask whether the actual behaviour of that species matches our expectations. To make it work we have to be able to define (1) 'Actors', who are able in some sense to make decisions about courses of action; (2) A set of 'strategies' characterizing the range of courses of action available; (3) A 'currency' in terms of which the costs and benefits of the different courses of action can be evaluated by some conscious or unconscious mechanism; and (4) A set of constraints which have to be taken into account by the different strategies, and which affect their pay-offs.[7]

This framework is not tautological. We are not saying that anything that exists must be optimal, but that, given what we know about the specific context and behaviour under study, we can predict what will be optimal, for example, the foraging strategy with the best return for a given amount of effort. We can then see whether we find it or not.

Despite the potential problems with optimization, for example the fact that other processes besides natural selection affect organisms' evolutionary histories, animal behaviour studies have shown that what animals actually do often corresponds very closely to the predictions of optimization theory.

A good example of such a study is an analysis of the economics of carrying a load for starlings bringing back food to their young (see fig. 1).[8] The size of the load clearly has an important bearing on the rate at which the young can be fed and therefore on their likely survival. This provides a good reason to believe that there should be ongoing selective pressure for efficiency in bringing back food.

It might seem obvious that the answer is always to bring back the biggest load possible, but the situation is actually more complicated than this. The starlings feed their young on soil invertebrates called leatherjackets, which they obtain by poking their beak into the surface vegetation and then opening the beak slightly to spread the vegetation and expose their prey. This can be done very efficiently for the first couple of leatherjackets, but as the starling's beak becomes increasingly full it becomes increasingly inefficient, so that it takes longer and longer to find another prey item. The question is, at what point does it pay to fly back to the nest with what has already been collected, bearing in mind the travel time that this involves? If we ask what is likely to be the best option in evolutionary terms, a plausible answer is that which produces the best possible delivery rate of food to the young, because starlings that do this are likely to be at a selective advantage over those that don't.

By observing starling behaviour it is possible to see how long it takes to obtain one prey item, how long it takes for two, and so on. If we plot the number of prey against the time taken to obtain them, we see there is a curve of diminishing returns (fig. 1a). But the travelling time to reach a specific site at a given distance from the nest also has to be taken into account. Once we know this and the time taken to obtain different numbers of prey, we can find

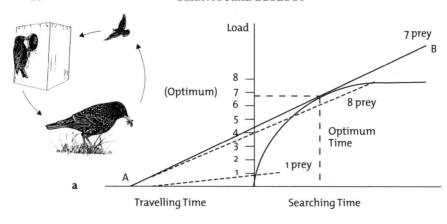

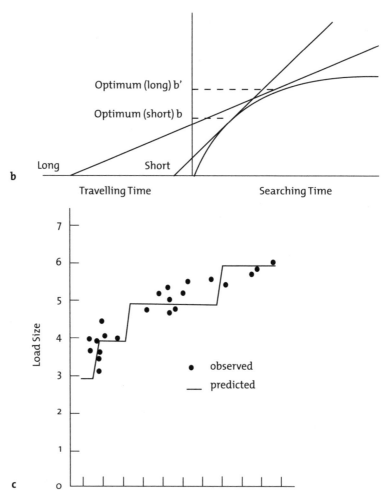

the most efficient load size. This is the straight line, taking into account the nest distance and touching the return rate curve, that gives the maximum slope. We can see from fig. 1a that in this case carrying a load of seven prey items gives the best return, better than eight and far better than one. However, this figure is not a constant. It depends on the distance of the feeding site from the nest (see fig. 1b). If the site is quite near, a better rate of return is obtained with a smaller load size. An experiment carried out by Alex Kacelnik[9] found that starling load-carrying behaviour matched closely the predictions of this model that starlings would be maximizing their delivery rate (see fig. 1c). The predictions derived from the hypothesis that they were trying to maximize their own energetic efficiency were not met. In other words, they were maximizing their delivery rate, not minimizing their own energy expenditure.

This leads to an important conclusion. Selection must have led to the evolution of proximate mechanisms which enable the starlings to behave in this way. They're clearly not drawing graphs in their heads! Selection is an important pressure which is not simply overwhelmed by all the other factors no doubt affecting their evolutionary history. Perhaps more important than this though is the fact that we gain information in those cases where our expectations are not met. This does not happen if we don't have the expectations. Without expectations we simply have another observation; with them we have an interesting puzzle.

1 *Finding the starling's optimum load size:* **a** *The horizontal axis shows time spent to obtain food to take back to the young. The vertical axis represents the load in terms of number of leatherjackets found and carried back to the nest. The curve shows the total number of leatherjackets found in relation to the time spent searching. The line AB represents the starling's maximum rate of delivery of food, which in this case is obtained by collecting and taking back a load of 7 leatherjackets on each trip. It takes into account travel time as well as search time. Two other lines, corresponding to loads of 1 and 8 leatherjackets, which produce lower rates of return, are also shown.* **b** *This shows how the amount of travel time affects the size of load that gives the best rate of return. When travel time is short the optimal load is smaller (at point b) than when it is longer (the optimum is at b').* **c** *This shows that starling behaviour did indeed correspond to the predictions of the model. As round trip time increased, the load size carried also increased. The predicted line is in steps because the load has to increase each time by one whole leatherjacket.*

LEVELS OF SELECTION

Thinking about behaviour as having evolutionary consequences in terms of the operation of selection raises complex issues about the way selection operates. If we are thinking about the evolution of the morphological features of an animal, for example, the evolution of fingers or flippers, we can see that potentially there is a clear relation between the specific form of the fingers or flippers of the individual and its reproductive success. The features concerned are specific to that individual. But this is not the case with behaviour, in a number of important ways. Suppose some aspect of the way beavers build their dams varies between beavers as a result of genetic variation between them. If variation in the resulting dams leads to some beavers being more reproductively successful than others, then in effect the beaver dams are under selection and we could even talk about a 'gene for dam-building'. In any event, the impact of the genetic variation extends far beyond the beaver's body. Similarly, if variations in an animal's signalling activities relate to genetic variation in some way, and if variations in the impact those signals have on other animals to which they are directed have an effect on the survival and/or reproductive success of the animal sending the signals, then these too will be under selection. A classic example of this is the manipulative signalling of young cuckoos begging for food in the nests of their foster parents, to the benefit of their own genes and the detriment of those of their foster-parents. This idea that the impact of genetic variation between individuals can extend far beyond the cells and body of the individual concerned is summed up in the term 'extended phenotype'.[10]

But this is not the only complicating consequence of seeing animal behaviour as under selection, nor is it the one that has produced the most, or the most heated, discussion. This has centred on an aspect of animal *social* behaviour, and specifically the issue of animal 'altruism', engaging in forms of behaviour beneficial to others rather than oneself. One of the most famous examples of such altruism proposed that the territoriality of male songbirds and the associated singing displays was a form of behaviour which was for the good of the species.[11] Birds arriving in the area would be able to assess whether it was already full or not. If it was, they would elect not to breed, because, if they did, they would be potentially threatening the adequacy of the food resources of the whole local population. This sort of explanation was rapidly shown to be unconvincing. If the decision to breed or not to breed had a genetic basis then the variant that selected for non-breeding would clearly stand no chance of spreading. More problematical still, if a mutation were to arise which led individuals to try to breed even if the area appeared to be full, then individuals with this mutation would be able to take advantage of the restraint of their potential competitors. Even if they had only limited success they would still be more successful than the 'altruists' so their genes would spread through the population, which would thereby become a population in which individual reproductive interests came first. Mathematical analysis demonstrated that in most circumstances selection for interests at the individual level will override interests at the group level, which tends to lead to the conclusion that competition between individuals is more important than cooperation.

However, if 'group selection' did not seem to work, how was it possible to account for what really did seem to be instances of animal 'altruism', for example, cases where an individual incurs danger by giving a warning of the presence of a predator and thus attracting notice to itself? Or those cases where two or more individuals cooperate to achieve some goal which seems to be to the benefit of only one of them? Two different answers have been provided to this question, both of which have been extremely influential; what they have in common is that both of them re-define altruism as a form of enlightened self-interest.

One is the concept of *reciprocal altruism*.[12] It was shown by Robert Trivers that cooperation could be maintained by individuals within a population, to their individual benefit, if the principle of their relationship was 'tit-for-tat'. Thus, if on first meeting one of the individuals offers a cooperative move, then the other will reciprocate. This will continue until one of the individuals makes a selfish, non-cooperative move, in which case the other will respond with a similarly selfish retaliation. While cooperation continues, both parties will benefit but no individual loses out more than once when interacting with another. In fact, 'tit-for-tat' turns out to be more or less the best possible strategy, in the sense that no other produces better returns. A great deal of work has been done exploring the 'pay-offs' of different interaction strategies between individuals and we will look at anthropological and archaeological applications of these ideas in Chapter 8.

One of the most famous animal examples concerns the regurgitation of blood by vampire bats.[13] It was discovered that bats which had failed to feed during the night often begged successfully for blood the next day in the roost from individuals which had succeeded in feeding, but this only occurred between close relatives or individuals that roosted together. Clearly, if such reciprocity is to work individuals have to be able to recognize one another and

refuse to feed any individual that has refused to feed them. It turned out that
bats which had received blood did reciprocate more often than would occur
by chance. It was also established that the gain to the hungry bat from being
given blood was greater than the loss to the well-fed one of giving it; in fact, it
could be the difference between life and death for the former, enabling it to
last long enough to try and feed again the next night.

The second answer to the question of the basis of altruism is the concept
of *inclusive fitness* developed by William Hamilton.[14] This involves the
assumption that variation in willingness to engage in self-sacrificial
behaviour is a genetically controlled trait. An animal which engages in self-
sacrificial behaviour may put itself at risk of death. However, the genetic
variant associated with greater self-sacrificial behaviour can spread through
the population if such self-sacrifice tends to lead to the survival of closely
related individuals. Thus, since offspring have 50% of their genes in common
with one of their parents, and full siblings are also 50% related, self-sacrificial
behaviour which leads to the saving of more than two offspring and/or
siblings can be successful in evolutionary terms, if the offspring and other
relations of non-altruistic individuals do not do so well. As usual in
evolutionary analyses, we have a calculus of the costs and benefits of
alternative strategies and those with the lower costs and higher benefits will
prevail.

It was the concepts of kin selection and inclusive fitness that made sense
of the otherwise extremely puzzling behaviour of such social insects as bees.
For specific genetic reasons female worker bees share 75% of their genes with
their sisters so that they gain a greater genetic benefit from rearing a reproductive sister than producing a daughter of their own.[15] This explains their
sterility, and also the suicidal behaviour of worker bees in stinging predators,
which leads to the death of the bee itself.

It is important to note that in accepting the idea of inclusive fitness we
have implicitly made an important shift in the level at which we see evolution
operating. Since we have seen that 'good of the species' arguments do not
work, and that genetic variants can persist and spread in a population even
when the variants are to the detriment of the individual that possesses them,
it seems clear that the level at which we have to look for the locus of evolutionary interest is not that of the population, and not even that of the
individual. Rather it is the genetic level: hence the selfish gene. Adoption of
the selfish-gene framework has been enormously stimulating of productive
new research in areas ranging from animal behaviour, where it has become

clear that groups of cooperating animals are usually closely related to one another, to the emergence of Darwinian medicine,[16] where it is now apparent that the 'interests' of the individual genes within an individual and those of the individual as a whole do not always coincide.

The idea that evolutionary studies should be gene-centred makes a lot of sense, since organisms die and only the genetic information continues through the generations. Dawkins suggested that individual organisms need be considered as no more than the temporary 'vehicles' for their long-lasting gene replicators. The latter, in effect, manipulate individual organisms into doing their will, or rather, acting in their interests. However, the philosopher David Hull suggested that it is better to consider organisms as 'interactors' rather than 'vehicles', because their role is more active than the latter word implies. Thus, an interactor 'denotes that entity which interacts, as a cohesive whole, directly with its environment in such a way that replication is differential – in other words, an entity on which selection acts directly'.[17] Evolution by natural selection is 'a process in which the differential extinction and proliferation of interactors cause the differential perpetuation of the replicators that produced them'.[18] Accordingly, accounts of both interactors and replicators are necessary if we are to study evolutionary processes. One cannot be reduced to the other.

This distinction also enables us now to see something which was initially not fully understood in the enthusiasm for gene-level selection. It was thought that by driving selection down, as it were, to the 'atomic' level of the 'selfish gene' then any idea of group selection had been finally eliminated. However, this is not the case. As Elliot Sober and David Sloan Wilson[19] have pointed out, we can agree that the genes are the replicators but that does not in itself determine what the relevant interactors are in a particular case. While individual organisms are very well-defined individual entities which can be seen as interacting and competing with one another, and within which there is relatively little internal conflict, this does not mean that they are the only possible interactors. It is increasingly clear that there are circumstances, such as strong inter-group competition, in which selection can act between groups and in which the coherence of the groups is not undermined by competition within the group at the individual level. Thus, while it is the genes as replicators that are transmitted through the generations, selection on interactors can potentially take place at a variety of different levels. We will have to explore this issue more fully in Chapter 9.

It is clear from this review of the evolutionary study of behaviour that it raises complex issues and these continue to be the subject of investigation and analysis by biologists and biological philosophers. In summary, behaviour can have an impact far beyond the body of the individual instigating that behaviour, in ways that have selective consequences for the individual concerned. Genetic interests are not restricted to individuals but dispersed through populations of related individuals. Reproductively successful strategies may be enhanced not only by competing with other individuals but also by cooperating with them under certain circumstances. Furthermore, because behaviour is a long way from genes in terms of causal chains connecting the two, it may be difficult to establish a link. The idea that there may be slight but systematic differences in behaviour between groups of individuals with different variants or versions of specific genes seems a reasonable one. Nevertheless, even this is not required: there may simply be genetic variation in sensitivity to environmental cues or in such general propensities as avoidance of unnecessary effort.

Of course, the evolutionary study of animal behaviour presupposes that the behaviour is oriented towards the achievement of survival and reproductive success. Nevertheless, the animals concerned are not aware that they have such aims. They are interested in much more proximate goals, such as obtaining the next meal, and even that not necessarily at a conscious level. But all this is immaterial to the operation of natural selection, which simply works on the outcomes of behaviour and their implications.

As we have seen in the case of starling load carrying, these ideas provide a basis for evolutionary biologists to build predictive models about what particular animals should be doing in a given set of circumstances, if their behaviour is governed by these evolutionary imperatives. Such predictions can then be tested in the field. Large numbers of studies carried out over the last 30 years in the field of animal behaviour amply testify to the ability of predictions based on these assumptions to make sense of field observations.[20] Furthermore, when evolutionary ecologists show, for example, that a certain animal foraging behaviour observed in the present is the one which produces the best returns in terms of energy per unit time, they are also implying that their conclusions are relevant to how that behaviour came to evolve in the first place, in the light of what we know about the emergence and continuity of the environmental conditions in which it is appropriate. That is to say, there was selection for a particular type of behaviour, or, in more complex animals, selection for the phenotypic flexibility, learning ability and sensitivity to environmental cues to respond appropriately.

THE BEHAVIOURAL ECOLOGY OF HUMANS

What about humans? As we have seen already, natural selection operates on organisms – on phenotypes, to varying degrees extended – but has its effects through the generations on genes. Those genes associated with better-adapted phenotypes are more successful than those associated with worse-adapted ones. Human phenotypes are more complex than those of other animals because culture makes up a far more significant part of them, a fact whose significance will be examined in detail in the next chapter. Since culture is not acquired genetically, the question arises whether our genes have any bearing on human behaviour. As we have seen, the answer to this question from the humanities and social science disciplines has always been a resounding no. In contrast, the dominant view among those who practice the behavioural ecological study of humans assumes that 'people tend to select behaviours from a range of variants whose net effect is to maximise their individual reproductive or inclusive fitness'.[21] This is not to say that people make conscious choices with this end in view, or that they lack intentionality. Nevertheless, the upshot of the decisions they make, consciously and un-consciously, is that they act in ways which an outside observer can recognize as conducive to their survival and reproductive success – to their fitness, in other words.

The reason for taking this view is that, as with other species, the history of evolution by natural selection has produced in us psychological capacities and propensities, not least our emotions, which predispose us to act in ways which lead to this end. Even though most of the variation we observe in people's behaviour arises through learning, by trial-and-error and from other people, the behavioural ecology expectation is that our inherited propensities will tend to make us 'opt for' fitness-enhancing behaviour.

As in the case of other animal species, this is the basis for the application of the principle of optimality to human behaviour, an application to which many have objected. Members of most human societies, they say, at least before the advent of capitalism, would not have optimized or maximized. To suggest that they did is to apply modern economic standards to societies where other, social, values would have been more important. More relevant, it is proposed, would have been 'satisficing', accepting what is 'good enough'.

As we have seen, however, the hypothesis of optimization is not self-verifying. We can predict what will be optimal in a given situation, for example, the foraging strategy that will give the best return for a given amount of effort. We can then see whether we find it or not. This is in contrast to the situation with 'satisficing'. As Eric Alden Smith and Bruce Winterhalder[22] point out, we do not have any basis for defining what is 'good enough'. The result is the kind of tautologous reasoning that has been so heavily criticized by those claiming that concepts of optimization are tautologous. In any event, in the evolutionary context what is 'good enough' at a given time is open to being superseded if something better comes along.

It has also been suggested that the concept of 'satisficing' is necessary to solve the problem that evolutionary actors never have perfect information about a given situation and therefore never know what is the best thing to do. However, we can gain much more understanding by assuming that information-gathering is a cost like any other, and including it in our optimization formulation. This point, in fact, plays an important role in recent theories about the origin of human culture, as we will see later on. In any case, as we saw earlier with the starling load carrying, studies suggest that complex animals have developed very effective cognitive 'rules of thumb' which lead to them making fitness-enhancing decisions on the basis of fairly simple environmental cues.

Finally, it is important to make clear that optimality principles are not immediately falsified by the fact that all cultures have their own particular standards of value and definitions of success. It is necessary to investigate empirically whether success in terms of the local criteria correlates with increased fitness; that is to say, whether the forms of behaviour which are successful in local cultural terms will tend to be successful in survival and reproductive terms for the individual that adopts them.

In conclusion, behavioural ecology provides a powerful and complex set of ideas for understanding animal behaviour in terms of its evolutionary consequences. In principle, since humans are a species which has evolved through natural selection, like any other, the same ideas can be applied to the study of human behaviour. Whether what people do corresponds to the predictions derived from optimality theory in particular cases is a matter for research rather than dogmatic assertion one way or the other. In later chapters of this book we will look in detail at the predictions of behavioural ecology with regard to a range of important areas of human social life to find out whether they fit or not. We will also have to deal with the specifically archaeological questions of how to apply the ideas when the evidence we have is not behavioural observation but the residues in the archaeological record.

Before doing this, however, it is necessary to examine the evolutionary consequences of the human reliance on learned culture, in particular the extent to which culture acts as an evolutionary system in its own right.

-3-

CULTURE AS AN EVOLUTIONARY SYSTEM

THE PREVIOUS CHAPTER left us with the idea that people have dispositions, shaped by natural selection, to use their capacity for flexible behaviour in ways likely to enhance their survival and reproductive success. Or at least this is a pretty good starting point for analysing human behaviour and its history as represented in the archaeological record. Furthermore, despite the complexity of the evolutionary study of animal behaviour, its general principles are now well understood and fall squarely within the general theory of Darwinian evolution. This is certainly not the case with the evolutionary study of culture, whose theoretical development is still very much ongoing.

It is important to be clear at the outset that the existence of cultural traditions complicates the study of human behaviour and its history from a Darwinian standpoint by adding two new possibilities to the way evolutionary change can take place:[1]

    1. Natural selection on people's survival and reproductive success can occur through selection on their cultural traditions, not simply on their genes via their genetically inherited dispositions.

    2. Processes of cultural selection can also operate, such that the frequencies of cultural attributes can change through time not as a result of natural selection affecting people's survival and reproductive success but as a result of conscious and unconscious decision-making based on a variety of criteria.

Sceptics might well ask why this latter sort of process should be considered from a Darwinian perspective at all. After all, isn't this the kind of thing archaeologists and anthropologists have studied successfully with well-established methods for a long time?[2] Even those who are favourable to the idea or are open-minded need to be shown why a Darwinian approach is justified and what it has to offer. For archaeologists, who deal with the 2.5-million-year record of human cultural evolution, the potential interest of an approach which claims to throw new light on cultural dynamics is obvious. Accordingly, the aims of this chapter are three-fold. The first is to present the argument that human culture can be considered as an inheritance system in quite specific and clearly defined ways, because if there is no inheritance there is no system for such Darwinian processes as selection to act upon. The conclusion that human culture does indeed have the properties of an inheritance system is reached on the basis of what we know about the mechanisms by which it is transmitted and of the patterns observable in various kinds of evidence. The second aim is to examine the routes of cultural transmission and the factors that affect what is transmitted, including the processes of selection, mutation and drift, as well as others that have no genetic parallel. Mutation, or more generally, change in what is transmitted, is also a requirement for the operation of a Darwinian system, for if inheritance were always perfect there would be no variation for selection and other processes to act on. Finally, we have to look at how and why such a parallel system for the transmission of adaptive information might have come into existence in the first place and why, once in existence, it had the potential to result in outcomes which run counter to the requirements of maximizing reproductive success.

INHERITANCE AND CULTURE

People tend to assume that the only valid model of an inheritance system is the genetic system based on DNA, but in fact this is only one very specific form of a much more generic process involving the transmission of information between entities. For example, epigenetic inheritance systems, that operate in the course of development rather than reproduction, are found in the cells of the body, ensuring that the functional and structural states of the cell continue to be perpetuated through cell divisions.[3] A very topical and unpleasant example of an inheritance system is 'mad cow disease'. Contact of normal brain proteins with the deformed shape of the prion proteins which are the disease agent leads to the prion as it were impressing its shape on the normal protein, which in turn becomes a new infective agent in a gradual process of degeneration.

In keeping with this general notion of inheritance I will follow the definition of it given by Eytan Avital and Eva Jablonka:[4] 'the regeneration of phenotypic traits and processes through the direct or indirect transmission of information between entities'.

We now need an appropriate definition of *culture,* that protean word that means so many different things to so many people and has been defined in so many different ways. The definition on which all the following discussion will be based is one given by Robert Boyd and Peter Richerson:[5] 'Culture is information capable of affecting individuals' phenotypes which they acquire from other conspecifics by teaching or imitation.'

The full implications of this rather terse definition will emerge in the course of the chapter, but it is important to draw attention to two features of it now. First, culture is not the same as behaviour; it influences behaviour's range of possibilities. What particular individuals *do* in any particular situation will be based on features of the situation in which they find themselves, as well as the cultural information they possess, consciously or unconsciously, relating to such contexts and ones like them. This was the point that the archaeologist Lewis Binford was making in his attacks on traditional culture-historical archaeology in the early 1960s.[6] What people do depends on factors in their environment (in the broad sense), as well as other things, not just on their stock of cultural ideas. When we see changes in the archaeological record we may be seeing changes in people's environments, physical and social, just as much as, if not more than, changes in ideas.[7]

Second, not all information capable of affecting people's phenotypes is cultural, only that acquired from other members of the same species. Thus, if I learn to make a stone tool by experimenting with striking pieces of stone together, what I learn does not count as cultural information. Rather, it is the sort of learning from interacting with the environment that is characteristic of many, if not most, animals. However, if my daughter learns by watching me then the practices she acquires in doing so count as cultural.

As we have seen, the significance of culture is disputed among evolutionists. Some behavioural ecologists and evolutionary psychologists see it as a relatively minor extension of biological evolution. Since the evolution of the human mind must have been shaped by natural selection, an individual's cultural attributes will be shaped by an adaptive rationale promoting beneficial decision-making even though they have been acquired by learning from a member of the same species.[8] On this view, culture, like any other learned behaviour, provides a means of achieving the normal evolutionary goals of survival, reproduction and successful parenting and doesn't have any cumulative consequences. To the extent that environments tend to remain the same through time, it will be appropriate to act in similar ways.

Those who adopt the dual-inheritance-theory framework described in Chapter 1, of whom I am one, do not accept that culture is to be regarded as little more than a minor extension of the phenotypic variation found throughout the natural world. In fact, some authors would argue the opposite: that the role of cultural traditions in evolutionary processes in the non-human animal world has been vastly under-rated.[9] These too, however, still maintain that culture must be seen in a Darwinian framework.

SOCIAL LEARNING

As we saw in the last chapter, most animals learn from their environment. Within an evolutionary context, learning may be seen as a form of adaptation which enables individuals to respond flexibly and appropriately to the contingencies they encounter. Like the blacksmith's strong arms, the knowledge acquired by an individual will not be passed on genetically to future generations. Genetic transmission will only be true of the capacity for learning, which will be selected for if the capacity is associated with greater reproductive success.

If learning is to provide a means of responding appropriately to contingencies in ways conducive to maximizing reproductive success, as the standard evolutionary view proposes, it requires the recognition of cause-and-effect relations, or the association between situations and events.[10] Individual trial-and-error learning has come to be distinguished from social learning, 'learning that takes some input from other individuals [of the same species]'.[11] In other words, social learning identifies, in broad terms, a way in which information is acquired, rather than a particular kind of information. The reasons why humans or animals should learn from other individuals of the same species rather than directly from their own experience are examined later in this chapter. The key point in the present context is that *social learning is the mechanism of cultural inheritance.*[12]

There is increasing evidence of the importance of social learning in a great variety of species and situations, albeit largely through quite simple cognitive mechanisms; for example, black rats in Israel have recently extended their range to include pine forests and young rats learn how to strip pine cones from their mothers.[13] Moreover, such work provides evidence not just of social learning but of the existence of learned traditions.[14] However, by common consent cultural traditions passed on by social learning play a far greater role in human adaptations than they do in those of other species. One of the most important reasons for this arises from the nature of those adaptations. While primate diets are largely composed of foods that are relatively easily collected, the most important food resources for human foragers are nutrient-dense plant foods and hunted game, whose exploitation demands

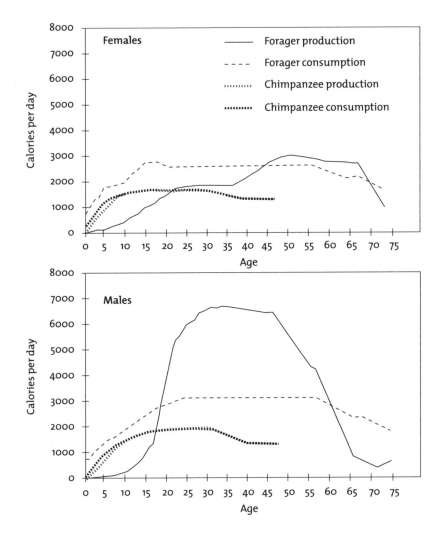

2 *Mean daily energy production and mean daily energy consumption per individual for males and females according to their age, calculated for chimpanzees and for human foragers, obtained by averaging over several groups.*

considerable knowledge. Acquiring such knowledge takes a long time: among the Hadza foragers of Tanzania, the tubers that provide the bulk of the calories are rarely acquired even by adolescents;[15] among the Ache foragers of Paraguay even 18–20-year-olds only acquire on average 1530 calories of meat per day whereas 25–50-year-olds acquire *c*.7000 calories per day.[16] A more general picture, based on several foraging groups, is shown in fig 2. The huge increase in male production from early adulthood is readily apparent. There is a similar but less marked pattern for females from late adolescence, although subsequent production is affected by child-bearing and it increases again when child-bearing years are over.

It is apparent, then, that the production of successful human offspring in a foraging context requires major parental investment, both in provisioning, and also in the transmission of relevant practical knowledge. The implications of this fact for human life-histories will be examined in Chapter 5. Significantly, one of the few instances where primates do make use of resources which are difficult to extract, the nut exploitation of the Tai forest chimpanzees in West Africa, provides one of the relatively few known examples of teaching in primates, and the techniques of extracting the contents of the nuts take years to learn.[17]

James Steele and I[18] compiled a table of information from ethnographic sources relating to the learning of traditional craft skills, such as pottery-making, and found that in all cases it was socially learned, and transmission was mainly if not entirely 'vertical/oblique' rather than 'horizontal'. That is to say, the learning path was from a parent or another individual of the older generation rather than from someone of the same age. In the vast majority of cases where the information was available, transmission was mainly from parent to offspring, and specifically to offspring of the same gender. In virtually all cases where information was available, the skill concerned took quite a long time to learn and was transmitted in the course of childhood/adolescence. In line with this, Barry Hewlett and Luca Cavalli-Sforza's[19] examination of the acquisition of day-to-day skills among Aka foragers in the tropical forest of Central Africa showed that the great majority of skills were learned from parents (in fact, the same gender parent in most cases), and that the learning process was largely complete by the age of 10 and almost entirely so by age 15.

An interesting study of this kind was carried out some years ago by Kenneth Ruddle,[20] who studied the acquisition of ecological and subsistence knowledge in a village in the Orinoco delta in Venezuela. Fig. 3 shows the ages at which particular tasks are learned. As children get older, for example, they are taken to the fields for the first time and boys are taught to use tools and techniques that require some physical strength, gradually moving on to

3 *The learning of task complexes on Guara Island in the Orinoco delta of Venezuela. The diagram shows the list of tasks, whether they are carried out by males or females, the age at which learning of them starts and the length of time it takes.*

Task	Sex		Age in Years (approx. range)
EARLY CHILDHOOD			
Household task complexes			
Messenger	X	X	2–5.5
Carry water and wood	X	X	5.5–8
Child care	X	X	5.5–8
Cooking	X	X	6–8.5
Laundering	X	X	6.5–8.5
Construction	X	X	6.5–8.5
Preparatory task complexes			
Identification of cultigens and animals	X	X	2–7
Care of domestic animals	X	X	3–8.5
Horseback riding	X	X	5.5–8.5
Use of machete	X		6–10
Swimming	X	X	2–4
Use of *piragua*	X	X	3–7
Line fishing	X	X	2–3
CULTIVATION			
Plant identification			
Plants in harvested state	X	X	2–4
Foodplants growing in dooryard garden	X	X	5–5.5
Ornaments and medicinals	X	X	5–6
Conuco plants	X	X	5–8.5
Natural vegetation	X	X	5.5–13
Harvesting			
Plants for home consumption			
Dooryard garden	X	X	5–7.5
Conuco plants	X		6.5–13
Larger root and tree crops	X		8.5–11.5
Berry and fruit	X		8.5–12.5
Coconuts	X		8.5–11
Commercial crops			
Observation	X		8.5–10.5
Packing crops	X		9.5–10.5
Cutting and harvesting own crops	X		11–13
Seed selection	X	X	
Sowing, Planting care			
Observation	X	X	7–8
Covering holes	X	X	8–10.5
Planting seeds	X	X	10–12
Use of digging stick	X		10.5–12.5
Transplanting tree crops	X		10.5–13
Interplanting	X		5–7
Weeding	X		
Cutting and Burning			
Observation – cutting	X		6–8
Cutting with machete	X		7–11
Cutting with axe	X		6–8
Observation – burning	X		9–10.5
Gathering and clearing	X		9.5–13
Actual burning	X		9.5–13
Marketing	X		9.5–13
Care and Construction of tools	X		
ANIMAL HUSBANDRY			
Identification and Care of			
Small Animals	X	X	2–4
Feeding Larger Animals	X	X	5.5–8
Herding Techniques	X		8.5–11.5
Taming and Training	X		8.5–13
Marking	X		8.5–13
Curing	X		8.5–13
FISHING			
Fish Identification	X	X	2–5.5
Line Fishing	X	X	5.5–8.5
Guaral	X		8.5–11
Casting Net	X		9.5–11
Harpoon	X		11.5–13
Bow and Arrow	X		12.5–13
Poisons	X		
HUNTING			
Animal Husbandry	X	X	2–5.5
Lizard Hunting	X		6.5–8
Netting Birds	X		8.5–11.5
Trapping Animals	X		9.5–13
Shooting Gun	X		9.5–13
Bow and Arrow	X		

more complex and difficult tasks. As fig. 3 also shows, there is quite a marked division between boys and girls in what is learned, which leads in adulthood to a corresponding difference in who does the teaching. The intensity of training is considerable. In fact, Ruddle found that the input of person-hours to instruction in food production made up 14% of the total labour input required for subsistence, a huge proportion of time which one suspects must have been under selective pressure,[21] although the paper gives no indication of this.

What it does make clear though is the implications of this teaching and learning process: the creation of a cultural tradition by a process of inheritance through social learning.

'A body of knowledge develops over generations to refer to the various activities involved in a given resource system, and takes on a linguistic form. For example, consider fishing:

> 1. Vocabularies define species, habitats, weather patterns, sea conditions, seasons, fish behaviour and the like.
> 2. A collection of "recipes" must be learned in order to fish both correctly and with consistent success.
> 3. Knowledge is also a channeling and controlling force that underlies fishing institutions.
> 4. In the persistence and crystallization of fishing institutions, knowledge becomes the objective description of the activity/institution.
> 5. An objective arena/field/ethnoscience of fishing develops in parallel with the activity of fishing.

This body of knowledge is transmitted to the next generation as an *objective truth* during socialization, and then it is internalized as *subjective reality*.'[22]

CULTURAL TRADITIONS

The studies described in the previous section have demonstrated the processes of cultural inheritance, as a specific variety of the more general inheritance process, but what about its outcomes? Boyd and Richerson[23] reviewed an extensive range of psychological and sociological evidence supporting the view that cultural transmission acts like an inheritance system, producing significant similarities between those passing on the information, either actively or by virtue of being observed and imitated, and those learning, which could not be accounted for by genetic transmission or continuity of environment. They concluded that, 'The calculated heritabilities for human behavioural traits are as high as or higher than measurements for behavioural and other phenotypic traits in natural populations of non-cultural organisms.'[24] In other words, when we look at the similarities and differences between parents and offspring in species where social learning plays no role and behaviour is governed solely by the consequences of genetic variation interacting with the environment, and compare the degree of similarity with that produced by cultural transmission in humans, we find that the measured heritability between parents and offspring is as great for traits passed on culturally as for those passed on genetically by biological reproduction: 'Thus, it may be that cultural transmission is as accurate and stable a mechanism of inheritance as genes.'[25]

Further evidence that cultural transmission is an inheritance system is provided by the existence of a cultural analogue of a phenomenon known as 'phylogenetic inertia'. In the case of biological evolution, change in a species may occur in response to environmental change, if the new environment favours the reproductive success of individuals with genes different from those that were previously successful. However, even if selection in favour of different genetic variants is quite strong, there is a limit to the speed with which change can occur. It is dependent, among other things, on the generation length of the creature concerned. If environmental change occurs more quickly than this, then for some time the distribution of characteristics within the species will not be the best possible one in the new circumstances. The fact that cultural traditions, like particular gene distributions, can persist in the face of changing environmental conditions to which different practices would be better adapted, suggests that they too act as an inheritance system which cannot respond instantaneously to new circumstances. People learn from older members of their society, who in turn learned from older individuals, and the knowledge passed on may be generations out of date if features of the social or natural environment start to change quickly. In these circumstances cultural patterns cannot be explained simply in terms of present-day adaptation but also need to be understood in terms of their past history.

A cross-cultural study by Guglielmino et al.[26] of a group of African societies examined a series of cultural traits characterizing different aspects of people's lives, material culture and organization, including family and kinship, economy, social stratification, division of labour by gender and physical features of the house. The object of the study was to examine the relative importance of vertical/oblique transmission and environmental adaptation in explaining the pattern of similarities and differences between the societies with regard to the traits concerned. It emerged that vertical/oblique transmission was the major process in accounting for the variation, having a major role with regard to the family, kinship and economic traits, and a significant one with regard to the social stratification and house attributes. In other words, it was the learning history of cultural inheritance from parents and other members of the older generation that largely determined what people did in many spheres of life, not what would be ideal from the adaptation point of view in the present circumstances.

Similarly, a study by Edgerton[27] of four East African groups examined the relative importance of culture history and ecological factors on a number of psychological variables. The results indicated that culture history played a major role in accounting for the patterns of variation.

Interestingly, the same phenomenon of phylogenetic inertia can also be seen in some animal traditions. A bird called the Mauritius kestrel traditionally nested in trees, but monkeys were introduced to the area and started preying on their eggs and chicks. The birds almost became extinct before they changed their behaviour and started nesting on rocks which were safe from predators.[28]

Of course, one of the major fields of evidence for the existence of cultural traditions which must have been passed on by social learning is the archaeological record and we will look at such archaeological traditions in the next chapter.

An important feature of traditions based on cultural inheritance is that they can be cumulative in nature, just as genetically-based evolution can be. In the case of genetic inheritance, misconceptions about its cumulative nature have led to inappropriate claims that random mutation and natural selection are improbable mechanisms for producing the complexities of the living world. They do not act like a whirlwind going through an aircraft factory and producing a Boeing 747 or monkeys randomly typing and producing the works of Shakespeare, to mention two widely cited comparisons. In fact, so long as innovations or mutations lead to an improvement in performance in some relevant sense, then, other things being equal, they will be retained and spread within the population by virtue of selection processes. Future possible innovations or mutations can build on them, leading to further improvements in performance which will in turn be positively selected. Jared Diamond's account of the differences in the architecture and decoration styles of the bowers of different populations of the same species of bower-bird in New Guinea suggests that animal traditions can also change cumulatively. Similarities between neighbouring bowers indicate that birds learn from their neighbours, while the role of learning in general in bower construction is very clear. Males take years to learn how to build good ones which will be attractive to females. Nor does ecological variation seem to account for the differences. The most plausible explanation seems to be the gradual accumulation of relatively arbitrary differences.[29] We need to develop an archaeology of bowers to find out!

A second important property of at least some forms of cultural inheritance is that it produces population level feedback effects. In other words, the frequency of a particular cultural trait within a population at a given time will depend on its frequency in the time period before, regardless of the features of the external environment. This is what is responsible for the phylogenetic inertia phenomenon that we saw earlier, but it obviously operates when selection is working in favour of a trait and not just against it. The prevalence of a particular positively selected trait cannot go from zero to 100% immediately, but only as a function of the strength of selection and the number of occurrences in the previous generation.

At this point we have arrived at the *dual inheritance theory* model described in Chapter 1 as one of Smith's three styles of evolutionary analysis. Humans have two systems of inheritance: the genetic system which they share with all living creatures and a cultural system which, although not unique to humans, is certainly developed to an unprecedented degree among them. As I have emphasized earlier in this chapter, we should not think of cultural inheritance as an unconvincing version of DNA-based genetic inheritance – both are versions of a more generic inheritance process realized in different ways and with their own specific features. Nevertheless, there are some attractions in exploring the analogies between the operation of the cultural inheritance system and the specifically genetic inheritance system. The processes of genetic transmission and evolution are much better understood than cultural transmission and evolution, so there may be something to be learned from exploring both the positive and negative analogies between the two systems and the way they operate. This process may lead to the development of useful theory which will help us to understand particular cases of cultural stability and change; equally, it may lead us in unhelpful directions, but even in the process of seeing why they're unhelpful we may learn something.

UNITS OF INHERITANCE

The natural question to ask when talking about inheritance is: what's being passed on? In the case of genetic transmission we know it is information embodied in strings of DNA, most importantly the genes, those sections of the DNA that code for the production of proteins. Exactly what is it in the case of cultural inheritance? This question is at the core of the best-known version of the analogy between cultural and genetic transmission: Richard Dawkins' concept of the *meme*,[30] already mentioned on a couple of occasions, which is based precisely on the idea of imitation as the passing on of copies of something from one person to another: 'A unit of particulate inheritance, hypothesised as analogous to the particulate gene, and as naturally selected by virtue of its phenotypic consequences on its own survival and replication in the cultural environment.'[31]

In other words, Dawkins sees memes as *replicators*, analogous to genes in the sense that they are things in the physical world that produce copies of themselves. They are subject to the same sorts of evolutionary forces as genes, especially selection, because they are inherited. They are, it is proposed, simply in a different medium: not DNA, but patterned neurological connections.[32] In order to be successful a meme must be characterized by (1) fidelity of copying, so that it changes only slowly; (2) by fecundity, in that it must be capable of generating multiple copies of itself; and (3) by sufficient longevity to be able to affect its own rate of replication. One consequence of this framework is that, just as genes can be considered 'selfish', in that the interests of the gene may clash with, or even override, the interests of the individual in whose body they are instantiated at a particular time, so memes too can be considered as 'cultural viruses'.[33] In other words, they parasitize the minds of individuals so that they act in the interests of the success of the meme rather than in their own interests (although what 'their own' means here raises a lot of questions!), or that of their genes. In an archaeological context, Ben Cullen[34] even suggested that items as diverse as pottery types and megalithic tombs could be seen in this way. The significance of the idea, and its own success in parasitizing minds, is indicated by the fact that it has now been taken up in the very practical field of marketing, where, in the field of fashion in particular, 'viral marketing' is now being adopted as a sales tool, with attractive individuals being seeded as points of contagion for members of their local peer groups.[35]

The question is, how satisfactory is it to see social learning as a process of memetic copying? Many authors have doubts about the meme framework.

Some emphasize social learning as a process of construction by the learner, involving interaction with a more experienced individual who provides 'scaffolding' for the learning of the task;[36] that is to say, certain parts of the task are controlled or assisted by the more experienced individual in a way which directs the efforts of the inexperienced individual in a particular direction, rather than actions being copies.[37]

Dan Sperber[38] criticizes the idea of learning as copying as a kind of essentialism which involves us exaggerating the similarities between things (for good evolutionary psychological reasons). Sperber's view is that what he calls 'representations', including everyday knowledge, do not replicate but transform in the process of transmission, and do so as a result of constructive cognitive processes. These go on both at the stage of representing inputs in the mind and at the subsequent stage of producing public outputs, whether these are words, movements or material objects. However, even though there may be all sorts of things going on in the mind, the resemblance between the inputs and the public outputs is often very striking, as the example of the continuity in many prehistoric pottery traditions clearly demonstrates.

Mark Lake[39] has differing reservations, pointing out that, 'Imitation is not a mechanism of cultural replication because it cannot effect the direct transmission of symbolic structure: the idea for an action is not directly transmitted, but retrieved from the action itself.' Clearly, this is very different from the way that genes operate.

Robert Boyd and Peter Richerson make a similar point, emphasizing that, when an act of transmission has occurred, we cannot assume that the information in the second brain is the same as that in the first. In fact, they cite a linguistic example to demonstrate that, in some cases at least, 'even though there is no difference in the phenotypic performance between parents and children, children do not acquire the same memes as their parents'.[40]

It appears then that the 'meme as replicator' model has considerable problems as the basis for a theory of cultural inheritance. Fortunately, accepting that culture is an inheritance system does not depend on the meme model. There are alternative possibilities. Harvey Whitehouse[41] has offered an account of cultural inheritance which rejects both the meme model and Sperber's view, based on Gerald Edelman's idea of neuronal group selection.[42] Eytan Avital and Eva Jablonka emphasize a developmental approach which incorporates all the many different ways in which information can be reproduced:

The crucial point is not the precise mechanism of acquiring a new preference or pattern of behaviour, but the circumstances that allow the transmission of this information in a way that ensures its trans-generational reproduction. Since a behaviour or preference has to be manifested in order for it to be acquired by other members of the social group, the focus must be the social and ecological conditions that lead to the manifestation and re-generation of essentially similar patterns of behaviour.[43]

It seems that we still do not understand the psychological mechanisms involved in cultural inheritance, which remain the object of ongoing debate and investigation. However, rather than worry too much about this and assume that we cannot make any progress until the mechanism is fully understood, the way forward for archaeologists and anthropologists, if not for psychologists, seems to be to ignore the psychological mechanisms and accept that, whatever they may be, they lead to culture having the character-istics of an inheritance system with adaptive consequences. Even if the meme concept in the strict sense is problematical, the word meme has been such a successful meme itself that it represents a useful shorthand way of referring to the idea that culture is an evolutionary system involving inheri-tance. Archaeology is particularly interested in those cases where the information passed on concerns ways of making and using artifacts. The artifacts produced on the basis of the information have consequences, for example in terms of how well they perform their tasks, which affect the lives of the individuals using them, and also affect whether the information required to make them continues to be passed on in the future. We can ask what are the population level processes characteristic of this inheritance system. This is what biologists did before they understood genetics. They could still measure the heritability of particular traits from one generation to the next without knowing the mechanisms involved. Indeed, it is well known that Darwin came up with his theory of natural selection while holding a completely erroneous view about how genetic transmission worked.

ROUTES OF TRANSMISSION

As a result of sexual reproduction, most of an individual's genes are inher-ited equally from their mother and father. Even where cultural practices are learned initially from parents, it is highly unlikely that they will be acquired 50% from each. In fact, as we have seen, it is much more likely that daughters will learn from their mothers and sons from their fathers. In this light, if we are thinking of possible genetic models, mother–daughter transmission of skills and knowledge is likely to parallel the inheritance of mitochondrial DNA. As we saw earlier, this is passed from the mother to offspring of both sexes but only female offspring can in turn pass theirs on to the next generation.[44] Father–son transmission will tend to parallel the inheritance of the genes on the male sex-determining Y-chromosome. Of course, there are many transmission routes that have no genetic parallel: learning from non-parents of the older generation (oblique transmission), for example. Furthest from the genetic route is horizontal transmission, when individuals learn from their contemporaries, but this has biological parallels in the spread of epidemic diseases. We can easily see some of the consequences of the different mechanisms. For example, in those aspects of life where practices are transmitted from parents to children, change is likely to be slower than in cases where they are passed among peers from one day to the next.

There are other relevant variations in transmission routes which have a bearing on the way practices will spread through a population. Cultural transmission does not have to be one-to-one; it can be one-to-many, as in the relation between a teacher and a class. By this means, new ideas and practices can be propagated very quickly across large numbers of people, producing a considerable degree of homogeneity. On the other hand, it can also be many-to-one, as when all members of the older generation insist on the same moral precepts or respectful practices in their interactions with individual children. The result is again uniformity but change is likely to be much slower. On the other hand, in those spheres where people learn solely from their parents there is likely to be much greater variation from household to household. The different routes and their implications are summarized in fig. 4.

Stephen Shennan and James Steele's[45] survey of ethnographic literature on the learning of craft techniques, already mentioned, found that transmission was mainly if not entirely vertical/oblique rather than horizontal. In the vast majority of the cases where the information was available, the transmission of knowledge was from parent to offspring, and specifically to the same gender offspring. As in the case of Ruddle's ecological study, the skills generally took a long time to learn and were transmitted in the course of childhood.[46] There are cases where the system of learning pottery-making goes from mother-in-law to daughter-in-law as part of a strong pattern of post-marital resocialization in a patrilocal group,[47] but this too maintains a strong vertical/oblique transmission through individuals who are closely related, albeit as affines.

	Modes of Cultural Transmission			
	Vertical or parent-to-child	Horizontal or contagious	One-to-many	Concerted or many-to-one
Transmitter	Parent(s)	Unrelated	Teacher/leader/media	Older members of social group
Transmittee	Child	Unrelated	Pupils/citizens/audience	Younger members of social group
Acceptance of innovation	Intermediate difficulty	Easy	Easy	Very difficult
Variations between individuals within population	High	Can be high	Low	Lowest
Variations between groups	High	Can be high	Can be high	Smallest
Cultural evolution	Slow	Can be rapid	Most rapid	Most conservative

4 *Different routes of cultural transmission and their suggested implications in terms of cultural uniformity and speed of change.*

Occasionally, even archaeological finds can be used to draw similar conclusions with greater or lesser plausibility. Thus, at the Central European late Neolithic lake-village site of Zürich-Mozartstrasse, ceramic crucibles for copper production were found over several phases, representing a span of about 70 years, in two houses only, suggesting the possibility that these restricted skills were passed on within the family from one generation to the next.[48] At another late Neolithic lake-village in eastern France, careful study of the pottery inventories of the individual houses, which could be shown to be contemporary with one another through dendrochronological dating, indicated that each house had its own pottery micro-tradition, suggesting that pottery-making was passed on in the same vertical/oblique way as the known ethnographic cases, with the predicted consequence of inter-household variation.[49]

The large-scale consequences of all these cultural transmission routes can be modelled mathematically using variations on existing population genetic and epidemiological models,[50] to see what sort of outcomes they produce at larger temporal and spatial scales. This has been one of the advantages of using genetic transmission as the basis for models of cultural transmission. A sophisticated mathematical apparatus already existed which did not have to be invented anew but could be modified to explore the consequences of the different transmission routes.

MECHANISMS OF CULTURAL CHANGE

So far we have seen that we are still in considerable ignorance about the precise psychological and other mechanisms through which cultural inheritance works, and that the routes it can follow are much more diverse than is the case with genetic inheritance. It's now time to ask what processes of change act on what is transmitted culturally, as the processes of mutation, selection and drift act on genes. The obvious starting point is to look whether these processes act on the cultural inheritance system as well, albeit perhaps realized in different ways. If they do not, we are hardly in a position to claim that a Darwinian perspective on culture is appropriate.

To start with, we need a mechanism of change in the content of the information that is transmitted. If the reproduction of cultural or genetic information was perfect every time then there would be no novelty on which other processes could act. Genetic mutations are 'blind', in that they occur randomly and are unrelated to the processes of selection which act on their outcomes. In contrast, cultural innovations are generally regarded as purposive. However, this need not always be the case. People can, in effect, make copying errors and alter the way they do things quite unwittingly. In the case of genetic mutations, many if not most will disappear very quickly and not make any difference to the genetic make-up of the population. If one person unwittingly decorates a pot in a slightly different way from the norm, this will not make any difference at all if there are many potters, unless some at least begin to deliberately copy the innovation. This sort of unintended copying error seems to be the basis for the rapid and divergent evolution of initiation ceremonies reported by Fredrik Barth[51] for the Mountain Ok of New Guinea. These were carried out in different local groups by small groups of elders at relatively rare intervals. They could not remember exactly how things were done last time and there were few people to check things with, so unintentional innovations occurred.

Nevertheless, sometimes innovations are purposive. In the framework developed by Robert Boyd and Peter Richerson[52] to describe processes of change in cultural traditions, purposeful innovation is referred to as 'guided variation': individuals change their way of doing something as a result of comparing the outcome of their existing method, most probably learned from their parents or another relative of the older generation, with that of a new method acquired by their own experimental, trial-and-error learning, and adopting the latter. For example, just because somebody has learned from their parents a particular way to make an arrowhead or the best time to plant a crop, does not mean that they will always follow it. They may experiment with alternatives and start using one of them, especially if their current way of doing things is not very successful. For the individual concerned this amounts to a one-step combined innovation-selection procedure.

Another difference between innovations and mutations is that the latter occur randomly with respect to time. This is the basis for the genetic 'clocks' which are used to calculate the time when different present-day species with a common ancestor split off from one another. Innovations do not work in the same way. Eytan Avital and Eva Jablonka[53] make this point in relation to animal behaviour. Animals do not change their behaviour when life is predictable but in situations where stress is present, so long as it is not extreme. Ben Fitzhugh[54] has recently made a similar point in a study of prehistoric technological innovation in the Kodiak Archipelago in Alaska, suggesting that conditions of greater risk sensitivity are likely to lead to more inventive behaviour.

However, as Fitzhugh is careful to point out, it should not be assumed that the element of intentionality in many innovations altogether vitiates the comparison between mutation and innovation. Just because somebody imagines that they have found an improved way of doing something does not mean that they really have, as the history of failed technological innovations shows. Moreover, even if a real improvement has been made, that does not necessarily mean that selection will act in its favour, as examples of technological 'lock-in' demonstrate; the history of the QWERTY typewriter keyboard is a particularly good example. The keys were originally arranged in this way on the keyboard to avoid the problem of them jamming when people typed quickly, but the arrangement is not ideal as regards the position of the most frequently used letters in relation to the fingers. Subsequently, other solutions to the key-jamming problem were found, which meant that the keys could be laid out in a more sensible way. However, by this time the investment in the old arrangement was so great, especially in terms of the number of people trained in the old system, that none of the improvements was ever adopted.

In other words, even if, at the level of the individual who produces it, innovation is a directed process, its ultimate fate in the population at large may have little to do with those initial individual intentions. It depends on selection processes. In a related context, we are all familiar with the idea that the intentions of authors may be very different from the way their work is understood by their audience.

Natural selection, of course, is the key process of biological evolution, but what role would it have played in the cultural context? Here we need to remind ourselves of the complications in the possible meanings of the term selection that were introduced at the beginning of this chapter. Natural selection can in principle act on people via their genetically inherited dispositions, in terms of their flexible behavioural responses to variations in the environment relevant to reproductive success, with cultural traditions playing little or no role. We'll see examples of this when we look at optimal foraging in Chapter 6.

The second possibility is that selection on people can operate through selection on their cultural traditions. In other words, particular inherited cultural attributes lead to some people having greater survival rates and reproductive success than others. In effect, this is a Darwinian version of the classic adaptive arguments made by Lewis Binford and other New Archaeologists in the 1960s. Sceptics about this process deny that most culture change has come about as a result of possessors of one cultural attribute being out-reproduced by those with another. However, even if this won't do as a general explanation, it certainly seems to have happened sometimes. Thus, it seems clear that inherited subsistence practices, for example, the adoption of the sweet potato in New Guinea in recent centuries or of cereal agriculture in the Near East in the early postglacial period, led to the populations which possessed them growing to a higher ceiling of density than populations which were still using pre-existing techniques, and out-competing them in classic natural selection terms. It is also certainly an aspect of the processes by which European populations have come to dominate large parts of the globe, the Americas in particular, over the last 500 years.[55]

However, cultural learning means that, in many circumstances at least, members of populations at the receiving end do not have to accept their fate but can pre-empt it by themselves adopting new cultural practices. This is something we will discuss shortly below when we examine those evolutionary processes which only act on variation that is transmitted culturally.

Apart from mutation and natural selection, the other important process in biological evolution is drift, variation in the frequency of genes through time entirely as a result of variations in survival and reproductive success unconnected with the role of the genes in question, but essentially the result of chance. In any finite population chance will always have some role in the survival of particular individuals and the propagation of their genes. If a population is very small, then the effects of chance can outweigh the strength of selection on the genes present within it. A particular group of individuals attempting to colonize a new island in Polynesia might well have been characterized by genes which would have enhanced their ability to survive, reproduce and be successful parents, but if their boat had sunk on the way and they had all been drowned, that would have been the end of the matter! On the other hand, if there was a large number of colonizers in a fleet of 50 boats, the odds are that at least some of them would have got through. In fact, there is strong evidence from the colonization of Polynesia that many islands were colonized by very small populations whose genetic composition was affected by precisely such chance effects.[56] Among such effects is the so-called founder effect. The initial members of a small group separating from a larger population are most unlikely to be a genetically representative sample of that population. If the pioneering group is successful in expanding and producing its own increasingly large group of descendants, their genetic repertoire will be based on the particular variants which characterized the founders, and it may well look very different from the descendants of the main population from which its founders initially separated.

The frequencies of all genes are affected by such chance effects in small populations, but some DNA variations are only affected by chance factors, however big the population. It was discovered in the 1960s that much of the DNA in organisms did not code for any functioning genes; in fact, it did not seem to have any functions at all and became known as 'junk DNA'. Since it did not have any function, selection could not act on it. If a mutation occurred in it, whether the mutation quickly disappeared or was reproduced and spread through the population depended entirely on chance. Understanding how genetic change occurs in these circumstances is the subject of the neutral theory of evolution.[57]

The same issues are relevant in the case of the transmission of culture. Some cultural attributes may be entirely neutral, just like junk DNA, in that no selective process acts on them. This is the basis of Robert Dunnell's[58] well-known distinction between style and function in artifacts. In his terms, stylistic attributes are those which do not have any selective value and whose frequencies will therefore change through time solely as a result of chance factors. For example, suppose that pottery-making is transmitted from mothers to daughters and a particular mother has more surviving daughters than others, who in turn have more reproductively successful daughters themselves. The result will be that the variations in pottery-making that characterized the mother who started the sequence will become more prevalent in the population, even though they are nothing to do with the reasons for the reproductive success and even if they were not copied by others. From the point of view of the ceramic attributes it is mere chance that they happen to be associated with a reproductively successful lineage of females.

However, it is important to understand that when populations are small, with culture as with genes, even the adaptive benefit of functional traits is likely to be overwhelmed by drift, especially if selection for them is weak. Thus, in the case of the Mountain Ok initiation ceremonies mentioned earlier, even if particular practices had some social significance, the copying errors introduced by poor memory were propagated through time as a result of drift arising from the small number of people involved, with the result that different groups became more distinctive in their initiation ceremonies over time. Cultural analogues of founder effect can also appear in the case of small colonizing populations and we will look at some possible archaeological examples later on.

One of the most interesting situations that cultural drift has been used to explain is the disappearance of apparently useful cultural attributes. This was the concern of the early 20th-century anthropologist W. H. R. Rivers[59] in a discussion of what he called 'the disappearance of the useful arts'. He noted that there were places in Oceania where the canoe had disappeared, clearly very puzzling from the practical point of view, for example in the Torres Islands.[60] Rivers discussed possible causes. The disappearance of canoes could not be accounted for by the destruction of forests or a decline in tools since forests were still present and tools were little different from those in neighbouring islands that still made canoes. He noted that in parts of Oceania canoes are only made by certain men and that the occupation is hereditary, so the canoe-makers are limited in number:

It is only necessary for such a limited body of men to disappear either as the result of disease or war or through some natural catastrophe, to account for the disappearance of an art. There is evidence that this dying out of skilled craftsmen has been the cause of the disappearance of the canoe in the Torres Islands, and Seligmann and Strong have recorded the dying out of skilled craftsmen as the cause of the disappearance of the art of making stone adzes in the Suloga district of Murua (Woodlark Island). The dying out of skilled craftsmen within a community is thus established as a cause of the loss of useful arts.[61]

However, it may not have been so much the loss of the manual skill that made canoe-building irrecoverable, but rather that the death of the crafts-men entailed the loss of the ritual knowledge whose application was essential to produce a safe canoe.[62] A practical craft could potentially be re-invented but the extinction of a tradition of ritual knowledge could not be reversed.

MECHANISMS OF CHANGE SPECIFIC TO CULTURAL TRADITIONS

This list of direct cultural analogues of the processes that affect gene fre-quencies in populations – mutation, selection and drift – does not exhaust the set of processes which affect cultural attribute frequencies, just as parent-offspring transmission does not exhaust the range of cultural trans-mission mechanisms.

Let us begin to look at mechanisms specific to culture by taking an example from a recent discussion in the literature.[63] In the middle of the 20th century snowmobiles replaced snowshoes as the preferred way of moving around when hunting among the Cree of northern Canada. This did not happen as a result of the action of natural selection on Cree populations, such that those who used snowmobiles were reproductively more successful and outcompeted those who used snowshoes, so that these gradually died out. On the contrary, people would have compared the relative merits of the two with regard to the various requirements of an arctic means of mobility, the costs involved and the skills and resources required for maintenance, and switched to the latter. They did not invent the snowmobile; it already existed. They presumably saw it being used by non-Cree individuals at various times and decided that in their situation the balance of costs and benefits was in favour of switching. This is the process described by Robert Boyd and Peter Richerson[64] as *directly biased transmission*. From the perspective of the people concerned it involves individuals changing their way of doing something as a result of comparing the outcome of the current way of doing it, perhaps inherited from a parent, with that of another individual. It is the practical evaluation of the consequences of the new model in relation to those of the inherited model that in this case led to adoption.

At this point we can introduce the next complication to our evolutionary framework. The decisions taken by the Cree hunters will have an effect on the frequencies of snowmobiles and snowshoes in use within the population. If the hunters continue with their preference for the new snowmobiles then snowshoes will die out. In this case, a major shift from snowshoes to snowmobiles suggests that previous history counts for little. The advantages of snowmobiles are obvious to all. This *is* an evolutionary process, not just some more or less plausible analogy to genetics. The snowshoe has a history of manufacture and use, no doubt involving changes – descent with modification in fact – over a long period of time, through the human generations. So with the snowmobile, although its history is much shorter and very different, including the invention of the internal combustion engine and its adaptation to use in very cold conditions.

We can trace these artifact histories through time, just as we can trace the histories of genes in biological evolution. However, as archaeologists have long been aware, we can't automatically assume that the histories of artifacts correspond to the histories of populations, precisely because of the variety of cultural transmission routes described earlier. Nevertheless, because both snowshoes and snowmobiles represented inherited traditions or lineages, linked through time by descent with modification, it is appropriate to think of them as subject to selection. A Cree hunter's choice of transport represents an arena of competition between the two types of transport system, where the selective environment for that competition is the human population, or certain elements of it.

As a more archaeological example, we can imagine two different ways of hafting an axe blade present within a Neolithic population,[65] one of long-standing and widely prevalent, the other novel and little-used. These methods of axe-hafting can themselves be considered in population terms and their population trajectories traced through time as the two types compete with one another. The selective environment in which the competition takes place is the human population of axe makers and users. Decisions will be taken about which forms of axe haft to make and use in the light of a number of factors – for example, the size of the trees to be cut down (which may change as clearance proceeds and primary gives way to secondary forest); the raw material sources used (which may affect the form and size of the axe blade); the ways in which axes are held and used, and so on – all within a broad least-effort framework which assumes that people would prefer to spend less time and effort cutting down trees rather than more, other things being equal.

Nevertheless, we should not exaggerate the competitiveness of this process. There will not have been a national centre for testing the properties of axes, nor does it seem probable to imagine that when young men reached the age of cutting down their first trees they took along axes hafted in six different ways and carried out a comparative performance analysis in terms of time taken, effort involved or the frequency of breakage. They would be far more likely to have used the kind of axe haft their father or some other older relative used, or the one that was most widely current. As we saw at the beginning of this chapter, in many areas of life it pays to follow what others do, just diverting from this occasionally when it is really obvious that it is better to adopt an innovation, as in the case of the snowmobile. With the hypothetical axes, it is not so obvious so the existing tradition continues, or alters relatively slowly. In other words, what we have is weak selection on ongoing cultural traditions with people as the environment and agents of selection.

In the case of the axes there is some relatively immediate indication whether the hafting is at least adequate. However, even here people are most likely to simply adopt some existing pattern rather than experiment with alternatives. In some spheres of life, whether the consequences of a particular action are good or bad may not be at all obvious until long after the event. This adds a considerable element of uncertainty to the generation and adoption of novelty and argues in favour of adopting existing modes of behaviour whose consequences in older individuals can be observed, or simply accepting what one first learned from a member of the older generation. The result is that such practices may be largely insulated from any evaluation and continue undisturbed.

Like guided variation, directly biased transmission is in one sense a kind of natural selection acting directly on cultural attributes, effected by human decision-making. That is to say, people make their judgments to continue with or to change what they do in terms of practical performance criteria. Such criteria, for example minimizing effort in cutting down trees, are quite likely in the long run to contribute to the maximization of survival probabilities and reproductive success. In this sense, people are trying to anticipate the effects of natural selection, in the strict biological sense of a force which leads individuals with certain attributes to be more reproductively successful than others. Instead, the cultural attributes themselves are either more or less successful in spreading through the human population and maintaining themselves within it.

A rather different process which affects the frequency with which infor-

mation is handed on to future generations, or even to next week, and therefore affects the frequency of cultural attributes in the population through
time is *indirectly biased transmission*,[66] where an individual adopts the cultural
attribute of another individual because that individual appears to be more
successful in terms of some locally accepted criterion, even if the attribute
concerned is not actually the reason for their success. An example is copying
the mode of speech or dress of successful musicians or actors. This may have
a genuinely positive result in that, as a result of this process, individuals who
adopt it may themselves be accorded higher prestige, for instance, than
would otherwise be the case. Adopting the characteristics of successful individuals you see around you is a pretty good rule-of-thumb for being
successful yourself without too much effort. It doesn't involve, for example,
the evaluation of alternatives that direct bias requires, and even if you adopt
some traits that are irrelevant, you nevertheless stand a good chance of
adopting traits that are significant in achieving success.

In fact, there is more of a distinction between direct and indirect bias
than might be apparent initially. In the case of direct bias, decisions are made
to adopt or not adopt on the basis of intrinsic features of the practice itself, in
terms of its performance characteristics, unrelated to its source. It is, as we
have seen, a kind of natural selection which is specific to culture. With indirect bias, practices are adopted on the basis of their source rather than their
merits, so the lack of contact with external reality which starts with people
imitating their parents, say, rather than learning by trial-and-error, continues. However, the practice will become more widespread to the extent that
indirect bias is effective. As Boyd and Richerson point out, such indirect bias
processes can have runaway properties:

If the average person prefers to accord high prestige to [and imitate the behaviour of] people with above average values of some indicator trait [e.g. people with
expensive cars], the preferences can continue to evolve, dragging the indicator
trait up another notch as well. We know this process as 'keeping up with the
Joneses'. In imitating the Jones' new car purchase, we may also have acquired the
Jones' heightened sensitivity to cars as markers of status, doing our bit to feed
the further evolution of the system.[67]

Since there are important distinctions in processes between genetic and
cultural transmission in human populations, it is no surprise that there are
important distinctions in patterned outcomes. Examination of the genetic
composition of the population of any given part of the world will show that

its members are extremely varied. Although there is some genetic variation *between* different populations, there is far more variation *within* them.[68] In fact, if you take the mean difference between any two world regional populations and compare it with the difference between two randomly chosen individuals from the same population, the difference between the two randomly chosen individuals from the same population will be greater. In contrast, with language and other forms of culture, at least in the period before modern world travel, you tend to find that the between-population differences were much greater than those within populations. How can cultural transmission processes produce this sort of effect?

One plausible possibility is what Boyd and Richerson[69] call *conformist transmission*: the idea that for any particular practice people simply look around them and do what most other people are already doing. When in Rome, do as the Romans. Of course, this too is a mechanism unique to cultural as opposed to genetic transmission. In general, it seems a very good approach to adopt when deciding how to do something. It doesn't require the evaluation involved in direct bias or learning by trial-and-error oneself, and the consequent possibility of making a mistake. It doesn't entail the risk involved in indirect bias that the successful individual is successful because of traits that are not well indicated by external appearance or behaviour. Finally, if most people are doing it, it must in principle be a good thing to do. However, it is important to note that, like indirectly biased transmission, it doesn't involve a reality check and that can be dangerous. We will see in Chapter 9 that this process and others may have resulted in group selection being much more important in human populations than in those of other animals.

THE ADVANTAGES AND DISADVANTAGES OF CULTURAL TRANSMISSION

A vital question that I have postponed addressing until now concerns the advantages and disadvantages of cultural transmission from an evolutionary point of view. Why should humans apparently place a lot more emphasis on learning from other members of their own species, as opposed to learning by trial-and-error, than most if not all other animals do? How would it ever have got started? What are the costs and benefits and what factors will cause the costs and benefits to vary?

In general, social learning is beneficial where individual learning is costly in terms of risk or time/energy expended, and where those costs can be cut by social learning. This would appear to suggest that social learning will always be superior to individual learning as a source of adaptive information that can be acquired at little cost.[70] However, things are in fact more complicated than this. At one extreme, if the environment to which individuals are adapting is unchanging, or only changing very slowly, a successful adaptation is likely to be reached by natural selection on genes, to produce a successful biological adaptation which does not involve costly investment in a complex cognitive apparatus capable of social learning, especially learning by imitation, and making decisions accordingly.[71] At the other end of the temporal spectrum a different problem arises. As social learners become more common, they are increasingly likely to have learned their behaviour from another social learner, who has also learned from another individual rather than by trial-and-error. If the environment is changing very quickly then information obtained by imitating others will be largely useless because it will always be out-of-date, so individual trial-and-error learning will be the only option.

Robert Boyd and Peter Richerson developed a model to explore the precise conditions under which social learning provides a better basis for learning about the environment than individual learning and concluded that its effectiveness depended on two factors:

1. The accuracy of individual learning (or the closely related cost of improving this accuracy).
2. The chance that an individual's social models experienced the same environment that the individual experiences.[72]

In general, when individual learning is not all that accurate in leading to the adaptively better decision, or obtaining the information to make an accurate decision is costly, and when the environment is changing, but not too quickly, then relying mainly on information from other members of the same species (whatever the mechanism involved) will be adaptively more successful than relying mainly on individual learning. Occasionally making use of individual learning, when the evidence for making a particular decision is very clear, is all that is required to keep the social learning system on track.

These conditions seem likely to have been quite widespread in the course of biological evolution so it is no surprise to find that there is increasing evidence for the importance of social learning in a great variety of species, as we noted earlier. There is a great deal of debate about the extent and nature of the uniqueness of the human case. Some authors[73] argue that humans are virtually unique in having cultural traditions that are cumulative.[74] This is because the cognitive mechanism involved in human social learning (and in bird song as well) is true imitation or observational learning, rather than the much simpler cognitive mechanisms that characterize most other species. As we have seen, however, Avital and Jablonka and others argue that any social learning mechanism will lead to cumulative traditions. They would see the unique elements of human traditions as arising from the symbolic possibilities offered by the evolution of language. Steven Mithen[75] has also pointed out that the existence of cognitively complex imitation cannot be the whole story with regard to the development of human cultural traditions. The Acheulean handaxes found in the archaeological record for well over a million years from 1.4 million years ago changed very little over that time, but certainly provide evidence for complex imitation in *Homo erectus* and later species that produced them.

What may be more relevant to the development of adaptations heavily based on socially learned traditions is increasing evidence from ocean sediment core-drilling programmes and other sources for exceptionally large and frequent environmental fluctuations during the Pleistocene period when hominins were evolving. As we have seen, too much stability tends to lead to genetically-based adaptations. Too little and only individual trial-and-error learning can keep up with the changes – socially-learned information will always be out-of-date. The climatic fluctuations which it is now possible to monitor at ever-higher levels of resolution seem to be at precisely the right sort of time-scale[76] for socially learned traditions to be adaptively effective.

If there are circumstances in which social learning provides the best means of individual adaptation, in the sense of increasing the chances of survival and reproductive success for the individuals who make use of it, does it have any down-side from this point of view? In fact, it does. An important result of the differences between the routes of genetic and cultural transmission is that cultural traits can spread through populations even when they have maladaptive consequences from the point of view of genetic transmission and reproductive success. This is the basis of the idea of the 'cultural virus' discussed above: cultural attributes that have the capacity to encourage their own adoption by others and thus increase their replicative success, without regard for the reproductive success of the individuals who adopt them. The idea is nicely encapsulated in Dan Dennett's slogan: 'A scholar is just a library's way of making another library'.[77] Or in George Williams' statement, 'There is no more reason to expect a cultural practice transmitted between churchgoers to increase churchgoers' fitness than there is to expect a similarly transmitted flu virus to increase fitness.'[78]

This is because the propagation of the practice does not depend on people reproducing themselves biologically but on their going to church. The two may even be entirely incompatible, as with the Shakers of the U.S. for instance, whose numbers have dwindled almost to the point of disappearance as a result of their ban on sex. These are relatively dramatic ways of putting it by Dennett and Williams and both imply a memetic framework for the analysis of cultural inheritance in Darwinian terms.

In fact, we do not need to accept the cultural virus or meme ideas to see how the processes of genetic and cultural transmission can lead to conflicting outcomes. We can remain agnostic as to the mechanisms, as I suggested earlier in this chapter. All we need to do is recognize that cultural inheritance exists and that its routes are different from the genetic ones. The conflicting outcomes simply follow from the mathematics describing the population consequences of the operation of the different transmission processes through time. Luca Cavalli-Sforza and Marcus Feldman[79] demonstrated this 20 years ago without invoking memes or any other specific mechanism.

In principle then, it is apparent that as soon as cultural transmission involves 'cultural parents' who are not biological parents – that is to say, in the jargon, when cultural and genetic transmission are asymmetric to one another – cultural transmission processes can lead to outcomes which override the genetically advantageous ones. How would a process of natural selection in the course of human evolution ever give rise to such a phenomenon? We have seen the answer already. It lies in the fact that it does not necessarily pay people to continue doing things in the way they learned from their parents. They may do better by copying someone else, whether by following the most common practice (conformist transmission) or following the practices of more successful individuals (indirectly biased transmission).[80]

The advantages of adopting a model different from the one you learnt when you were growing up may be considerable. In a mathematical model which I used to explore the effects of group size on individual fitness,[81] a directly biased transmission process, comparing the fitnesses of a small set of individuals and adopting the traits of the individual with the highest fitness value, gave fitness values up to 100 times greater than simply adopting the value of a genetic parent. Nevertheless, as we have seen, the process has the side effect that in some circumstances it can lead to genetically maladaptive consequences. Authors differ in their assessment of the potential significance of this effect. Those of a more behavioural ecology persuasion tend to assume that such effects will be eliminated by natural selection – culture is on a short leash. Dual inheritance theorists, on the other hand, believe that there is no guarantee that such 'corrective' mechanisms will be effective. In principle, of course, we should seek to establish the answer empirically, on a case-by-case basis.

Conclusion

In culture humans have a second inheritance system, in addition to the genetic one, that is more developed than in other species. This second inheritance system – encapsulated in the general idea of the meme – operates through a different mechanism from that of the genetic one – social learning – and because of that, what is transmitted is affected by different processes – or rather by additional ones. This does not make cultural transmission less Darwinian than genetic transmission. Both are specific instances, with their own properties, of a more general category of information transfer processes that lead to the production of heritable variation and its modification through time: 'descent with modification' in Darwin's term. We can remain agnostic about the precise psychological mechanisms of cultural inheritance processes.

People are to some extent (but only to some extent) capable, in effect, of anticipating the potential effects of natural selection by directly biased decision-making, and changing what they do when they see that something appears clearly advantageous. This means that cultural attributes can wax and wane in frequency through time independently of human population sizes, although ultimately limited by them. Conversely, populations can increase and decrease in size as a result of natural selection operating on the culturally inherited attributes of individuals. Other forces specific to cultural transmission, such as indirect bias, can also produce complex effects. The fact that the routes of cultural transmission and genetic transmission are different from one another means that successful responses to selective pressures on cultural traditions will not necessarily produce outcomes enhancing the survival and reproductive success of the individuals in the population concerned. The result is that histories of people and histories of cultural traditions are linked to one another but they are not the same thing,[82] although they may come close to coinciding in certain circumstances, for example when there is strong vertical transmission.

Histories of artifacts, in other words, histories of passing on information about how to make and use them which result in the actual production and use of artifacts, are of central importance to archaeology. They represent lineages or traditions linked by descent, as we saw in the case of the hypothetical Neolithic axes, on which all the various evolutionary processes described in this chapter can operate, modifying their form and frequency. The agents of these processes are human individuals conducting their lives in the light of the cultural inheritances they have received, whose aggregate decisions, conscious or not, produce evolutionary patterns. Except in the case of artifacts or artifact attributes which change solely as a result of drift processes, those decisions are based at least partly on the characteristics of the actual artifacts concerned. Information relating to the manufacture and use of successful artifacts will be kept through time by the individuals concerned and passed on to others. From this point of view the distinction made by David Hull that we saw in Chapter 2 – between organisms (or other entities) as 'interactors' and genes as 'replicators' – is at least as important in the case of culture, even if we do not accept the strict memetic perspective that cultural attributes can be regarded as active replicators in the way that genes are. In the case of artifacts not only are the individuals who make the decisions 'interactors', but so are the actual artifacts themselves, as distinct from the information required to make and use them correctly, since they conform entirely to the definition of 'an entity that interacts as a cohesive whole with its environment in such a way that replication is differential'.[83]

It should be clear by now that the properties of cultural transmission processes are such that the dynamic outcomes of their interactions through time are not easily predictable. The caricatures of the implications of Darwinian approaches to culture which are sometimes found in the archaeological literature simply betray their authors' lack of knowledge and understanding. It does not necessarily follow from the adoption of the perspective described in this chapter that the specific features of historical trajectories will inevitably be overwhelmed by the impact of natural selection, although they may be. The interplay of transmission and evolutionary forces will be a recurrent theme throughout the remainder of this book, starting with the archaeological documentation of cultural traditions in the next chapter.

-4-

THE EVOLUTIONARY ARCHAEOLOGY
OF CULTURAL TRADITIONS

WE SAW IN THE PREVIOUS CHAPTER that evolutionary processes act on cultural phenotypes – real artifacts and practices for example – whose characteristics are based in part on culturally inherited information. As a result of those processes, more diverse than in the case of genes, the frequency with which that information is passed on and used as the basis for new phenotypes can change. It can even go extinct, as we saw in the case of the Torres Island canoes. Since evolution in the human species operates largely on what is inherited culturally in the form of cultural traditions, without identifying and characterizing those traditions we have no basis for understanding how or why human evolution has taken the course it has done. The only source of direct information about such traditions for most of human history is archaeology. If this makes archaeology essential for understanding the evolutionary processes at work in the human past, it also specifies what the first task of archaeology should be: documenting those traditions or cultural evolutionary lineages.

Such traditions potentially exist in many if not most areas of human (therefore social) life. Artifact-form traditions are best known to archaeologists but examples of others might be ethnotaxonomies – indigenous ways of categorizing the world in general and nature in particular – or agricultural practices or ways to organize inter-personal relations. Plenty of questions spring to mind about such lineages. How stable are they? Do some change more quickly in response to external factors than others? Do specific artifact lineages through time correlate with specific traditions of subsistence practices? Do traditions of social organization in different areas converge on similar patterns because of functional constraints? Is there any correlation between documented artifact traditions and inferred language or gene histories?

The object of this chapter is to look at how such traditions may be identified and characterized archaeologically and what general features, if any, they may have in common. We will also have to look at some of the processes that create and maintain them, although that is a task that will continue to be developed in subsequent chapters.

THE CULTURE HISTORY TRADITION IN ARCHAEOLOGY

Identifying and documenting cultural traditions was, in fact, the task with which prehistoric archaeology as a distinct discipline began in the late 19th and early 20th centuries. It originated with Gustaf Kossinna and Gordon Childe in Europe and with authors such as Alfred Kroeber and Alfred Kidder in North America,[1] but it had earlier roots in German Romanticism. Those roots lay specifically in the beginnings of nationalism and a concern with identifying supposed 'national character'. 'Peoples' were conceived as having essences which could be traced into the past.[2] Kossinna in particular proposed an approach that he called 'settlement archaology', which assumed that sharply bounded cultural provinces could be identified with the territories of past peoples. Accordingly, by identifying the cultural features of those areas which Classical sources suggested were occupied by Germanic tribes at the dawn of recorded history, the ancestors of those cultural features could be traced back much earlier into prehistory, and an original German 'homeland' identified. The dangers of this sort of approach emerged very clearly in its subsequent application to justifying German claims to territory in eastern Europe, very much one of the nationalist Kossinna's intentions. The dangers have also become apparent again much more recently with the rise of new nationalisms and the demands of national minorities, both often based on claims derived from supposed culture histories based on archaeological evidence.[3]

The links between these sorts of nationalistic ideas and the existence of traditions in different areas of life, maintained day after day and generation after generation by the handing on of information, are obvious. To the nationalist it is these traditions that give the *Volk* its essence. We will see later in this chapter that culture histories are much more complex than this, but right from the beginnings of the discipline of archaeology, the power of the basic idea of tracing traditions and their spatial extent through time was recognized by archaeologists who had no time for any of its ideological implications. In fact, it would not be an exaggeration to say that nowhere in the world have archaeologists been able to do without it, not least because it has provided a spatial and chronological framework for archaeological evidence: the archaeological timetable as Sir Mortimer Wheeler called it.

Rather typically, the Europeans adopted a qualitative approach to the task of describing cultural traditions and the Americans a quantitative one. Thus, the Europeans identified 'cultures' on the basis of artifacts found together with one another at sites in a given geographical area and on this basis produced distribution maps of the 'cultures' of a region in a particular period. The prehistory of an area could then be represented by a series of distribution maps (e.g. fig. 5).

American archaeologists, on the other hand, were more concerned with

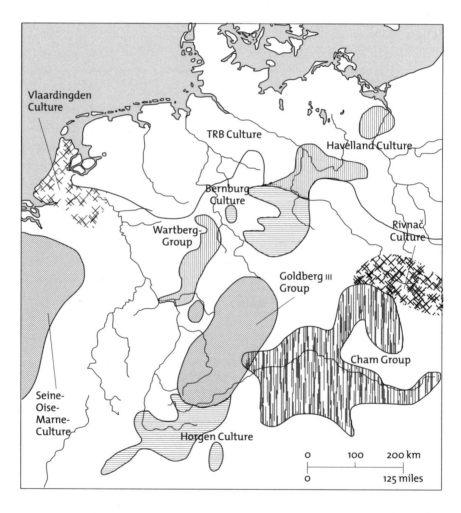

5 *A characteristic distribution map of the kind produced by the European version of the culture-historical approach to archaeology. In this case the map shows later Neolithic cultures in part of Central Europe.*

constructing chronologically ordered sequences showing the frequencies of different types through time.[4] The idea was to define, for example, a series of different types of pottery, then count the number of each of the types in the successive layers of a site. You could then produce diagrams like those shown in fig. 6, in which the frequencies of the different types are arranged in chronological order. On this basis it was possible to see specific types appearing at a certain point in time, gradually increasing in popularity and then decreasing, until finally they disappeared. These diagrams came to be known as 'battleship curves', because the shape of the curve of the ordered frequencies looked, at least to the imaginative eye, like the plan view of the hull of a battleship. Through their use it was possible to characterize through-time patterns in cultural traditions. In modern parlance this technique is known as *frequency seriation*.[5]

What both the European and American versions of culture history had in common was an interest in describing culture change and a set of assumptions which made it possible to explain it. The most important assumption was the one we have just seen, that the spatial or chronological uniformities identified represented the traditions of human groups. It followed from this that major changes in the archaeological record could only occur through the replacement of one tradition, and therefore one group, by another, at least in those cases where material culture production was domestic rather than in the hands of specialists. Within European archaeology, at least, this fitted in with the relatively short time-scales available for change in later prehistory. These were bounded by historically known dates for the Mediterranean Late Bronze Age at around 1200 BC at one end and estimates of the beginning of farming at around 3000 BC or even later on the other. This idea also fitted in with the nationalistic view of present-day peoples as historical actors having both pasts and destinies. As we have already commented, this nationalistic view of peoples was one of the main sources for the idea of culture history in the first place, so the affinity is hardly surprising.

The American archaeologist Lee Lyman and his colleagues[6] have recently had a close look at the ideas behind the development of North American culture history and noted both their closeness to Darwinian ideas and their rejection of that closeness. Thus, Alfred Kidder in 1915 talked about different pottery styles in terms of ancestor-descendant relationships; in other words, it was intended that the types he defined should be informative not only about chronological change but also about phylogenetic relationships (relationships of descent) between artifacts.[7] Some years later

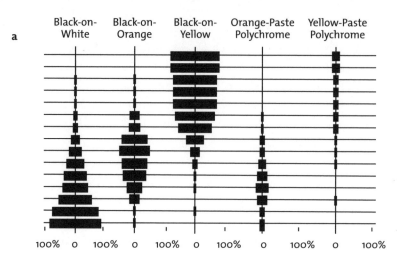

6 *Examples of the outcome of frequency seriation. If types can be ordered in this way, so that a pattern of increasing then decreasing frequency corresponds to their chronological order, then they can be regarded as representing historical lineages produced by a process of cultural transmission. Example **a**, above, shows a sequence of pottery types from a prehistoric Hopi pueblo in Arizona; example **b**, opposite, the changing popularity of different grave-stone motifs at different places in New England, from 1700 to 1830.*

the anthropologist Alfred Kroeber was emphasizing the importance of distinguishing analogous similarities (those arising from common function) from homologous ones (those derived from common descent) in both biology and anthropology if we are to understand evolution:

The fundamentally different evidential value of homologous and analogous similarities for determination of historical relationship, that is, genuine systematic or genetic relationship, has long been an axiom of biological science. The distinction has been much less clearly made in anthropology, and rarely explicitly, but holds with equal force.[8]

In contrast, J. O. Brew in the 1940s was very clear that, 'Phylogenetic relationships (i.e. relationships of descent) do not exist between inanimate objects',[9] and simply did not consider that evolution could involve anything other than biology and genes. Furthermore, where others saw 'types' as somehow naturally reflecting cultural group traditions, Brew pointed out that there was no such thing as a single 'natural' classification of a set of artifacts. There were only different classifications for different purposes, making use of different attributes of the artifacts concerned.

b

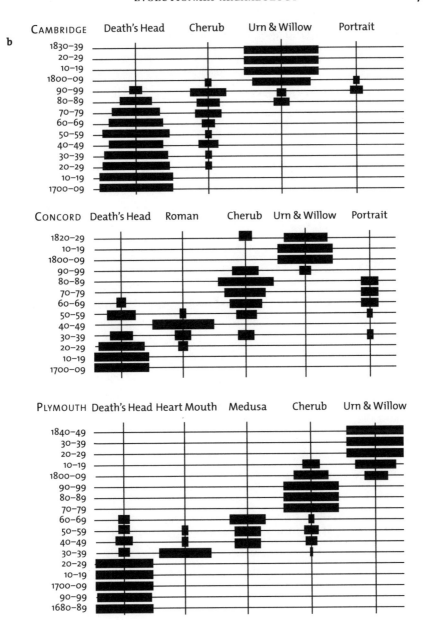

Irving Rouse took a similar line to Brew on the point that classifications had to be defined by the archaeologist and devised with a purpose in mind,[10] but then specifically focused on the construction of historical/chronological types which could be interpreted in an essentially phylogenetic or homologous way as the outcome of conformity to the norms or mental templates of a set of artisans. The types thus constructed were then seen as reflecting the variations in popularity of such norms, which could also be 'replaced' or 'go extinct'. Indeed, a thread common to the great majority of the culture historians was the idea that those types which were useful for constructing chronologies based on changing styles worked as they did precisely because they represented variation through time – changing fashions – within a single cultural tradition, that is to say, ancestor-descendant homologous relationships.

When the New Archaeology emerged in the 1960s, there was some interest in developing culture historical concepts,[11] but the dominant strand of the New Archaeology, based on Lewis Binford's ideas,[12] rejected any interest in norms and traditions. It took the view that, in broad terms, the key to understanding culture change was to see the artifacts produced by human communities in terms of their role as means of adaptation,[13] rather than as reflections of population replacement or cultural influence. The result of taking this perspective was the conclusion that the cultural complexes defined by the culture historians either didn't exist or didn't matter. What was left of the issues that they raised was subsumed under the heading of 'style', which was regarded as a residue, that variation in artifacts which didn't seem to have any obvious functional explanation.[14]

The only large-scale systematic attempt to transform this culture historical tradition in the light of the early stirrings of the New Archaeology and parallel developments in other disciplines, such as Geography, was David Clarke's *Analytical Archaeology* (1968).[15] This development and systematization of the culture historical tradition by Clarke was never followed up; it remained moribund for over 20 years in Anglo-American archaeology and indeed has no real descendants.[16] However, as we have seen, it follows from the idea of cultural traditions as evolutionary lineages discussed in the last chapter that an updated culture history is essential to the realization of a Darwinian archaeology. Since the end of the 1980s this has led to renewed interest in the issues that culture history raised.[17]

THE DARWINIAN ANALYSIS OF CULTURAL TRADITIONS

The remainder of this chapter will address a number of key issues in the evolutionary archaeology of cultural traditions.

– How do we construct demonstrably homologous cultural lineages? That is to say, traditions linked by historical continuity based on the transmission of information through time.

– What evidence do we have for the extent to which lineages relating to different aspects of material culture and other practices are transmitted together through time as parts of larger cultural packages?

– Can we distinguish whether particular cultural traditions originate or change as a result of hybridizing and mixing processes or branching and splitting processes?

– What basis, if any, do we have for the view that histories of artifact forms and cultural practices evidenced in material culture will be similar to histories of languages and genes, in the light of the point made in Chapter 1 that increasingly it is language and genes that are being used as the evidence to write the history of human populations?

CONSTRUCTING CULTURAL LINEAGES

The key question here is how to distinguish homologous from analogous similarity and it is common to all evolutionary analysis, biological as well as cultural, as we have seen. If two artifacts or reconstructed cultural practices are similar to one another, is the reason for this that they are linked through the transmission of information, or because they represent convergent solutions to particular situations? Those situations might represent adaptive problems posed by getting a living in a particular kind of environment, or successful ways to keep large communities from fragmenting, or indeed anything else. It will be very clear from the preceding chapter that we cannot define *a priori* a set of functional attributes or types which are the result of adaptive processes and a different set of stylistic features which simply reflect learning and interaction histories. Every practice that is socially learned, whether it is a way to hunt or a way to decorate a pot, in other words, whether it is obviously functional or not, will have a history of descent. Furthermore, in any given case we will not be able to establish whether or not the presence of a particular feature in several different nearby cultural contexts arises from a common convergent adaptation or a common history without first carrying out a phylogenetic analysis, that is to say, a reconstruction of cultural descent. Adaptation can only be properly understood on the basis of a diachronic approach which recognizes this. Equally, it is not helpful to see style as a residue after the function has been taken out. Style is simply a 'way of doing'. Some of these 'ways of doing' are designed to have immediate practical consequences, but that doesn't mean that they lack a historical signature.

In fact, the problem of distinguishing homologies from analogies exists in two different versions. In the diachronic, or through-time, version the problem is that of deciding whether a particular sequence – for example, the pottery types in successive layers of a site – are linked together by a process of cultural inheritance, so that one can be considered ancestral to another. In its synchronic, or snapshot, form the issue is to decide, for example, whether similar-looking kinds of pottery dating to a given period and found in a number of different sites or regions are similar because they have a common ancestor or because of independent, convergent development.

The archaeologists who have given most attention recently to the problem of constructing cultural lineages are Mike O'Brien and Lee Lyman.[18] The methodological solution they propose to the problem of identifying homologous cultural lineages through time is the application of the techniques of occurrence and frequency seriation, developed, as we have seen, by culture historians in the early 20th century. These techniques involve the measurement of similarity between archaeological assemblages in terms of the *occurrence* of shared cultural attributes or types, or their *frequency*. The types might be different forms of pottery for example. The aim is to arrange the assemblages in an order in such a way that the more similar the two assemblages are, the closer they are in the order and the closer they are in time. If particular attributes or types make it possible to seriate in this way the assemblages in which they occur, then those attributes or types can be said to be linked historically by a process of descent or information transmission, and the resulting ordering represents a cultural lineage. It is important to understand that chronological seriation is not a tautologous or self-verifying procedure. Valid seriations don't automatically result from attempts to use seriation techniques; closeness in order of similarity, for example, does not necessarily correspond to closeness in time.

As O'Brien and Lyman[19] point out, the first requirement for seriation of some attribute to work is that drastic change in its frequency should not be instantaneous. We saw in the previous chapter that such instantaneous change is not characteristic of traditions passed on by cultural inheritance since, by definition, the frequency of occurrence of some feature at time t depends to a considerable extent on its frequency at time t-1. A type representing a cultural lineage – what O'Brien and Lyman[20] call a historical type – will have a continuous presence through time. It will start as the result of a local innovation,[21] increase in frequency and then eventually decline and go extinct. Next, the assemblages to be seriated must represent similar lengths of time, so that

Variants and Variant Frequencies

7 *Simulation of the joint effects of drift and neutral innovation on cultural variant frequency through time. During each of 400 time periods, individuals learn variants from a randomly chosen model. They then have the opportunity to replace this variant with a novel variant that has never been seen in the population before. The probability that this happens is the innovation rate. In this case the innovation rate is 0.01 (in other words there is a 1 in 100 chance of an innovation occurring), the population size is 50 and the population contains a single variant in the initial time period. Drift and innovation combine to produce variant frequency patterns through time that show rises in popularity then decline and disappearance.*

their positions in the sequence relate to their age rather than their duration. Third, the assemblages must come from the same area so that variation between assemblages in time does not become mixed up with variation in space.[22] This increases the probability that the assemblages will belong to the same tradition but does not guarantee it. However, if there has been a significant break in tradition during the period being studied, then the continuity criterion of cultural transmission, already mentioned, will not be met.

The extreme case of cultural transmission is when there are no selective forces acting on the tradition at all, in other words the attributes concerned are 'neutral' in the sense we saw in the last chapter. In these circumstances, the only factors affecting changing frequencies of attributes through time are the rate of innovation and random processes of cultural drift. Fraser Neiman[23] showed by computer simulation that these processes are all that is needed to generate precisely the kind of 'battleship curve' on which the seriation procedure is based (fig. 7).

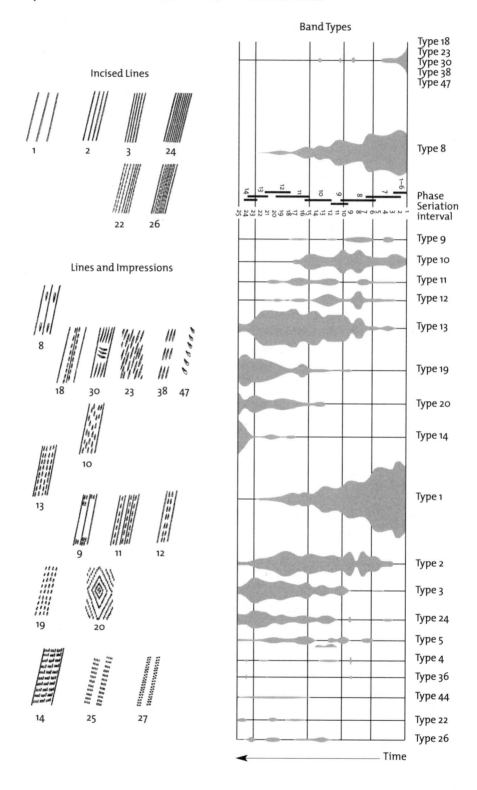

However, it is important to emphasize that ceramic decoration does not always change solely as a result of the neutral drift processes described in Neiman's study, nor is drift the only process that produces 'battleship curves'. Fig. 8 shows the results of a seriation of pottery assemblages in terms of the frequency of vessels decorated with different types of impressed band motifs.[24] The vessels come from a small group of settlements belonging to the early farming Linear Pottery Culture in Germany. The time span represented is about 500 years, from $c.$ 5350 to 4850 BC, within which a number of different settlement phases have been identified. It can be seen that the early forms of decoration found in the first phases are already present in high frequency. This is to be expected, because the occupation of this area almost certainly occurred as a result of colonization by a group of farmers from a neighbouring area where this pottery tradition had already been developed. We can then trace the local development of the pottery through time until the abandonment of the area. The pattern of change in this tradition is produced not just by drift but by selection both for and against novel forms of decoration, as we will see in a later chapter when these early farming communities are discussed again. So long as cultural inheritance has a significant role in affecting the occurrence of artifact types and cultural practices through time, then the classic 'battleship curve' seriation pattern of changing frequencies will exist.

These diachronic material culture patterns are real and are not an epiphenomenon of anything else. They have their own internal logic, in the sense that the way they change depends on their own state at a given time: this is the essence of an evolutionary process. Change can only operate on the forms or practices inherited from previous generations. New social conditions, for example, may lead to changes in pottery-making, but those changes will be responses of the existing practices and organization of pottery-making. Moreover, the sort of knowledge we acquire from describing and explaining these patterns is in no sense an inferior kind of knowledge to that obtained by talking to people or reading written sources.

8 *The results of a seriation of pottery assemblages from a group of early farming sites in Germany, dating to c. 5350–4850 BC, in terms of the frequency of vessels decorated with different types of impressed band motifs, which are also shown. The seriation was carried out by means of correspondence analysis and its chronological validity checked against independent evidence. The classic 'battleship curve' pattern of the frequencies of the band motifs through time is readily apparent.*

However, as we have seen, demonstrating that individual through-time patterns represent cultural lineages doesn't exhaust the question of distinguishing analogies from homologies, because we have to address the question of the links between different traditions. If we find similar historical patterns in neighbouring areas, is that because they arose independently or because they had a common ancestor? The tools for dealing with this problem go under the name of *cladistics* and will be examined towards the end of this chapter. We now need to address the question of the extent to which cultural traditions relating to different areas of life are linked together.

CULTURAL COHERENCE AND THE TRANSMISSION OF CULTURAL PACKAGES

A continuum of possibilities exists as regards cultural coherence.[25] At one extreme, whole cultures may be transmitted from one generation to the next, hermetically sealed from others, each characterized by its own world view. This is the possibility favoured by ethnic nationalists, past and present, going back to the German Romantics of the early 19th century already mentioned, and by others who regard cultures as unique constellations of meaning, understandable solely in their own terms. Unsurprisingly, in the light of what we saw above about the origins of culture history, it is also the position closest to that of the first archaeological culture historians. Even those who came afterwards and subscribed to the approach but not its ideological background still tended to see archaeological cultures as essences. They defined their cultures in terms of uniform characteristic artifact types and ignored the fact that distributions of these types did not coincide with one another.[26] This characterization of the nature of cultural traditions seems implausible given that diffusion of information between cultural traditions certainly occurs, and that it is simply impossible to identify perfectly coherent spatial blocks in which all the different cultural attributes mapped have exactly the same distribution.[27]

At the other end of the spectrum of possibilities we have a situation where there is no spatial or temporal coherence: people always make their own decisions about how to carry out any specific activity on the basis of their own trial-and-error experience and the alternatives to which they are exposed. The temporal coherence we see in the archaeological record, together with the importance of social learning shown in the last chapter, indicates that this extreme is as unlikely as the first.

More likely than either of the two extremes are two intermediate possibilities that Robert Boyd and his colleagues propose.[28] One is the suggestion that there are core traditions whose components stick together over time and provide a basic cultural framework. The core has a major influence on social life but does not by any means organize everything, so that there also exist 'peripheral' cultural elements not closely tied to the core. The other is the idea that there may be no single cultural core but rather 'multiple packages' – a series of separate groups of cultural elements, each with its own distinctive pattern of descent and quite possibly very different rates of change. In some cases, such as the initiation rituals of the Mountain Ok in New Guinea mentioned earlier, the rate of change may be so fast that any similarities due to common descent rapidly become dissipated. There is no reason to think that either the 'cultural core' view or the 'multiple packages' view is right or wrong. It seems plausible to suggest that in some cases there are genuine, powerful cultural cores and in others there are not. The point is not to decide the issue *a priori* in principle but to find out which is relevant in a particular case and why. The answers are of great importance to understanding long-term human history but do not even arise if one does not adopt a Darwinian perspective.

Boyd *et al.* cite a number of anthropological cases where such core traditions seem to have been maintained over long periods of time. One example is a study by Scott Rushforth and James Chisholm[29] of the traditions of certain North American groups speaking languages belonging to the Athabaskan language family. The authors found a link between the social behaviour of the groups and the languages spoken which they explained by proposing that language and social traditions were related historically by 'culture birth', in that both originated together in a single ancestral group. They concluded that the cultural beliefs and values of these groups were 'genetically related' to one another, in the sense that they 'originated in and developed from a common ancestral cultural tradition that existed among Proto-Athabaskan peoples; this cultural framework originated once and has persisted (perhaps with some modifications) in different groups after migrations separated them from one another.'[30]

Similar ideas have recently been discussed by Michael Rosenberg,[31] who also favours the idea that cultural cores exist: what he calls, following Stephen Jay Gould and Robert Lewontin,[32] the cultural *Bauplan*.[33] A culture remains itself, 'as long as the systemic integrity of its *Bauplan* is maintained'.[34] On this view though, in contrast to that of the processual archaeology of the 1960s and 1970s, a culture is not an adaptive system but a self-replicating reservoir of information which is differentially used by different real actors in the world, whether individuals, families or larger entities such as communities. Because the elements of the *Bauplan* are tightly linked together, not only are they not easily changed but they can themselves constrain innovation and lead to cultural stasis.

A recent archaeological characterization of such a cultural core, albeit not conceived in quite these terms, is Scott Ortman's[35] study of metaphor and material culture in the American Southwest. On the basis of generalizations derived from cognitive linguistic research on the nature of metaphor, he proposes that pottery designs from the Mesa Verde area of the American Southwest during the Great Pueblo period (AD 1060–1280) were conceptualized as textile fabrics.[36] The basis for the claim is a comparative analysis of the designs on pottery and on preserved basketry and other woven materials. Ortman shows, for example, that details which were not intentionally woven into textiles but arose as inevitable consequences of particular weaving processes were actually deliberately produced in pottery designs. He also demonstrates that pottery designs not related to known weaving patterns, or combining them in impossible ways, are very rare in the ceramic assemblages. The fact that they occasionally occur suggests that potters occasionally tried them but that they were regarded as unacceptable by others and never caught on.

Ortman uses many other examples to support his case, but one of the most interesting is evidence that exposure of potters to different weaving traditions affected what they did. Thus, in the eastern part of his study area, the pottery designs tend to emphasize coiled basketry features and in the west they emphasize features characteristic of loom-woven cotton cloth. Direct evidence of cotton production and weaving is much more common in the latter area. The inference is that local potters based their designs on the features of weaving products and practices that they knew well. Ortman's conclusion is that, "'POTTERY IS A TEXTILE" describes an ancient mental phenomenon that really was shared among Mesa Verde potters and that is decipherable from archaeological remains alone, without the benefit of native consultants.'[37]

The question is obviously, why did they have such a view? The answer appears to be that it is part of a larger worldview based on container imagery. The underground ritual kiva structures of Mesa Verde were sometimes decorated in ways similar to the pottery decoration, while their roofs were constructed in a way that appeared similar to a coiled basket. This in turn may relate to the fact that in some modern Pueblo cultures kivas are regarded as representing a cosmos made of an earth bowl and sky basket (see fig. 9).

As Ortman points out, the result of this sort of situation is that these different cultural attributes are transmitted through time as a linked set, not easily infiltrated by novelty that is not in keeping with it, as his example of the rejection of non-textile pottery designs illustrates. Interestingly, such non-textile designs were clearly 'thinkable' occasionally by potters working within this tradition but were not acceptable for wider adoption and transmission. While we do not know about the transmission routes for Mesa Verde pottery-making, it seems reasonable to suggest that if decoration patterns were indeed connected with cosmological beliefs then, in addition to

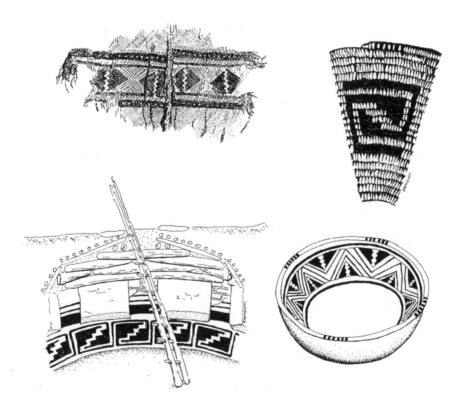

9 *Examples (clockwise from top left) of cloth, basketry, pottery and a ceremonial kiva structure from the Mesa Verde region of the American Southwest, showing the similarity between the decoration on them and the dependence of the pottery decoration on textile/basketry motifs. The similarities may relate to the cosmological dimension of the kiva as an expression of an earth-bowl, sky-basket cosmos.*

the usual one-to-one parent-offspring transmission which operates in the case of learning craft techniques, there may have been broader many-to-one pressure encouraging conformity to cosmologically acceptable community norms, strengthening still further the resistance of this cultural core to external influence.

The power and usefulness of the contrasting 'multiple packages' idea is well illustrated by a recent examination of the adoption of bow-and-arrow technology in prehistoric western North America, by Robert Bettinger and Jelmer Eerkens.[38] It revolves around the idea that identifying precisely what features are transmitted together as a package is itself an extremely informative exercise that can tell us about cultural transmission processes operating in the prehistoric past. Their study starts from what appears to be a classic question of arid archaeological typology: why is it that in Central Nevada the weight and the width of projectile points were strongly correlated with one another, while in eastern California correlation between the two was non-existent? The explanation that Bettinger and Eerkens propose centres on a difference in transmission mechanisms. In eastern California, bow-and-arrow technology was spread and maintained by the process of 'guided variation' that we saw in Chapter 3. In other words, the lack of correlation between weight and base width arose because people experimented with the two variables until they got what they wanted, in a situation where there were no strong design constraints determining what the relationship should be. In Central Nevada, on the other hand, the technology was acquired and maintained by 'indirect bias'. That is to say, the correlation arises because all the attributes of arrow point design were adopted and subsequently copied locally as a package. The idea is borne out by the fact that the same pattern of strong correlation between point attributes in Nevada and lack of correlation in eastern California is also found when other attributes are analysed. At a later date historically known Numic-speaking groups spread into Nevada at the expense of existing populations.[39] One of the reasons for this was certainly that they possessed superior adaptive strategies; however, the question arises, why did the pre-existing populations not respond and adopt some of these strategies themselves? Perhaps, Bettinger and Eerkens suggest, it was because of the prevalence of indirectly biased cultural transmission, since this would largely have insulated people from the possibility of responding to adaptive pressures.

In summary, there will be a number of different factors leading to the maintenance or disintegration of patterns of correlation between sets of attributes characterizing a particular artifact type, or between practices in different areas of life. These include external limiting constraints, such as functional requirements; particular world views; and the extent to which the different activities or elements are transmitted from one person to another in similar ways; as well as variations in the pattern and strength of social sanctions concerning appropriate ways of doing things.

THE ORIGINS OF CULTURAL TRADITIONS: BRANCHING OR BLENDING?

In the previous sections of this chapter we have seen that the evolutionary lineages based on cultural inheritance whose existence was demonstrated in Chapter 3 can be recognized in the archaeological record, and that they can come in packages of varying sizes. The question we now need to look at is how these lineages and packages originate, and in particular whether their origins are characterized by 'branching' or 'blending'. Within biology, the course of evolution is generally represented by branching phylogenetic trees showing the splitting of existing species and the consequent creation of new ones, where specific evolutionary lineages are characterized by shared mutations. Branches which diverged at an early date will be differentiated by a large number of mutations which have occurred independently on the two branches since the time they split. As you move towards the tips of the tree, species which are closely related will share most mutations which occurred in that specific evolutionary line. They will be differentiated by only a small number of very recent ones. The construction of such trees is based on the principles of cladistics, which will be described below in more detail when we come to look at the relations between genes, languages and cultures. These principles provide a basis for solving the synchronic, or snapshot, version of the problem that we have already had to look at in a diachronic context: distinguishing similarities between species which arise from a shared history of descent (homologies) from those which have arisen as a result of convergent adaptation (analogies), where each species in effect represents a distinct evolutionary lineage. Thus, if we find that all the species which share a particular adaptation are widely scattered in different places on the family tree, it suggests that the adaptation arose independently rather than as a result of a common evolutionary history. Traditionally, such trees were based on the phenotypic form of the species existing at a particular point in time, but for species still existing today they are now largely based on molecular genetics.

Do such trees represent an appropriate way of understanding the evolution of the cultural traditions created by social learning? Certainly, historical linguists think so and have been producing phylogenetic tree diagrams showing the relationships between languages, based on histories of shared linguistic 'mutations', for well over 100 years.[40] In recent years it has been suggested that the model can be applied to non-linguistic culture too. Thus, William Durham's[41] proposal of 'Evolutionary Culture Theory' is based specifically on the assumption that such splitting is the key process of culture change. The paradigmatic example where this kind of approach has been applied concerns the cultural patterns arising from the human colonization of the Pacific. Patrick Kirch,[42] following Ward Goodenough,[43] suggested that a process of branching differentiation could be traced from a founding form of 'Ancient Polynesian Society', as new islands were colonized and underwent their own local processes of cultural and social evolution. In this case, because the process of colonization involved the successive splitting of populations, the pattern of cultural differentiation correlates with the linguistic and genetic classifications, all reflecting essentially the same history.

These attempts to derive branching (often referred to as cladistic or phylogenetic) classifications of human cultures and societies have been strongly criticized by some. John Moore[44] has argued that phylogenetic taxonomies linking cultural traditions, languages and biological attributes presuppose the homogeneity and boundedness of human societies, which are highly questionable. He also argues that such classifications of species in biology are based on qualitative features of non-interbreeding groups, whereas cladistic classifications of different populations within a species are more open to question, especially if they are based on quantitative variations in particular features, rather than qualitative characters.

Moore's alternative to seeing the histories of human populations, languages and cultures in terms of phylogenetic classification is to see them in terms of what he calls 'rhizotic[45] theories', which emphasize 'the extent to which each human language, culture or population is considered to be derived from or rooted in several antecedent groups',[46] a process which he calls 'ethnogenesis'. The outcomes of such 'rhizotic' processes are representations of descent relationships not as a branching tree but a braided stream, with different channels flowing into one another and then splitting again (see fig. 10). John Terrell and colleagues[47] make a broadly similar set of points in their critique of phylogenetic approaches, arguing that they assume that the societies concerned were 'primitive isolates'.[48]

10 *The traditionally assumed form of biological and cultural evolutionary trees.* **a** *A biological tree. Once the branches representing different species have separated they never come together again.* **b** *A cultural tree. Cultures and their specific attributes can separate from one another and then come together and hybridize at a later point in time.*

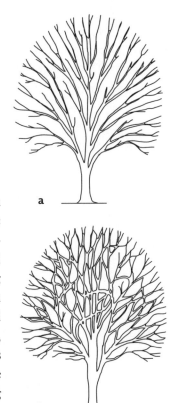

In short, the key argument made by both Moore and Terrell *et al.* against the phylogenetic approach is that populations have always interacted; that 'tribes' have constantly formed and re-formed; and that homogeneous long-lasting cultural/ethnic units have never existed, even though the oral traditions of many groups would have us believe that they have done. However, even if we grant all these points, the question is whether they have the implications that Moore and Terrell claim, in terms of the overwhelming role of blending as a cultural process. Whether or not long-lasting cultural/ethnic *units* have ever existed, long-lasting cultural traditions with recognizable coherence certainly have done, as the archaeological record demonstrates very well. Ortman's study of textiles as a metaphor for pottery shows clearly the way in which blending processes may be hindered. The basketry and textile metaphor which seems to have operated as a general worldview created a powerful pressure for coherence that led to the exclusion, for example, of pottery decoration that did not correspond to the metaphor. Other processes, described in the last chapter, may produce the same effect. Thus, the fact that much cultural learning takes place in childhood means that what Dan Dennett[49] calls 'mental filters' are installed in people at an early age and can render them less susceptible in later life despite exposure to new possibilities.[50] Conformist transmission – when in Rome, do as the Romans – certainly has this effect. Other social processes which lead to people continuing to do what is expected of them will be explored in Chapter 8.

The way barriers between traditions can be difficult to cross and therefore be maintained over time has been clearly shown by Pierre Pétrequin's[51]

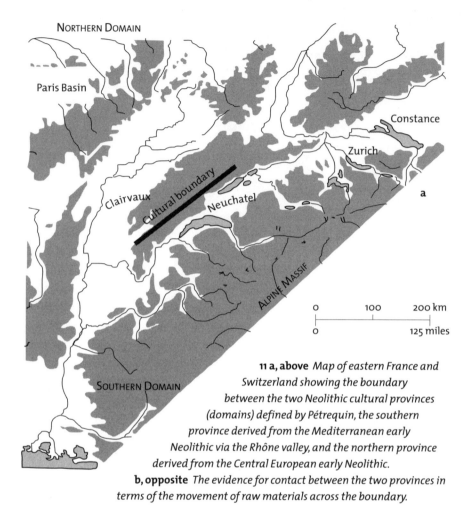

11 a, above *Map of eastern France and Switzerland showing the boundary between the two Neolithic cultural provinces (domains) defined by Pétrequin, the southern province derived from the Mediterranean early Neolithic via the Rhône valley, and the northern province derived from the Central European early Neolithic.*
b, opposite *The evidence for contact between the two provinces in terms of the movement of raw materials across the boundary.*

study of Neolithic technical traditions in the area of eastern France / western Switzerland. This is a zone where two broad traditions with different histories came together. One was the Central European Neolithic tradition, which had spread from Greece through Central Europe via the Balkans; the other was the Mediterranean tradition, which had spread from the same source but along the north coast of the Mediterranean and then up the Rhône valley. In the zone where the two traditions met a shifting cultural frontier was formed.

Pétrequin showed that there was a great deal of interaction across the boundary, in terms of the exchange of raw materials (fig. 11). Nevertheless, a cultural border was maintained despite the interaction. Thus, in the third

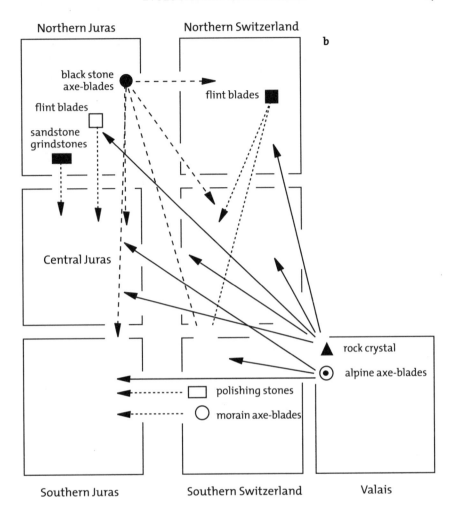

millennium BC, the Corded Ware pottery beaker, which originated on the eastern side of the frontier, became known on the western side and 'clumsy attempts [were made] at imitating them',[52] before they were rejected. Certain aspects of the Corded Ware ceramic assemblage were adopted but Pétrequin shows how difficult was the acceptance and learning of a new technical process.

In particular, the communities on the western side of the frontier were used to making round-bottomed ceramic vessels, but changed to making flat-bottomed ones (fig. 12). However, this was not straightforward. It required the learning of a new technique of building up the vessel and a sequence of stages in moving from a round-bottomed to a flat-bottomed technique which

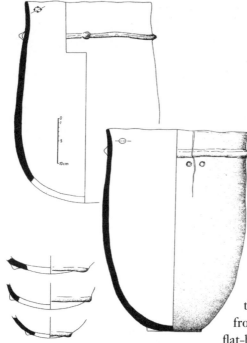

12 *Stages in the transition from round-bottomed to flat-bottomed vessels, an innovation which took a long time to cross the boundary.*

seems to have taken 2–3 generations (known because of the dendrochronological dating of the sites producing the vessels):

To make a flat bottom, the potters first built up a round bottom with a horizontal stabilising cordon; sometimes the round bottom was even hidden by adding clay along the inside of the annular cordon; from the outside it looked exactly like a flat-bottomed vessel, built up directly from a lump of clay. In this case, the technique of the true flat bottom became known and adopted only after a long period of trial-and-error; the idea had been transmitted without a proven technique to go with it.[53]

In other words, it is not sufficient to introduce a new form into local cultural environments and assume that people can easily 'reverse engineer' it and produce it themselves. The relevant skills need to be taught and learned and this will not be easy when it does not fit in with local traditions.

A similar distinction between the two zones existed with regard to the use of the axe and the adze, the two having very different cultural lineages, one derived from Central Europe, the other from the Mediterranean. In each area the hafting system changed in response to the same selective pressures derived from the changing nature of the forest to be cleared – from primary forest with large trees to secondary forest with saplings and bushes – but the changes maintained the distinct axe and adze traditions. As with the distinction between round- and flat-bottomed vessels, there is more to the difference between axes and adzes than first meets the eye; as Pétrequin[54] points out, 'the working positions, the gestures and the norms for sharpening the stone blades of the two tools are radically different'. Even where innovations from outside were adopted, those selected tended to be from communities with similar traditions, thus reinforcing the differences between the two sides of the frontier.

The sort of process much more likely to lead to blending will arise when transmission and selection forces leading to the maintenance of cultural traditions do not exist. A prime candidate, therefore, is cultural drift, which, as we saw earlier, presupposes that the only processes affecting a particular tradition are innovation and interaction rates, i.e., who is in contact with whom. Fraser Neiman[55] has demonstrated the operation of this process in a study of decorative variation in Woodland-period pottery assemblages of the first millennium AD in the North American Mid-West. As we saw in Chapter 3, drift represents the chance element affecting the prevalence of practices: even if we assume that all potters and/or all decorative motifs are equally likely to be taken as models in an episode of social learning and subsequent ceramic production, in any finite population not all potters or motifs will be copied the same number of times.

Innovation in this case refers to the introduction of novelty into the decorative repertoire of a particular group. This can come from local innovation or from the adoption of new motifs from other groups. To the extent that groups are in contact with one another, the drift-driven changes in the different groups should go in step with one another. Neiman carried out a simulation to demonstrate that, for a given population size, higher levels of inter-group transmission produce lower values of inter-group divergence. A specific consequence follows from the theory and its mathematical specification when drift and neutral innovation are the only forces operating: as differences between assemblages decrease, variation within assemblages will increase, and vice versa.[56]

An analysis of the differences between a number of Woodland ceramic assemblages from different sites, for a series of seven successive phases, showed a trend of decreasing then increasing difference between them. It also showed the pattern of inverse correlation between intra- and inter-group variation just mentioned: as inter-assemblage differences went down, the variation within assemblages increased. Neiman therefore concluded that the trends through time in inter-assemblage distance were indeed a function of changing levels of inter-group transmission, which started low, reached their highest level in Middle Woodland times and sank to new low levels in the Late Woodland period. The Middle Woodland was also the time of a phenomenon known as the 'Hopewell Interaction Sphere', evidenced by the widespread appearance of exotic trade goods.

In fact, although at first sight Neiman's study appears to support the 'blending' view, it does not do so in a straightforward way. On the basis of precisely the sort of argument which has been made in this chapter and the last, he argued that successful transmission of ceramic traditions requires a long-lasting relationship between teacher and learner. Accordingly, he went on to suggest that since the attribute being studied was decoration on cooking pots, the changes in level of inter-group transmission must relate to changes in the level of long-term residential movement of potters between groups. That is to say, the most likely way to get cultural blending is by the mixing together within the same community of people from different cultural backgrounds. What is interesting about this is that it implies a link between people and pots of the kind imagined by the culture historians. Equally interesting though is the further implication that there are likely to be major evolutionary differences between societies where material culture production is domestic and those where it is in the hands of specialists. In the latter case the producer-consumer identity is broken; the consumer choice of objects produced by others does not involve a long learning period and may be much more open to outside influence.

It appears that inherited cultural traditions in particular areas of life are at least to some extent insulated from external influence and are not simply a product of interaction rates. In other words, even when change effected by outside influences occurs, 'phylogenetic continuity' is maintained. In this light it seems plausible to suggest that splitting rather than blending processes are likely to have played a greater role in cultural origins. Where they are based on blending, it is likely to have been blending of a very particular kind. Whether these suggestions are more likely to apply in societies without developed specialist production, or simply more likely to be archaeologically detectable in these circumstances, isn't entirely clear.

In situations where we are dealing with the formation of new cultural cores or *Baupläne*, Michael Rosenberg[57] has suggested that this is more likely to occur in small groups physically separated to some degree from their larger parent population, because the social sanctions which help to maintain the existing *Bauplan* are likely to be weaker. The new core which emerges will have a strong stochastic element to it: founder effects, in terms of those elements of the cultural repertoire which exist within the small sub-population; chance effects of transmission in the small population, relating for example to the number of children particular families have; and the compatibility of specific elements of the old cultural *Bauplan* with the new practices.

Such situations arise particularly in the context of migration processes, Rosenberg argues, which have consistently produced punctuated change.

In fact, even if we imagine the origin point of a new core tradition as arising from a blending process, say members of two or three different groups which have been decimated by warfare coming together and producing a hybrid tradition, everything we have seen suggests that it will propagate itself through time by being resistant to outside influence and expand by a process of fission.

On the other hand, where we are dealing with what we have called 'multiple packages' as opposed to cultural cores, it is far from obvious that these conclusions follow. This is clearly an important area for future research, to establish the relative frequency of cores versus multiple packages as types of cultural lineage, and then to explore the transmission and selection processes associated with the individual packages. One process which is almost certainly important when significant socio-economic centres exist is that they become centres for the diffusion of prestigious innovations, which represent individual packages with their own dynamics. In some cases they may be associated with a combination of self-organization and social learning processes rather than the latter alone, a subject we will return to in Chapter 9. For example, in the Upper Xingu area of Brazil a number of different groups belonging to traditions with different histories and areas of origin, speaking different languages and with some very different cultural practices, have ended up in the same area as a result of the dislocation associated with the arrival of European colonizers. In the time since they have been in the same region, although they have maintained many of their cultural differences, they have developed a series of common cooperative social institutions, including inter-group rituals and specialization in particular spheres of production.[58]

Genes, languages and cultures

If integrated culturally inherited packages can come in different sizes and contain a greater or lesser variety of different things inside them, then the largest package it is possible to imagine is one which includes not only most cultural practices but also a specific language, not to mention the addition of a package of specific genes. Such a package implies that specific cultural practices and genes, as well as a language, are all being passed on through time together. Three questions immediately suggest themselves. Is there any evidence for such packages? If there is, how might they come into existence? What processes could produce them? These questions have resulted in a huge amount of debate in recent years and it will only be possible here to touch on some of the issues raised, which have already generated several books in themselves.[59]

In a way it is easier to start with the second question and follow Patrick Kirch and Roger Green[60] in quoting Kimball Romney, making some allowances for his 1950s formulation of the issue:

Physical type and language, we would say, have no causal relationship; there is no functional reason why a given physical type should occur within a given language family. Therefore when these two variables do show significant concordance in their distribution this may well represent an important historical fact, namely that the explanation for their concordance can be traced to a common point somewhere in the past. A demonstration that these two factors are also uniquely accompanied by a systemic culture pattern...strengthens the belief in a common origin.[61]

Romney's argument thus presupposes that we have a group of present-day populations with evidence of biological, linguistic and cultural similarities, and that the explanation for this pattern in the present is that the populations concerned can be traced to a single origin at some point in the past. The mechanism that links past and present is demographic expansion. In effect, some cultural feature, such as a subsistence innovation, provides members of the population with a selective advantage, and an essentially accidental association of cultural practices, language and specific genes at the origin becomes propagated with the expanding population through processes of vertical and oblique transmission. The relation between cultural practices and language history in the case of Athabaskan-speaking groups and its explanation in terms of the common origin of both has already been mentioned. Over time the result is diversification as populations become separated from one another and independent changes occur within them. In other words, the origin and spread of maximal packages depends on a demographic branching process. It is important to understand that it is the transmission processes, and the selective forces acting on what is transmitted, that determine whether the various different elements of the packages stay 'in step' with one another. In fact, the implicit assumption is usually that selection on most of the elements (except that responsible for the expansion) is weak or non-existent.

By and large it is language that has played the dominant role in such discussions, and particular examples where this sort of phenomenon is argued to have occurred include the spread of the Austronesian languages into the Pacific, the spread of the Bantu languages in Africa and of the Uto-Aztecan languages in western North America.[62] At least part of the reason for this role is that the processes of change in language are better understood than those affecting other areas of cultural practice, and the fact that a diversifying tree model generally seems to fit linguistic change extremely well,[63] not to mention that vertical transmission is usually assumed to play an important role in language learning.

Despite their apparent attractiveness as tools for reconstructing the history of populations, genes are more problematical, even the mitochondrial genes and Y-chromosome genes which aren't reshuffled with every reproductive event. This is because histories of individual genes are not the same as histories of populations; they are linked but separate.[64] Thus, any population which is not very small indeed will usually include within it individuals with different versions of the same gene, so tracing any specific version does not represent the population history. Furthermore, although genetic techniques make it possible to estimate the coalescence time of particular genes, in other words the last point at which the different versions had a common ancestor, that could easily be well before the time the gene first appears in a particular population whose history we are interested in tracing.[65] Languages in contrast represent speech communities. The same may be said in general terms for cultural practices, despite specific variations in transmission patterns. However, cultural attributes may be more open to hybridization than linguistic ones and the possible role of selection cannot be neglected.

Nevertheless, we are not totally without recourse in analysing these issues. As we have seen already, the key problem is to distinguish characters which are similar because they share a common recent evolutionary history from those which are similar for other reasons, and we can do this using cladistics,[66] already mentioned above as the set of principles and techniques designed to produce classifications that represent descent or phylogenetic history. In the biological context there are in fact three different ways that a group of species can be similar to one another. One is convergence, which we've seen already. Another is similarity among ancestral characters that a lot of other species also share. An example of this might be warm-bloodedness as a feature that humans and chimpanzees have in common. This is true but it is shared by a lot of other species as well and the evolutionary link lies a very long way back. Such similarities are known in the rather complex jargon of cladistics as *symplesiomorphies*. A third kind of similarity is the one of interest from the point of view of distinguishing different descent relationships from one another: the similarity shared only by the group of species under consideration, as a result of descent from a recent common ancestor; for example, those that distinguish humans and chimpanzees from gorillas. Such features are known in the jargon as *synapomorphies*.

Computer programs have been written that take a set of characters and attempt to construct the best evolutionary tree, in terms of the history of hypothesized descent relationships that are most consistent with the data.[67] Furthermore, it is possible to assess the extent to which the data are consistent with tree-like transmission. Not only are such trees interesting in themselves as pictures of descent history, they also create other interesting possibilities. For example, given the pattern of characters on which the analysis is based and the cladistic tree, it is possible to hypothesize the ancestral state of the characters. In addition, once the tree has been constructed, it provides the basis for what is known as the comparative method,[68] a rigorous approach to distinguishing homologies from independent analogies. Indeed, as I suggested at the beginning of this chapter, it is very difficult to understand adaptations unless we have a reconstructed history.

Applying these techniques to understanding the history of human cultural and linguistic traditions and adaptations is clearly an attractive proposition and the possibilities were illustrated some years ago by Ruth Mace and Mark Pagel.[69] Their phylogenetic analysis of the subsistence practices of a number of East African groups made it possible to distinguish those groups which had adopted pastoralism independently from those which were pastoralists as a result of having a pastoralist common ancestor. In fact, as I noted above, the principles used by historical linguists to reconstruct the relations between languages bear a close relation to those of cladistics, and specifically cladistic methods can be used to analyse languages. Cladistic methods have also been applied to archaeological data and an example of such work that Mark Collard and I have carried out will be described in a different context later in this book. Moreover, to return to the question with which this discussion of cladistics began, we can use the methods to assess the elements that belong to our cultural packages and see which ones do go together. Thus, if we take the language tree as probably the best picture of descent relationships between populations, then we can map other cultural attributes on to the tree and see to what extent similar pottery types, for example, belong to groups on closely related branches of the language tree; or we can construct distinct language and cultural attribute trees and compare them with one another.

In this context of evaluating the existence and implications of combined gene, language and culture packages and their relation to population histories, it is worth concluding this section with two examples of phylogenetic approaches, both concerned with what we have already noted as a classic example of cultural and linguistic branching processes: the human colonization of the Pacific.

Pacific phylogenies

Russell Gray and Fiona Jordan's recent study[70] contrasts what has become known as the 'express train' model of Polynesian expansion with the 'entangled bank' model.[71] The former suggests a rapid dispersal of Austronesian speakers from a homeland in Taiwan around 6,000 years ago, the latter that the Polynesian colonizers derived from a population in eastern Melanesia which had been there for tens of thousands of years, and that the cultural and linguistic patterns which are visible among the Polynesian islands arise at least as much through continuing contact subsequent to initial colonization, as through the colonization process itself.

Gray and Jordan took the series of archaeological/geographical steps suggested by the 'express train' model (see fig. 13) and mapped these onto the cladistic language tree which they produced (see fig. 14). Their analysis indicated that the links predicted by the model represented a very close fit to the language tree, much closer than would be predicted to occur by chance. As they point out, proponents of the 'entangled bank' or 'braided stream' model argue that culture, language and genes are constantly combining and recombining, so that patterns of language relationships say very little about the history of language speakers, and only reflect geographical proximity. Gray and Jordan's results largely conflicted with this latter pattern: proximity on the language tree did not correspond to geographical proximity. They did note cases where discrepancies existed between the language tree and the predictions of the express train model and suggested that these could have arisen through contact and resultant borrowing. Overall, however, 'The patterns apparent in linguistic relationships are integrally tied to the movements, contacts and activities of language speakers.'[72]

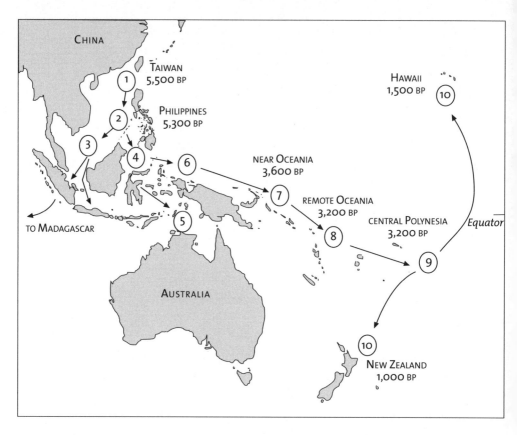

13 *The stages postulated by the 'express train' model for the spread of Austronesian languages into the Pacific from an assumed origin in Taiwan. 'BP' signifies years before the present.*

The second example represents what can only be described as the out-standing example so far of the application of a phylogenetic approach in anthropology, Patrick Kirch and Roger Green's *Hawaiki, Ancestral Polynesia* (2001), an updated and greatly amplified version of the earlier work already mentioned. Although it does not use specifically cladistic methods as such, it uses historical linguistics to the same end of constructing an evolutionary tree of the relations between different Oceanic languages. This is linked to the archaeological record of Pacific colonization, on the assumption that the language of the first colonizers of a remote island group will be the ancestor of the language spoken there in the present, so long as the initial population was reasonably substantial and there is no archaeological evidence for replacement of the founding cultural tradition. The language tree is also used to infer the dispersal centres for successive stages of Pacific colonization

14 *If the 'express train' model is broadly correct, then the links between the languages should parallel the successive stages of the expansion that the model postulates. Thus, in **a**, the language in location 1 should be ancestral to that in location 2, which in turn should be ancestral to that in location 3. If this is the case, it should be reflected in the family tree of language relationships, as shown in **b**. If it is not the case, then the relationships between the languages should not relate to their locations in the same way, as shown in **c**. This would be expected if relations between languages reflected subsequent patterns of contact rather than an initial population expansion. The results of Gray and Jordan's analysis largely supported the 'express train' model.*

associated with specific language sub-groups, in particular the Polynesian homeland of Samoa–Tonga.

Once this history of colonization and cultural and linguistic descent has been constructed, Kirch and Green use linguistic, ethnographic and archaeological evidence to reconstruct Ancestral Polynesian culture, including economy, society and religion, by a process of *triangulation*. This involves evaluating each line of evidence independently to see the conclusions they lead to, then bringing them together. However, even this is not an end in itself, but a step towards further goals:

These are the study and explanation of cultural change, 'evolution' if you will, represented by the diversification and differentiation of the myriad Polynesian cultures that descended from the ancestral 'Hawaiki'. By defining the cultural content of the ancestral node or root, we set the stage for a more comprehensive analysis of subsequent cultural change, through the individual trajectories of daughter cultures and societies.[73]

CONCLUSION

This chapter has shown that the long archaeological tradition of studying culture history becomes revitalized by recognizing that cultural inheritance is part of a Darwinian evolutionary system. Indeed, documenting culture histories once again becomes a central archaeological task. Seriation also regains an important role as a basis for distinguishing historical lineages from through-time patterns created by other processes. The evolutionary approach to cultural traditions transcends the essentialism of the old culture historical approaches with their implicit ethnic foundations by showing that cultural packages come in different sizes. A consequence of this is that the different cultural practices and artifact forms that are found within a population at a given time may have different descent histories. Some may be transmitted together and others not, and they may be affected by very different selective pressures. This is perhaps especially likely to be the case in complex societies, and represents an obvious subject for investigation.

Nevertheless, there are cases where large sets of cultural attributes are linked together in time and space – core traditions – and there are grounds for thinking that these may often, if not always, be associated with particular populations, perhaps especially in those cases involving relatively recent history where links with languages can be established. However, we should be very careful about referring to these as ethnic units, if by this we mean political or social units, since by and large the spatial scale of these traditions far exceeds the likely scale of any such units,[74] nor do we have any basis for assuming that the people concerned had any ethnic consciousness. It seems likely that the main processes associated with the origin and spread of these large packages are branching ones relating to demographic expansion. The situation with multiple packages is a lot less clear and needs a great deal of work. Part of that involves demonstrating that such multiple packages do in fact exist and here, as with analysing patterns derived from population histories, cladistic techniques may be very useful. Indeed, we can agree with Gray and Jordan that, 'In the future, phylogenetic methods may provide a common methodology and analytical framework to integrate data from ethnography, archaeology, linguistics and genetics. This is an important step towards a unified approach to biological and cultural evolution.'[75]

However, the immediate task of this book is to examine the demographic processes which lie behind many of the issues discussed in this chapter and have a long and chequered history in archaeological arguments. As we will see, in contrast to the emphasis in this chapter on the evolutionary dimensions of cultural traditions, population questions immediately lead us to start thinking about natural selection in the conventional biological sense, about matters of survival and reproductive success.

HUMAN LIFE HISTORIES AND THEIR POPULATION CONSEQUENCES

ARCHAEOLOGISTS HAVE LONG GIVEN a role to demographic processes in their explanations. The adaptive explanations of the New Archaeologists placed a great deal of emphasis on population pressure as the key to understanding a whole range of different phenomena, from the origins of agriculture to the appearance of hierarchical societies and the emergence of civilizations and states. Lewis Binford's proposal for the origins of Near Eastern agriculture[1] presupposed a foraging population that became sedentary as a result of exploiting wild plant resources, expanded as a result of becoming sedentary, and then found out that the population was outstripping the availability of wild resources. The problem was compounded as a result of land being lost to rising sea levels at the end of the last Ice Age. Under this pressure, the solution was to adopt cereal cultivation rather than simply collect from wild cereal stands. This was a classic explanation of the kind proposed by the agricultural economist Esther Boserup in her book *The Conditions of Agricultural Growth* (1965),[2] where the emergence of a subsistence problem under population pressure leads to a technological solution, in this case crop cultivation, at the expense of decreased efficiency, in the sense of diminishing returns for increased effort. As these agriculturally based populations grew, new daughter settlements budded off and moved to new areas, taking their agricultural economies with them and gradually rolling out across the neighbouring parts of the Old World in a great population wave.

The emergence of social hierarchies was also seen as an adaptive solution to the problems caused by increasing population. Chiefly managers could organize the redistribution of agricultural products from different parts of their territory and thus maintain higher population levels. Furthermore, increased populations and the resulting increased social interactions led to the failure of existing methods of dispute settlement and the emergence of central figures to take on this role. Colin Renfrew[3] proposed that the reason for the appearance of megalithic tombs and other monuments in the early agricultural societies on the Atlantic fringes of Europe was that they acted as territorial markers. The need for territorial markers arose as a result of population pressure. This in turn arose because the agricultural communities which had expanded across Europe from the Near East now had nowhere left to go; they had run out of road. Finally, Robert Carneiro's famous theory of the origin of the state[4] sought an explanation for it in terms of 'social circumscription'. This could arise in a variety of ways, but all of them ultimately produced a situation in which pressure arose on resources, leading to hostilities between different groups and ultimately to one of the groups becoming victorious and incorporating the others.

The time when all these explanations were being proposed was also just when the first doom scenarios were emerging concerning the implications for humanity's future if population growth and resource use continued at current rates. These scenarios provided both a source of ideas and a justification for the whole approach of seeing population as a prime mover in bringing about potentially disastrous change.

Then population pressure models were largely rejected by archaeologists. It was argued that population could not be regarded as an autonomous, independent factor affecting the rest of the socio-economic system and beyond human control. On the contrary, it was suggested, decisions about fertility were very much under control. Contrary to the usual beliefs, non-industrial populations were not at the mercy of the 'passion between the sexes' as Malthus had put it, but provided plenty of evidence for measures such as abortion and infanticide designed to control population. Furthermore, when people examined actual population levels in foraging societies, for example, these turned out to be well below what the area could theoretically support – its so-called 'carrying capacity'. The conclusion was that population pressure was a 'non-explanation'.[5] On the contrary, it had to be explained why, when foraging populations had clearly been successful at keeping their levels static for thousands of years, this had changed. Needless to say, this sort of finding had a pretty damning effect on explicit population pressure models and it was confirmed by further comparative studies of the relationship between population size and density and various measures of social complexity and inequality,[6] which showed that a lot of the putative relationships between them did not in fact exist.

Archaeological understanding of population processes has remained in the state reached in the 1970s and, therefore, models of change involving population have remained largely out of fashion. It is the aim of this chapter to show that things have changed. First, archaeological understandings of population processes are now 20 years out of date. Second, an understanding of past population patterns is essential to understanding cultural change, although not in exactly the way that the adaptationist archaeologists of the 1960s and 1970s assumed.

The basis for the first of these claims comes from the development of *life history theory*, which addresses the key question raised by the critics of population pressure models: what motivates people at the individual level when they are making reproductive decisions? No theory that lacks an answer to this question is going to be satisfactory.

LIFE HISTORY THEORY

Life history theory is a set of ideas from evolutionary biology concerned with the effect of natural selection on how organisms allocate their limited resources through the course of their lifetime. Like many fruitful ideas in the study of evolution it can be traced back to Sir Ronald Fisher.[7] It is concerned with such questions as: how much effort should be allocated to growth at a particular stage of the life cycle? How much to reproduction? As far as reproduction is concerned, to be successful is it best to devote most effort to mating or to parenting at a particular stage in life? Will it be more successful to produce a large number of offspring without caring for them much, or a smaller number in whose care a great deal is invested? Those individuals will be most successful in natural selection terms which come up with the optimal allocations in the light of the specific constraints they face, so over time selection should lead to genetically evolved life histories that produce higher fitness. Clearly, there is no single answer to this question: the optimum allocation for ants will not be the same as it is for elephants, because the genetic and other constraints affecting them are very different. That is to say, different species have arrived at different solutions to these trade-offs, depending on their own characteristics and the characteristics of their environments. Furthermore, many, if not most, are capable of varying their reproductive strategies, depending on cues they can perceive to variations in the environment. The point of life history theory is to explain how and why life history allocations within and between species vary over the lifespan. An early example of such a study was David Lack's[8] investigation of bird clutch size. He found that there was a trade-off required between the number of eggs produced and the number of chicks which could be successfully fed and brought to maturity, which depended on the food available.

The starting point for the application of life history theory to humans, of course, is that they are the same as the rest of the living world, in the sense that, as the outcome of millions of years of natural selection, they should have a propensity to maximize their reproductive success. It is important to be clear that this does not necessarily involve conscious motivation, although elements of it might do – in general, for example, people consciously want to take care of their children. It obviously does not involve conscious motivation in animals, and in humans, as in other living creatures, some of the mechanisms related to the aim of achieving reproductive success are entirely physiological.

Life history theory illuminates a lot of features of human demography which are otherwise extremely puzzling, and have certainly been so to archaeologists trying to make sense of past population patterns. To begin with, we need to see that achieving reproductive success is not just about maintaining high birth rates: it is no good producing children every year if they die in infancy because it is impossible to care for several of them at the same time. In fact, a better measure of an individual's reproductive success is not their number of children but their number of grandchildren. That is to say, one must not only produce children, but also ensure that they do not die in childhood. In addition, it is necessary to invest in their upbringing, so that they in turn become successful adults who have a high probability of reproducing their parents' success.

To achieve this will, in principle, involve a number of trade-offs which among mammals, including humans, are likely to differ between the sexes. For example, it is females that are obliged to bear the costs of both gestation and lactation. Humans are no exception to this requirement for trade-offs. This is why it is mistaken to take evidence that the birth rate is not being maximized as evidence that there is no propensity to maximize reproductive success. This is what the critics of population pressure models did not realize when they saw evidence of population regulation in traditional societies: a regulated birth rate could potentially produce the maximal reproductive success in the circumstances prevailing. Of course, the idea that this might be the case also goes against the assumption of the population pressure critics in the 1970s that people were restraining their reproduction for the good of the group, to keep it below carrying capacity. In an earlier chapter we have already seen reason to reject this form of altruistic group selection as an explanation: the altruistic strategy is open to infiltration and exploitation by cheating. It makes much more sense to see the processes of fertility regula-

tion observed ethnographically and historically as responses in the individual's interests to the current prospects for reproductive success, which may
require, for example, much longer intervals between births than those which
are theoretically feasible.

Since fertility rates contribute directly to fitness, it seems likely that they
are under relatively strong natural selection.[9] It follows that the ability to
respond appropriately to differing conditions is heritable and evolved as a
result of selection. These adaptive response patterns are known as 'reaction
norms':[10] they result in an adaptive ability to match variations in environmental conditions with variations in behaviour and other aspects of the
phenotype. This is part of the reason why looking at human behaviour from
the perspective of evolutionary ecology is less about identifying human universals, although that should not be discounted,[11] and much more about
offering explanations for precisely why human behaviour varies between different environments in the way that it does.

It is these varying conditions that affect the best pattern of trade-offs
between current and future reproduction and quantity and quality of offspring. In other words, at any given age humans, like other animals, face the
optimization problem of allocating their lifetime 'income' in terms of
energy, among investments in survival, improving the possibilities for future
income, and in reproduction (including parental investment), to give the
solution that maximizes the energy for reproduction at that age.[12] Thus,
female nutritional status, for example, has a considerable impact on fertility.
The closing down of the female reproductive system under conditions of
nutritional stress is often seen as a pathological phenomenon, but from the
life history perspective it is better seen as an adaptation. It makes much more
sense under these circumstances to devote current resources to survival
rather than to reproduction, which will probably fail anyway, and to wait for
the possibility that resources will improve in the future and make successful
reproduction more likely. It is the returns over the lifetime as a whole that
matter.

The most extensive and detailed study of the life history patterns of traditional foraging people is that carried out by the American anthropologists
Kim Hill and Magdalena Hurtado among a group called the Ache living in
eastern Paraguay.[13] In the past, the Northern group with whom Hill and
Hurtado worked lived by foraging in the primary forest, but after contact in
the 1970s and depopulation as a result of contact-related disease they began a
transition to life on a reservation. On the basis of an enormous amount of

careful and detailed work, especially in the construction of marital and fertility histories, Hill and Hurtado were able to build up a picture of the main features of Ache life history.

The first part of the lifespan is normally given over exclusively to growth, but when should allocation of resources to growth stop? Should it stop at the same age for males and females? In general, it is the case that fertility varies positively with body size in mammals. In their study of the demography of the Ache, Hill and Hurtado found that there was an association between body weight and fertility for both men and women, but that it was stronger for men. Ache males grow for two years longer than females and reach a greater body size, because the effect of body size on fertility is greater for males and because males have a longer reproductive span than females over which to gain the benefits of increased body size.[14]

This brings out the point that if the expected future lifespan is short, then it doesn't pay to invest in future growth or 'earnings'; instead, resources should be allocated to immediate reproduction. Thus mortality rates are part of the equation as well. Eckart Voland[15] points out that, on average, the higher the prevailing mortality, the younger and more frequently humans marry.

In the case of the Ache, the importance of parental investment is very clear at the most basic level: when they lived in the forest, before they were settled on a reservation, death of a child's father or mother led to a great increase in child mortality, as did divorce. But equally, the parental investment must be looked at from both the child's and the parent's point of view. For the child the maximum amount of parental investment is desirable, but for the parent the investment in any given child must be taken in the context of the trade-offs already described, so that, at the point that diminishing returns set in, it may be time to adjust the investment pattern accordingly. Hillard Kaplan[16] points out that data from traditional societies show that children are given less food than would maximize their growth rates and chances of survival.

What is very clear is that humans are committed to major amounts of parental investment. As we saw in Chapter 3, in foraging and horticultural societies children produce much less than they consume and production does not exceed consumption until the age of 18–20 years.[17] In fact, among Ache men returns from hunting increase four-fold between the ages of 18 and 25 (see again fig. 2). Kaplan sees this as arising from the fact that, unlike other primates, humans are dependent on nutrient-dense food resources which require considerable knowledge and experience to extract.[18]

This idea has been developed further by Hill and Kaplan.[19] They argue that the shift to a learning- and skills-based energy production system in the course of human evolution would have been associated with lower juvenile mortality and a lengthened juvenile period which would also have resulted in larger body size. The difference in both juvenile and early adult mortality between chimpanzees and human foraging societies is very clear from fig. 15. Chimpanzee rates are consistently much higher. Furthermore, such an investment in skills and learning could only be viable if there was a subsequent long period to pay back the initial investment; in other words, the juvenile period of investment in skills acquisition should have co-evolved with a longer adult productive lifespan, because the investment in skills led to high levels of energy production which could be maintained over a long period of adult life. This is borne out by the differences between chimpanzees and human forager populations in their probability of survival to different ages (fig. 16).

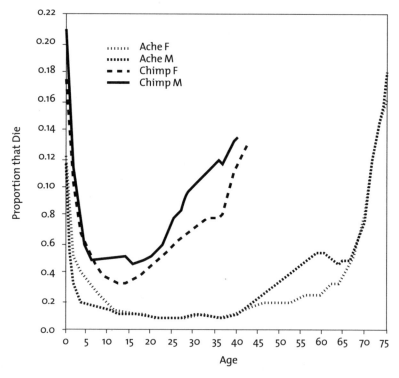

15 *Yearly mortality rates for the Ache compared with those for chimpanzees. Chimpanzee rates are consistently much higher.*

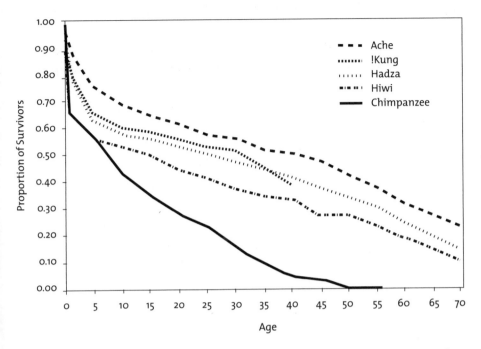

16 *Survival curves for four forager populations compared with that for chimpanzees. The probability of surviving to a given age is much greater for human foragers.*

The comparison of human life histories with those of chimpanzees and other primates brings out another phenomenon which is actually rather surprising. Despite all the parental investment and the long juvenile learning period, humans have higher fertility rates than great apes. The great apes have very long inter-birth intervals which are primarily due to long lactation periods.[20] In the great apes weaning generally takes place when the infant is around 5 times neonatal weight or more, whereas in the case of humans the average is 2.6 times neonatal weight. The result is that humans have short lactation periods and short inter-birth intervals. In fact, humans not only have higher fertility than chimpanzees and other apes, they also have longer lifespans, longer reproductive spans and higher offspring survival. Similarly, where chimpanzees are often near demographic equilibrium, most traditional human populations that have been described are growing rapidly.[21]

Humans have usually been seen as a characteristically high-investment, low-reproductive-rate species (*K*-selected in the jargon), but in the context of their evolutionary ancestors it appears that humans evolved in the direction of a higher reproductive rate species (*r*-selected). This would have had the effect of giving them a much greater potential to respond to the opportunities provided when large quantities of resources became available. Hill and Hurtado[22] suggest that humans might be seen as a 'colonizing species' of ape, able to expand at high rates when the opportunity arose. But high reproductive rates are in the end the victims of their own success. At the end of their remarkable study of Ache ecology and demography,[23] Hill and Hurtado raise the question of the role of rapid population growth and periodic crashes in human evolutionary history. They speculate that our high reproductive capacities can only be understood in the context of frequent population crashes, and propose that many human reproductive traits may have evolved under density-independent conditions, while others may have been selected for under a regime of periodic extreme crashes. We will return to these issues later in this chapter, and also in Chapter 8 in a different context.

Life history theory then provides us with a framework which enables us to understand the processes going on at the individual level which affect population patterns at the larger scale. People have been selected by their evolutionary history to maximize their reproductive success. External conditions have a bearing on the best way of doing this and individuals are sensitive, including physiologically, to these conditions. Birth rate is only one of the requirements and has to be traded off against a whole series of other considerations which are relevant to the production of grandchildren. It is impossible to have both maximum birth rate and maximum offspring fitness and it is the successful raising and social placement of offspring that decides lifetime reproductive success. In difficult conditions, the number of children who can be produced and successfully brought up will, on average, be lower than when more resources are available.

If this is true, then one implication is that those who have more resources will be more reproductively successful.[24] This prediction has been consistently confirmed by ethnographic and historical studies, especially for males. Hill and Hurtado[25] found that a man's hunting rank was strongly correlated with both his fertility and the survival of his children among the Ache in the period before they settled on reservations, while on the reservation male socio-economic success was of key importance. Among Turkmen pastoralists wealth was associated with reproductive success,[26] while Eckart Voland,[27] in his study of the 18th-century agricultural community of Krummhorn in Friesland, Germany, found that elite male farmers had much greater reproductive success than the general male population, especially over the long term. Clearly, the inheritance of resources becomes relevant in some of these cases, and this is a topic to which we will return in a later chapter, as we will to the whole question of the differences between males and females. In the meantime, it is important to be aware that, even among the Ache of the forest period, where there were no resources to be inherited, there was a strong correlation between the lifetime reproductive success of fathers and their sons, although no such correlation in lifetime reproductive success was found for mothers and their daughters.

It follows from this correlation between wealth and reproductive success that when resources are tight there are likely to be considerable reproductive differentials between individuals who are wealthy or successful at hunting and those who are not, but when resources are plentiful such differences will be less marked. Thus, Tony Wrigley[28] showed that the increase in population in England in the 18th century was a consequence of an earlier age at marriage, which in turn arose as a result of increased economic opportunities.

Eckart Voland[29] cites a number of factors which will, in general, lead to increases in the number of children produced and a correlation between fertility and achieved reproductive success, and which are of considerable importance if we are to understand the circumstances in which populations would have expanded in prehistory:

– If the costs of parental investment are low.

– Where parental investment is low in efficiency. That is to say, increasing investment does not lead to increased survival and reproductive success for offspring. Thus, if childhood mortality is affected by external risks which parental investment does not affect, for example childhood infectious disease, then the better method of ensuring reproductive success is likely to be increased fertility rather than increased investment in existing offspring.

– Where there are low opportunity costs. That is, where the cost of having one child does not interfere all that much with the possibility of having another. This may be more relevant to males than to females, because for females the costs of reproduction are always high but for males who can avoid supporting their offspring they may not be.

– Relative resource richness, such that the trade-offs involved in the different aspects of achieving reproductive success are not too severe, in which case increased fertility, by starting reproduction earlier and/or shortening inter-birth intervals, can lead to increased reproductive success.

– Promising dispersal opportunities. This is really the same as the previous one, in that it implies less severe trade-offs, but the resources available are non-local. In fact, the benefits of local resource-richness are likely to be cut off quite quickly by increased successful fertility unless dispersal opportunities are also available.

– Demographic competition for expansion. This is a non-intuitive implication of the life history perspective which actually acts to increase the fertility associated with promising dispersal opportunities. In terms of the competition for reproductive success and the trade-offs described, it makes no sense to postpone reproduction if an expansion opportunity exists of which others are already taking advantage. There is no option but to join them.

– Reproductive returns of children. This will be relevant if the benefits of older children acting as 'helpers at the nest' for younger ones outweighs the costs incurred in providing for them.

In short, as Voland[30] indicates, population effects, including population growth, are not targets of biological self-regulation but are *consequences* of numerous locally adaptive individual 'decisions', some of which are genuine decisions while others are physiological responses. Moreover, all these decisions are ones which discount the future; in other words, they operate on the 'bird in the hand is worth two in the bush' principle. What good is a big gain in the future that may never be realized? The future is uncertain. What matters is the reproductive opportunities within a given lifetime and if mortality rates are high then waiting may leave things too late.

We have already seen examples of the way that reproductive success corresponds to the availability of resources at the level of individual lives: the earlier marriage ages which led to the population growth of 18th-century England; and the greater reproductive success of Krummhorn male farmers. We can also see the phenomenon at a larger scale even where we can't trace it at the individual level. In their account of the history of the New Guinea Enga, Polly Wiessner and Akii Tumu[31] show that population shifts and migrations were the most prominent catalyst for change mentioned in Enga historical traditions, and that the population shifts were ultimately set off by the new opportunities which arose after the introduction of the sweet potato. Population increased from an estimated 10,000–20,000 to 100,000 within around 220 years; as populations expanded, clans grew and split more rapidly. The environment could support this expansion and it was only around the time of European contact that population pressure on land began to limit opportunities.

Apart from so-called endogenous changes within the population system, there can also be exogenous ones. In other words, population levels do not simply respond to changes within the system, for example, the gradual emergence of density-dependent responses as population increases. External factors can also be relevant if they affect resource levels, as we will see in the next chapter; climate change is one example, and technological development another. In the case of the Ache, discussed above, and also of the Yanomami of the Amazon region, both of whose populations were growing at the rapid rate of 2% per year at contact, the reason for the expansion was probably the fact that competing groups had been decimated by colonial expansion, making available a niche which was previously occupied. In the case of New Guinea, as we have seen, it was the introduction of the sweet potato. In the case of 18th-century England it was the economic growth associated with the beginning of the Industrial Revolution that broke through the old agrarian population resource limits which were the basis of Malthus' assumptions. Moreover, as Wrigley[32] puts it, in a comment which can be widely generalized, 'Contemporaries knew little of this though it shaped their destiny so powerfully.'

However, it should not be thought that increased fertility is the only mechanism that makes such growth possible. Renée Pennington[33] shows, for example, that fertility can stay the same and adult mortality even increase, but if rates of infant mortality are reduced, for example through the introduction of better weaning foods, then population will still increase.

It is worth concluding this account of life history theory with a final point. Since it was first suggested by Marshall Sahlins[34] that hunter-gatherers were 'the original affluent society', many archaeologists have often been puzzled by how humans could have let themselves be thrown out of the 'Garden of Eden' since they apparently did have control of their reproduction. In other words, why isn't evolution about increasing the sum of human happiness? Apart from the fact that there are good grounds for not accepting the 'original affluent society' premise,[35] the answer should now be clear. Controlling reproduction is about putting parental investment into ensuring that existing children survive to adulthood and can reproduce themselves, in situations where there have to be trade-offs between different goals. While, in any given generation, there might be individuals who did not attempt to allocate their resources to maximizing reproductive success, they would always be out-reproduced by those who did and who used any extra resources that came their way for this purpose. By definition, a propensity not to reproduce could never gain a foothold.

LIFE HISTORY THEORY AND ARCHAEOLOGY

It should be clear from this account of life history theory that it gives a new lease of life to models that see population as a key variable in the understanding of cultural change. Indeed, it is worth reiterating here that the relation between population and resources is at the core of the whole theory of evolution by natural selection. Life history theory spells out the 'choices' at the individual level associated with the allocation of resources to maximizing reproductive success. As we have seen, the best measure of this is the number of grandchildren an individual has, not maximizing the number of births, as some archaeologists still appear to believe. This will only be the best strategy for maximizing reproductive success in limited circumstances.

Of course, the archaeological record is not a source of information that gives ready access to the life history 'decisions' of past individuals. Nevertheless, that does not mean that the theory is irrelevant. On the contrary, it provides the theoretical underpinning for understanding the factors affecting the larger-scale population patterns in prehistory that archaeology *is* able to tell us about. Indeed, it follows from life history theory that identifying patterns of population growth and decline offers the archaeologist a powerful source of information about past human adaptations and their success. Population growth, for example, becomes an indicator not of population pressure, as the conventional wisdom has it, but of the availability of new resources, which may stem from technological innovation, environmental change, or simply from being forced by the over-exploitation of traditional resources to use resources that were always there but were previously deemed unproductive.[36] It is population stability that indicates population pressure on resources, and the presence of density-dependent checks on population, as Robert Bettinger[37] has pointed out.

It follows from all this that the archaeology of population has three tasks: (1) to characterize regional population patterns through time, (2) to identify the factors affecting these, and (3) to examine the impact of population size and density on other spheres of human activity and social institutions. These last two tasks are linked together to some extent, since the effect of population on resources at one time will lead to a reciprocal effect of resources on population at a later time. Nevertheless, the causes and consequences of population patterns are broader than this. As we noted earlier, population trends can be affected by external factors, such as climate change, not simply by their intrinsic relationship to resources. Furthermore, population patterns have an impact on a wider range of cultural processes than simply subsistence patterns. In the remainder of this chapter we will examine these issues from an archaeological perspective, concluding with a more extended case study that brings many of them together. We can start, though, with the key link between population and resources.

POPULATION AND RESOURCES

As we have just noted, natural selection as a process presupposes the potential pressure of populations, including human ones, on resources, for the reasons indicated by Eckart Voland:[38] population effects are not targets of self-regulation but *consequences* of individual adaptive 'decisions' about reproductive strategies which will always discount the future. This is why populations tend to expand towards and beyond the capacities of the resources currently being used.[39] As we will see in the next chapter, people are forced down an optimal foraging hierarchy of resource exploitation towards decreasing rates of return. If the next resource down has a low density and low rate of increase, then population will decline, because the rates of reproductive success previously achieved cannot be sustained. However, if resources lower down the order have a high density and/or a high reproductive rate, then life history theory tells us that people will take advantage of the possibilities created by the new resources to increase their reproductive success. In these circumstances, the trade-offs required by different elements in the life history investment process will be less severe: it will be possible to have more children *and* bring them up successfully. Local population will increase. The next chapter will show that this is what happens in the case of acorn exploitation in prehistoric California and also with the origins of agriculture in the Near East. Such developments may be linked to technological innovations but that is certainly not always the case. Mark Basgall[40] argues convincingly that technological innovation was not the key to acorn exploitation in California. On the other hand, towards the end of the last Ice Age in the Old World, innovations such as the bow, which made possible the exploitation of highly productive but difficult to capture resources such as hare and partridges, may have played a key role in making possible increases in local populations.[41]

One of the clearest examples of demographic responses to new opportunities is provided by the extremely rapid spread of agriculture from the Near East into Europe and the Mediterranean. A dramatic example of this is the evidence now available for an early overseas migration of farming communi-

ties from an adjacent area of the east Mediterranean coast to the island of
Cyprus, involving a sea crossing of 70–100 km to an island that was most
probably deserted. This occurred in the 8th millennium BC, at a time when
·domestic livestock still did not show morphological signs of domestication.[42]
With the exception of certain coastal areas and river valley situations where
marine and freshwater aquatic resources were already sustaining high population densities, there were extensive areas in Europe and the Mediterranean
where existing occupation density was low that were amenable to the new
form of exploitation. This situation satisfies several of Voland's criteria for
there to be a high correlation between birth rate and achieved reproductive
success: relative resource richness, reducing the severity of reproductive
trade-offs; promising dispersal opportunities enabling increased fertility to
be successful even when local resources were beginning to come under pressure; and demographic competition for expansion, increasing the fertility
associated with promising dispersal opportunities.

There is extensive debate in the literature about whether this was the
result of a 'wave of advance' of expanding population originating in the Near
East, which was increasingly diluted as the wave spread to the west by successive mixing with existing populations. Indeed, albeit in modified form,
this remains the most likely hypothesis.[43] In some respects, however, this formulation is a misleading one. Even if the process had been initially one of
local foragers adopting an agricultural economy, once they did so, at least in
the favourable environments where early agriculture was practised, then
population growth would automatically have followed. The basis for this is
not the claim that farmers have higher population growth rates than foragers. On the whole, the evidence is that on average they are pretty similar;[44]
both can expand very rapidly in favourable circumstances. The significant
factor is that in general, away from areas with significant aquatic resources,
agriculture will support more people per unit area, so higher population
growth rates can continue for longer. Even so, because demographic
processes work so quickly, at least from the point of view of archaeological
time-scales (see below), the time still won't be very long. There are then three
possibilities, not necessarily mutually exclusive: population can stabilize,
innovation can make it possible for the population to continue growing, or
people can make use of dispersal/migration opportunities and move to areas
where expansion opportunities still exist. In the context of a situation like
the spread of agriculture where high-density areas are adjacent to low ones,
the result will be the 'wave of advance' of population.[45] This does not depend

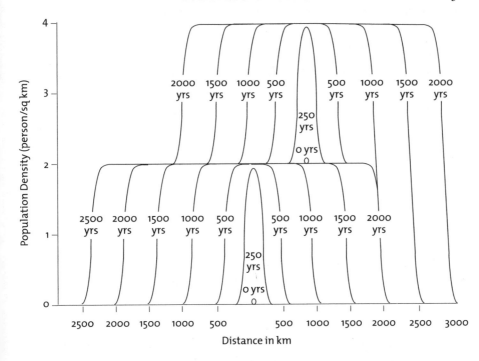

17 *The classic 'wave of advance' of an expanding population from a point of origin. The outcome of an initial low-density expansion may be overlaid by a subsequent one of higher density.*

on agricultural areas becoming completely saturated with people, but simply on the balance of local costs and benefits tipping in favour of migration rather than settling locally, for any number of possible economic or social reasons (see fig. 17).

We can see this process of population growth in microcosm in some places. From the 1960s to the 1980s an area of several square kilometres around a small stream called the Merzbach near the western border of Germany with Belgium was almost completely excavated in advance of strip mining for brown coal. A number of settlements of the earliest European farmers were found, covering the period *c.* 5300–4850 cal. BC.[46] The settlements consist of groups of long houses and pits scattered in groups of varying size. Detailed analysis of the sites and finds has made it possible to subdivide the sites into a large number of phases and as a result of this it was possible to trace the process of local population growth through counting the number of houses occupied in each phase (fig. 18). At initial colonization the number of houses was 3; less than 200 years later it was 16. This five-fold

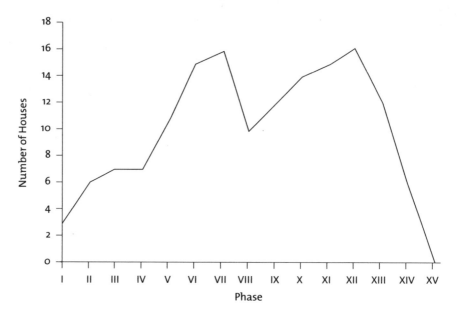

18 *Numbers of houses by phase in the Merzbach settlement micro-region of the first farmers in west Central Europe. The number rises rapidly in the early phases to a peak, then falls back slightly before rising to another peak, followed by a rapid decline to regional abandonment.*

increase in such a short space of time is comparable to that seen in New Guinea with the introduction of the sweet potato, and shows the potential that the new economy offered. However, the example also shows the limits. In the following phase the number of houses dropped to 10 and then over the next few generations gradually rose to 16 again before the area was abandoned altogether; we will have another look at this example in Chapter 9.

Chris Meiklejohn and colleagues[47] have also looked at the transition from Mesolithic foraging to a Neolithic mode of subsistence from the demographic point of view and offer us another local microcosm of the global process. They make use of a comparison by Mary Jakes[48] between the skeletons from three cemeteries in Portugal, two Mesolithic and one Neolithic. This study found a high representation of juveniles in the Neolithic sample and concluded that the Neolithic population was growing at a rate of close to 1% per year. The theoretical basis for linking skeletal age to birth rate was established by Lisa Sattenspiel and Henry Harpending,[49] who showed that the birth rate is roughly equal to the inverse of the mean age at death. Thus, so long as you can show that the skeletal sample is not biased by deposition or recovery factors, the higher the poportion of younger skeletons, the higher the implied birth rate. The problematical nature of estimating mean age at death led Jane Buikstra and colleagues[50] to suggest an alternative measure which had the same relationship with birth rate but could be more reliably measured from skeletal samples.

Meiklejohn *et al.*[51] concluded that the Mesolithic populations were relatively stable, with low mortality, while the Neolithic population had a high mortality rate but was nevertheless growing, pointing to increased fertility. A similar analysis of North European Mesolithic cemetery populations also found that the best interpretation of an example from Denmark was that it represented a stationary population, one neither growing nor declining, with low fertility and low mortality.

Other archaeological evidence from Denmark[52] suggests population growth in the middle-later part of the Mesolithic but not the latest part, prior to the transition to agriculture, perhaps an indication that density-dependent checks had begun to set in. One of the interesting features of the spread of agriculture from Central to Northern Europe was that it took a long time. Farming had spread right across Central Europe into the plains of Central Germany and almost to the Atlantic coast before 5000 BC, but it was another 1000 years before it was adopted by the foraging populations further north on the Baltic coast. The reason for the delay is likely to have been the high-density forager populations in this region, successfully based on aquatic resources. These could mount a successful opposition to farming expansion, demographically, and no doubt in terms of warfare and the strength of their cultural traditions as well. The ways such a successful adaptation could be gradually undermined as a result of contact with neighbouring farming populations have been described by Marek Zvelebil.[53]

In short, we can say that population will tend to grow when the opportunity arises, because people will tend to increase their own reproductive success when they can. The opportunity will arise when resources are sufficiently plentiful that life history trade-offs are not very severe and high birth rates and reproductive success go together. Because, in general, agricultural adaptations are more efficient, in the sense of supporting larger numbers of people on a given area of land, they will tend to spread in the way we have seen and to overwhelm existing low-density exploitation patterns and their populations by processes of displacement and assimilation.

POPULATION PATTERNS

The outcome of the availability of new resources is initially a rapid increase in population, followed by a slowing of growth until eventually it stops at a ceiling. This produces the shape of the famous logistic curve of population size against time, a key element in archaeological discussions of population pressure in the 1960s and 1970s. However, computer modelling of population processes subsequently made it clear that population size would not necessarily gradually increase to a ceiling at a fixed value. It might oscillate around a given value before eventually converging on it. It might continue oscillating, in what is known as a stable limit cycle, without ever converging. In this case the population keeps overshooting the limit and then under-shooting it, before overshooting again. Finally, the oscillations might actually become larger through time, so that in the end the population concerned would become extinct during an oscillation when its low value touched the zero level. The different possibilities are shown in fig. 19.

Theoretically then, so-called endogenous population-resource processes can lead to population fluctuations, not to mention external factors like climate change that have already been mentioned. Is there any indication that such fluctuations are any more than a theoretical possibility as far as human populations are concerned? In fact, there are several lines of argument to suggest that they may well have been important. First is the general pattern of world population growth over the period of the Pleistocene. The issues have recently been spelled out by James Boone.[54] If you take a plausible esti-mate of the world population at the end of the last Ice Age and work out the past growth implied to achieve this, it comes out at around 0.01% per year, or one person per 10,000 per year. This does not fit with the fact that most of the world was colonized by humans during this time, most probably at least twice over. Nor does it fit with what we know about human life histories in terms of their intrinsic potential for population growth. As we saw above, Hill and Hurtado suggested that humans should be called the 'colonizing ape', while known fertility rates for foragers range between about 0.7% and 3% a year. The implications are cogently spelled out by Peter Richerson and his colleagues in a recent paper:[55]

Suppose that the initial population of anatomically modern humans was 10,000 and that the carrying capacity for hunter-gatherers is very optimistically one person per square kilometre. Given that the land area of the Old World is roughly 100,000,000 square kilometres, then the [original population density divided by the Old World land area tells us that the population starts at 0.01% of world carrying capacity]. Then [solving the logistic equation for the length of time needed to reach a given level of population pressure] assuming $r = 1\%$ a year, Eurasia will be filled to 99% of capacity in about 1400 years. The difference between increasing population pressure by a factor of 100 and by a factor of 10,000 is only about 500 years!

The implications can only be that human population history is one of periods of rapid growth interrupted by frequent crashes, caused no doubt by both density-dependent and external factors.[56] Such a suggestion is also supported by computer simulations which model the effects of resource acquisition on human population growth rates, the effects of changing prey densities on resource selection and the effects of resource exploitation on prey population densities.[57] The outcome of these simulations was the appearance of oscillations in the human population size. If one adds to this the impact of occasional external factors, like adverse climate, then the

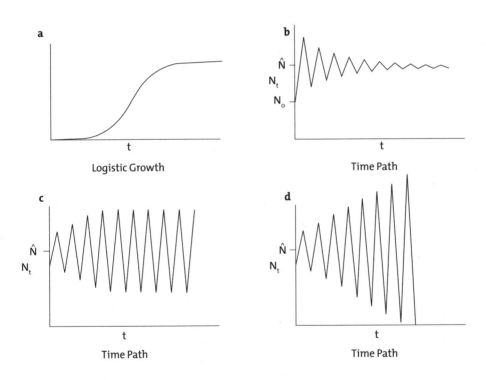

a Logistic Growth

b Time Path

c Time Path

d Time Path

19 a *The theoretical logistic curve of population growth to a ceiling;* **b–d** *Possible alternative population patterns: gradually decreasing oscillations in size to an equilibrium limit, a stable limit cycle with continuing oscillations, increasing oscillations leading to extinction.*

potential for more uncontrolled fluctuations, and even extinctions, is clearly apparent.

Charles Keckler[58] has also suggested the possibility of a 'biphasic' population pattern of rises and crashes to account for human population history, in which growing populations are intermittently hit by what he calls 'decimation events', leading to the extinction of local sub-groups (fig. 20). He shows by simulation that such a process could also account for a puzzling feature of the age distributions of skeletons that one finds in cemeteries. Population age-at-death distributions are normally characterized by high proportions of infants and old people, except of course that the absolute numbers of the latter are much lower because of the reduced numbers of people that reach old age. Cemetery populations generally have too many adults for such normal demographic processes, but including an element of catastrophic mortality at intervals produces the observed pattern of large numbers of adults.

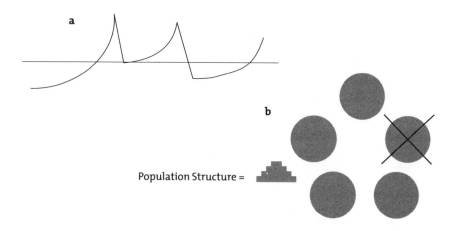

20 a *Keckler's so-called biphasic population pattern of growth followed by sudden decline;* b *The decline phase takes place as a result of events which lead to the elimination of specific local sub-groups, so that the overall regional population structure remains the same. The stepped feature in the diagram shows the population age structure of any given local sub-group, with large numbers of children at the bottom and the numbers shrinking for each older age group. When a group goes extinct, for whatever reason, the population of the region declines, but that decline is not detectable in the regional population age structure because all the age groups of the local group die off when it disappears.*

A further line of argument pointing in a similar direction comes from the anthropological genetics research of recent years, which has provided us with specific evidence of population expansions and crashes. These have become best known in the context of the origin of modern humans. It is now widely accepted that the human population of the world is so homogeneous genetically because it went through a bottleneck *c.* 100,000 years ago in which the population was extremely small, thus current human variation has evolved from a very narrow range. A similar bottleneck seems to have occurred again rather later, after the modern human population had begun to expand out of Africa, leading to population fragmentation.[59] However, bottlenecks and expansions are by no means restricted to the Pleistocene. As we have seen, an ethnographic example is given by the Yanomami, whose territory, at least until very recently, had expanded by perhaps as much as 2–3 times in the last 100 years,[60] while other groups went extinct. Expansion took place through a process of population growth and village fission[61] which led to marked genetic micro–differentiation as a result of stochastic processes of drift and founder effect.

With very few exceptions, archaeologists have not appreciated that past populations might have fluctuated in this way, or considered its implications. One of the reasons for this is that there was little evidence of population fluctuations. For example, the main effect of the early use of absolute dating methods such as radiocarbon was to put back the dates of many developments, thus lengthening the period over which they could occur and making gradualism a more viable possibility. What the new techniques did not do was increase the precision of dating for individual sites or layers within a site – in fact, they had the reverse effect. The site phases were floating within much longer time spans and it was natural to assume that, within a given archaeological phase, the evidence was reasonably evenly spread out within it.

Now, however, we have increasing archaeological evidence for population fluctuation. For example, in favourable circumstances, thanks to such developments as dendrochronology, we can now see that site occupation was often discontinuous, with short phases of occupation followed by longer periods of abandonment. With high-precision dating the past becomes much more dynamic and in the course of doing so the potential role of population fluctuations, albeit at local scales, becomes greatly increased, as we appreciate the scale of the gaps in our schemes and the instabilities behind our assumed continuities.

One example is represented by the work of Pierre Pétrequin and his colleagues on the Neolithic of eastern France.[62] Another is the work of Joop Kalis and Andreas Zimmermann[63] on the prehistory of the region of western Germany where the early farming villages of the Merzbach valley already described are situated. They analysed pollen data, using statistical methods on the frequencies of different species indicative of human impact to create a single summary variable representing changing human impact through time. The picture which emerged (see fig. 21) indicated a pattern of strong fluctuations. R. G. Matson and colleagues[64] noted similar patterns of occupation and abandonment in the Cedar Mesa area of Utah between AD 200 and 1300, as well as in adjacent regions. While Terry Jones *et al.*[65] have suggested that western North America was widely affected by demographic crises caused by decreased environmental productivity arising from climate change in the period AD 800–1350.

In short, we have increasing independent evidence for past regional population trends from a variety of sources. It is apparent that they were characterized not by a smooth upward trend and a levelling out but by major fluctuations. The spatial scale of such fluctuations – how big an area was at a peak or in a trough at the same time – is a matter of archaeological investigation in particular cases and clearly relates to the scale of the phenomenon

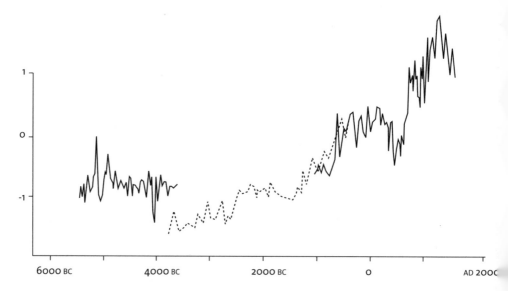

21 *The changing intensity of human influence on the environment in the Jülicher Lössbörde area of western Germany on the basis of quantitative changes in the pollen diagrams. Each of the three lines represents a different diagram. The pattern suggests fluctuating population sizes.*

responsible for the fluctuations.[66] The chronological scale is a different matter. As we have seen, quite conservative rates of population growth can lead to humans colonizing the whole of the Old World in less than 1500 years, which didn't happen. Accordingly, at long time-scales population growth by itself cannot be the explanation of such developments as the origins of agriculture. Peter Richerson et al.[67] sum things up as follows:

If people are motivated to innovate whenever population pressure rises above an innovation threshold, and if, in the absence of successful innovation, populations adjust relatively quickly to changes in [carrying capacity] by growth or contraction, then evidence of extraordinary stress, for example skeletal evidence of malnutrition, is likely only when rapid environmental deterioration exceeds a population's capacity to respond via a combination of downward population adjustment and innovation. Thus, for parameter values that seem anywhere near reasonable to us, population growth on millennial time-scales will be limited by rates of improvement in subsistence efficiency not by the potential of populations to grow, just as Malthus argued.

On this basis, and in the light of what we have seen already, it would appear that specific demographic phenomena created by such things as technological innovations or new dispersal opportunities are likely to play themselves out over time-scales of much less than a millennium, perhaps more like 500 years, as the Linear Pottery Culture micro-settlement area that we discussed above suggested. Clearly, cultural phenomena that are attached to demographic processes are likely to play themselves out over the same period. It is to such population consequences that we now turn.

POPULATION CONSEQUENCES

In the earlier discussion of population and resources we have already seen that life history theory provides a basis for reasserting many of the claims made by 1970s archaeologists about the consequences of population growth, for example in terms of its relationship to processes of subsistence intensification. Another frequent effect is likely to have been increasing regionalization and territoriality. An analysis of this kind of process has recently been presented by Bruno David and Harry Lourandos[68] in a study of the regionalization of rock art styles in the Cape York region of northern Australia (see fig. 22).

David and Lourandos show that the late Holocene period, c. 2,000 years

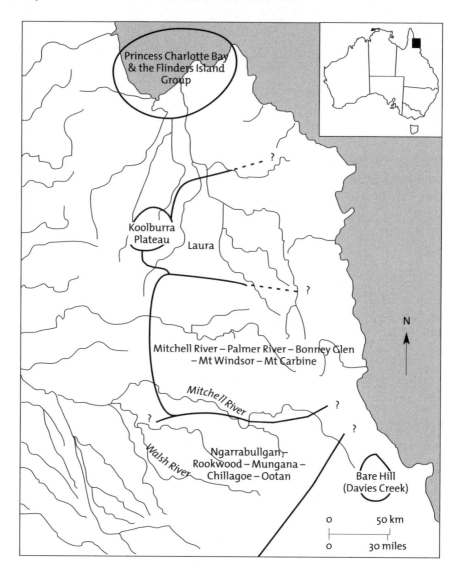

22 *Southeast Cape York, Australia, showing the locations of the regional rock art styles which emerged in the late Holocene as a result of population growth and the emergence of new territorial systems.*

ago, saw innovations in subsistence, including the first evidence for the systematic exploitation of grass seeds, as well as in stone artifact types. At the same time there were increases in site and regional occupation, in addition to the regionalization in rock art styles. The authors suggest that there was a population increase in the early to mid-Holocene, at a time when rainfall and

biological productivity were at a high level. In the late Holocene drier conditions returned and people responded by broadening their diet and making
use of new resources which were much more localized, a development which
involved innovations such as new stone tool types. The resources had considerable potential for supporting large numbers of people, including
occasional mass feasting. Ethnographically, it is known that groups of more
than 500 people sometimes congregated for weeks at a time. Another consequence was the emergence of increasingly formal group territories,
especially in areas rich in resources. At the same time, regionalization developed in rock art styles, with the implication that the different styles
represented claims of ownership by different groups.

However, population growth and decline can also have impacts that are
not usually considered in archaeological discussions. Attention was drawn to
some of these potential implications when we looked at genes, languages and
culture at the end of the last chapter. If a population expands, its cultural
inventory will spread with it, regardless of whether that inventory has anything to do with the reasons for expansion. We saw that some of the major
expansions of specific languages and cultures in different parts of the world
– for example, the colonization of the Pacific and the Bantu expansion in
Africa – are likely to be explicable in this way. Is there any means of detecting
in the archaeological record smaller-scale cultural expansions arising from
such demographic processes, in addition to gaining chronologically controlled information on site sizes and regional site densities? One way is to
focus on those aspects of material culture which there is good reason to
believe were largely vertically or close to vertically transmitted and involved a
long learning process in childhood and adolescence, as we saw in the last two
chapters. In other words, it involves a more nuanced and theoretically
informed version of the kind of approach long used in culture history. As we
might expect from earlier discussions, one of the concepts most successfully
used in this way is that of technological style: the ways in which objects are
made; these are not easily copied and often require long and intensive learning processes. Michelle Hegmon et al.[69] describe a series of case studies from
the southwestern United States where this sort of information has been used
to trace large-scale population movements. Their own study of the presence
of a new kind of pottery – indented corrugated ware – in the eastern
Mimbres region of southern New Mexico in the 12th century AD, indicated
that it was locally made but that some was in the technological style of the
area to the north, while other vessels were imperfect imitations. Given that

village size increased at this time, the authors suggested that at least some of the pottery in the foreign style was made by immigrants moving into the area in small groups which joined existing communities.

In a recent study of the technical knowledge involved in New Guinea pottery traditions, Pierre and Anne-Marie Pétrequin[70] have suggested that the techniques of pottery-making by paddle and anvil can't easily be acquired by imitation because of the long apprenticeship they imply. Accordingly, they suggest that their appearance must have involved the movement of maritime communities from eastern Indonesia, where the techniques were well established, to coastal locations in New Guinea, perhaps connected with the development of exchange in bird-of-paradise feathers (see fig. 23).

In many respects, however, the archaeology of demographic expansion is well established. What is much less well developed is the archaeology of demographic decline. Given what we have just seen about the probable growth and crash character of human population history, it seems likely that decline and extinction processes were frequent events and are therefore of considerable importance to understanding the past in general and the

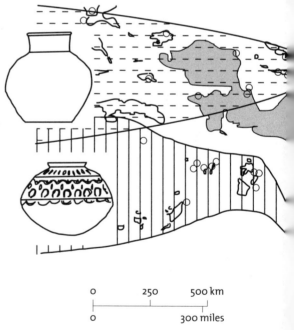

23 *The distribution of pottery types made using paddle-and-anvil methods in eastern Indonesia and New Guinea. The spread of the complex techniques of paddle-and-anvil pottery construction from eastern Indonesia, where they had a long history, to coastal New Guinea most probably involved the movement of maritime communities, perhaps connected with the development of exchange in bird-of-paradise feathers.*

| 0 | 250 | 500 km |
| 0 | | 300 miles |

archaeological record in particular. As we saw earlier, if a population declines or goes extinct then those distinctive cultural attributes with a strong element of vertical transmission will probably go extinct with it. Extinction represents, in effect, the pruning of branches of a particular evolutionary tree. R. M. W. Dixon[71] has emphasized the likely importance of extinction events in the history of languages, but they are also likely to have been impor- tant for the kinds of material culture and cultural practices that archaeologists study. Furthermore, the chance drift processes described in Chapter 3, affecting what is culturally transmitted when populations are small, will be operating not just at the early stages of expansion processes, when, as we saw earlier, it can be a significant factor affecting new cultural origins, but also during phases of population decline. Fraser Neiman's[72] computer simulations, described earlier in a different context, also demon- strated very clearly that when drift is the only process operating, the mean time to disappearance of any cultural attribute being transmitted within a small population will be much shorter than when it is large; cultural variation will rapidly disappear (see fig. 24).

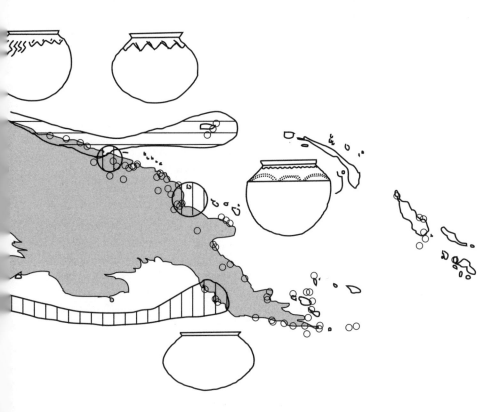

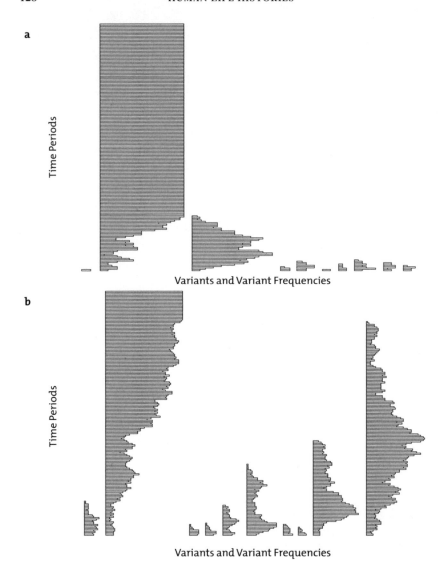

24 *Simulation of the effects of drift on a set of cultural variants (e.g. pottery decoration motifs) being copied by a number of individuals over a series of time periods. During each period individuals learn variants from a randomly chosen model or teacher. The figure shows the distribution of the frequency of the variants across the time periods. In both cases there are 10 variants whose frequencies in the initial time period are equal. The upper part of the figure, **a**, shows the changing frequencies of the variants through time for a population of 20, the lower part of the figure, **b**, for a population of 100. In this random copying process it is apparent that the average lifespan of a variant is much greater in the larger population, which takes far longer before a single type takes over completely.*

It is especially important to remember that the effective population size for many if not most kinds of cultural transmission is likely to be much less than the overall population size. Thus, for example, if we imagine a situation where a population is made up of 50% sub-adults and some craft skill is largely if not entirely transmitted by adults to their same gender offspring, then the effective population size for transmission is only 25% of the total population size. In situations where transmission is 1:many, say a specific elder transmitting a ritual to a group of initiates, then the effective population size may only be one. Thus, even where a particular local population does not actually go extinct, it may suffer significant cultural loss, as we saw in the case of the disappearance of the Torres Island canoes described by Rivers.

Finally, even if a group does not become totally extinct physically, it can still disappear culturally, as its remaining members join more successful groups and are absorbed into them. If this process was a common one, as the evidence we have seen suggests it might have been, it has considerable implications for the processes of social evolution that we will look at in Chapter 9.

POPULATION AND CULTURAL PATTERNS IN THE LATER NEOLITHIC LAKE VILLAGES OF THE ALPINE PERIPHERY

The high degree of chronological resolution provided by the tree-ring dates from the Neolithic lake villages of the European Alpine region gives us an excellent opportunity to look at prehistoric population patterns in detail.

Fig. 25 shows the dates of tree-felling activity identified on the wood used for piles and house construction at Neolithic settlements dating between 4000 and 2400 BC around the shores of Lake Constance in southern Germany, on the border with Switzerland. They are shown in relation to the forest clearance history and the names of the local archaeological cultures.[73] The most striking feature is the fluctuations in occupation that they suggest. A similar pattern is also seen in the results of pollen analysis work from the same region, which shows a series of phases of cereal cultivation, separated by shorter gaps. The dendrochronologically dated wood from the lake villages also provides evidence for patterns in the development of the woodland itself, in which repeated periods of clearance are succeeded by regeneration and the development of secondary forest.

Precisely the same sort of situation is to be found during the later Neolithic on the much smaller lakes of Chalain and Clairvaux in the French Jura, in the western foothills of the Alps.[74] Again, dendrochronological

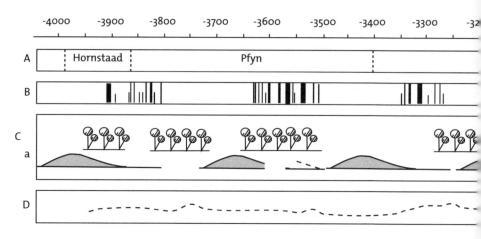

25 *Later Neolithic occupation around Lake Constance, on the Swiss-German border, showing the cultural sequence A, dendrochronologically dated timbers from settlements B, woodland history C, and inferred demographic history of population fluctuations D.*

information is available. The left-hand column of fig. 26 shows the number of settlements around the two lake shores, from 4000 to 1600 BC. Pierre Pétrequin and his colleagues see this pattern as a series of demographic cycles of population growth and decline which is also reflected in the gaps in the evidence for agricultural activity in the pollen analysis results, as well as in the dendrochronological evidence of woodland clearance. Similar patterns are also found around the lakes of both eastern and western Switzerland.

Not everyone accepts that these patterns can be interpreted in demographic terms. The fluctuating numbers of settlements are correlated, although by no means perfectly, with lake-level fluctuations. The number of settlements known from low lake-level phases is much greater than for higher levels. One possible explanation, therefore, is that because the settlements which would have been occupied at times of high lake levels were never submerged, they are poorly preserved, so the wood to provide dendrochronological dates has not survived. Accordingly, the fluctuations in settlement numbers could simply be a result of fluctuations in preservation.[75]

However, the fact that variations in human impact are apparent in both the pollen diagrams and in the evidence for woodland history suggests that population fluctuations are at least a significant factor. Moreover, there is a

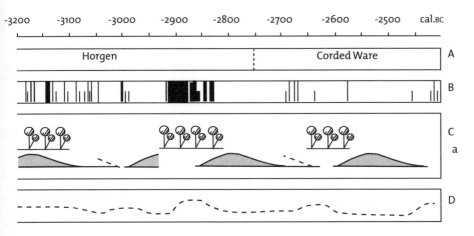

further source of evidence which points in the same direction. It is now generally agreed that the lake-level variations are a result of climatic variations,
with cooler, wetter phases corresponding to high lake levels and warmer,
drier phases to low levels.[76] The pattern of rises and falls correlates closely
with the high-resolution record of variations in the $\Delta^{14}C$ concentrations in
the atmosphere, as measured from tree rings (see fig. 26, column B). These
relate to levels of solar activity. High concentrations reflect low levels of solar
energy and a consequent increase in the amount of cosmic radiation reaching
the earth, which increases ^{14}C production. Low concentrations reflect high
levels of solar energy. The variations in solar energy affect patterns of atmos-
pheric circulation, leading to changed weather conditions. Historic evidence
indicates that at the latitude of Central Europe low levels of solar energy correspond to the sorts of weather conditions seen during the Little Ice Age of
the 16th–18th centuries AD, with shorter, wetter and cooler summers, hence
the rise in lake levels, as well as other indications of climatic deterioration in
the Alps.[77]

How would this have affected population levels? Christian Maise[78] uses
historical records from Western and Central Europe to show that cooler,
wetter conditions led to frequent crop failures because the growing season
was shortened. Mortality rates increased as a result.[79] The same problems are
likely to have arisen in prehistory. Calculations based on evidence from a
village on Lake Zürich dating to around 3700 BC suggested that about two
thirds of the calories would have come from plant foods and the remainder
from animals.[80] Cereals would have contributed about half the calories. The
evidence from this site, like most of the others, comes from a period of
favourable conditions but, even in this case, the model suggested, the subsis-

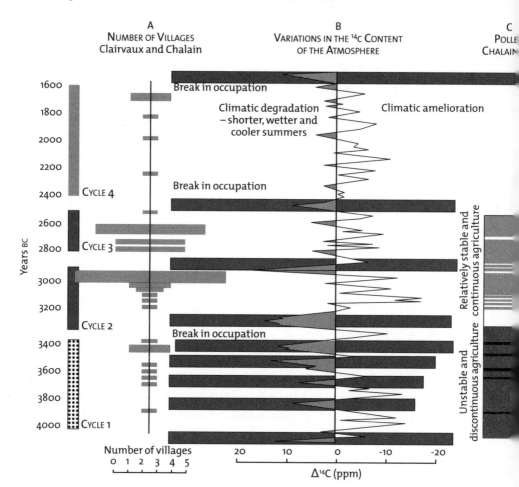

26 *Later Neolithic occupation in the Chalain/Clairvaux area of the Jura region, eastern France. The figure shows the demographic sequence A, variations in the ¹⁴c content of the atmosphere as a climate proxy B, the pollen sequence C and the cultural sequence D. The horizontal bars in A represent the number of villages occupied in that period.*

tence economy was vulnerable, in terms of the margin between what would have been needed by the population and what the economy could provide. A climatic downturn leading to cool, wet conditions and a shorter growing season would have produced severe problems. In the light of what has been said earlier about the sensitivity of reproductive decision-making, infant mortality, and parental investment to external conditions we would expect such events to have significant demographic consequences.

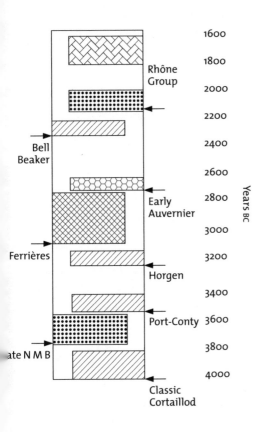

D
CULTURAL SEQUENCE

Rhône Group

Bell Beaker

Early Auvernier

Ferrières

Horgen

Port-Conty

ate N M B

Classic Cortaillod

Years BC

1600
1800
2000
2200
2400
2600
2800
3000
3200
3400
3600
3800
4000

In summary, even if the fluctuations in site numbers around the lake shores are partly a result of variations in preservation conditions arising from variation in the lake levels, the climatic conditions which produced high lake levels would probably have had a negative demographic effect. The conditions that led to low lake levels would have been more conducive to sustaining higher rates of reproductive success.

Finally, now that we have seen the evidence for the population fluctuations and the climatic factors which seem to have had an important role in producing them, it remains to examine their consequences. Most importantly, it appears that the cultural patterns are intimately linked to the demographic ones. If we look again at the pattern for Lake Constance (fig. 25), we see that the initial Pfyn culture occupation lasted for a little more than 50 years, then there was a gap in occupation of 150 years before reoccupation, by communities which again had Pfyn culture inventories. After this there was another 150-year gap before Horgen culture communities appeared and a similar pattern was repeated. They in turn were succeeded by Corded Ware communities after a further gap.

It is likely that over time some of these gaps will be filled or shortened, but a much fuller set of dendrochronological dates for eastern and western Switzerland collected by the archaeologist Claus Wolf of Lausanne[81] shows essentially the same picture. Most of the cultural transitions fall at gaps in the record. It seems probable that significant cultural changes took place when populations were relatively small and were perhaps more subject to drift processes, in the way suggested by Michael Rosenberg[82] that was described earlier. When subsequent more favourable conditions led again to population expansion, the new cultural complexes then emerged into the archaeological light. In some cases these complexes came from outside the local region, as in the case of the appearance of the distinctive pottery types belonging to the wider group known as the Corded Ware in eastern Switzerland around 2780 BC.[83]

Cultural novelties from outside do not always appear in such gaps though. In contrast to eastern Switzerland, the earliest Corded Ware pottery in western Switzerland appears at the time of a local population peak, around 2750 BC, in the form of small numbers of locally made, culturally distinctive Corded Ware sherds in settlements of the local cultures. These almost certainly represent the movement of small numbers of people from communities with a tradition of making and using this very different pottery, in the same way as Michelle Hegmon and colleagues suggested the corrugated pottery came into the communities of the eastern Mimbres region, as we saw above. However, the subsequent transformation of the local culture 100 years later, into one where the overall pottery repertoire was now a specifically local version of the Corded Ware tradition – the Auvernier culture – again followed a demographic trough.[84]

The broader regional dynamics show a similar picture based on demographic processes, with the expansion of the population characterized by Horgen pottery having a significant impact over a wide area, not just in terms of pottery but also of the spread of new forms of village settlement, which persisted in many regions when the pottery produced changed as a result of close contact with groups from a different tradition.[85] The pattern is summarized in figs. 27 and 28 (see pages 136, 137).

In sum, it appears that population dynamics have a considerable effect on cultural patterns. That is, perhaps, no surprise in the light of the evidence for cultural transmission processes that we saw in Chapter 3.

CONCLUSION

It seems very likely that past populations have been much more dynamic, in terms of processes of expansion and contraction, than we have appreciated until very recently. Our review of life history theory, as well as population resource modelling and world population patterns generate this as an expectation, recent historical/ethnographic evidence supports it, but perhaps most importantly it is very clearly apparent in the archaeological record when we are in a position to look at this with the necessary high levels of chronological resolution.

However, perhaps the most important lesson of this chapter is that it provides a coherent framework, based on life history theory, for the archaeological study of population. The theory tells us that the human reproductive system is very sensitive to external conditions, and provides us with a series of micro-scale mechanisms at the individual level that specify how variations in external conditions will be translated into variations in reproductive 'decisions' (many of which are physiological). The repetition of numerous individual decisions leads to macro-scale outcomes at the population level – these are unintended outcomes, not goals of regulation. The archaeological record can, if approached in the right way, provide us with the evidence for these macro-scale population outcomes over time in individual regions, and therefore of reproductive success histories. Through life history theory we can postulate well-founded models. One feature which emerges very clearly from such models is that population processes have specific time-scales, medium- rather than long-term ones. These make sense of many patterns in population history and their relation to such processes as the spread of agriculture which are inexplicable in terms of traditional frameworks. Furthermore, the population patterns have major implications in the cultural domain. The adaptive processes associated with reproductive decisions in particular times and places produce specific population histories which can carry cultural traditions with them and also lead to their demise. This is certainly not the only process through which cultural patterns are propagated and disappear but it is an important one.

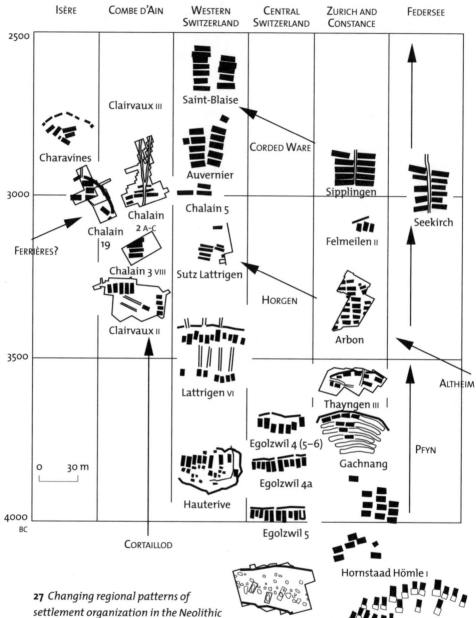

ISÈRE   COMBE D'AIN   WESTERN SWITZERLAND   CENTRAL SWITZERLAND   ZURICH AND CONSTANCE   FEDERSEE

27 *Changing regional patterns of settlement organization in the Neolithic of the circum-Alpine lake-villages, 4000–2500 BC. From around 4000 BC there are two different village construction traditions represented in the lake-villages north of the Alps, a western one in which houses are constructed at right angles to the lake shore and an eastern one where the long area of the house is parallel to the shore. With the Horgen expansions the eastern tradition spreads rapidly to the west, where it remains prevalent for over 500 years.*

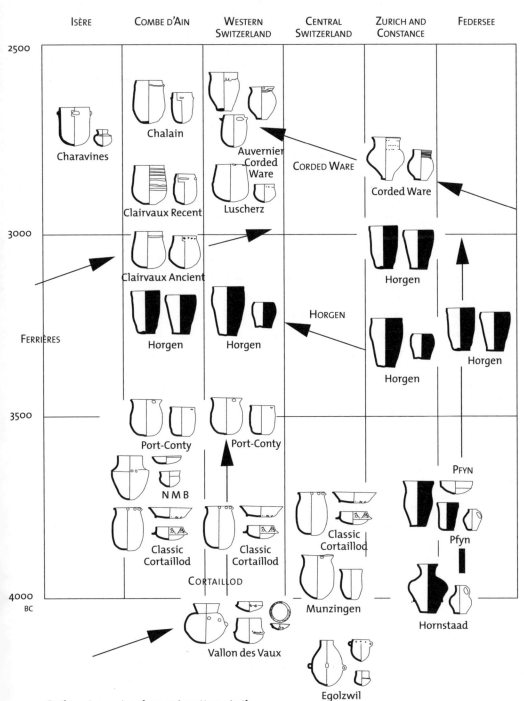

28 *Changing regional ceramic patterns in the
Neolithic of the circum-Alpine lake-villages, 4000–2500 BC. In contrast to the village plans,
the ceramic styles are more susceptible to outside influence in the latter part of the period.*

The Archaeology of Getting a Living: Long-Term Patterns in the Human Exploitation of Resources

IT IS CLEAR FROM the previous chapter that the life history strategies people adopt, consciously and unconsciously, and the population patterns that ensue, depend to a major extent on people's strategies for survival. This chapter looks at the evolutionary answers to the question of how and why people get their living in the many and varied ways that they do, and the implications that these have. In order to do so, the first requirement is to look at the evolutionary theory employed in such studies, then the evidence that is relevant to humans, before finally turning to the specific issues raised by applying the ideas to archaeology. These revolve around three key questions. The first concerns how we can test our evolutionary ideas using archaeological data. This is a prerequisite for addressing the second two questions. To what extent do we need to invoke a role for cultural traditions in accounting for how people get their living, as opposed to simply basing our hypotheses on the capacity for flexible, fitness-maximizing behaviour possessed by all higher animals? Does archaeology have anything to add to the short-term studies of people's decisions carried out by ethnographers who adopt the second style of evolutionary analysis in Eric Smith's classification that we saw in Chapter 1: human behavioural ecology? We need to begin, though, with some history.

CULTURAL ECOLOGY

Questions about how people got a living from their environment only began to interest archaeologists in the 1940s and 1950s. Before that the subject had not generally been considered very relevant to understanding the past and many archaeologists considered that retrieving the bones from their archaeological sites was not worth the trouble; as for plant remains, they were barely even aware that these existed.

The theoretical framework that began to provide an important role for questions about how people got a living from their environment was 'cultural ecology', developed by the American anthropologist Julian Steward in the 1930s and 1940s.[1] It was concerned with the relationships between society, technology and environment. Cultures were conceived as having a core, formed by those activities related to extracting energy from the environment, especially the subsistence technology, while other aspects of the society, like religion, depended on the core but were more open to being affected by the result of such processes as diffusion. As Robert Kelly[2] explains, Steward tried to show how society was shaped by technology and by the environment. These defined the adaptive possibilities of the society and how it might change. So, for example, he suggested that, in the case of many hunter-gatherer societies, the limited possibilities of exploiting environments by means of foraging using a simple technology would have led to low levels of production and limited population size. In turn, these would lead to a relatively simple type of social organization which would be found wherever such conditions were met: the foraging band. Because hunter-gatherer societies were considered to be so simple, in Kelly's words,[3] 'There was nothing for the core to determine, since hunter-gatherer society was nothing but cultural core!'

Many anthropological studies in the 1950s and 1960s were conducted within the framework of cultural ecology and their main tenor was to show how cultural practices of various kinds assisted societies in adapting to their environments. In this it was not so different from the functionalism that had come to be characteristic of British social anthropology in the 1920s and 1930s. The object was to show, in effect, that cultures formed harmonious wholes, and that even what appeared to members of Western societies to be outlandish practices in fact had a functional or adaptive logic. Thus, the use of burnt caribou scapulae as part of a process of divination to decide where to hunt by a Canadian Indian group was seen as a way of randomizing hunting expeditions which was actually very efficient in an area of scattered and mobile prey.[4]

The potlatch feasts of some of the societies of the Northwest coast of North America, in which chiefs destroyed or gave away large quantities of wealth, such as blankets or sheets of copper, to gain prestige with their neighbours, were explained as devices to create debts in neighbouring communities which could be called in if necessary in times of food shortage: so-called 'social storage'.[5] Perhaps most famously, the anthropologist Roy Rappaport[6] saw the cycle of ritual pig feasts of the

Tsembaga of New Guinea as, among other things, a means of preventing the local pig populations from getting out of hand. Other studies explained cannibalism in terms of local protein shortages and warfare as a means of population regulation.[7]

Many archaeological studies were in a similar vein. The origins of agriculture, for example, were no longer seen as a triumph of human inventiveness but as a response to population pressure.[8] Colin Renfrew[9] suggested that a possible explanation of the growth of civilization in the Early Bronze Age of the Aegean region was the need for someone to redistribute subsistence products between different local micro-environments, following the 'chiefdom' model of Elman Service.[10]

These cultural ecological studies were an enormous advance on anything which had gone before because they actually attempted to address processes of change in the past, rather than explaining them as arising in some supposedly self-evident way from migration of peoples or the diffusion of influences. Moreover, studies of local adaptation still continue, producing interesting scenarios about how and why cultures changed in the past in response to adaptive pressures. Nevertheless, the cultural ecological approach eventually came under attack, on a variety of different grounds.

In many respects the accounts it offered were 'just-so' stories that never actually provided evidence for the claims the cultural ecologists wanted to make. Thus, the explanations of the potlatch in terms of the need for subsistence security never demonstrated any relationship between a measure of subsistence security and measures of village prestige and rank;[11] they simply asserted it. The whole approach, indeed, was symptomatic of the attitude that if a particular type of behaviour exists, it must be adaptive. If it wasn't adaptive it wouldn't exist. It followed from this that societies in general could be assumed to be at equilibrium.

Another problem with the cultural ecological approach was its implicit belief in the importance of the group, as opposed to the individual, as the adaptive unit. This belief runs deep in all the social sciences with the exception of economics but, as we have seen in Chapter 2, it raised problems for studies of animal behaviour. There are many contexts in which the same issue comes up in the ecological study of human behaviour.

As we saw in the last chapter, a good example concerns the study of population, where it was argued in the 1970s that people, especially foragers, practised population control measures for the good of the local group, often maintaining a population level well below the 'carrying capacity' of the local environment. This would have had the effect of keeping the population in balance with the environment and enabling them to survive the occasional bad year when resources were much poorer than normal. However, as we have already seen, this is a problematical idea, since the self-sacrifice of some can be exploited by the self-interest of others, perhaps especially in foraging societies, where group membership is very flexible, so that it may be relatively easy to avoid the disapproval of other members of the community by going elsewhere. The alternative explanation will be apparent from the last chapter: those individuals who produce fewer offspring may actually be more successful in bringing up more to adulthood than individuals who initially produce more.

It was the perceived inadequacies of cultural ecology, especially its Panglossian[12] view of adaptation, that led many archaeologists and anthropologists to reject it during the 1970s, some in favour of the Darwinian approaches with which this book is concerned.

In what follows I want to argue that many extremely interesting, illuminating and, above all, answerable questions arise if we make the assumption that human ways of getting a living from the environment, like those of other animals, have been conditioned by natural selection. Although this view has found little favour until relatively recently, over the last 40 years a small number of archaeologists have been attracted by this assumption and have made use of it in their work. Perhaps the most single-minded in this respect was the Cambridge economic prehistorian Eric Higgs, originally a sheep farmer himself, who took the view that over the long term evolutionary principles always prevailed and cases where they apparently did not could be dismissed as short-term aberrations. In fact, the application of such principles to understanding past ways of getting a living raises issues which go well beyond archaeology. They have great consequences for modern debates in society at large about humanity's relation to nature. Only the archaeological record has the information to tell us about the history of these relations: about the extent to which human history has been characterized by 'noble savages' living in harmony with nature, or by the kind of short-sighted exploitation which we regard as specifically characteristic of the capitalist, profit-obsessed present.

OPTIMAL FORAGING: THEORY AND ETHNOGRAPHIC EXAMPLES

As we saw in Chapter 2, the key assumption that provides the basis for testable hypotheses in this context is the idea of optimization: that individuals will relate to their environments in ways that maximize their reproductive success. This is not a tautological claim about the world in the way that cultural ecological claims about adaptation were. It is a framework for trying to find out about the world and possibly being proved wrong. Foraging provides the context in which we can formulate optimization models most straightforwardly. This is done most simply by assuming that the foraging strategy which will be most successful in fitness terms will be the one that is most efficient in providing the maximum amount of energy for the minimum amount of effort on the part of the individual doing the work.[13]

There are a variety of reasons why this sort of efficient behaviour might be correlated with increased fitness. For example, if individuals forage efficiently they will have more time for other socially, and potentially reproductively, important activities, such as parenting. In this context it is time that is important. Individuals will gain by obtaining a given amount of food in as short a time as possible. If foraging is dangerous, for example because of predators, it is again likely to be beneficial to keep foraging time to a minimum. However, perceptions can change depending on the animal's state of hunger. Experiments showed that sticklebacks placed less emphasis on vigilance when they were feeding if they were very hungry than when they were less hungry.[14] Moreover, specific constraints affect particular species in particular ways. Thus, it has been shown that moose, when foraging, will seek to maximize energy efficiency, but subject to the constraint of the size of their stomach and the need for a given level of sodium intake.[15] In summary, animal studies clearly suggest that foraging strategies are under selective pressure even in circumstances where actual food shortages are not a problem.

We can apply the same sort of optimal foraging principles to understanding human foragers. At first sight it might seem obvious that the best way to exploit an environment is to make use of those resources that are most widely available. In fact, this is not the case. What is known as the *diet breadth model* predicts that the resources that will be exploited are not those that are most widely available, but those which provide the best return for a given amount of effort. The effort or cost is divided into two components: the time taken to find the prey item and the handling costs which arise when it has been found, such as the butchery of game or the processes required to make acorns suitable for eating. Search costs will vary with the density of the resource concerned, but also with the technology available for searching, such as the use of the horse in bison hunting. Handling costs will likewise vary depending on the technology available.

When a forager encounters a resource, a decision has to be made about whether to make use of it or pass it by and try to find something better. The diet breadth model predicts that individuals will ignore the resource if they think they can soon find something that gives a better rate of return; otherwise, they will decide to exploit it. Accordingly, if we know something about the resources available, in terms of the average time taken to find them, the amount of time it takes to kill/collect and process them, and the energy return from them, we can predict which resources will be used if the aim is to maximize extractive efficiency. Thus, resources can be ranked in terms of the returns they produce once they have been encountered and we can find out which combination of resources will produce the maximum returns, taking into account the time it takes to locate them. The highest return diet will only include the small number of highest return resources. If the inclusion of a specific resource in the diet mix leads to a decrease in net returns, it is not included. Even if certain resources are plentiful in the environment they will not be included if the handling costs are large and the return rates in terms of calories per unit time are low.

What would lead to change in the optimal diet? One possibility would be a technological innovation which drastically reduced the capture/handling costs of one of the low-ranked resources initially not in the diet and thus made it worth exploiting. Another possibility would be the situation that arises when the highest-rated resources become rarer as a result of exploitation, so that search times increase. In these circumstances too the exploitation of resources not originally in the optimal diet might become worthwhile. In fact, where optimal foraging assumptions hold, as environments are increasingly exploited, return rates go down, the diet breadth increases as people have to look to other resources, and they have to do more work to maintain the same levels of production as before, unless the opportunity of migration to less heavily exploited areas is available.

Ethnographic studies of foragers, such as the Ache of Paraguay, which have collected the relevant information[16] suggest that their foraging behaviour does indeed match the predictions of the diet breadth model, in that those resources which give the maximum return are included in the diet and those which would lower it are excluded (see fig. 29). However, the male and female resource rankings are different, for reasons we will look at in a later chapter. A similar study of aboriginal women foragers in Australia produced the same result, in that they only gathered the three most profitable foods and ignored the most abundant ones available, because the returns on processing the latter would have lowered their net return rate.[17] Similarly, seeds dropped out of the diet of Aboriginal women as soon as commercially produced flour became available.[18]

Ethnographic studies also support the model predictions as regards the impact of technological change. The possibility has already been mentioned that a new technology, for example fishing with a net as opposed to a line or spear, might increase the return rate of low-ranked resources which then become worth including in the diet. Another possibility is that technology can cut pursuit time for the highest return resources and thus make it possible to restrict the diet again and improve return rates. The use of the shotgun, for example, as opposed to bows and arrows, increases hunting efficiency and therefore raises net return rates.[19] As predicted, hunters decrease their diet breadth when using shotguns, but clearly this can only continue for a certain time, before return rates again start to decline.

The diet breadth model makes the simplifying assumption that resources are evenly distributed across the environment and that foragers search randomly, with the result that they encounter different resources in proportion to their density in the environment. This seems an unreasonable assumption for any given foraging expedition. On the other hand, the idea that over the course of a large number of expeditions this requirement is met is much less implausible. Therefore, as Robert Kelly[20] points out, the model may be an especially useful one for archaeologists because the

29 a *Return rates expected from resources exploited by Ache men in order of descending profitability from left to right. The vertical axis shows the return rate expected on encounter with each type of resource. Circled resources are sometimes ignored when encountered whereas other resources are always pursued when encountered. Note that 27 of 28 resources handled by Ache men are characterized by higher return rates on encounter than can be expected from overall foraging.*
b *Return rates expected from resources exploited by Ache women. Note that women do not exploit most game resources taken by Ache men. The solid line shows the foraging return rate for women if time travelling between campsites is viewed as search time. The dotted line shows the return rate for women on days when they do not move camp and all foraging time is spent in search or handling of resources.*

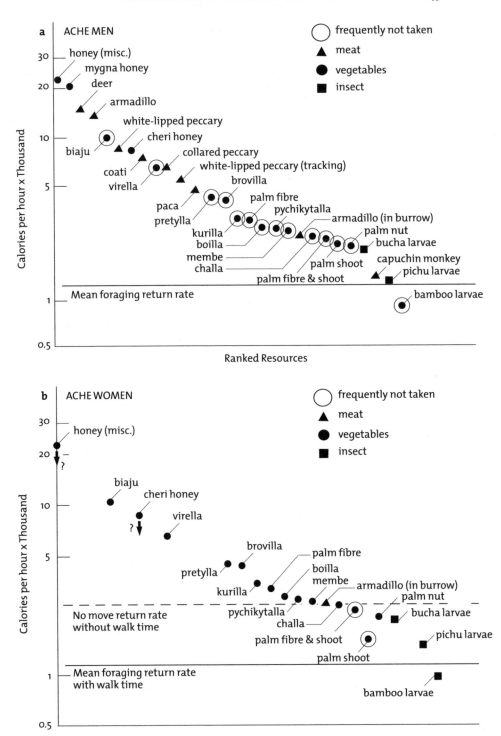

assemblages of plant and animal remains which they study are almost invariably the aggregate outcome of large numbers of events.[21]

In addition to the diet breadth or prey choice model, an alternative model has been developed by behavioural ecologists studying foraging behaviour, to take into account the fact that resources are normally distributed patchily rather than evenly in the environment. Unsurprisingly, it is called the *patch choice model* and instead of asking which resource types should be included in the diet, it asks which patches should be searched and how long the search of a particular patch should last before the forager moves on.[22] Normally, when a forager starts searching a patch, returns will be high but as the resources are used up – the plants gathered and the animals hunted – returns will diminish, because search times will increase. The prediction is that, if foragers are energy-maximizers, then they will leave a patch once the returns to be gained have fallen below the average for the environment as a whole. This is the so-called 'marginal value theorem'[23] and we will return to its significance below. The point to note at the moment is that on these assumptions it is time to move on well before the resource patch is completely exhausted.

Patch studies which have been carried out have tended to find that the outcomes predicted are not met. Thus, a study by Jim O'Connell and Kristen Hawkes[24] in which Alyawara Australian Aboriginal women were offered jeep rides to resource patches of their choice found that on nearly half the occasions they chose to go to mulga woodland patches which produced overall net returns lower than sandhill patches. However, the woodland patches produced better meat returns, indicating that, as with the moose and its sodium requirements, maximizing rates of calorie intake will not necessarily be the whole story. Despite these problems, we will see later in this chapter a very productive archaeological application of the patch selection idea.

Nevertheless, the point raised in the last paragraph brings us back again to the issue of what happens when the predictions of such models are not met. Those who are sceptical about the value of applying scientific approaches to the study of human behaviour say that such a lack of fit shows that humans have free will, and that they have very different goals from those assumed by the models. They therefore dismiss the use of what they regard as deterministic models of human behaviour altogether. Like Steven Mithen,[25] I take the view that the ability of people to make the best use of the environment to achieve their goals should not be seen as a determinism which effectively makes people robots. On the contrary, it is a reflection of their capacities and their creativity in learning about their environment and making the best possible use of it. As we have seen already, where the models do not fit we gain information by going on to ask further questions about why that might be, but from within the same framework. Finding that feathers fall more slowly than apples is not a reason for rejecting the laws of physics but for asking what factors affect feathers more than apples, and why. In the case of the Alyawara women just mentioned, and a number of others, it is clear that there is a preference for meat rather than just simple calories. However, this preference may not be mere cultural choice, it may derive from a need for nutrients which are only, or at least far more readily, obtainable from meat.

The differences between male and female resource rank orders among the Ache have already been mentioned. Patterns of male hunting fit very well with the predictions of the diet breadth model, even to the extent of showing why men dig armadillos from burrows in one season but not another.[26] The digging involves a lot of time and effort. At the season when this is done the armadillos are very fat and the returns from digging them out, once they have been encountered, average 3900 cal/hour, in comparison with an overall average hunting return of 1340 cal/hour. In the season when they are not taken the armadillos are thin and produce an average of only 1220 cal/hour.

However, while the Ache men maximized their meat calorie returns, they often ignored plant foods which would have given them much higher overall return rates of energy intake. Women, on the other hand, avoided pursuing profitable game resources for the most part: they could hunt but avoided doing so. Kaplan and Hill[27] believe that this is probably because of the reproductive costs potentially arising from pursuing dangerous mobile prey. We will take another look at male and female goals in Chapter 7. For the moment we can simply note that while the diet breadth model seems to give good predictions *within* plant resources and animal resources, it does not seem to work so well *between* them, probably at least partly because energy is not the sole criterion of value as far as food is concerned.

There is far more to be said about ethnographic foraging models than we have the time or the space to go into here. But before turning to the archaeological implications of the ideas it is necessary to consider briefly the role of these ethnographic examples in our argument. As we saw at the beginning of the chapter, evolutionary theory provides us with a set of principles. Those principles work themselves out differently, depending on the specifics of local conditions, both natural and human. Thus, we do not have one set of principles applying to hunters who have shotguns and another applying to those who have bows and arrows. We have a single set of principles that will give predictions about the hunting choices of foragers with the two weapon types, in the light of the differences in returns they offer and the costs they entail. The ethnographic examples illustrate that the principles do have some validity, rather against the odds one might have thought at the outset, given how much they simplify reality. The examples also illustrate that when the models do not fit, the reasons for the lack of fit are interesting and potentially comprehensible within the same framework. The examples certainly do not lead us to the conclusion that thinking about non-capitalist societies in this way is an ethnocentric imposition of alien and inappropriate microeconomic values, any more than we could make the same statement about the application of optimal foraging models to lions or blackbirds.

THE ARCHAEOLOGY OF OPTIMAL FORAGING

The archaeological application of optimal foraging theory is different from its use in an ethnographic context in two major respects. First, there is the matter of methodology. It is impossible for archaeologists to go out with the foragers they are studying, time how long they are hunting or collecting, and then calculate the calorific value of the food they have obtained. Archaeologists must find a way of obtaining equivalent information from the residues surviving on archaeological sites. Since plant remains tend to survive less well than animal remains and are also more problematical to quantify, the majority of such archaeological studies have looked at animal bones. As we have just seen, one of the key tools for testing whether optimal foraging theory assumptions are met is the diet breadth model: the highest return diet will only include the small number of resources that provide the best return for a given amount of effort. When these are scarce, foragers do not have the option of passing up those giving low returns. They have to include these as well, so the number of species taken increases. Accordingly, one of the ways in which archaeologists can explore optimal foraging theory ideas is by finding a way of using assemblages of animal bones to measure diet breadth or alternative indicators of the exploitation of high-return versus low-return resources.

Important though these methodological issues are when it comes to actually operationalizing the ideas of optimal foraging theory in an archaeological context, they would be irrelevant if archaeology did not differ from conventional ethnographic human behavioural ecology in another important respect: the window it offers on human environmental exploitation in the past, and the extent to which it followed optimal foraging principles. Nobody ever systematically wrote down such things and the pictures the ethnographers provide are no more than static snapshots of a single moment in time. By ethnographic observation it is possible to establish whether people's actions at a particular moment fulfil optimal foraging predictions, but that doesn't tell us about the long-term history of resource exploitation – for example, what people actually did when their highest return resources became too rare to produce a living, or indeed what happens to the human population when such resources decline. Over the long term that archaeologists are interested in, people do not just have an impact on resources; the availability of resources has an impact on people, as we saw in the last chapter.

Finally, archaeology is the only source of information that can help resolve a specific issue which is often raised in critiques of ethnographic optimal foraging. This is the suggestion that insofar as modern people living traditional lives follow optimal foraging principles, it is because they have been 'contaminated' by capitalist values as result of their involvement on the periphery of the modern world-system over the last 500 years. Archaeology can tell us whether or not people behaved as optimal foragers even in the Palaeolithic.

In the next section we will look at some archaeological case studies.

LONG-TERM PATTERNS

The first case study is Joel Janetski's analysis of changing hunting patterns in the Great Basin of the arid western United States during the Fremont phase (AD 400–1300).[28] This is an interesting example because the Fremont people were farmers with investments in land and residential facilities, as well as foragers, and so could not easily move in response to the decline in wild resources that generally takes place around a residential base once people have been there for a while. The problem is how to explore archaeologically whether such a decline took place and, if so, what its consequences might have been.

Janetski starts from the optimal foraging assumptions of energy efficiency in foraging already described. Thus, it is assumed that high-rank items are always taken but lower-rank items only come into the diet as high-rank ones diminish, increasing the search time required to find them. In terms of hunting, one of the best measures of a resource's profitability and therefore its rank is its body size. Within limits (very large animals may be too dangerous for instance), larger body sizes give better returns. Archaeological bone assemblages give us direct evidence of prey body sizes so, generally speaking, an assemblage with more large mammals will be indicative of a more efficient strategy, in terms of rate of energy return, than one with many small mammals.[29] If, over time in a particular region, we find an increasing number of small mammals in the bone assemblages, and there is no evidence of corresponding environmental or technological change, it suggests that the larger ones are becoming increasingly rare, forcing the hunters to widen their diet breadth to include what were originally unprofitable prey items not worth including in the diet. Accordingly, an appropriate way of measuring this, which we can derive from our bone assemblages, is the ratio of large to small mammals in the assemblage. In Janetski's case an appropriate measure of this was the so-called 'artiodactyl index', obtained by dividing the number of specimens of artiodactyls (deer, antelope, mountain sheep, i.e. large grazers) by this total plus the number of lagomorphs (hares and rabbits, i.e. small grazers). There was a clear trend over the period from AD 600 to 1300 in the direction of smaller mammals (see fig. 30).

Janetski considered a variety of possible explanations for the increasing focus on small mammals, including a number of methodological issues,[30] as well as climatic factors, technological change, and the possibility that human predation had resulted in a decline in the available resources. Eventually he concluded that the trend towards smaller animals was a result of local resource depression caused by the increasing population, for which he had independent evidence. This led to people staying in the same place longer. Indeed, Janetski points out that local resource depletion is characteristic ethnographically wherever one finds so-called 'central place' foraging strategies. These occur when people are reluctant to move for some reason, in this case because of the agricultural aspect of their way of life.

This sort of approach has been taken further by Lisa Nagaoka,[31] using a version of the patch choice model to understand changing patterns between c. AD 1300 and 1450 in the use of sea and land resources at the site of Shag

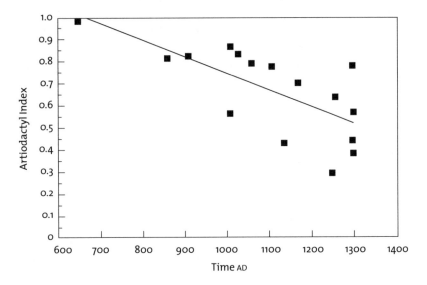

30 *Changing hunting patterns in the Great Basin of the western United States during the Fremont phase. The vertical axis shows the artiodactyl index, the proportion of large mammals among those found in the bone assemblages. The value declines over time, indicating an increasing proportion of small mammals.*

River Mouth in New Zealand. This involved looking not just at the different species represented in the bone assemblage, but also at the different bones of the different species, to assess the extent to which people were interested in obtaining every last scrap of meat from the prey they caught or just used the better parts. In the light of their large body size, seals were argued to be the highest-ranked marine resource and moas, a large flightless bird, the highest-ranked on land. As these high-ranked resources declined, Nagaoka found that the exploitation of seals and moas developed in different ways. Seals were used more intensively, with more different body parts being found at the site. Moas were used more selectively, as evidenced by the body parts represented. The difference is explained in terms of transport costs. Seal transport costs were low, either because they were exploited locally or could be easily moved by canoe. The declining numbers of moas locally led to hunters seeking them further afield, where encounter rates remained high, but transport was an issue. Hunters would use the low-value parts of the moas at their hunting camps and only bring back the parts with the most meat.

Similar foraging-theory arguments were invoked by Mark Basgall[32] to account for the history of acorn exploitation in aboriginal California.

Acorns were a dietary staple in historic times in much of the area, a situation which suggested that they must have been a preferred high-quality resource. On the other hand, the archaeological evidence suggested that large-scale acorn use was a relatively recent phenomenon. If they were a high-quality resource, then the only reasons for acorns not to be exploited by a particular subsistence economy would be either a lack of oak trees in the vicinity, or the lack of the required technology to get rid of the toxic tannic acid, or possibly that people had not yet properly 'settled in' to the area and therefore were not yet making the best use of the potentially available resources.

Basgall examined each of these suggestions in turn, starting with the proposal that the key factor was the invention of the leaching process for removing tannic acid. As he points out, given the earliest occupation dates for California and the dates for the beginning of large-scale acorn exploitation, we would have to conclude that leaching remained unknown for 6,000 years or more. This seems unlikely in view of the sophistication with which ethnographically known foragers exploit their environments. Furthermore, if acorns were a resource waiting to be exploited as soon as the technique was available, it would be reasonable to expect that the technology would diffuse rapidly through local populations, who would therefore have started acorn exploitation at more or less the same time. In fact, acorn economies appear in different parts of California at different dates.

The 'settling-in' idea is similarly unconvincing in the light of what we know about foragers' environmental knowledge. It involves assuming that in the early period people would have been using a subsistence strategy that gave rise to seasonal stress because they didn't think that the acorn crops surrounding them were a possible resource. Finally, there is no reason to believe that the climatic changes which affected California during prehistory would have had the effect on oak distribution which has been claimed.

Basgall argues, in contrast, that the reason why acorns only became a major part of the subsistence strategies of Californian groups at a relatively late date was because they were a low-ranked resource. The reason for their low rank is revealed by looking at the ethnographically known processes involved in the gathering and processing of acorns, which were extremely laborious and therefore gave very low rates of return. So-called 'broad spectrum' plant-focused economies had existed in the area for several thousand years, but the demands on the more productive resources eventually reached the point where it was worth adding acorns to the diet, mostly as a result of local population increase. It is this that explains why large-scale acorn exploitation began at different times in different places, since the threshold for exploiting acorns was reached locally, as a result of local demographic processes.

However, the demands of relying on acorns had further repercussions; for example, the need for large-scale storage, because they are only available seasonally. In California the result of this reliance in contexts of high population density was the intensified use of smaller areas of land, decreased mobility and the emergence of formal group territories.

HUMANS AS CONSERVATIONISTS?

A final California study leads us into one of the most important issues concerning present-day human societies and their relations to the natural world: what are the best strategies for conserving resources and maintaining biodiversity? The history of past human subsistence economies provides information and lessons that are illuminating for discussion of this subject, because it tells us about the attitudes to environmental exploitation of ourselves and our ancestors over the last two million years. Evolutionary arguments provide us with a basis for understanding those attitudes, not least the endlessly criticized short-sightedness which is certainly evident today. It would seem sensible to devise policies that work with the grain of these demonstrated attitudes rather than against them. As we noted above, the archaeological evidence of prehistory is especially important because it tells us about economies which cannot possibly have been influenced by attitudes ultimately derived from capitalist markets, which is potentially the case with all ethnographic studies of 'traditional' economies.

The intensification of resource use which leads to the extraction of more resources from a given area at the expense of decreases in rates of energy extraction, which we saw reflected in the growth of acorn exploitation, is also seen in the prehistoric exploitation of many other resources in California. One of the most carefully documented examples has been presented recently by Jack Broughton[33] in a paper which looks at through-time patterns of fish exploitation. In this case the argument focuses on changes both within and between prey populations.

As Broughton explains, any animal population being over-exploited will show demographic indicators of this harvest pressure, in that the mean and the maximum age of the individuals taken will tend to decrease. Fish continue to grow throughout their lives, so that harvest pressure can be measured by looking at decreases in mean and maximum size over time, if we can find relevant samples within archaeological deposits on which to carry out measurements. A shell mound in San Francisco Bay dated to between 2400 and 700 years ago provides the source of Broughton's evidence (see fig. 31). He argues that the highest-ranked fish in the area, and also the one most sensitive to harvest pressure, would have been the white sturgeon. Through time this declined as a proportion of the fish assemblage at the site, leading Broughton to conclude that the encounter rate of

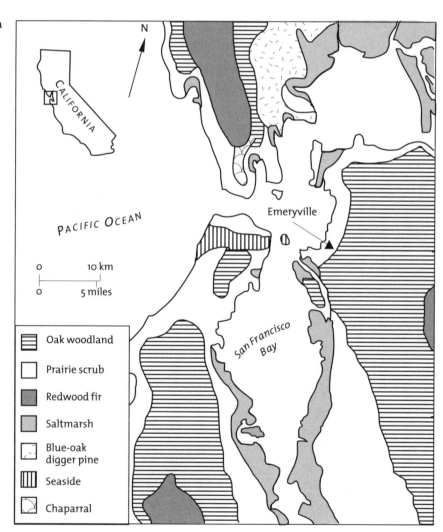

sturgeon had declined and therefore the efficiency of fish exploitation had decreased. There appear to be no environmental reasons for this to have occurred so the obvious alternative is human harvest pressure. If this was really the factor involved then, apart from the declining proportion of sturgeon in the bone assemblage, it should also be visible in the declining size of the fish taken. Comparison of sturgeon sizes from different levels of the shell mound established that there was indeed a decrease through time in the mean and maximum size of the sturgeon taken, thus confirming the fishing pressure hypothesis.

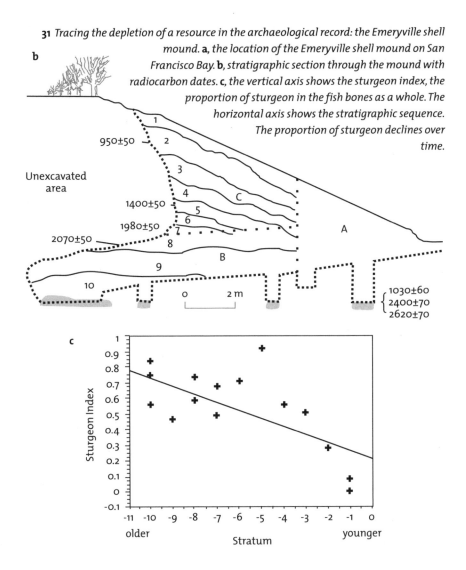

31 *Tracing the depletion of a resource in the archaeological record: the Emeryville shell mound.* **a,** *the location of the Emeryville shell mound on San Francisco Bay.* **b,** *stratigraphic section through the mound with radiocarbon dates.* **c,** *the vertical axis shows the sturgeon index, the proportion of sturgeon in the fish bones as a whole. The horizontal axis shows the stratigraphic sequence. The proportion of sturgeon declines over time.*

Similar patterns are found in the mammal faunas of this and other shell mounds in the vicinity. Indeed, whether we take fish, land mammals or sea mammals, we find increasing reliance on smaller prey in the later prehistoric period of California, consistent with the harvest pressure hypothesis and also with the arguments for the development of acorn exploitation.

The situation described in these studies is by no means unique. Work by Virginia Butler[34] on mammal and fish remains from sites on the Columbia River in Oregon dating to the last 2000 years also found that in the later period there was a decline in the use of higher-ranked resources, including large fish, which resulted from human predation pressure. However, the human population of the region collapsed at the beginning of the 19th century as a result of European contact, and in the subsequent decades resource populations were able to recover, a situation reflected in the increased use of high-ranked resources after contact. As Butler points out, the results have considerable implications for views about prehistoric subsistence economies derived from the ethnographic descriptions of the region in the last 100 years. These all emphasize the importance of the salmon, both as a source of food and as the basis for the complex social organization in the region. In fact, the historically observed emphasis on salmon may be a product of the reduced foraging pressure that resulted from depopulation.

Apart from these examples, the role of human populations in the extinction of the flightless birds and other resources of the islands of the Pacific is well known.[35] Evidence has also been found for harvesting pressure on shellfish populations by later Palaeolithic foragers in Italy and Mesolithic foragers in southern England.[36] Perhaps most surprising of all, there are now indications of harvesting pressure on tortoise populations in the Near East more than 40,000 years ago.[37] Tortoises, and indeed most shellfish, are not very resilient in population terms, because they take a long time to mature and, of course, are not very good at escaping when discovered.

How do these findings tie in with the often-heard suggestion that prehistoric people, and non-capitalist or industrial communities generally, were conservationist in their attitudes and made use of practices such as food taboos to restrict the exploitation of certain resources? This subject has recently been examined in some detail by Michael Alvard.[38] Alvard argues that resource conservation is not nearly as common as people used to think, and that the misconception has arisen because people have mistakenly taken the existence of sustainable harvests as evidence in itself of conservation. Often the conservation is 'epiphenomenal', a consequence of the fact that small groups will generally only have a minor impact on the resources they exploit (unless the resources are very sensitive, like the Near Eastern tortoises studied by Mary Stiner and her colleagues). Moreover, behaviours which have a conservation effect need not be undertaken for conservation reasons. Alvard[39] cites the example of the exploitation of male Stella's sea lions, which are easier to kill during the breeding season than females. The result is a kill pattern biased towards males which also happens to be preferable from the resource conservation point of view.

As for food taboos, most claims that these make a difference from the conservation point of view have not been based on empirical data but simply on adaptive assumptions of the kind already criticized. One of the very few such studies that has been conducted found out that, even though the Central African Lese horticulturalists and Efe foragers studied had large numbers of food taboos, in fact individuals often invoked 'exception rules' to permit themselves to eat taboo items, with the result that 'less than 2% of calories were restricted for the Lese and less than 1% for the Efe'.[40]

Michael Alvard proposes defining conservation as 'when individuals reduce their level of resource use below what would be fitness-maximizing in the short-term, in exchange for long-term, sustainable benefits in the future'.[41] This excludes situations where behaviour has 'conservation-like' consequences as a side effect of activities undertaken on the basis of short-term self-interest. One specific example of this has already been mentioned, but another more general situation where this applies should also be noted. It follows from the optimal foraging patch choice model described earlier. As we noted then, foragers will generally leave a resource patch when the returns from exploiting it fall below those of the local environment as a whole, not when every last food item has been exhausted, because it makes sense in optimal foraging terms to do so. This short-term maximizing behaviour can have positive conservation consequences, but does not represent conservation in terms of Alvard's definition.

Maximizing long-term rates of return for any given species would involve biasing exploitation towards males, and those individuals that have lower reproductive value, namely the older and the younger individuals. Alvard's own ethnographic studies of hunter-horticulturalists found no evidence of attempts to avoid killing prime adult prey, or to bias kills towards males. Other studies lead to the same conclusion that hunters maximize their short-term rates, including the Inuit[42] as well as the Ache, whose subsistence strategies have already been mentioned earlier, and who show 'a complete absence of any practices designed to check over-harvesting of resources'.[43] A recent archaeological study of long-term marine resource exploitation on San Clemente Island, California, over a period from 7000 BC to AD 1400 came to similar conclusions. Fur seal and sea lion bones mainly represented females and juveniles, indicating that exploitation of island rookeries was based on short-term self-interest rather than conservation principles. Sea mammal populations declined, then bounced back during periods of site abandonment.

The key reason why active conservation is likely to be uncommon is one we have already seen in a different context in the last chapter, when we were discussing the logic of passing up good reproductive opportunities, 'a bird in the hand is worth two in the bush'. Some uncertainty attaches to the two in the bush. You may be unlucky in your efforts to catch them, or someone else may get there before you. Furthermore, you may get more benefits from exploiting the resource now rather than waiting, because the current gain may compound in some way. For example, it may help to feed your young offspring who will then be more likely to survive and reproduce.

The lack of certainty will be particularly acute in cases where the resources are open access. In these circumstances 'tragedy of the commons' situations arise, where any holding back on one person's part is likely to be exploited by somebody else. The issues here are well summarized by Judith Porcasi and her colleagues in their explanation of why the prehistoric Californian coastal community they studied exploited migratory sea mammals with the short-term priorities that they did. Since evidence shows that these mammals were hunted wherever they came out on land,

The same animals that gave birth on San Clemente Island and avoided pursuit there were subsequently hunted by other Native peoples on other islands or the mainland. Effective management of these populations would have required hundreds of Native communities up and down the west coast of North America to adhere to mutual conservation-oriented hunting policies. This seems extremely unlikely in light of high human population densities during the late Holocene in California and Oregon.[44]

In principle, of course, ownership is one means of cutting down the possibility of 'tragedy of the commons' situations because the owner(s) are more likely to enjoy the benefits. However, in the case of migratory sea mammals that is not even an option. Even when ownership is possible, though, it is not a guarantee unless owners are prepared to pay the costs of defence. It is certainly not a no-cost option. Moreover, although ownership and territoriality may increase the rewards for conservation, they certainly do not ensure that it will occur.

The archaeological examples we have looked at tend to suggest that it is the short-term values that have prevailed over time, because resources have been consistently depleted. We will return to some of the issues raised by the kind of cooperation and social norms which are required for conservation to work in a later chapter. For the moment, though, we can use Alvard's[45] suggestion that plant and animal domestication represent nascent conservation strategies to take us into the next set of issues to be explored from the evolutionary perspective. Agriculture turned out to be a sustainable economy for unprecedentedly large numbers of people.

ORIGINS OF AGRICULTURE IN THE NEAR EAST

How and why did people in certain parts of the world switch from foraging to farming at various times following the end of the last Ice Age, and how are we to see the transition in the context of the optimizing framework which has been developed in this chapter? Michael Alvard has offered one thought-provoking suggestion, that domestication might have been a conservation measure. An interesting alternative within the same framework has been offered by Bruce Winterhalder and Carol Goland[46] and is one of a number of recent attempts to see agricultural origins from this perspective.

Winterhalder and Goland's model is rather different from the ethnographic optimal foraging models described earlier. As we have noted above in passing, these all focus essentially on the short term, in effect at the scale of a single forager lifetime. The result is that we look at the forager's effect on the resource population but not the impact of the changing resource through time on the forager population. Even the archaeological examples just presented argued that resource intensification was a product of population increase but did not examine the impact of resource intensification on population in the way required to understand the processes going on at an archaeological time-scale, as we saw in the last chapter. This is what Winterhalder and Goland's model does and it relates directly to the issues discussed by Alvard, for it shows how, over time, the effect of a resource on the foraging population depends not only on its net return rate but also on its sustainable yield under exploitation. This in turn is a function of the resource's density and its intrinsic rate of increase.

Taking the latter two factors into account solves what initially appears to be a problem for diet breadth models of the origins of agriculture, which see it as a response to declining efficiency in foraging and a move to low-rank resources. If this is so, how is it that agriculture is generally associated with increased population densities? Winterhalder and Goland's model shows that the answer to this depends on the characteristics of the low-ranked resources that are gradually brought into the diet as foraging efficiency declines. If the lowest-ranked resource brought into the diet has a low density and a low rate of increase, then forager population density will decline. However, if the resource has a high density and/or a high reproductive rate then forager population density will increase despite the low net-return rate. Resource density has the greater effect because, once the resource rate of increase is high enough to bring the resource level back up to its carrying capacity after each harvest, higher rates of increase do not make any difference. In short, 'A population increase can be initiated by a low-net-return-rate resource so long as it has a sufficiently high sustainable yield.'[47] This does not depend initially on the population becoming sedentary or defending the territory that contains the resources, although it seems plausible that it might lead to these consequences.

Ofer Bar-Yosef[48] has recently summarized current ideas about the origins of agriculture in the Near East. In the late Palaeolithic of the Levant, towards the end of the last Ice Age, there is evidence of increased diet breadth and the incorporation of more plant resources in the diet, but also for the existence of new ground-stone technologies that probably increased return rates on the use of such resources by cutting handling costs. Then c. 13,000 years ago we see the beginning of the so-called Natufian culture, which is now widely agreed to have played a major role in the emergence of the first farming communities. The core area where the Natufian originated was in a region of open forest, where there were grasses with high frequencies of cereals. One of the innovations in stone tools associated with the Natufian are the so-called 'sickle blades'. These are blades showing a gloss which experimental studies indicate were used for harvesting grasses, including cereals. It is thought that using sickles rather than beaters and baskets would have improved the yield from a given area.

The suggestion is that, in the early Natufian, sedentary hamlets were established in response to environmental change that shifted the resource rankings in favour of cereals and thus required a change in resource scheduling, both in space and time: that is to say, the new resources demanded that people be in particular places at particular times which were incompatible with what they had been doing previously. The evidence for sedentism comes from a variety of sources, including the presence of such species as house mice at greater frequencies than in foraging sites, and studies of the teeth of gazelle, which represented the main animal prey at this time. These showed that prey animals were killed by the inhabitants of particular settlements in both summer and winter. The investment in the construction of substantial semi-subterranean houses can also be seen as an indicator of at least semi-sedentary occupation.

This way of life was severely affected by the onset of the very cold climatic phase known as the Younger Dryas at the end of the last glaciation. This seems to have led to a decrease in the natural production of plants such as cereals and a reduction in the distribution of wild cereals, a situation perhaps further exacerbated by local human over-exploitation. Bar-Yosef[49] suggests that in response to this situation communities would once again have become more mobile, returning to a more flexible scheduling of resources. The hamlets of the earlier period were abandoned but at some there are numbers of secondary burials, indicating the possibility that communities maintained some sort of ancestral relation with them, returning there to bury their dead. Following on the expectations of Winterhalder and Goland's model of diet breadth and population change, we have to conclude that this climatic down-turn would have meant a further broadening of the diet breadth. In doing so, the deterioration in cereal resources must have led to the inclusion of resources of lower density, otherwise there would have been no reason to shift from the previous sedentary pattern. It seems highly likely that a fall in human population density would have been a concomitant of this.

It is only at the end of the Younger Dryas cold phase, c. 10,300 years ago, that we see the reappearance of the kind of elaborate and relatively sedentary cultural system which characterized the Natufian, with the appearance of the so-called 'Pre-Pottery Neolithic A', but now on a much larger scale. The largest sites were 3–8 times as large as the largest Natufian sites; houses had stone foundations and unbaked mudbrick superstructures. Associated with these sites, there is not only extensive evidence of pounding tools but also direct evidence of the exploitation of barley, wheat and legumes. This time there was no Younger Dryas to bring things to a halt and agriculture and its consequences took firm hold. In terms of the Winterhalder-Goland model, the improving climatic situation would have led to the reappearance of dense wild cereal stands and a growing human population taking advantage of them for the sorts of reasons we saw in the last chapter. How the innovations associated with agriculture itself occurred is not clear, although it is plausible that the descendants of the early Natufian populations had not lost all the cultural and organizational traditions that had existed prior to the Younger Dryas and that these were a relevant factor in providing a foundation for further innovations soon thereafter.[50] The demographic consequences that ensued have been discussed in the last chapter; the social consequences will be examined in Chapter 8.

Agricultural societies

It might seem from all that has been said in this chapter so far that the application of optimization models to understanding how and why people get a living in the way that they do is only relevant to foraging societies; or, at most, to understanding how people in certain regions ended up becoming agriculturalists. We are back to Richard Bradley's distinction between foragers who have ecological relations with hazel nuts and farmers who have social relations with each other. Although it is true that most, if not all, the explicit archaeological and anthropological optimization studies which have appeared in recent years have focused on foraging groups, nothing could be further from the truth than the idea that optimization considerations are irrelevant to agriculturalists.

   In fact, the idea that such considerations are relevant to the understanding of agricultural economies goes back to the early 19th century and Johann von Thünen's famous book on the spatial organization of land use, *The Isolated State* (1826). Von Thünen postulated the existence of an isolated population centre in the middle of a uniform plain and showed how the zoning of land use around the centre, for such purposes as market gardening, timber for fuel and construction, cereal cultivation, and grazing, would depend on the labour and transport costs associated with the different uses in relation to the returns to be gained from them. Grazing, for example, would tend to be further away because labour inputs required were low and space needs were high, while market gardening would be close to the centre because tending the produce was time-consuming and it needed to be brought to market frequently, since it always had to be fresh.

Of course, in von Thünen's case a Darwinian framework was lacking, but it was there in the 1960s when Eric Higgs and his colleagues invented their technique of 'site catchment analysis',[51] on the basis of von Thünen's ideas and subsequent developments of them by geographers such as Michael Chisholm.[52] Higgs was interested in finding out about prehistoric subsistence economies. He postulated that people would generally settle in locations that gave them the best access to the resources which were most important to them; those groups that did not would not last very long. Accordingly, if archaeologists went to sites known to have been occupied during a particular period and evaluated the resources available at particular distances from the site, for example the quality of the soil, they would be able to infer the main subsistence preoccupations of the site's inhabitants. In practice, there were many problems with this, for example sufficient attention was not always paid to the possibility of local environmental change between the past and the present, such as the erosion and deposition of soils. Nor was it always appreciated that, even if a place was not ideal for a particular purpose, it might still be the best there was in the local region. Nevertheless, over time many of these issues were addressed and site catchment analysis came to have an important role, both in identifying general settlement tendencies and in providing an optimization-based prediction of what people *should* be doing at a particular place, which could then be compared with the evidence of the animal bones and plant remains excavated from the site.

At about the same time that Higgs was developing the site catchment approach, the agricultural economist Ester Boserup published her book, *The Conditions of Agricultural Growth*,[53] mentioned in the last chapter as one of the major sources of the population pressure arguments adopted by archaeologists in the late 1960s and 1970s. Although her own theoretical foundations were certainly not Darwinian, her arguments about the nature of agricultural intensification can be seen to fit squarely into the optimal foraging framework presented in this chapter. Boserup proposed that complex forms of agriculture, such as those involving the use of the plough, did not arise from a human urge towards progress, but represented a process of agricultural intensification resulting from population pressure. Thus, initial agricultural systems would have been so-called 'slash-and-burn' systems. In these the land is cleared of trees by cutting and burning and crops are grown on the cleared land, making use of the accumulated nutrients of the forest soil and of the residues from burning. After a few years the plots are abandoned, as yields decline, and the clearings left to regenerate. As populations grew, however, it would no longer have been possible to leave clearances so long to regenerate. The result would be a 'short fallow' system, representing an increased intensity of exploitation in terms of the use of the land and decreased efficiency in terms of returns for a given amount of work, because of the greater effort involved in the clearance and use of land under secondary forest. As populations became denser still, it would have become worthwhile to resort to yet more intensive methods, such as plough agriculture or irrigation. These increase the yield from a given area of land, but at the expense of the greatly increased effort of building irrigation works or the maintenance of draught animals and the much more thorough land clearance required for the use of the plough. In other words, as intensification increases, the returns for a given extra amount of labour input gradually decrease.

As social science models go, Boserup's has been extremely successful in accounting for variation in agricultural systems worldwide, but it has also been subject to many criticisms. Many of these criticisms are misplaced, or arise from the fact that she did not explicitly spell out her assumptions about the circumstances in which the model holds;[54] others do not apply to the broader Darwinian optimization framework in which her work can be placed. For example, the argument that there can be stimuli for intensification other than land shortage, such as market incentives or risk reduction, remains firmly within the cost-benefit evolutionary framework; it is a matter of identifying the key factors in a particular case and showing why one is more important than another.

In fact, like all good theories, Boserup's is illuminating in situations where its predictions are not confirmed. A recent archaeological case study around Wupatki National Monument in the Arizona desert provides an excellent illustration of this.[55] The area suddenly became fertile in AD 1064 as a result of a volcanic ash fall and archaeological survey suggests that more than 2,000 people moved into the area in the following 100 years. The authors examined the ecological conditions of the area and found that it offered almost no opportunities for irrigation and only minimal ones for floodwater farming along stream beds. Agriculture would have depended on rainfall, which was scarce and unpredictable. In such a situation it would have been positively counter-productive to invest increased amounts of effort in land plots at risk of failing because of lack of rain in any given year. The only viable strategy was an extensive form of farming, with fields in different locations. For any given community, the key to survival and success was the ability to back up claims to land. The result of these competitive pressures and the lack of an intensification option was the growth of two major communities, about 10 km apart, during the 12th century AD, whose expansion was probably too fast to have been the result of natural increase and must have resulted from immigration. The advantage of working with archaeology, of course, is that we know what happened afterwards. By the mid-13th century the area was abandoned: following a climatic deterioration the competitive, high-population land control system could no longer be sustained.

We will return to these competition and group organization issues in Chapter 9, but here we can note that the Boserup framework gives us a powerful basis for seeing agricultural societies from an optimal foraging perspective as well. Even when its predictions do not hold, the theory provides the basis for explaining why that is and leads us on to explore a different aspect of the relationship between population and resources, in this case the formation of competitive social groups and claims to land control.

EXCHANGE AND COMPARATIVE ADVANTAGE

At this point the reader may think that I have already stretched the initial idea with which I began this chapter more than enough. Certainly, the prevailing view would probably be that if optimal foraging ideas are valid and relevant at all then they apply to subsistence production only, and certainly not to exchange. The object of the next part of this chapter is to argue that exchange can be viewed from within the same framework too, perhaps less surprising when we remember that many of the principles of Darwinian evolution started their lives in economics. In fact, just as Boserup's proposal about the nature of agricultural growth came from a different theoretical background to optimal foraging theory but can now be seen as fully within its sphere of relevance, so there also exists a very long-standing principle in the economics of exchange which can be seen in the same light: that principle is the law of comparative advantage, developed by the economist David Ricardo in the 1840s. It may be something of an exaggeration to describe this as the only proposition in the whole of social science that is both true and non-trivial,[56] but it certainly has profound implications which have largely been ignored in archaeology and anthropology.

Ricardo's law states that it is not worth producing commodity x yourself, even if you could easily do it, if you are better off producing commodity y and obtaining commodity x in exchange for it; in other words, by specializing. What matters is the exchange value in relation to the costs of production and transport. Of course, such situations are not without a context; they presuppose, for example, that people want the items exchanged rather than being prepared to do without them. But if this is the case, then specialization can occur which will be to *the individual benefit of all*, although, as we shall see, not equally to all. Furthermore, it will raise the level of production of the region to a level higher than it would otherwise have been.

This idea goes against the usual approach to exchange within archaeology, and indeed anthropology more generally, which presupposes that the reason why people exchange things, if not simply to maintain social links with one another, is to import items and raw materials not locally available and to export things to have something to exchange for their imports. In this section we will look at an ethnographic example which does not follow the standard approach and then consider its implications for the analysis of a prehistoric exchange system.[57]

In studies of the reconstructed 19th-century regional and inter-regional economy of the Cameroon Grassfields in West Africa, Mike Rowlands[58] and Jean-Pierre Warnier[59] showed that the exchange patterns were not simply the result of ecological distributions of resources but of economic specialization. The basis of the specialization was that the costs of production in some areas were lower than others, partly for ecological reasons and partly because of local variations in the social organization of technology; the two reinforced one another. The result was that people obtained better returns by specializing and producing for exchange rather than trying to produce everything locally. All members of the regional system benefited from being part of it, in the sense that all gained some access to the increased regional production that specialization produces. But these benefits were unequally distributed, because the less productive members were in the position of having to accept poorer terms of exchange.

Warnier[60] showed that the exchange rate of palm oil for iron was such that 50 hours of iron production obtained 100–150 hours of oil production.

Indeed, the palm oil producers were the worst off of all those involved in the regional exchanges because of their low productivity, a situation which was further compounded in two different ways. First, the low-productivity work of palm oil production was further socially devalued by those in the central part of the exchange system, and those who carried it out were despised as savages. Second, because the exchange rates were stacked against them, the palm oil producers were always poor, which prevented them from obtaining the status items common in richer areas.

I suggested that the same principles might also be relevant to understanding the factors affecting the production and distribution of copper in earlier Bronze Age Europe (*c.* 2000–1400 BC).[61] Copper was produced by small autonomous communities living in settlements from which people travelled to the local mining and smelting sites, and where copper was concentrated before being exchanged. The copper sources were in the Alps, on the periphery of the main settlement area where the consumers of the copper lived. In fact, the essence of copper production was that it was production for exchange; it would have taken very little to satisfy the needs of the communities themselves. Producing the copper was arduous and involved a series of time-consuming processes, from the mining itself, through the ore preparation, to the final smelting. It therefore seems possible that the productivity of the whole process was relatively low, placing the copper producers at an exchange disadvantage. In effect, they may well have been in the same situation as the Grassfields palm oil producers, making something which everyone in the region wanted but able to gain only a slight benefit from it.

The reason why communities immediately outside the mining region did not engage in primary copper smelting may seem obvious: the ore was not locally available. But this has not prevented primary smelting being carried out some distance from ore sources in other times and places.[62] The answer may be that such communities could get higher returns on their labour by engaging in other activities, such as cattle-keeping for example, and obtaining their copper by means of exchange. Mountain-dwelling communities would have gained less return on agricultural activities because of inferior growing conditions and thus could not have competed in production for exchange on this basis, even though they kept animals for their own use.

Even if people knew of the locations of alternative copper sources nearer to hand than existing ones, and knew how to produce metal, we cannot assume that such sources would have been exploited to produce copper for exchange. They would have had to produce a better return than alternative activities such as cattle-rearing, and be competitive in exchange terms with the productivity of other copper producers at different sources. One suspects that the major sources that we know were extensively exploited in prehistory were naturally more productive, in the sense that it took less labour to produce more copper, even if only to start with, and that this gave the communities involved an edge in exchange transactions.

The very fact that certain communities were specializing in production for exchange suggests the relevance of such cost-benefit considerations, but other indications also exist. We have evidence that in the plains adjacent to the mining areas copper had come to acquire some of the functions of a 'primitive money', as store of value, standard of value and means of exchange. This evidence consists of hoards of copper ingots of standardized weights. This commodity approach to metal and its equivalence, as well as the specialized production itself, suggests that relative productivity considerations were probably also relevant in the Central European Bronze Age.

TECHNOLOGY, HISTORY AND ADAPTATION

This chapter has shown that the theory of evolution by natural selection leads to a set of principles with specific predictions about the way animals should forage in their environments. A common prediction, but by no means the only possible one, is that they should attempt to maximize their rate of calorific intake. Observation of animal and human behaviour suggests that individuals often act in ways that fit such predictions. The archaeological examples we have seen indicate that people have exploited their environments in such ways for a very long time. Their foraging has been largely governed by short-term considerations which have led to resource depression, and to the need to shift down resource hierarchies to exploit previously ignored resources giving poorer rates of return. Sometimes this has led to the inclusion of resources, especially plants, which can sustain much higher local population densities, despite lower rates of return, because population growth can carry on for longer before shutting off. As we saw in the last chapter, such systems will have a tendency to spread at the expense of those that support lower densities. This is the basis of the recent claim by Peter Richerson and his colleagues[63] that agriculture was impossible in the Pleistocene – because rapid climate fluctuations prevented the development of stable plant communities that humans could rely on – and mandatory in the Holocene – because the stable climate conditions of this period allowed high-density plant-based systems to develop and, once these are sustainable, they will tend to out-compete others.

With the exception of the exchange discussion, the account has contained little that would distinguish the factors affecting the pattern of human exploitation from those of any other higher animal: behavioural flexibility responsive to environmental cues. However, this cannot be taken at face value because in fact the responses are based on specific cultural traditions, in the form of technological knowledge, based initially on the invention and diffusion of innovations but then passed on through the generations by the methods described in Chapter 3.[64] The significant thing about such innovations in the context we have been discussing is their effect on the costs of resource exploitation. Although some innovations would have helped to improve encounter rates with prey, for example the adoption of the horse in North America, in general maximizing encounter rates depended on years of acquiring ecological knowledge, on moving through the landscape and maintaining information networks.[65] Pursuit and handling costs are a different matter. We have already noted in passing the use of the bow and arrow to cut the pursuit costs of mobile prey in the late Palaeolithic, giving people access to a significant food source which previously had been largely unobtainable, as well as the use of such mass-capture techniques as nets and fish traps. Such innovations may do more than simply mitigate the effects of sliding down the resource hierarchy, they may actually move resources up the ranking so that people obtain improved rates of return, although the effect at an archaeological time-scale may be temporary, depending on the density and the productivity of the resource concerned. In the context of agricultural production Boserup believed that prior to the Industrial Revolution all innovations that increased overall production were associated with decreased productivity. However, here too productivity-enhancing developments sometimes occurred. A study by Robert Hunt[66] which compared slash-and-burn rice cultivation with irrigated rice agriculture found that the latter was more productive in terms of the output-per-unit time, and led to the production of surpluses.

The other key component of resource exploitation is the handling costs involved. These are of particular importance in the exploitation of plant resources, which in many cases require a major investment of time to make them edible. We have already seen the issues involved in Basgall's analysis of the factors affecting acorn exploitation in prehistoric California. Even though processing techniques were known, acorns only began to be used on a large scale when there was no alternative. Nevertheless, if handling techniques can be improved, then return rates will improve likewise. With the shift to increasing use of plant resources in many parts of the world since the end of the last Ice Age, there is increasing evidence in the archaeological record of investment in technologies to improve plant-processing rates, especially such items as grinding stones for seed processing. Jason Bright and colleagues[67] have recently analysed the factors involved in investing time in different technologies. If you only exploit a resource occasionally and it is not an important part of your diet, then there is no point in putting a great amount of effort into a technology for reducing its pursuit and/or handling costs. Bright *et al.* show that the shift from an investment of large amounts of time in producing such lithic items as projectile points to producing ground stone items and basketry, which improved the rate of processing seeds, is explicable in terms of a shift towards the exploitation of plant resources which is independently evidenced. The development of the production and use of pottery can be seen in a similar light.

Once such innovations were adopted by a local population, it is easy to understand that there would have been selective pressure to maintain them from a variety of the sources described by Boyd and Richerson,[68] including copying of the most effective methods (direct bias), copying of the most prestigious individuals (indirect bias) and copying the most commonly used local practices (frequency-dependent bias). But what about the invention and innovation process itself? We saw in Chapter 3 that the existence of a problem won't necessarily lead to a solution, while a supposed solution may make things worse rather than better. While acknowledging that any innovation may not have the intended effect, Ben Fitzhugh[69] has suggested that in certain situations of stress people may become less averse to risk and more inclined to experiment, generating new possibilities on which selection and decision-making forces can operate.[70] Obviously, this is much more likely to happen if people think there is a large and significant gain to be made by finding a new way of doing things than if the projected gain is only small.[71] History may or may not be important in this process. For example, the fact that ground stone technologies have developed wherever people have become significantly dependent on plant foods, especially seeds, suggests that in some circumstances a problem leads to an adaptive solution with little role for historical contingency. In other cases the opposite may be true. Since most innovations in a given place are adoptions of something that originated elsewhere rather than local inventions, patterns of contact are likely to have been important in many cases. In fact, this is the basis of Jared Diamond's explanation[72] for the technological dynamism of Eurasia in comparison with the other continents: large-scale, long-distance contacts were easier because of the nature of Eurasian geography.

However, it is important to appreciate that even when particular technologies are adopted they do not always have the same trajectories wherever they occur. An interesting example of this sort of situation is the decline of the plough, the wheel and domestic animals in late pre-modern Japan.[73] Thus, far from the plough being the obvious solution in all circumstances to the problem of increasing production in the face of population pressure, in Japan people gave up the plough for the hoe in the 17th century, as population increased. While religious reasons may well have played a role, we should not make the mistake of thinking that the existence of a different pattern obviates the whole cost-benefit approach that we have been adopting. It is simply that the selective pressures in terms of costs and benefits were different. Given the high population that needed to be fed and the mountainous nature of the Japanese landscape, land could not be spared for grazing, nor could crops be spared for fodder, while population increase meant that human labour became cheaper than alternatives.[74] In other words, while specific historical events led to the introduction to Japan of domestic animals, the wheel and the plough and their incorporation into traditional agricultural practices, following transmission routes that the authors of the study do not discuss, there came a point where trial-and-error and directly biased decision-making processes, based on assessing costs and benefits, led to selection against them, so that they gradually declined in importance.

As in all areas of human life, information passed on by cultural transmission processes – whether it is details about animal habits or successful technologies – is important in getting a living, but in this field in particular that knowledge can be used flexibly in response to changing local situations. To over-simplify, within broad limits set by knowledge and technology it is the cost-benefit situation rather than the cultural tradition which determines courses of action. Furthermore, the importance of

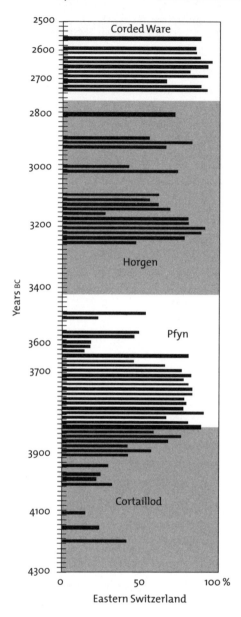

performance criteria means that subsistence patterns can vary relatively independently of the traditions seen in other areas of life. For example, an ethnographic study of the subsistence patterns of two groups in Chitral, Pakistan, one Muslim, the other following a traditional local religion, showed that it was the local environment rather than ideology/religion that was the key to understanding subsistence practices, which were largely identical in both groups.[75]

Another case study using the same high-resolution data from the circum-Alpine lake-villages that we saw in the last chapter enables us to address the issue of the relation between cultural traditions and subsistence patterns on an archaeological time-scale.

Fig. 32 shows the relative frequency of domestic (as opposed to wild) animal bones from a series of sites, and layers within individual sites, in eastern Switzerland. The order of the bars and the distances between them correspond to the date of the site or layer concerned. The cultural attributions of the different phases are also shown. Fig. 33 shows the

32 above *Percentages of domestic (as opposed to wild) animal bones from a series of Neolithic sites, and layers within individual sites, in eastern Switzerland. Cultural phases are also shown.*

33 opposite *The absolute densities (i.e. numbers of bones per standardized excavation unit) of the domestic and wild animal bones found at Neolithic sites around Lake Zurich, showing rapid fluctuations over time, together with a general trend for densities of domestic animal bones to increase and wild animal bones to decrease.*

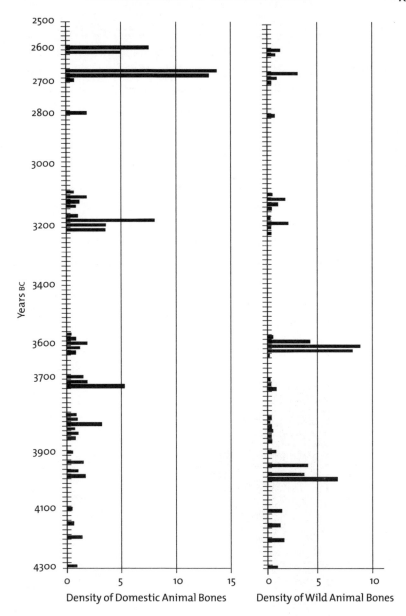

Years BC

Density of Domestic Animal Bones

Density of Wild Animal Bones

absolute densities of the domestic and wild animal bones found at a subset of these sites, those around Lake Zurich.[76] Both the relative and absolute figures show considerable variation within any given cultural phase, although there is a tendency for the number and proportion of wild animals to decrease through time.

The cultural phases largely represent ceramic traditions, which will have been passed on by social learning within communities and households, as we have seen. It is very apparent that there are no corresponding inherited cultural traditions or templates dictating that agriculturalists should only exploit domestic animals. Rather, they exploit their environment opportunistically, with considerable variation sometimes even from one short period to the next. The high rates of exploitation of wild animals that suddenly appear around 3600 BC are related by Jörg Schibler and his colleagues[77] to a climatic downturn that would have led to poor conditions for cereal growing. The long-term trend towards lower numbers of wild animals in the diet is related not to cultural traditions or preferences but to the fact that the availability of wild animals decreased as human populations increased, leading to a growth in the area of land permanently cleared for agriculture.

Pierre Pétrequin and his co-authors[78] in their analysis of changing economic patterns in the lake-villages of the French Jura around 3000 BC

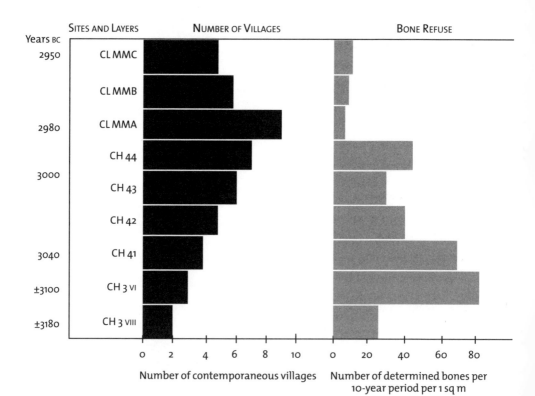

come to conclusions that are similar to Schibler's in some respects but different in others. Fig. 34 shows the relationship between animal exploitation and population over time. As the number of contemporaneous villages increases, the amount of bone refuse, indicating meat consumption, remains quite high and is mostly made up of wild animals. During this time domestic animals were actually decreasing; those that were kept were probably fed on forest resources, such as leaf fodder. However, at the point

34 *From left to right: the changing number of Neolithic settlements on lakes Chalain and Clairvaux, the absolute number of identified bones per sq. m, the percentage of domestic animals, percentage of elm twigs and the percentages of cattle and pig bones, all shown by phase. As the number of villages increases the amount of hunted meat consumed remains high. Then suddenly the amount consumed drops drastically and wild animal resources are replaced by domesticated ones. The decline in wild animals and the increase in domestic ones is associated with an expansion of pasture and a decreasing need to feed animals with leaf fodder.*

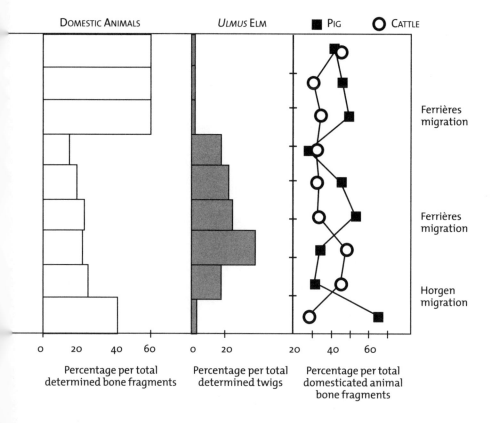

where the number of villages reaches its peak, the situation suddenly changes. Hunted resources decrease and domestic animals increase, while evidence for the feeding of animals on elm leaves also ceases. At the same time, the absolute amount of meat consumed decreases significantly. At this time too, cereal growing seems to have expanded and pollen evidence suggests that animal husbandry became based on grazing. It appears that all this was associated with the establishment of permanent fields. In this case though, the lack of a cultural connection is less clear-cut since the authors associate the demographic peak – the time of the major changes just described – with the arrival of new settlers in the region from the southwest, so the changes may not simply be the kind of intensification response to population increase that we have seen earlier, but the introduction of different subsistence practices.

Overall, it appears that the predictions of optimal foraging theory based in evolutionary theory are very often met when we analyse people's subsistence decisions, but in some circumstances they will not account for the patterns we find. It is important to remember that optimal foraging theory presents us with a powerful and illuminating predictive framework from which we can learn even when its predictions are not met. In the case of humans, as opposed to other animals, technology and its development play a key role in defining patterns of costs and benefits, but particular technological trajectories cannot be assumed to be inevitable.

-7-

MALE-FEMALE RELATIONS IN EVOLUTIONARY PERSPECTIVE: THE ROLE OF SEXUAL SELECTION

THE PREVIOUS TWO CHAPTERS have examined life history and survival strategies in different human groups and the extent to which they are explicable in evolutionary terms, including the way they affect, and are affected by, specific cultural traditions. They went on to look at what archaeology has to offer to the evolutionary study of human behaviour in these areas, and the methodological issues that need to be taken into account to make such a contribution possible. The next three chapters will be concerned with patterns of human social organization, starting with a subject which is central to the evolutionary study of any species, the relations between the sexes. As before, the approach is to look first at the general ideas that evolutionary ecologists have developed in this field, then at applications of the ideas to understanding these relations in different human societies and finally, to the contribution that the ideas can make to understanding patterns in the archaeological record, taking into account the specific problems posed by addressing such questions using archaeological information.

Archaeological work on the subject of gender has expanded exponentially in the last decade.[1] There is now an enormous number of different approaches to the subject, based on a wide variety of different theoretical positions. The one position that virtually all of them share is that gender has little, if anything, to do with biological sex. To suggest otherwise is often seen as an advocacy of biological determinism, implicitly or explicitly supporting conservative political positions. A further feature of most work on gender and archaeology is that it has mostly been by, and about, women,[2] usually from a feminist perspective. In the light of the inequities in women's positions in contemporary society, including academic professions such as archaeology, not to mention the default assumption of maleness in most reconstructions of the past, this situation is entirely understandable. There is a lot that needs to be done. Nevertheless, it has led to some extent to a ghettoization of the subject of gender relations as one more archaeological special interest, most relevant to women.

35 *'I'd like to find a man who's sensitive in general, and macho in emergencies.' One view of desirable male attributes.*

The object of this chapter is to argue for the importance of an evolutionary approach to male-female relations, based on the centrality of reproductive differences and the role of sexual selection (see fig. 35). Such an approach makes sense of a great deal of what we know about cross-cultural patterns of difference in male and female behaviour and provides the basis for an exciting and potentially productive programme of archaeological research. In the course of doing this I hope to show that male-female differences have much less to do with biological determinism than critics of evolutionary approaches normally suppose, and that the evolutionary approach makes male-female relations central to the archaeological study of past societies.

A prerequisite for this endeavour is the need to spell out a basic point about theory which archaeologists often fail to grasp, especially those who are sceptical about generalizing approaches. Generalizing theory is not about claiming that everything is the same, when we all know that it really isn't. Theory is concerned with explaining variation. Nowhere is this point more important than in studies of male-female relations, because one of the key arguments often advanced for rejecting biologically oriented approaches is that these relations differ from society to society. The conclusion is therefore drawn that such relations are culturally specific, they are not open to generalization. As other authors have pointed out, this is rather like taking the fact that birds and aeroplanes fly as a refutation of the laws of gravity. The scientific approach to the issue does not do this. It shows how and why certain mechanisms and techniques enable the force of gravity to be overcome in certain circumstances. Similarly, variation in male–female relations in different cultures does not exclude the possibility of developing productive generalizing approaches. The requirement of such theory is that it should provide an explanation of the variation: why one set of relations holds in one context but very different ones in another. For example, in the context of male–female relations, such a theory has to explain why women may be warriors or hunters in some situations even though they are usually not. Behavioural ecology provides us with a framework for doing precisely this, as it does in the case of getting a living that we saw in the last chapter. It does not claim that this is all there is to be said on the subject; simply that no approach that fails to take into account the Darwinian dimension can possibly be satisfactory.

The answer to the question of why the behavioural ecology approach to archaeology makes male–female relations central should be clear by now. The archaeology of the past made production and its organization the central process in the study of society. In the evolutionary approach production is only a means to the end of reproductive success. At the centre of the process of achieving reproductive success are male–female relations; these are associated with their own specific set of evolutionary processes, especially those that Darwin described under the heading of sexual selection. Hence these relations and processes must be at the centre of an evolutionary archaeology.

The reasons why the approach does not lead to biological determinism are more complex. They will be outlined here but will become clearer in the subsequent discussion and description of specific examples. As usual, the starting point is the assumption that both males and females have evolved to have a propensity to maximize their reproductive success. However, because they have different roles in the reproductive process, the life history tactics that lead to the maximization of reproductive success are not the same in males and females: what is successful for females will not necessarily be successful for males, and vice versa. The biological difference in reproductive roles has led to far greater differences in interests between males and females, and the trade-offs to which they are subject, than differences in other biological capacities. There are some differences in other capacities, such as physical strength for example, but there are big overlaps in male and female ranges of values with respect to these capacities. As regards the differences of interests, the specific form they take and the specific 'tactics', conscious and unconscious, which lead to the maximization of male and female reproductive success will not be the same in all social and environmental contexts.

The situation is exactly analogous to the one we saw in Chapter 5, with regard to issues of fertility and parental investment. It is only in certain circumstances that maximizing birth rate will lead to maximizing reproductive success. Humans, like other animals, have evolved to be very sensitive to variations in circumstances and to respond to them appropriately. The forms which male-female relations take will likewise respond to different constraints and opportunities. The genetic determination does not involve specifying particular behaviours, but behavioural flexibility in response to various relevant cues, conditional on potential differences in male and female reproductive interests. If a particular set of circumstances relevant to male and female decisions has remained constant over a long period of time, then we would expect the pattern of decision-making likewise to have remained unchanged over this period. Correspondingly, when the circumstances change, the pattern of male and female decisions connected with the best way of maximizing reproductive success will change as well. This is the essence of the phenotypic flexibility which is so characteristic of humans. In summary, biology has dictated interests, rather than general capacities, and certainly not destiny.

SEXUAL SELECTION: THE EVOLUTIONARY ECOLOGY OF SEX

It is important to put the human situation in the broader comparative context of biological evolution and differences in male-female behaviour within and between species. The variation here is enormous, much more so than that within humans, but it is explicable in evolutionary terms. Biologists do not simply throw up their hands in horror, overwhelmed by the sheer diversity of life.

The essential difference between females and males is that between individuals with large gametes (sex cells) and those with small ones. The large and small gametes fuse in the process of sexual reproduction. Bobbi Low[3] asks us to imagine a population of jellyfish-like creatures reproducing by releasing gametes into the sea to combine with another gamete to produce a new offspring. The gametes vary in size. The smallest ones will be the cheapest to produce and are also likely to travel further in currents and thus have the greatest probability of meeting another one. The largest ones have the resources in the cell to live longer and also to provide offspring with the most resources once they have fused with another. The strategies for success of small gametes are associated with their being mobile and cheap to produce, for large ones they are associated with providing the resources for a successful fused zygote. Medium-size gametes get the worst of both worlds.

Given that the strategies for success in small gametes are not the same as those for large ones, there has been selection for individuals to specialize in the production of small ones (males) or large ones (females). Far fewer resources are involved in the production of male gametes, so they can be produced in extremely large numbers. The potential for producers of small gametes to produce offspring is thus much greater than for those with large ones, since the latter can only produce more by speeding up the production of young, whereas the former can do so by fertilizing the large gametes of many different females. This specialization in different reproductive roles leads to a corresponding tendency towards specialization of reproductive effort, towards mating effort, on the one hand, for producers of small gametes and parental effort on the other, for producers of large ones. The commitment to parenting effort (which may involve much more than the production of large gametes) arises because of the ceiling on the number of offspring that can be successfully produced in a lifetime. Seeking large numbers of extra mating opportunities is not going to make a great deal of reproductive difference.

Commitment to mating effort can potentially produce a much larger number of offspring, since far fewer resources are put into any single one. However, because the reproductive potential of individuals that invest little in their offspring is much greater than that of individuals who invest a lot, the result is competition between the low investors (usually males) to mate with the high investors (usually females).[4] Inevitably, in such a competition there is strong selection for those characteristics that lead to success in mating with the high investors. Equally inevitably, while some individuals may be extremely successful in the competition, others will not be successful at all. Being successful as an investor in mating effort is likely to involve different strategies from those required to be successful as a parental investor.

We can regard the differences just described as a kind of theoretical baseline derived from evolutionary considerations, from which to generate plausible predictions about what we should expect when examining actual male-female differences in different species. The theory that explores these issues is the Darwinian theory of sexual selection.

The evidence of male competition for females is extremely widespread in the animal world and often takes such obvious forms as fighting,[5] either directly for females or for resources on which females depend. Less obvious ways that biologists have discovered include 'sperm competition' within the female in many cases where females are fertilized internally.[6] Such competition represents one kind of sexual selection. Another revolves around female choice, since, by the nature of the competition, it is the parental investor (usually female) who will be selecting from among the mating investors. Furthermore, because the basis of success as a parental investor is access to resources for the offspring, a competing male that can offer the best resources has a high probability of being chosen. Thus, male bullfrogs, for example, compete for the best territories and females choose those that have been most successful.[7] The best-known examples of female choice are cases of elaborate male displays, such as the peacock's tail. Experiments have shown that such displays really do lead to greater mating success for those individuals that have the most developed version of the trait. In such cases it is not a resource that is being selected but it may be some genetic benefit; for example, there is some evidence that ability to put on a good display is related to resistance to parasites.[8]

It is a strength of sexual selection theory that it is not simply defined in terms of males versus females but of large investors versus small ones. In many species parental investment extends far beyond gamete production, to looking after the young. Accordingly, it follows that if instances arise where males are the greater investors, then we should expect them to be the ones making the choices, with the females competing for them. This is precisely what we find in species such as the moorhen, where it is the males who spend most time incubating the eggs.[9]

It is the specifics of life history and physiology, together with ecological circumstances, which lead to variation in mating and parental care systems. Thus, in birds there has been selective pressure for maximizing the rate at which food is provided for the young. This can be achieved better by two parents rather than one and both parents have the same interest. The result is a tendency to monogamy.[10] In mammals, on the other hand, the commitment by females to gestation and lactation, a much greater investment than males and one in which they cannot share, means that they tend to be polygynous, one male with several females.

Even in cases where there is no male parental care, there is a great deal of variation in mating systems, depending on variation in resource distribution, which in turn affects the distribution of females and the possibility of defending them. A classic case where they are defendable is the elephant seal, since the breeding grounds are localized and the females are grouped together. The strongest males have the largest harems but are rarely able to maintain their position for more than a season or two before losing to another that will dominate in his turn.[11]

In this case, since males do not contribute parental care, the females probably do not lose anything from the situation and probably gain in the sense that by mating with the dominant male they are increasing their chances of being the mother of such a male in the next generation. However, it is important to understand that, in a given mating system, interests have to be considered from both the male and the female point of view and they will not necessarily be the same. Moreover, even within a given species, the mating system may be very variable, depending on circumstances.

Both of these points are well illustrated in John Krebs and Nicholas Davies' account of the mating system of a song-bird called the dunnock.[12] This species shows examples of all the different kinds of mating systems, including monogamy, polygyny (one male and two females in this case) and polyandry (one female associates with two males). For the male, most reproductive success is obtained with polygyny, because, although his efforts are split between the two females, with the result that their individual broods will be smaller than they could be, nevertheless, his total output is greater than it would be in the other circumstances. For the female the balance of advantage is the other way round. If she has two males assisting with parental care she is likely to be able to rear a larger brood, but the two males have to share the paternity of the brood. In some cases one male is unable to drive off the other and neither female can drive off the other, so two males share two females. The specific outcome that emerges in a particular case depends on the competitive ability of the individuals concerned and the local sex ratio.

A general constraint on breeding systems arises from the fact that species sex ratios are usually 1:1.[13] This arises because of the way selection acts at the level of the individual. If the population is largely female then any male will have much more reproductive success than any female, so a mutation that allows individuals the possibility of biasing their offspring towards males would quickly spread. The converse would be true for a population with a heavily male-biased sex ratio, hence the equilibrium value is 1:1. However, Robert Trivers and Dan Willard[14] suggested that there might be circumstances where the sex ratio could really be biased in favour of one or other sex, in at least part of the population, if the future reproductive prospects of the offspring were somehow dependent on the current state of one or both parents. Thus, if the current state of the parent means that the offspring are likely to have good reproductive prospects then, given the option, it would make sense to have male offspring. As we have seen, this is because the variance in male reproductive success is greater than for females, so the best males will do better than the best females. Conversely, if the prospects for the offspring are poor then it makes sense to invest in female offspring, since a poor female will do better than a poor male.

The validity of this in many ways remarkable prediction has been borne out by field studies in a number of species. In red deer, for example, dominant females who have access to good feeding sites and as a result can produce and feed offspring that are large and strong, tend to have males, with a good chance of being successful in inter-male competition. Subordinate females tend to produce daughters.[15]

As with the breeding systems, a key point to note is the flexibility of the system and its responsiveness to particular situations.

SEXUAL SELECTION IN HUMAN MATING SYSTEMS

There is a lot of evidence that similar considerations to those just described affect human mating systems and account for some of the variation between them. This section will examine some examples that illustrate this point.[16]

That human males have a bias towards mating effort and females towards parenting effort is indicated by the fact that the variance in reproductive success for males is greater than it is for females. The most successful males have far more offspring than the most successful females, although the extent of this difference varies with social and economic conditions. The contrast is easily demonstrated by a look at the *Guinness Book of World Records*, which reveals that the largest known number of children produced by any male is 888, while the corresponding figure for a female is 69.[17] Conversely, far more men are completely unsuccessful. In biological terms this means that humans are, in effect, polygynous.

The extent of the difference between males and females in the variance in reproductive success is a measure of the strength of sexual selection.[18] Because males are competing with one another for mating opportunities, it is females who are in the position of choosing, although that doesn't necessarily mean that they set the terms of the competition. In terms of female reproductive interests as a parental investor, apart from good genes, the most important factor is adequate resources for herself and her offspring. For males, then, a key means of succeeding in competition for females is to be able to offer resources. The evidence that in humans there is a female preference for males with resources is very considerable, both in terms of expressions of opinion in survey questionnaires in modern societies[19] and of reproductive outcomes. We can illustrate this with some examples.

Resources and reproductive success

We saw in Chapter 5 that Ache male hunting success was strongly associated with both fertility and offspring survival during the time they lived as foragers in the forest.[20] Now that they are on the reservation the association is between fertility and male socio-economic status, not hunting success. This shows the plasticity and flexibility of the response to male resource patterns. We are not dealing with a genetically programmed response to variation in hunting skill which has been selected over hundreds of thousands of years, but an ability to recognize and respond to cues concerning resource differentials, whatever they may be. Another significant aspect of the Ache example is that the association between resources and reproductive success is stronger for males than for females, as the theory outlined above would predict.

Many other examples of the link between male wealth and status and reproductive success are known, from very different kinds of society. In the case of the Yanomami horticulturalists of Venezuela and Brazil, the village headmen were polygynous, a practice restricted to a few of the most powerful men in each village, and left approximately twice as many offspring as other men.[21] The anthropologist James Neel also pointed out that in the four villages he and his team studied in detail, males whose fathers were powerful and polygynous were likely to have more wives and children themselves, so that some men had much higher numbers of grandchildren than others: 'Among 61 men in the four villages who were born before 1909, there were four who had 41, 42, 46 and 62 grandchildren respectively. Moreover, two of these men are fathers of the other two. For comparison, no female born before 1909 has more than 31 grandchildren.'[22]

Eckart Voland's study of reproductive success in relation to wealth in 18th-century Krummhorn, north Germany[23] has already been briefly mentioned in an earlier chapter. Krummhorn is an interesting case. It is a very fertile area in which a market-oriented agriculture developed early and enabled the accumulation of considerable wealth in certain families. A single heir inherited the estate, usually the youngest son, while those who did not inherit received cash or some other equivalent. It was landownership that defined the local social structure, with a major difference in every aspect of life between landowners and others. Voland used a variety of contemporary records to reconstruct Krummhorn's demography. He demonstrated that elite male landowning farmers in the area were more successful reproductively than other males. This differential increased over the long term, as a result of better child survival, marrying younger women, and providing more marriage opportunities for their own children: 'In short, a prosperous farming couple of the 18th century had almost twice as many gene replicates in the local population 100 years after their wedding as an average family.'[24]

Voland looked specifically at the subject of female mate choice in this context, noting that the average age of Krummhorn men at marriage was *c.* 30 years, with very little in the way of social differences. On the other hand, the brides of wealthy farmers, at 24.9 years of age on average, were 2.3 years younger than those of propertyless workers. Voland argued that this arose as a result of female choice. The younger women were, the more demanding they were in terms of the resources provided by their husband, and therefore the greater was their likely reproductive success. As they got older they became less demanding in their choices. Thus, of those women who were under 20 when they married, almost one in three married a farmer, but less than one in ten of those over 30 did so. Correspondingly, one in five farmers, but only one in 25 other married men, married women under 20.[25]

As Voland says, since it is reasonable to assume that young women would have been equally attractive to men of all social groups, the pattern is best explained as the outcome of systematic female choice based on a preference for wealthier/more successful men. The pattern is even clearer when attention is focused specifically on those women who married up, rather than into their own social class. The former were on average 2.3 years younger on marriage than the latter. Furthermore, those women who married down into a lower social class were on average 1.3 years older at marriage than those who did not. These differences were directly related to the reproductive success of the women concerned, since this decreased with later marriage and rose with increased social status.[26]

Another example of the role of female choice in the context of differential male wealth comes from Monique Borgerhoff-Mulder's work among the Kipsigis agropastoralists of Kenya.[27] Here too wealthier men were more reproductively successful, and in this case the value of younger women was reflected in bride-prices, which were higher for young women with early menarche. However, Borgerhoff-Mulder was also able to show that women new to the area were more likely to marry men who could offer them more land, i.e. land which would be available to them as individuals, taking into account the land already allocated to other wives. Total male wealth, in terms of the total amount of land possessed by the man without taking into account the division between wives, was not correlated with the chances of obtaining a mate. In other words, women were making choices in terms of their own specific interests. Just as with the Ache, however, the Kipsigis also demonstrate how flexible the system is in terms of choices based on patterns of advantage. In more recent years people are producing fewer live births and investing more as parents in the survival and education of those children that they do produce. The result is that the pattern of paying a higher bride-price for earlier-maturing girls has now disappeared.

Although there are many other cases that could have been mentioned,[28] we will finish this review of cases where male wealth and status correlate with reproductive success by looking at James Boone's[29] study of the demography of different groups within the Portuguese nobility over the period AD 1380–1580. He defined four groups, ordered by status and wealth. For males, wealth/status category at birth was a significant determinant of the number of children produced, with a mean of 2.9 for men of the highest rank and 1.5 for the lowest. At least part of the difference was due to the higher number of reported illegitimate children for the highest category. When attention was restricted just to males who had been married, the mean number of offspring for those born into the highest category was 4.1, compared with 2.4 for the lowest category. The difference appears to relate, at least in part, to the increased probability of marrying more than once for males in the higher categories.

When we make the comparison for females the picture is different,[30] in that the number of offspring produced does not increase with status at birth. In addition, the range of variation between the wealth/status categories is much narrower than for males, with a mean of 3.8 for the highest category and 3.3 for the lowest. In contrast, when the number of children is examined in relation to the husband's status, a significant difference is found, essentially between the three upper categories, which are all very similar (between 3.6 and 4.0), and the lowest, with a mean value of 2.6. In other words, marriage to higher-status males improved females' reproductive success. The pattern, then, is similar to all the other cases we have looked at, in that status/wealth makes a bigger difference to reproductive success for men than for women, and similar to Krummhorn (the data are not available for the other cases), in that being married to a higher-status/wealthier man also increases the reproductive success of the women who are married to them.

A further pattern that emerges from the Portuguese nobility data is that while high-status males are more reproductively successful than high-status females, as we would expect given the greater use of wealth for males in terms of mating investment, this is not so for members of the lowest-status category. Here females are reproductively more successful than males, a result of the fact that some women who were born into the lowest-status category were able to marry up. This too corresponds to the expectations of the general sexual selection model outlined at the beginning of the chapter, where it was predicted that competition between males for reproductive success would be more severe than that between females, so that males at the lower end of the range lose out significantly more than females.

Differential investment in male and female children: the Trivers-Willard hypothesis in human societies

The patterns just described have further consequences. One such group of consequences concerns inheritance. We have already seen that even among the Ache and the Yanomami, who do not have any heritable resources as such, the lifetime reproductive success of sons is strongly correlated with that of their fathers. It follows too, from everything that has been said so far, that when there are significant resources to inherit they are likely to make a much bigger difference to the reproductive success of males rather than females. Accordingly, such inheritance is likely to be biased towards sons rather than daughters. Since reproductive success depends on wealth and since, when health is inherited, the wealth of the next generation is predictable to a considerable degree from that of the current generation, we have a situation where the Trivers-Willard hypothesis described above should be relevant, just as it is to the red deer, if such evolutionary considerations affect human reproductive systems. That is to say, if the current state of the parent means that the offspring are likely to have good reproductive prospects, then it makes sense to invest in male offspring; if the prospects are likely to be poor, it will be better to invest in females.

Accordingly, in the case of the medieval Portuguese nobility, we would expect parental investment to be oriented towards male offspring among families in the highest-status categories and towards females in the lowest. James Boone shows that this is precisely the pattern we find. Daughters of the lower nobility were not only more likely to marry than their brothers, but also more likely than women in the higher social categories. In this case the existence of investment in daughters is quite clear because marriage of daughters involved payment of a dowry. In the lower-status families where only a limited amount of wealth was available, it was better used as a dowry for a daughter than an inheritance for a son, because it would buy status for the daughter and her offspring, increasing her reproductive success, as we have seen. Furthermore, whereas high-status males were more likely to inherit and establish themselves in Portugal, low-status males were more likely to spend their lives in warfare, often abroad. The result was that the percentage of warfare deaths was lowest for the highest-status males and highest for the lowest.

The Trivers-Willard hypothesis also appears to account for the situation found among the Mukogodo in present-day Kenya.[31] They are a low-status group who until early in the 20th century were foragers speaking their own language. Since that time they have been gradually absorbed into the dominant Maasai pastoralist system, adopting their language, values and pastoralist way of life. However, this transformation has led them to a position at the bottom of the local socio-economic hierarchy, poorer than other groups and despised by them. As a result of this situation, Mukogodo men only have low probabilities of getting bridewealth in the form of livestock to marry women from neighbouring groups. However, Mukogodo women can marry up, to wealthier men of neighbouring groups, and their families acquire bridewealth as a result. Lee Cronk found that in the 0–4 age group the sex ratio was the equivalent of 100 girls to 67 boys. Furthermore, daughters were nursed longer than sons, taken more frequently to the baby clinic, and showed better growth than boys in terms of height and weight for their age. What is particularly interesting about this case is that the outcomes of what people do contrast with their expressed values, since the Mukogodo claim to share the general regional preference for male offspring which is characteristic of Maasai pastoralist values, but actually invest more in their daughters, as the Trivers-Willard hypothesis predicts they should.[32]

However, the patterns can be complex. Eckart Voland[33] found that among the rich Krummhorn farmers, the probability of sons dying in childhood was greater than that for daughters, suggesting the existence of greater parental investment in the latter. He explained this in terms of circumstances described already. Only one son was needed to survive and inherit the estate and thus continue both the property and the lineage. Because the landscape was full, with a fixed number of farms, other males of the farmer class had very little probability of owning property and, therefore, of achieving significant reproductive success. Daughters, on the other hand, had a chance of marrying the inheriting sons of other families of the farming class. In contrast, not far away, in the Leezen area of north Germany, it was landowning girls who had the highest mortality and landowning boys who had the lowest. In this area the landscape was not saturated and expansion was still going on. This offered the possibility of successful competition to all the sons of the landowning class, not just the one inheriting the estate, who were more successful than those with fewer resources behind them.

In fact, greater parental investment in male rather than female children seems to be more prevalent cross-culturally than the converse, visible in male-biased sex ratios at the onset of the juvenile period. The differences seem to arise from a combination of differential infanticide and neglect.[34] Among the Ache, Magdalena Hurtado and Kim Hill[35] found much higher male than female survivorship rates until age ten, and lower rates from age 20 onwards. They suggest that this type of pattern is characteristic of societies that prefer male children and is indicative of female infanticide, homicide and childhood neglect. Elsewhere they estimate that about 14% of male children and 23% of female children were killed before the age of ten, during the period when the Ache were living in the forest and for which Hurtado and Hill were able to collect figures.[36] Moreover, this was in a period when, as we saw in the previous chapter, the Ache population was growing rapidly. In his Yanomami study, James Neel[37] had access to demographic data from a total of 29 villages and found a sex ratio of 301 male children to 216 female. He explained this in terms of the known existence of infanticide, preferentially directed towards newborn females, at a rate of some 25% if one assumes the standard male:female birth ratio of 105:100.

It is hard to see precisely why female offspring need to be traded off against male ones unless such societies are moving towards being resource-limited, and in the case of the Ache and the Yanomami this does not seem to be true, because both were expanding rapidly. However, the examples we have seen of differential investment in terms of inheritance, bridewealth and dowry among the Portuguese nobility, the Krummhorn farmers and the Mukogodo point to differential reproductive possibilities being a key issue.

Competition, coercion and choice: differential male and female interests

So far, the argument has emphasized male control of resources, inter-male competition for mating opportunities and female choice in explaining the differences between male and female reproductive patterns and the differential parental investment which exists. Those males with more resources are more likely to be chosen by females and will be more reproductively successful. But this is not the end of the story. Various other factors deriving from the sexual selection theory framework outlined above need to be taken into account, including competition between females and male attempts to control females and their sexuality directly, not just by means of the resources they need. In what circumstances do these factors vary in significance?

A key factor in the whole equation is the dependence of females on male resources. If a woman can succeed in providing for herself and her children without male support, then she has less reason to take account of male interests and male control. In turn, this is likely to be associated with greater female sexual freedom and correspondingly low certainty for males that they are the father of their wife's children. In traditional contexts this is most clearly seen in matrilineal and matrilocal societies, that is to say, those where socially significant descent relations are through the mother and where married daughters tend to live in the same place as their mothers rather than moving somewhere different. In these societies a woman's closest relations are with her maternal kin, who also provide most of the food production. Female independence is high because investment by a husband is not required.[38] John Hartung's[39] analysis suggested that matrilineality probably evolved and was maintained because of its benefits to women, rather than to men. The argument that it developed because it is beneficial for a man to invest, if at all, in his sister's children rather than his own when paternity certainty is low is less plausible. For such a benefit to outweigh the cost for males the level of paternity certainty has to be very low indeed.

Clare Holden and Ruth Mace[40] carried out a statistical analysis of the relationship between matrilineality, patrilineality and pastoralism. They concluded that, in terms of probable historical patterns of social change, the sequence of events is likely to have been that matrilineal societies became pastoral and these pastoral societies then became patrilineal, presumably because females became more dependent on males for parental investment as heritable resources became more important. Inherited resources tend not to be significant in matrilineal societies. As we have seen earlier, there tends to be a much greater correlation between the reproductive success of fathers and sons than of mothers and daughters, and inherited resources generally provide greater reproductive benefit to males than to females, so it is more likely that when such resources exist they will be passed on from father to son. Certainly, bridewealth is crucial to male reproductive success in pastoral societies.

If a relatively small proportion of the men in a population control a large proportion of the resources and those resources (i.e. male parental invest-ment) are important for the success of women themselves and their children, then there is likely to be competition between females for the best males, as well as the usual competition among males. One indicator of such inter-female competition has already been mentioned in the context of the Portuguese nobility study: the institution of dowry, which was preferred to investment in male children by less wealthy and lower status families. Steven Gaulin and James Boster's study[41] found that dowry was most likely to occur in highly stratified monogamous societies, especially those in which females are dependent on male resources. It may be that the direction of marriage payments gives an indication of the strength of inter-male versus inter-female competition.

If males are going to invest in parental effort, they are likely to be partic-ularly concerned with the issue of paternity certainty and therefore female chastity. This reaches its peak in stratified polygynous societies,[42] where those men who are at the top of the wealth and reproductive pyramid are not only concerned about their parental investment but specifically have to cope with the threat of large numbers of sexually disenfranchised males. The result is high levels of sexual control of women,[43] including claustration in harems, as well as severe penalties for adultery. As Elizabeth Cashdan points out, mothers of daughters collude in such customs because they are con-cerned with their daughters' reputation for chastity in the competition for high-quality mates.

It is clear that in such situations women do not have a great deal of choice. If they need the resources controlled by men then they are potentially open to coercion arising from the interests of male resource owners. Their vulnerability will be even greater if the situation is one with high levels of inter-female competition for the best resource holders. In such contexts there is likely to be a spiralling intensity of sexual selection in terms of crite-ria defined by the interests of male resource holders.

A particular context where female interests arise is that of polygyny and the extent to which women benefit from it or suffer costs because of it. The so-called *polygyny threshold model* views polygyny as the outcome of female choice, in that, in societies with marked inequality, a woman may get access to more resources by being the second or third wife of a rich man than the only wife of a poor one. However, it is clear that while polygyny is always going to be a good reproductive strategy for successful men, it is often detrimental to individual women's reproduction. Beverly Strassmann's study of the Dogon of Mali in West Africa[44] found that the greater the ratio of married women to married men in the family, the greater were the odds of death for Dogon children. Strassmann was unable to identify a specific factor producing this effect but postulated that the cause of polygyny was the average eight-year age difference between spouses. This meant that there were more females than males in the marriage market, with the result that many females had to accept polygyny.

Dan Sellen and colleagues[45] looked at the same situation among Datoga pastoralists in Tanzania, predicting that, since women appeared to have considerable autonomy in their marital choices, there should be no deleterious effects when they decide to marry polygynously. In fact, women with a single co-wife produced fewer surviving offspring than monogamously married women,[46] a difference that was most marked for women married to poorer men. The deleterious effects arose because such women had reduced access to livestock, which affected children's growth and survival. Despite the apparent autonomy, there appear to be constraints on female choices.

Social stratification is also likely to have an impact on inter-male competition. Interestingly, reproductive stratification occurs in a number of animal species and refers to a situation where there are alternative male reproductive strategies which are either permanent or change in the course of a lifetime. For example, in the case of bullfrogs, males of younger ages (and therefore smaller sizes) cannot compete directly with those that are larger and older, and therefore adopt different tactics.[47] It seems likely that social class stratification in complex human societies acts in a similar fashion, because the heritability of resources and status is such that men in the lower classes are not in the same competition as those in the upper classes.

Bobbi Low[48] suggests that variation in male and female reproductive success should be divided into two components: a non-behavioural component based on the morphological characteristics and heritable resources of individuals and a behavioural component where variation in success is associated with active competition and striving. Where there are distinct social strata based on inherited resources, the behaviour patterns associated with success in striving aggressively for resources within a particular stratum may be different from one another. Those strata within which there is the greatest variation in reproductive success will be those which are most competitive. Low[49] also found that whether or not the education of sons teaches them to compete aggressively depends significantly on the extent to which reproductive success is largely determined by heritable resources. Where it is, the emphasis on such competition is much reduced.

Male and female activities

By and large, it is not the subjects just described that have interested archaeologists working on gender. There has been far more interest in the subject of male and female activities. Low[50] points out that although the physical differences between human males and females are slight, in terms of their behaviour humans are extremely sexually dimorphic, much more so than other primates. This is less true of foragers than agriculturalists, but nevertheless the differences are still marked. In her study of !Kung forager gender roles Patricia Draper[51] noted that because of child dependency, roles that conflict with female reproductive success are generally either avoided by women of their own volition or denied to them by other interested parties, such as their kin. In comparison with males, females have to be cautious both in economic and reproductive terms, because they have only limited ability to recoup losses, whereas men may have more to gain by taking risks.

Draper also proposed an explanation for the ethnographically observed substantial gender equality that has been observed among the foraging !Kung. It existed because inter-male competition was strictly limited by the low potential for extracting resources from the harsh environment in which they were living. This situation changed when the !Kung became sedentary. The ceiling on inter-male competition was raised and a variety of further distinctions arose between male and female behaviour. These were similar to those described by Gilda Morelli[52] in her comparison of the development of gendered behaviour in childhood between the foraging Efe and their agricultural Lele neighbours in Central Africa. Young girls in the agricultural society were more likely to spend time involved in household economic activities than boys, but there was no such distinction among the Efe. Similarly, among the Lele, young girls watched and participated in female activities but adult male activities largely took place outside the village and children spent little time in male company. Among the Efe, on the other hand, men and women work together in sight of children, the main difference between them being that women rarely accompany men on hunts.

We have already seen such a distinction in the roles of men and women in hunting among the Ache. It is not that women physically cannot hunt, but the returns from the risky activity of hunting are more useful for males than females. On the one hand, as we have seen, women have more to lose from risky activity, if harm comes to them or they fail to provide for their children on a regular basis. On the other, the gains from hunting large game which are shared outside the immediate nuclear family are likely to be more useful to males than females, in terms of the exchange relations they create and their contribution to mating effort, for example extra-marital affairs in exchange for meat, as opposed to investment in parenting.[53] Males are prepared to accept reduced efficiency in foraging in exchange for these gains.

Cross-cultural studies cited by Low[54] indicate a number of activities which are predominantly or exclusively male, in addition to warfare: hunting big game, whether aquatic or terrestrial, mining or quarrying (although not necessarily the repetitive and labour-intensive processing of the material, such as ore-crushing), ore-smelting and metal-working, chopping down trees, woodworking and boat-building, among others. Activities done mainly by women included fuel-gathering, the gathering and preparation of plant foods, cooking, drink preparation, water-fetching and spinning. Nevertheless, when these and other activities become specialist activities producing for a market then males often tend to take over.[55] Low's general conclusion about the distribution of tasks between men and women corresponds to the explanation we have already seen as to why women among the Ache, the Efe and the !Kung tend not to hunt large animals. Much of the effort which males put into high-risk, high-gain activities can be seen as mating effort, from which women in general have little to gain. Conversely, the fact that women's reproductive success comes from parental investment, including pregnancy, lactation and childcare, means that activities inconsistent with these are not in their interest.

Nevertheless, this is not the whole story with regard to activity differences, even if it provides the starting point. As we saw when looking at differential marriage patterns, the question of whether women have control of their own interests is closely related to whether they and their children are dependent on male parental investment; when there are significant heritable resources this tends to be the case. So the question of differences between male and female activities cannot be divorced from the issue of male power and control. If women remain at home engaged in such activities as spinning and weaving this may be more a matter of male interest in female claustration than of female interest *per se* in activities compatible with parental investment.[56] Furthermore, it is very clear that in virtually all societies such activity differences become the object of enormous symbolic elaboration around male-female gender differences and the legitimation of male power. As we saw in Chapter 3, such cultural patterns can have their own logic and dynamic arising from the process of cultural transmission, since the factors affecting the transmission of cultural traditions are not necessarily the same as those that affect variations in reproductive success. Nevertheless, it is important not to assume *a priori* that such cultural factors will always be dominant. Changes in the balance of interests, and therefore decisions, in the reproductive system can occur extremely quickly in response to exogenous changes, as the changes described above in bridewealth priorities of the Kenyan Kipsigis and in the requirements for male reproductive success among the Ache demonstrate. There is no sign of cultural inertia here.

Summary

It is worth summing up some of the main features to emerge so far from this treatment of the relations between men and women in terms of sexual selection. There are predictable constellations of relations between males and females. These arise out of their different reproductive interests and responses to the specifics of local social and ecological contexts. They are not genetically hard-wired. First, inter-female competition will be particularly strong in conditions of high wealth differentials, both with and without monogamy. Second, the form and strength of inter-female competition will vary depending on the likelihood and need of male parental investment. Third, inter-male competition will tend to be more muted in stratified than unstratified societies, because by and large males from different strata do not compete with one another. Fourth, the correlation between wealth and reproductive success is stronger for males than females, as is the correlation between parent and child reproductive success. Fifth, female sexuality will be more strongly controlled in situations of high male investment. These variations operate against a broad mammalian background in which males tend to invest more in mating and females in parenting, with the result that competition between males is more intense and females choose between them on the basis of their attributes, especially resources.

THE EVOLUTIONARY ARCHAEOLOGY OF MALE-FEMALE RELATIONS

The findings presented above with regard to male-female power, property, behaviour patterns and interests have all been derived from a comparative approach to male-female differences across species and across societies, through the application of sexual selection theory to data from biology and anthropology. Palaeoanthropology and especially archaeology have played little role, despite the fact that the claims made by comparative work often involve assumptions about processes which actually occurred in the prehistoric past. It seems that archaeology and behavioural ecology should have a mutual interest in these issues for two reasons. On the one hand, archaeology can potentially provide data about trajectories of change which can be used for testing hypotheses generated by comparative models. On the other, as we have seen already, the theory provides a coherent framework for developing hypotheses about the significance of aspects of the archaeological record which relate to sex and gender relations. Indeed, as we saw at the beginning of the chapter, investigating these relations becomes absolutely central to an evolutionary archaeology.

The archaeological investigation of male-female relations from a sexual selection perspective is more of a prospectus for the future, on the basis of the ideas presented earlier in this chapter, than a framework for much work that has already been done, at least partly because archaeologists have been unaware of the sexual selection framework and what it has to offer. Of course, the other issue that arises is the need for an archaeological methodology that will throw light on male and female roles and interests, and life outcomes, in the prehistoric past. It seems reasonable to predict that such methodologies will be developed as interest in the subject increases. Indeed, work on such subjects as distinguishing different male and female activity and post-marital residence patterns has developed considerably in recent years.[57] Despite the undeveloped nature of this field, however, there are some examples of archaeological work which can throw light on the issues described above, even if not all of them were conceived from this perspective.

One example is the hypothesis of Marek Kohn and Steven Mithen[58] that sexual selection was a factor in the production of handaxes by ancestors of modern humans between c. 1.5 million and 250,000 years ago (see fig. 36).

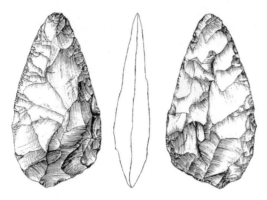

36 *An example of a carefully finished handaxe from an old river channel in southern England.*

0   5 cm

The authors point out that some handaxes seem to be 'over-engineered' in terms of the care devoted to their production in relation to any likely practical function. In particular, a great deal of effort seems to be directed to ensuring the symmetry of the handaxe. The authors relate this to the considerable evidence[59] that among animals and birds bodily symmetry is a character that reflects the health of the individual concerned, and that it is used as a criterion for mate choice by females. In this case the argument is that the making of fine handaxes with a high degree of symmetry might have been a male display on which females would make judgments of male quality, like the bowers of the bower birds that we saw earlier. As we noted then, imitation seems to be an important part of trying to build an attractive bower and it takes years for males to become good enough at building bowers to be selected by females, so the analogy may not be so far-fetched. Of course, it is hard to imagine how Kohn and Mithen's hypothesis would be testable and we have no basis for knowing whether handaxes were made by males or females, or both. Nevertheless, the study is an interesting attempt to account for some of the very puzzling features about handaxes that have long eluded convincing explanation.

A second example concerns the making of hunting decisions. The last chapter showed that optimal foraging theory provides a powerful framework for the understanding of subsistence decisions. We do not have to assume that its predictions will always be met in order to be able to use it heuristically as a basis for evaluating evidence. Nevertheless, the examples given in that chapter were generally cases where optimal foraging principles based on the assumption that the main goal of foragers was calorie maximization did seem to account very effectively for the patterns observed. Another study carried out by Mithen[60] came to different conclusions. He modelled the foraging decision-making processes of Mesolithic hunter-gatherers from Northern

Europe using foraging theory and a knowledge of likely environmental conditions and compared the predictions of his models with the content of the archaeological bone assemblages of the area and period he was modelling. In doing this he had to take into account all the other various factors that affect the composition of archaeological bone assemblages, especially preservation factors. He found that the predictions and the assemblage composition did not match up. His conclusion was that the assumptions of his decision-making model were wrong. Hunters cannot have been trying to maximize their calorific intake after all. In fact, he concluded, they seem to have been attaching greater importance to the hunting of large game than they should have done if calorie maximization was their priority, and he proposed that the successful hunting of large game was most probably associated with gaining prestige, based on the distribution of meat beyond the family. For the same reasons as those described already above, Mithen suggested that the hunters were most probably male and that the hunting of big game should be seen in the context of mating effort, following Kristen Hawkes' 'show-off' hypothesis,[61] because there would have been a female preference for more successful hunters, whether for long-term or short-term relationships. Sexual selection for reproductive success was more important than natural selection for survival in terms of hunting goals, according to Mithen.

Although the perspectives adopted have been very different, the nature of male-female relations has been on the agenda of European prehistory for a long time. In fact, the evolutionary analysis of male and female strategies and their relation to resources which has been presented above provides new theoretical foundations for some long-standing views on this subject, going back to Engels' discussion of the origins of patriarchy.[62] Gordon Childe[63] raised the issue, as did the Czech prehistorian Evzen Neustupný,[64] who argued that the introduction of plough agriculture into Europe in the later fourth millennium BC transformed the division of labour between men and women, since the latter were now removed from agricultural activity and men came to have patriarchal authority. The evolutionary approach leads to the same conclusions as the Marxist analysis, for similar reasons.

We have seen that males investing large amounts of resources in parental effort are likely to be concerned about paternity certainty and female chastity. On the other hand, where women can provide for themselves and their children without male support, they have less reason to take account of male attempts at control and are likely to have greater sexual freedom. Since plough agriculture is historically and ethnographically a male-dominated activity,[65] there are clearly good grounds for believing that it would have led to a dependence of women on male-controlled resources which had not previously existed, or at least to nothing like the same extent. The process is likely to have been compounded for other reasons.

Plough agriculture involves the use of fixed fields rather than temporary clearances in the forest. We know from such evidence as pollen analysis that fairly permanent clearance was becoming more widespread in Europe at the end of the fourth millennium, at a time when animal traction, including the use of the plough and the cart, had recently been introduced.[66] We also know that the appearance of permanent pasture at the same time, by cutting the need for the provision of leaf fodder, began to lift the constraint on the number of animals that could be kept, especially cattle. Although it is difficult to imagine that archaeologists will ever succeed in proving it, it seems likely that investment in such long-term resources as fields and larger herds, including plough teams,[67] would have been associated with the increasing importance of the institution of private property and inheritance. As we saw earlier, the lifetime reproductive success of sons is correlated with that of their fathers, and inherited resources generally give greater reproductive returns to males than to females, so when they exist it is most likely that they will be transferred from father to son, at least for males at the upper end of the wealth distribution. We saw too that Holden and Mace's analysis of the evolution of patrilineality and pastoralism[68] led to the conclusion that, if matrilineal societies become pastoral, then they are likely to become patrilineal as inherited resources become more important. As a consequence women become more dependent on men. It seems likely that, whether or not earlier societies were patrilineal, plough agriculture and permanent clearance began to have the same sorts of consequences in terms of the emergence of new patterns of male control of women that had not previously existed. At the same time, as we have also seen, competition might well have developed between women themselves for the best male resource holders for long-term parental investment, involving strategies conditioned by male interests such as paternity certainty.

Although male-female symbolic distinctions had always been important, they certainly seem to have received a new emphasis in many parts of Europe at the end of the fourth millennium. The lake-villages serve us well here too. In the western Alps about 3100 BC we find a new emphasis in the archaeological assemblages on bows and arrows, stone hammer axes and flint daggers. At the same time there is an increase in the frequency of items of personal ornament, including for the first time pendants in the form of male genitals, while bows and arrows, axes and daggers become symbolic male attributes. Pierre and Anne-Marie Pétrequin[69] suggested that there was an asymmetry between men, who were competing with one another for access to exotic materials obtained by exchange for such things as hammer-axes, daggers and arrowheads, and women, whose tools were made of local materials.

An analysis of north Italian petroglyphs dating to the same period by John Robb[70] led to similar conclusions. In hunting scenes weapons were used by males while in others, halberds (a kind of dagger blade hafted like an axe), axes and especially daggers were consistently used to distinguish males from females (see fig. 37). Furthermore, although we know from bone assemblages that a variety of animals was hunted, the only one commonly represented in art is the deer, and in particular the stag with its antlers; if the gender of the hunters is represented it is male, distinguished by a phallus. Images of ploughing show a similar pattern – oxen are represented in particular by their

37 *Late Neolithic stelae and Early Bronze Age rock art from the Alps showing male symbolism of daggers, axes, bows and halberds.*

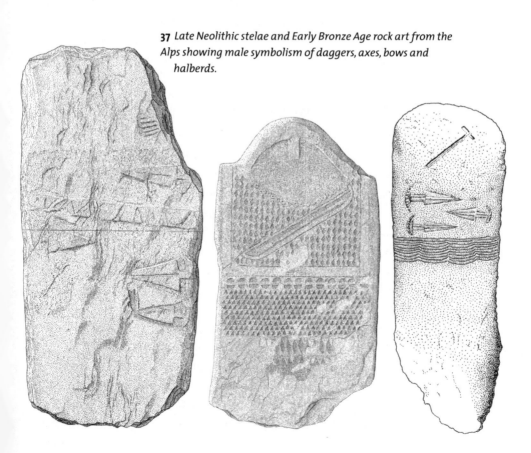

horns and those using the ploughs frequently identified as male. Robb suggested that these representations would have contributed to an ideology of male power, in which the male-female distinction was a hierarchical one, although relations between males were ranked rather than stratified at this point; stratification developed later, during the Bronze Age. Such an ideology of male power, together with growing male control of important agricultural resources, would have provided the basis for the constraining of female choice and competition into forms consonant with dominant male interests.

Clearly, such suggestions are speculative and there are alternative possible explanations of the increasing emphasis on male-oriented symbolism in much of Europe at the end of the fourth millennium. One of the best-known is that of Maria Gimbutas, who proposed that it resulted from the invasion of patriarchal Indo-European tribes from the steppes north of the Black Sea.[71] Even if this is not a convincing idea, however, it seems implausible that such a symbolic universe was invented independently wherever plough agriculture, long-distance exchange and male competition became increasingly important. It must have emerged somewhere and then spread because of its affinity with the newly emerging pattern of social relations.

Sexual selection and ornamentation

In a cross-cultural ethnographic study Bobbi Low[72] suggested that variations in male and female ornamentation might be related to processes of sexual selection. Recently Amanda Giles[73] has begun to explore this idea archaeologically, using the information from the inhumation cemeteries of Bronze Age Europe, which follow on, a millennium later, the developments described above. These are cemeteries of individual burials in which people were clearly buried in their local costume and it is possible to identify the age and sex of the skeleton from the bones, so that the relation between the biological characteristics and the social identities indicated by dress can be studied.

On the basis of the results of Low's ethnographic analysis, Giles suggested that marital status would probably be the most widely signalled attribute in women's dress and ornamentation, while men would be signalling wealth and status. She pointed to the conclusions of a study by Marie-Louise Sørensen[74] of female costume in Middle Bronze Age Europe which identified two different categories of women on the basis of evidence

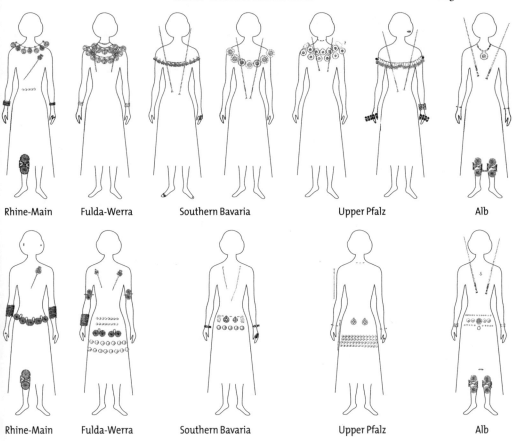

Rhine-Main Fulda-Werra Southern Bavaria Upper Pfalz Alb

Rhine-Main Fulda-Werra Southern Bavaria Upper Pfalz Alb

38 *Female costume in Middle Bronze Age Europe, suggesting two different social categories of women, one on which ornamentation is concentrated around the waist and hips, the other on which it is focused on the neck and breasts.*

from ornamentation on different parts of the body (fig. 38), as well as other aspects of costume, such as hair decoration. Sørensen's proposal was that the two categories might be linked to stages in the female life cycle, such as marriage. Such a distinction was not visible in male grave goods, including those related to dress. According to Sørensen, variation between males was defined in terms of 'degree of wealth, possession, access to prestige objects, or possibly physical age',[75] factors which again fit in with the patterns suggested by Low's ethnographic study. Finally, the fact that male grave goods often included weapons was also predictable from the sexual selection perspective adopted by Giles, 'and might be interpreted as symbols of physical prowess or ferocity mimics, analogous to displays by males in other species'.[76]

As we have seen already, in stratified societies, where the social distribution of resources is very unequal and is controlled by men, women are heavily dependent on male resources to provide for the welfare of themselves and their children. In these circumstances there will be considerable efforts on the part of elite males to control women and their sexuality to guarantee paternity certainty, and women will not be in a strong position to resist; indeed, it may be in their reproductive interest to play the game. Giles points out that there is indeed some evidence for female restrictedness in the European Bronze Age: some female burials wear pairs of leg-rings linked by a short chain which would have restricted movement (see again fig. 38). The elaboration of these leg-rings, and indeed their association with other elaborate costume items, are not consistent with an interpretation in terms of slave status for the individuals wearing them. Giles' proposal is that they should be interpreted 'as female ornaments of sexual restriction, or claustrating devices, designed to impair female freedom of movement', analogous to Chinese foot-binding.[77] These items first appear in the Middle Bronze Age, but become more widespread in the Late Bronze Age, a time when other evidence suggests that social inequality had increased markedly in comparison with earlier periods. Indeed, even apart from the chained leg-rings, high-status female ornamentation in the Late Bronze Age and Early Iron Age is characterized by very heavy jewellery, including leg-rings without chains, which would have been very restrictive.

The evidence from male graves and other sources of these same periods has been interpreted in terms of the emergence of a distinct warrior status,[78] in which elite males owned elaborate weapons produced by specialist craftspeople and made use of toilet articles suggesting a strong concern with appearance, especially their hair. Social hierarchy is strongly correlated with polygyny and competition among elite males, linked with the signalling of wealth and status. The pattern of increasingly restrictive elite female ornamentation as society became more hierarchical in the Late Bronze Age is paralleled by increasing levels of display in male costume, such as the elaborate armour which made its appearance at this time.

Finally, Giles addresses an issue which has been an object of discussion in work on Bronze Age social organization for more than 25 years, since Susan Shennan noted a pattern of grave-goods distribution at the Early Bronze Age cemetery of Brač in Slovakia[79] in which the richest burials in terms of grave goods were those of females with elaborate ornaments, and the numbers of such rich female burials exceeded those of their male equivalents. Shennan explained the pattern by suggesting that the 'wealth' in the female burials came from their husbands or other male relations, and that the smaller number of male than female burials at the top end of the grave-good 'wealth' scale arose because high-status males were polygynous. Elizabeth Rega[80] criticized this interpretation as androcentric, and suggested that it might be indicative of real female control of important resources like metal, obtained by exchange. Ethnographically, however, the wearing of elaborate ornamentation is negatively correlated with women occupying powerful social roles,[81] as Giles points out. Furthermore, there exists other possible evidence for male control of the economy, as we have seen, as well as possible indications of female exogamy – women leaving the community of their birth on marriage – in the form of burials of 'foreign women'.[82] That is to say, burials of women found in cemeteries in one region wearing costumes foreign to that region but the normal form of female dress somewhere else; female exogamy tends to be associated with low levels of female solidarity, as well as with patrilineal descent and inheritance. Giles[83] concludes that we have evidence of the sort of situation, 'in which we would expect low female economic and sexual autonomy and gender inequality to exist. In this light it appears most likely that female wealth and ornamentation was indeed related to male status.'

The key general point is that Darwinian sexual selection theory, and its predictions of material culture correlates in such areas as ornamentation, provide a basis for making predictions about the linkages between the different phenomena we observe in the archaeological record, and therefore why they pattern in the way they do. Because most archaeological work, especially on the subject of gender, rigorously eschews these sorts of generalizing, comparative approaches, we simply have little more than a series of disconnected observations and reconstructions, local in scope, and limited in their implications because of the shortcomings of the archaeological record. The field is wide open for this to be changed.

In the case of sexual selection, the role of historical processes in altering the nature of social and economic contexts, thus changing patterns of male and female interests and the way they are played out, is very apparent. At this stage, however, the role of specific cultural traditions in channelling these changing constellations of interests is less clear. However, they do seem to be relevant to the forms of male-female ideology and symbolism that were adopted in different parts of Europe.

-8-

THE HISTORY OF SOCIAL CONTRACTS
AND THE EVOLUTION OF PROPERTY

THE OBJECT OF THIS CHAPTER is to show how the Darwinian perspective can be used to throw new light on the way past societies were organized and on the kinds of questions archaeologists should be asking if they want to find about past forms of social organization. Obviously, a great deal has been said about this subject in previous chapters. It has been shown that male-female relations vary markedly in relation to overall patterns of hierarchy and inequality in society, which affect the extent of female economic autonomy and the potential success of male strategies for controlling women and their sexuality. It is also apparent that patterns of parental investment in offspring vary according to such factors as family wealth. In this chapter it will be suggested that the Darwinian perspective makes a difference to our understanding in three other, more general, areas: our perspective on the history of human societies; our understanding of the mechanisms by which societies operate and change; and the factors which affect those mechanisms. These topics have long been a central subject of interest in anthropology and archaeology and they have been approached within the framework of 'social evolution'.

SOCIAL EVOLUTION

The term 'social evolution' (sometimes used interchangeably with 'cultural' or 'sociocultural' evolution), as commonly used by archaeologists and anthropologists, refers to the history of what are conceived as the key long-term trends in human history: from foraging to farming; from farming to the origins of civilization and the state; from agrarian civilizations to industrial and now post-industrial society; accompanied by such developments as increased population, greater social complexity and more complex technologies. Such directional schemes have a long history in human thought, although they vary in their view of whether the movement is good or bad: the Greek and Roman idea of the decline from a golden age can be compared with the Christian idea of a movement towards salvation. More secular schemes originated during the Enlightenment, in the 18th century, but the schemes which have been most influential are those which developed in the 19th century, especially those of Marx and Engels. Nevertheless, even these bear a marked resemblance to the Christian scheme, with the demise of the initial, pre-Fall state of primitive communism followed by an historical movement towards the fulfilment of a socialist utopia with the withering away of the state. In the 19th-century industrial societies where the secular schemes were increasingly elaborated, such developments as complex technologies and increased production were seen as improving humanity's lot, and therefore as progressive. In a similar vein, the process of domination of traditional societies by industrial, imperialist ones was seen as a natural and inevitable process of Darwinian competition, in which weaker societies succumbed to stronger ones.

While the idea of directional evolution was a central part of the intellectual background out of which archaeology and anthropology emerged in the later part of the 19th century, it was less prominent in the first half of the 20th century. In Britain, anthropology adopted the theory and method proposed by Bronislaw Malinowski and Alfred Radcliffe-Brown. This involved rejecting the conjectural history of past states of society which had characterized 19th-century anthropology and emphasizing the study of the functioning of specific present-day ones. Most archaeologists were preoccupied with culture-historical concerns of the kind described in Chapter 4. The outstanding exception to this archaeological emphasis was Gordon Childe, a Marxist by persuasion. As well as playing a key role in the development of culture history, he was also deeply concerned with understanding the broad patterns in the evolution of human society and with presenting them to the general reader. Childe's approach was not an inflexibly unilinear and deterministic one, as the titles of such books as *Man Makes Himself* (1936) clearly demonstrate. However, he did regard the origins of agriculture (the Neolithic Revolution) and the emergence of urban societies (the Urban Revolution) as major steps in the progress of human societies, because they represented improved adaptations of humans to their environments, witnessed by the greatly increased populations which could now be sustained. Nevertheless, progress was not automatic. Childe argued that the civilizations of the ancient Near East, which had initially been progressive, eventually became stagnant and fossilized as a result of the effects of despotic leadership and social control. Further progress took place elsewhere, he suggested, when the Bronze Age Near East handed on the baton of technological development to the societies of prehistoric Europe. Because these did not have despotic forms of leadership they were able to take the innovations which had developed in the Near East, such as metallurgy, and turn them in new directions.[1] The result, in Childe's scheme, was a kind of direct line of evolution from independent European Bronze Age metal producers to Greek democracy and on eventually to the Industrial Revolution!

In North America, too, evolutionary ideas were not so prominent in the first half of the 20th century. The anthropologist Franz Boas emphasized the particularistic study of the history of individual cultures which then came to dominate North American anthropology, although it has been argued[2] that there were still ideas of progressive unilinear evolution behind the culture-historical schemes. However, the two individuals who brought evolution back to centre stage were Julian Steward,[3] who was concerned with the adaptive trajectories of particular societies, as we saw in Chapter 6; and Leslie White,[4] who revived a much more generalizing view of evolution on a global scale.

White saw cultural evolution as an extremely general process, in which societies progressed as a result of harnessing increasing amounts of energy from the environment thanks to the process of technological innovation. At the beginning of the sequence were hunting and gathering societies, simply extracting energy from plants and animals available in the environment. At the other end of the scale were present-day industrial societies, not only producing food in intensive ways but actually able to drastically increase their energy throughput as a result of gaining access to fossil fuels created in the remote past.

A problem with White's idea of cultural evolution as increased energy throughput was how to relate it to the analysis of individual societies so that they could be placed within the scheme. The answer was provided by Elman Service, who proposed that a proxy measure of energy throughput could be obtained by examining how energy was invested in social structure. He suggested that structure could be characterized in terms of four successively more complex social types: bands, tribes, chiefdoms and states.[5] Broadly speaking, bands corresponded to the majority of hunter-gatherer societies, with very few links between local groups. Tribes were generally seen as practising some sort of agriculture and as having certain social institutions that linked individual communities together, such as fairly formal kinship structures. Chiefdoms had a central agency responsible for such activities as redistribution, in which goods are collected from members of the community and then handed out again in some way, often through the organization of feasts. Finally, there was the state, which involved the presence of a much more centralized decision-making apparatus, dependent on provisioning by the population at large.

Societies were regarded as moving through these stages by responding to adaptive challenges. Thus, redistribution was conceived as a means of organizing a territory with a diversity of economic potentials, such that communities could benefit from all the resources in the territory as a whole, as opposed to just their particular part of it. It was also suggested that societies with more complex organization would tend to be more successful if competition between different groups occurred.

Anthropological archaeologists eagerly adopted such schemes. Not only did they seem to encapsulate the key patterns in human history, they also seemed to offer an appropriate scale of resolution for archaeology, as a discipline that has evidence for long-term patterns in the past, but evidence that is usually coarse-grained in temporal resolution and in detail often open to a variety of interpretations.[6] For instance, Service provided a list of the characteristics of the chiefdom stage, and Colin Renfrew[7] went through the list checking off the diagnostic features of the archaeological record of late Neolithic Wessex, to see if the societies which produced such monuments as Avebury and Stonehenge could be counted as chiefdoms. He argued that between the early Neolithic, with its long burial mounds and causewayed earthwork enclosures, and the late Neolithic, with its enormous 'henge' monuments, such as Avebury, Wessex society must have evolved from the tribe to the chiefdom stage.

As with cultural ecology, to which it is closely related, a great deal of useful work has been done within this framework, mainly devoted to tracing patterns of changing complexity in past societies on the basis of the archaeological record and then attempting to explain the changes observed. Nevertheless, the criticisms that the approach has attracted are many. The 'complexity' scale was seen as one in which 'complex' societies were more highly valued than simple ones, with dubious Eurocentric moral overtones.[8] Moreover, many of the archaeological sequences in different parts of the world failed to show much evidence of increasing complexity. Either these periods and areas had to be left on the sidelines of history, or, more usually, the archaeologists working on them, not wanting to be left out of things, had to become ever more ingenious at showing that some slight increase in social complexity could actually be observed.[9] In any event, it seemed unrealistic to many to squash all social variation onto a single dimension of 'complexity', and worse still to divide that dimension into a series of discrete stages.

These attacks on conventional directional schemes of social evolution have left social archaeology in a state of crisis. Much of prehistoric archaeology has moved in a post-modern direction, with no very clear agenda in terms of the issues it should address. One response has been the interest in the phenomenology of perception of landscapes and monuments referred to in Chapter 1. Apart from the question of whose perceptions they really are, the problem with these approaches is that the perceivers and their claimed perceptions largely float free of any more down-to-earth reality, while the nature of their social relations is generally left vague in the extreme, often involving no more than an implicit acceptance of the reconstructions of social evolutionists. Another response has been a concern with individual 'agency', where individuals with capacities and resources, symbolic and material, are seen as negotiating with others to achieve their aims. But what those aims might be and why is usually far from clear, and material constraints rarely play a role in the discussions.

In fact, the issues that the social evolution approach was supposed to address remain as important as ever, as Bruce Trigger[10] has recently emphasized. It is the assumptions behind the approach that have been shown to be problematical. This emerges very clearly in the processes social evolutionists have regarded as important, especially their focus on the role of elites and social control. In effect, archaeologists have been seduced by the same great monuments and concentrations of wealth that were designed to overawe local populations into believing elite propaganda and imagining that issues of social control are the only ones that matter.[11] As Richard Blanton points out,[12] other important dimensions of change that impinge on governing institutions, such as the development of commercial institutions, have been largely ignored. The same is true of domestic institutions, despite the fact that many aspects of social change are located at the domestic level, including production and consumption decisions and the reproduction and sexual selection issues discussed in previous chapters. Furthermore, many authors have pointed out that attempts at domination always invoke a corresponding resistance: we need to look at what social processes are going on at the bottom as well as at the top.

If 'social evolution' does not provide an adequate framework for the study of the prehistory and history of human societies, what, if anything, do we put in its place? This chapter proposes a broader agenda, of which social evolution only represents a part: the history of human social orders; in other words, the different social contracts which have characterized human populations over time. We also need a theoretical framework that provides a convincing set of principles for identifying and explaining the key aspects of those social orders. Finally, of course, we need a means of putting our ideas into effect so that we can make appropriate observations on the archaeological record.

The only serious candidate for such a framework is provided by the developments in Darwinian evolutionary theory that have taken place over the last 40 years and whose implications this book has been pursuing. First, they provide a general theory of ultimate human motivations and their consequences for human decision-making and action, as previous chapters have shown. Second, they acknowledge that human social orders have an evolutionary history which has had a bearing on subsequent possibilities.[13] Third, they do not assume the existence of societies as functioning entities, but raise the question of how any sort of social order can come into existence and provide tools for addressing these issues. Fourth, they illuminate various aspects of inter-group relations, not least the nature of warfare. Finally, they represent evolution as a process of branching differentiation rather than a directional trend. If there are any directional trends in the evolution of human societies, as indeed there appear to be, they emerge as a by-product of directionless selection processes in specific local contexts, just as the major transitions in biological evolution did.[14] These subjects will be the focus of this chapter and the next.

CREATING AND MAINTAINING SOCIAL ORDERS

The traditional social evolutionary view was based on the premise that the entities that evolved were social groups, which adapted by means of social institutions to the natural and social conditions surrounding them and attempted to maintain an equilibrium. The so-called 'post-processual' archaeologists who reacted against these ideas in the 1970s and 1980s argued that such perspectives took away any concept of human autonomy and agency because people were reduced to being examples of groups, functions and systems. There was no possibility of them changing the conditions in which they found themselves. It was proposed that more attention should be given to individuals as the basis for understanding stability and change in societies.[15] One of the sources for this idea was the 'practice theory' of the French sociologist Pierre Bourdieu,[16] based on analysing the way individuals make and change their societies from day to day by interacting with others using the material and institutional resources available to them to achieve their ends. Others criticized this perspective, claiming that such individuals are only found in recent and modern capitalist societies, and that some societies do not have any idea of an individual at all.

As we have seen already, the starting point for the evolutionary approach is the theoretical position known as methodological individualism. This is the view that larger-scale entities emerge from interactions between individuals. Individuals exist in all societies, in the sense of living creatures with a specific genotype, developmental history, birth, lifespan and death, and propensities to achieve goals which have been favoured by natural selection. Even identical twins are not the same person because of variations in the course of phenotypic development. How communities construct and conceptualize these individuals in the course of their lifetime has varied with time and place. In some they have had considerable autonomy, in others they may be conceived as having no individuality at all. This latter situation is not an argument against the existence of individuals, as some naïvely believe. On the contrary, it is an argument for raising the question of why it is that such constructions of individuality vary. This is precisely the question the anthropologist Mary Douglas approached[17] when she suggested that societies could be characterized in terms of their position on two dimensions: 'group', the extent to which individuals are subordinated to group values; and 'grid', the extent to which societies have strong social categories which distinguish people from one another and affect what they can do. The Indian caste system would be an example of a society with a very high value on the grid dimension. Cults which demand total loyalty from their members, even to the extent of mass suicide, would be examples of societies at the high extreme of the group dimension.

As we saw in Chapter 2, not dissimilar issues have arisen in evolutionary biology, concerning the identification of valid levels of individuality at which evolution can be said to occur. It was explained that one of the key breakthroughs in understanding how evolutionary forces affect social behaviour was the rejection of the group selection view that individuals would act for the good of the species. It was shown that individuals that did so would lose out to individuals who put their own reproductive interests first. Accordingly, individuals in the basic sense defined above have to be our starting point in understanding the evolution of social behaviour: individuals with a specific genotype, developmental history, birth, lifespan and death, and propensities to achieve goals which have been favoured by natural selection. Nevertheless, as we also saw in Chapter 2, the situation is not clear-cut, for a number of reasons. First of all, even though all the genes that characterize an individual have a common interest because they share a common fate, there is nevertheless evidence for so-called 'intra-genomic conflict'; that is to say, genes producing effects which are for their own benefit rather than for the benefit of the organism as a whole. Furthermore, the evidence for the existence of apparent altruism within animal societies does not make sense if individuals are the only relevant entities for evolutionary purposes, because no individual should put itself at risk for the sake of another. The key concept in resolving this – William Hamilton's idea of inclusive fitness, described in Chapter 2 – inevitably has the effect of dispersing the individual in certain respects and is of course one of the pillars of the 'selfish gene' concept. Furthermore, others have argued that, despite the demise of earlier concepts of group selection, selection between higher-level entities than individuals is the main mechanism which produces major evolutionary change. This view is a key part of Niles Eldredge and Stephen J. Gould's 'punctuated equilibrium' theory of biological evolution over geological time.[18] It has been generalized by authors such as Elliot Sober and David Sloan Wilson[19] into the idea of multi-level selection. Finally, all theoretical schools, including those that are sceptical about other levels of evolutionary process than that of individual inclusive fitness, recognize that such interests may often be served by cooperating rather than competing with other individuals of the same species.

In what follows we will start by looking at how individuals interact and then at how the nature of the resources available to people affects those interactions. The first task is to provide an appropriate set of tools for doing this. We can then go on to examine the implications of analysing interactions in this way for an understanding of how societies work and how they change, before looking at how we can use these ideas for understanding patterns of stability and change in the archaeological record.

GAME THEORY, COOPERATION AND THE NATURE OF SOCIAL INSTITUTIONS

At this point we need to introduce a major theoretical innovation, only mentioned in passing up to now. Interactions cannot be analysed with the straightforward optimization framework that has largely been used so far because, when individuals interact, the best thing to do in a given set of circumstances depends on what the other person decides to do, all the more so if they have different interests. The tools used to explore the implications of this sort of situation are those of *game theory*.

Perhaps the classic game is Prisoner's Dilemma; classic because it raises the key issue for the existence of societies: in what circumstances will people forego a certain amount of self-interest to produce an outcome which is good for both of them, but not as good as it could have been for one of them at the expense of the other. The eponymous version of the game presupposes that two people who committed a crime together are being held by the police in separate cells and being asked to inform on each other. If neither of them informs, then the police will only have the evidence to convict them on a lesser crime, so each will get one year in prison. If one informs and the other does not, then the one who informs will get away free while the other will have to take all the blame and will get a three-year sentence. If they both inform on each other, then they will share the blame and each get a sentence of two years. If the game is only played once, the only sensible thing to do is inform, since otherwise the outcome may be the worst possible; thus, both informing is the equilibrium result. On the other hand, if they had cooperated by not informing on one another both would have done better.

As it stands, all this sounds very artificial, but in fact there are a number of types of real-world situations which seem to correspond in structure to Prisoner's Dilemma. Perhaps the best known is the so-called 'tragedy of the commons', mentioned in Chapter 6, which can arise in the exploitation of common resources. Suppose a fishing ground is being over-fished. It would pay all concerned to stop fishing there for a year to allow stocks to recover. This is fine if everyone agrees to do it, but if some people cheat and ignore the agreement they will get the benefit of everyone else's restraint. Unless some arrangement can be reached, the best available pay-off will be produced by carrying on fishing and obtaining at least some share of the diminishing resource. As we saw earlier, this sort of situation is probably very relevant to the over-exploitation of seal resources on the North American Pacific coast.

Where games are repeated, however, and people can make use of their previous experience, contingently cooperative strategies can lead to the establishment of cooperation. The best known of such strategies is tit-for-tat,[20] mentioned in Chapter 2, in which players start by cooperating and then respond in kind to whatever their opponent played on the last occasion they met. This leads to cooperation and reciprocity, to the long-term benefit of those concerned, in that no other strategy can do better than it in terms of the pay-offs it provides. The problem from the point of view of understanding how societies work is that reciprocity tends to break down in these models when groups become larger than 6–10 individuals, because reciprocators can be infiltrated by selfish individuals who take advantage of them and gain better pay-offs as a result.[21] Nevertheless, there are various ways round this problem that raise interesting issues for the nature of cooperative forms of social organization.

One possibility is that there is selection at the group level which is stronger than that at the individual level, thus leading to the differential survival of groups with greater degrees of cooperation. We will return to this question in the next chapter. Another possibility is that cooperation could be maintained by sanctions, including sanctions on those who fail to apply sanctions when they should. Robert Boyd and Peter Richerson[22] show that in these circumstances any behaviour can be stabilized in a population, even if it is maladaptive. Of course, someone has to pay the costs of punishment; and this presents another Prisoner's Dilemma. As James Boone[23] explains, one possibility is that there may be a special interest group within the larger population that has more to gain from the maintenance of group cooperation than the rest and is therefore willing to pay the extra costs to ensure this. Political entrepreneurs might be one such category of people. Indeed, paying such costs might be one way to increase the regard in which such individuals are held. A simpler possibility though is that the entrepreneur benefits in a variety of ways from having a larger rather than a smaller group of followers.

However, there are other possible ways in which cooperation may be maintained without either group selection or the development of hierarchies; for example, if individuals use their memory of previous encounters to refuse to interact with those who have previously acted in a non-cooperative fashion.[24] Indeed, this is one way of producing a more general phenomenon: the development of correlated game strategies.[25] If we do away with the assumption of random encounters between individuals and assume that similar strategies (and strategists) will meet one another more often than dissimilar ones, then, even with a small amount of such correlation between strategies, the possibility of selfish, non-cooperative states of equilibrium, i.e. states where these strategies do best, is greatly reduced.[26] One way in which such correlation can occur is if cooperators can recognize fellow cooperators. Another is the case where similar individuals cluster together spatially. As a result of such correlation the short-term interests of classical economic game theory can be overcome in favour of cooperative interactions.[27] Brian Skyrms suggests that many human social institutions have the function of generating and maintaining such correlations.

These ideas have recently been taken forward by Samuel Bowles and Herbert Gintis[28] in a study of the evolution of what they call prosocial norms, defined as norms, or rules of conduct, whose increased frequency in a population enhances the level of well-being of members of that population, in the context of what are known as coordination problems, like those seen in Prisoner's Dilemma. As we have just seen, in these circumstances the pursuit of self-interest leads to inferior outcomes for everybody but prevails because it gives the best guaranteed minimum returns in the absence of other considerations.

Bowles and Gintis focus their argument on the existence and nature of communities – organizations that lack centralized institutions capable of making decisions binding on their members. They show that a variety of effects associated with frequent interaction with the same people lead to the emergence of pro-social norms which enhance the average well-being of members of the communities concerned, in terms of the pay-offs that individuals receive for particular kinds of behaviour. Furthermore, they do so in the absence of specific tendencies to conformism in the adoption of particular norms and in the absence of group selection, which are often considered of major importance for the development of within-group cooperation. Populations whose interactions are structured in such a way that coordination problems are successfully overcome will tend to grow, to absorb other populations and to be copied by others.[29]

But apart from its implications for an understanding of how cooperative communities can emerge and be maintained, Bowles and Gintis's game theory model, and others like it, has important implications for the assumptions on which game theory is based. Many people have objected to game theory on the grounds that it posits hyper-rational and perfectly informed individuals attempting to optimize as they interact. The weakness of this objection had already become apparent with the successful application of game theory to understanding animal behaviour,[30] which showed that mechanisms other than conscious rationality must exist that respond to the predicted pay-offs. In Bowles and Gintis's model a rough learning rule replaces conscious optimization. All that is required is for individuals to be capable of recognizing more successful forms of behaviour, in terms of the benefits they get from interacting with others in particular ways, and copying these.

Peyton Young[31] has developed a general theoretical framework for linking individual strategies to social structures through evolutionary game theory, which takes further the points made by Skyrms and Bowles and Gintis. The agents in Young's models are not perfectly rational and fully informed. On the contrary, they only have access to fragmentary information and have only a partial understanding of the processes they are involved in; they do not think very far ahead, but they are not completely irrational. Young's individuals take action on the basis of expectations, and those actions in turn become a precedent influencing the behaviour of agents in the future.[32] Finally, Young assumes that such processes never arrive at a perfect equilibrium but are constantly being affected by small shocks of one kind and another.[33]

At any given time a society is likely to be near equilibrium, in that the vast majority of people will do what is expected of them and they are happy to do this given what they expect of others.[34] However, there will always be a small number of people who do not follow the expected behaviour pattern in some aspect of life and occasionally a new behaviour pattern will spread to so many others that the society's behaviour pattern will tip to a new equilibrium in this respect. Some of these equilibria, i.e. widespread patterns of expected behaviour, turn out to be inherently more durable in the face of shocks than others and thus will tend to persist longer when they are reached, and the equilibrium is likely to tip back to them more often. Young's model predicts that if one pattern of behaviour is even a bit better than the other in terms of the pay-offs it provides for the individuals who use it then it will be stochastically stable, in the sense of being the most likely equilibrium, invulnerable to minor chance disturbances. However, it may take a long time to get there, because the existing equilibrium may have a great deal of inertia. On the other hand, when people make decisions on the basis of very little information and interact regularly with only a very small number of others, a new equilibrium may be reached very quickly. Equally, however, it is more likely to be dislodged by further random events in favour of a less satisfactory alternative.

The nature of social institutions

It is important to appreciate that the account just presented gives us a powerful way of characterizing social institutions. Such institutions are the outcomes of individual interactions – game conventions. These outcomes are the best responses it is possible to give in a particular kind of interaction, conditional on other people sticking to the convention.[35] Most people follow the conventions most of the time. However, not everyone does, and sometimes the new way of responding will take over and become a new convention. Institutional change may arise from internal or external, inter-group processes.

This characterization of institutions has further implications relevant to the whole argument that has been made so far about the nature of cultural traditions. We have assumed that these gain their continuity through space and time essentially as a result of cultural transmission via social learning. We are now saying that there is an additional way in which uniformities in practice through space and time can arise. That is through the emergence of social conventions which are maintained because of the pay-offs they give to those who follow them; social adaptations in other words. Furthermore, those conventions can actually have a selective impact on the prevalence of individual-level traits – social norms – that are passed on by social learning.[36]

Most games have many potential equilibria, so that different societies whose members do not interact are likely to have different social institutions (equilibrium expected behaviour patterns); what is standard in one society may not be standard in another. Such inter-group differences in social institutions may be further accentuated by the conformist transmission of cultural behaviour patterns – the tendency described in Chapter 3 to acquire the most common behaviour exhibited by members of a society – as well as by sanctions against deviant behaviour. Furthermore, as we saw in Chapters 3 and 4, there is considerable evidence that distinct social norms and institutions can be maintained by different groups even in the presence of considerable interaction between them. In other words, history matters.

Nevertheless, there should be some tendency for the preferential spread of certain institutions if they offer manifestly better solutions to coordination problems, either by expansion of certain populations and the absorption of others, or by their preferential adoption by members of other groups. The former process is apparent in such well-known cases as the absorption of the Dinka by the Nuer in southern Sudan, as a result of their better organization for cattle raiding and warfare.[37] The latter process provides the basis for some phenomena which have long been recognized in archaeology, such as Colin Renfrew and John Cherry's 'peer polity interaction' process.[38] The peer polity interaction concept is based on the observation that many social developments, for example the emergence of complex society in the Aegean Bronze Age, seem to occur simultaneously over a broad area, far too large to have been the territory of a single political entity. The adoption of successful organizational innovations by neighbouring groups seems to be the process involved.

The extent to which this goes on may well be a function of the strength of competition between the groups involved. As Bruce Trigger[39] has pointed out, where competition is weak even inefficient social arrangements can last a long time. Furthermore, while there may be only a few ways to be a successful state, and perhaps, in the light of the collapse of communism, only one way to be a successful post-industrial state, there may have been a whole range of different ways of being a viable horticultural, pastoral or agricultural non-state society.

At this point we need to sum up the argument so far concerning the relations between individuals and groups. If we do not start at the individual level, it is impossible to understand how and why groups form and why they have the character they do. We do not even see that coordination problems and their solution or otherwise represent a key aspect of human social interactions. The unrealistic rational actor assumptions of classical game theory can be abandoned; all we need are individuals that are not completely irrational. The social construction of the nature and autonomy of those individuals in specific societies is not something which undermines the concept of the individual but an aspect of the nature of local social norms, passed on by social learning. Social institutions are local equilibrium game outcomes arising out of interactions between individuals. They maintain their continuity through time as a result of the pay-offs they provide for group members. Because there is always a large number of possible equilibria, groups with different histories are quite likely to have different social institutions, although contact and competition may lead to the spread of more successful ones.

In the remainder of this chapter we will look at the nature of the interactions *within* social groups and their relation to the nature of resources. In the next we will look at interactions *between* groups and the factors affecting their outcomes.

THE ORIGINAL SOCIAL CONTRACT?

By and large the social evolutionary schemes of the 19th century took the initial forms of human society to be some sort of opposite of the society of the schemes' proponents. The neo-evolutionary schemes of the 1960s and 1970s took the 'band'[40] and 'egalitarian society'[41] as the original social forms. The basis for these categories were such forager groups as the Shoshone of the Great Basin in the western deserts of North America, and especially the San foragers of southern Africa. The latter provided the classical model of what an original hunter-gatherer band should look like, with their small-scale egalitarian form of organization, and even more so with their apparently non-materialist Zen value system.[42] Indeed, in neo-evolutionary terms, if the San had not existed it would have been necessary to invent them, because the neo-evolutionary scheme presupposed an initial undifferentiated form of organization out of which more complex forms developed. It now turns out, however, that the San were in a sense invented, at least as representatives of some original pre-Fall state of human society. Work has shown that they have a complex history of interactions with neighbouring groups, including episodes of pastoral activity.[43] There is no reason to believe that they provide a valid model for the hunter-gatherers of the past.

However, we do have an alternative to the construction of rhetorical oppositions. Rather than looking for early human social orders in mythically characterized modern foragers, another possibility is to characterize them on the basis of comparative inter-species analysis and evolutionary history, as the biological anthropologists Robert Foley and Phyllis Lee have attempted to do in a number of publications.[44] They have proposed a general set of categories designed to characterize variation in ape social systems, based on the distribution of males and females in relation to their kin and in relation to one another. Their proposals are summarized in fig. 39.

The distribution patterns depend on sex-specific dispersal at adulthood. The most common pattern among monkeys is for males to leave

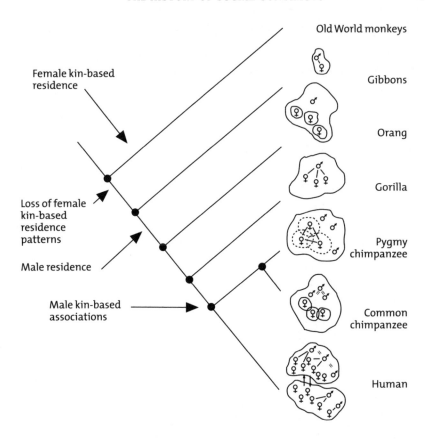

39 *An evolutionary tree of the relationships between the different primate species showing the forms of social organization characteristic of each species and the points on the tree at which specific social innovations occurred.*

the group, so the group is female kin-bonded. Consequently, female kin gain the advantage of cooperative control of patches of rich resources. Male kin-bonding, on the other hand, involves females leaving the group and is much less common. It appears to be linked with the control of females as a resource with a dispersed and patchy distribution. After the splitting off of the gorilla from the chimpanzee and human branch of the evolutionary tree, an innovation in social organization occurred, with the establishment of larger male kin-bonded communities, over and above smaller sub-groups, and female dispersal at maturity.

Of course, the reconstruction of the social organization of extinct forms of early hominins[45] is much more problematical than that of extant primates, but the evidence that *Homo ergaster* 1.5 million years ago had a different diet and metabolism from earlier forms of hominin[46] suggests a change in social organization, in Foley's view, towards further development of male alliances, because these provided an advantage in terms of foraging in new ecological conditions. Females would have preferentially associated with larger male groups, which would have provided better protection. On this basis Foley[47] proposes that the ancestral social condition of modern humans would have been characterized by a number of features:

    – Moderately large communities based on male kin-based coalitions and unrelated females attached to one or more males.

    – An element of inter-generational lineage structuring with a patrilineal bias given the male kin-bonded group pattern and the increased individual longevity which had developed by this time.

    – The male-bonded groups would have been at least to some degree closed to one another and mutually hostile, and larger groups would thus have been at an advantage.

    – Nevertheless, when groups reached a certain size they would have split, which would tend to lead to dispersal.

Foley's scenario for the characteristic form of modern human social organization is far removed from the San, with their flexible and egalitarian organization.

In the light of the Darwinian framework that this book has presented we can suggest various possible features of the social processes going on in such groups. A centrifugal tendency would have been competition between males for reproductive success. A cooperative pressure would have been the potential for inter-group competition. Another force encouraging cooperation is likely to have been inclusive fitness considerations among the patri-centred group members. If Hillard Kaplan and his colleagues are correct[48] and male provisioning of females and children was essential to their own reproductive success, leading to pair bonding of greater or lesser stability, then it would have been impossible for a very small number of males to dominate a group's reproduction. Food sharing would also have been a factor in limiting competition. Studies of food sharing among the Yanomami, for example, have shown that it operates on a reciprocal altruism principle.[49] In another case study, this time of the Yora of the Amazon lowlands in southeastern Peru, Lawrence Sugiyama and Richard Chacon[50] demonstrated that in cases where injury or illness to the best hunter has a big impact on other members of the group, then they have an interest in ensuring that he is provided with resources to recover.

However, another consideration arises from the structure of the resources themselves. If a large meat package is available then, once those most closely involved in hunting it and their relations have had their fill, it is of limited further value. This is the basis of Nicholas Blurton-Jones's 'tolerated theft' model of sharing.[51] If your consumption of a resource you control has reached the level of diminishing returns, the costs of defending it against someone whose consumption has not reached that level are likely to be greater than the benefits.

Ritual knowledge

It is important to appreciate, though, that control of food is not the only possible basis for inequality in foraging societies. Another is inequality in access to ritual knowledge. In many foraging societies, the transmission of ritual knowledge and control over it through initiation and other rites play a central role in social activity.[52] Indeed, control of the transmission of such knowledge may be the only legitimate locus for the generation of inequality among their members.

This point emerges very clearly from David Whitley's[53] discussion of the rock art of the foragers of the North American Great Basin. As described by Julian Steward,[54] these foragers are generally regarded as one of the classic egalitarian societies that support the traditional social evolutionist view of early human society. However, Whitley presents a very different picture. Not only was there inequality between men and women, there were also differences among men, in particular between those who were shamans, and thus had access to supernatural power, and those who were not. Local group headmen were almost always shamans, and shamanism, like leadership, was largely hereditary:

It was only through the acquisition of shamanistic power that men could truly become political actors and gain prestige and status in Numic society. In turn this advantaged them in a number of ways: women desired such men as marriage partners, and the population at large respected them, largely out of fear of their potentially malevolent [power]. And in that shamanistic power was partly inherited, but in any case limited to a small segment of the population, it is apparent that a very restricted, incipient elite group, composed of shaman/headmen, existed within the ostensibly egalitarian Numic society.[55]

A related argument was developed at length by David Riches[56] in a discussion of the role and significance of shamanism. He pointed out that the cosmologies of nomadic hunting and gathering societies are predominantly shamanistic and he associates the presence of shamanism with relatively decentralized forms of organization. However, this is not to say that they are thoroughly egalitarian. Among the Canadian Inuit on whom his discussion is mainly focused, although superior hunting ability is not allowed to form a basis for the development of social inequalities, the role of shaman does provide such a basis. The success or failure of the hunters is seen as depending on the community's relations with the spirit world and maintaining these in good order depends on the observation of taboos. The shaman is the mediator between the two worlds and has the responsibility for the cultural evaluation process in terms of which some actions are regarded as taboo. The role is seen as a highly skilled one requiring a specialist and the skills are passed on from expert to novice through an apprenticeship. As a result of his mediating position with the spirit world, the shaman has power, privileges and position which are unavailable to anyone else.

On the basis of this and other evidence, I proposed that a key locus for the generation of social inequality in forager societies was the cultural transmission of ritual knowledge, even in the absence of material inequalities.[57] Furthermore, if the rules for the control of cultural transmission are different from one group to another and have an effect on the longevity and survival of the groups concerned, then they can potentially also provide a basis for cultural group selection (see next chapter). However, for present purposes, the main point to note is that if you share details of a ritual with somebody, you do not have any less of it yourself. In other words, ritual knowledge is a resource of a very particular kind.

Prestige

Another resource that can provide a basis for social inequalities in the absence of significant material distinctions is prestige. The status of an individual is not so much something that the individual possesses but a feature of the perceptions that other members of the group have of that individual, which is then reflected in how they behave towards them.[58] Moreover, status is a relative quality, defined by an individual's position in relation to others. Being of high status can have advantages of various kinds. For example, game theory experiments cited by James Boone and Karen

Kessler[59] indicated that people were prepared to accept lower returns playing against high-status individuals than low-status ones, suggesting that status can be translated into material benefits.

They also cite evidence that at times of crisis high-status individuals and groups had priority access to resources, which meant that they were far more likely to survive such crises than ordinary members of the population. Even if such status distinctions were relatively unimportant under normal conditions, they played a key role in defining priorities at times of adversity.[60] In fact, the authors show by simulation that, under plausible conditions, investing in the gaining of status to the detriment of reproduction can lead to greater fitness in the medium- to long-term if populations are characterized by regular crashes. If those of higher status are significantly more likely to survive the crashes, then even crashes which only produce population reductions of 20–25% are sufficient to have this effect. In the light of the archaeological evidence for population fluctuations at the local and regional scale that we saw in Chapter 5, it seems possible that this effect of prestige may have been an important one in prehistory.

However, the attainment of prestige entails costs as well as benefits. The benefit is social power, defined as 'the ongoing capacity to extract or defend a disproportion of the fitness-affecting benefits in the form of goods and services produced collectively by members of a social group'.[61] Prestige does not necessarily depend, as wealth does, on the ownership of resources and hence its significance will not be restricted to the sorts of societies and economies where resources are owned. However, it does depend on investing in the ability to provide benefits for the group in some way in order to gain prestige, and also on outdoing potential competitors. One way of achieving the latter is to impose a cost on them which they cannot afford to pay. For example, if the key to gaining prestige is successful big-game hunting, then the hunter with greater ability who is able to achieve success more quickly may be able to impose an unacceptable cost in time on a rival with less ability. In other words, the individual with the greater ability pays a lower marginal cost for a given increase in the intensity of competition. Such competition could potentially be very costly in terms of time and effort to the individuals concerned but the outcome would be directly informative to other members of the group, not least potential sexual or marriage partners, of the relative capacities of the individuals concerned, with potential reproductive benefits on both sides. This sort of behaviour is known as *costly signalling* and is an example of Amotz Zahavi's 'handicap principle',[62] formulated to account for the way in which certain animals and birds, for example male peacocks, expend huge amounts of energy on conspicuous displays, as we saw in the consideration of sexual selection in the last chapter.

As already mentioned, Sugiyama and Chacon's analysis of the effects of illness and injury on hunting success among the Yora of the Amazon lowlands points in a similar direction.[63] Being the most successful hunter can provide a reason for other people to support you when you are ill which is to their benefit as well as yours. The authors extend this argument to the provision of any difficult-to-replace benefit, such as ritual intervention or superior craft skills. If, in any given group, there is clearly only one person who can provide a particular type of benefit there is not a problem, but if there is more than one there is likely to be competition for the position and the benefits that accrue to it. Thus, 'Shamans, for example, wage spiritual warfare against each other in battles for status that are a chronic feature of Jivaroan life.'[64]

Boone and Kessler's model shows that it can pay to invest in costly signalling, even at the expense of immediate reproductive success, if the high-status position obtained leads to better treatment, and therefore better survival rates, at times of crisis. Nevertheless, the evidence described earlier in the book would tend to suggest that usually no conflict arises between achieving high status and reproductive success: the two tend to go together. In other words, high status leads to higher reproductive success at times of population growth and expansion as well as high survival rates when times are bad. Even so, as groups become larger and as the range of status differences increases, the costs of maintaining a status position in the competitive rank order can increase very considerably. Investing less may lead to loss of position altogether, so there may be no option but to keep meeting the costs for as long as possible, even if there is no apparent rational justification.

Archaeological discussions of social competition and the emergence of social hierarchies have made extensive use of the concept of prestige but have rarely been very specific about its nature. Nevertheless, there are some studies that relate directly to the issues just discussed.

One example is the attempt by DeeAnn Owens and Brian Hayden[65] to understand the nature of the rituals associated with the production of cave art, and especially the involvement of children and adolescents in those rituals, which is indicated by the small size of some of the hand and foot prints found deep in the caves. On the basis of a comparative analysis of ethnographic data on rites of passage among what Hayden calls transegalitarian foragers,[66] they propose that the cave sanctuaries would have been used for the initiation of adolescents into secret societies. This is consistent with the well-known role of secret societies in holding and transmitting esoteric knowledge available only to members and thus restricted in distribution within the society. Such knowledge provides a basis for gaining social power and status, as we have seen above. Initiation into secret societies appears to be precisely the kind of investment in prestige creation discussed by Boone and Kessler, but it is also parental investment of the kind described in Chapter 5. Not only do adults have to invest in prestige-generating activities on their own account if they are to be successful; they also have to provide investment in prestige-building for at least some of their offspring – a kind of inheritance that may exist even in the absence of ownership of resources – so that their competitive abilities are enhanced.

Ethnographically, there is evidence that high-ranking males in more socially differentiated forager societies received longer, more severe and more specialized training than other males, which no doubt put them in a better position to compete for positions providing hard-to-replace benefits, while higher-ranking females underwent more elaborate puberty ceremonies. Furthermore, initiation into high-ranking secret societies or to high grades within them often involved expensive payments. As Owens and Hayden[67] point out, differentiation in the area of initiation rituals and other rites of passage would no doubt have been greatest in those societies where there was also differentiated ownership of material resources, inherited within specific corporate groups. However, prestige would still have been a valuable resource on its own, worth investing in and passing on to offspring. As we saw with the Ache foragers in Chapter 5, the reproductive success of sons was correlated with that of their fathers, indicating that the latter had an effect on the success of their sons even in the absence of any control of material resources by anybody.

In summary, there are a number of factors which would have put a ceiling on the degree of competition and inequality in male-centred foraging groups of the kind proposed by Foley and Lee. Not the least important of these would have been the limit on returns available from controlling such food resources as animal carcasses and the requirement for male parental investment, which would have restricted the possibility of polygyny and reproductive monopoly. Other resources, such as ritual knowledge and prestige, would have provided a basis for generating inequalities, including inequalities that could persist through more than a single generation, but, despite their undoubted importance, neither of them provides a basis for transcending the limits imposed by the first two factors.

WEALTH, PROPERTY AND INHERITANCE

In the light of what we have just seen, the question arises of what is the effect of material wealth on this sort of situation. Or rather, in what circumstances did notions of wealth and the concept and practice of ownership come into existence, and what was the result? All foraging groups have territories and even in cases where population density is low and the territory is not defensible from other groups, it is still normally required that people should ask permission to make use of the resources in another group's territory. The extent to which such territories are likely to be defensible and to need defending is likely to be dependent on the local population density. However, such issues raise questions about inter-group competition that we will consider in the next chapter. What concerns us here is the possibility of differential resource ownership within groups.

A key factor is the characteristics of the resources themselves, specifically, the extent to which they are excludable and divisible and thus amenable to some sort of divided ownership. This requires such resources to be predictable and defendable. Many important foraged resources are neither densely nor predictably enough distributed to meet this requirement. This seems to be particularly the case with the big-game animals which are at the top of the optimal foraging hierarchy.[68] Others, however, certainly do satisfy the requirement, particularly those that come to be exploited when groups intensify and have to shift down the hierarchy of preferred resources, for example, stands of plants producing edible seeds.

Contest competition

The existence of such ownable resources changes the nature of social interaction in two important ways. First, it leads to new forms of competition, with new social implications, specifically to a shift from *scramble* to *contest* competition. This is a distinction made by evolutionary ecologists which is relevant to competitive behaviour in many different species. The implications are described by James Boone.[69] In the case of scramble competition, the name indicates exactly what is involved. If you imagine throwing some coins into a crowd where all the individuals are similar in size and strength, then the number of coins any individual obtains will be dependent on the size of the crowd. The same is true of foragers exploiting a resource which cannot be controlled. The share obtained by any one forager will be dependent solely on the size of the group and any differences in foraging abilities.

Contests, on the other hand, involve competitions between pairs of individuals over particular resource patches,[70] where the outcome in the simplest case is that one or the other individual wins or holds the resource. If an individual is holding a resource, the addition of further individuals to the group is not going to affect that individual's fitness, except insofar as it increases the intensity of competition. In any given case, especially from the point of view of a latecomer to the group, at least some of the best resource patches will already be occupied, so there is not a free choice. In these circumstances the individual's share of resources, and hence fitness, will not be equal but will depend on the quality of the resource patch they are able to obtain.

As Boone[71] makes clear, such resources provide a basis for social hierarchies to develop, as a density-dependent phenomenon, in the sense that latecomers to the local population have to accept resource patches of lower quality if it is worthwhile for dominant individuals or groups to defend their higher-quality resources. If they are not able successfully to defend their higher-quality resource then the competing group will take it over, but structurally the position will remain the same. At a larger spatial scale, however, the situation presupposes that 'latecomers' do not have the option of going elsewhere at a cost lower than that of remaining within the group.[72] Where plentiful dispersal opportunities are available they will have such an option.

Contest competition provides a particular variant on the well-known Hawk-Dove game in game theory.[73] This is a game in which two individuals are competing and have two possible strategies open to them. The 'Hawk' strategy always fights to injure the opponent physically and at the same time risks injury to the individual using it. The 'Dove' strategy simply makes a threatening display but never actually engages in any serious fights so the individual concerned is never injured. If everyone acts as a Hawk then there is a high probability of being injured and the Dove strategy will do better. Equally, if everyone is a Dove then the Hawk strategy will be more successful. However, a population of mixed Hawks and Doves, or individuals who play Hawk some of the time and Dove the rest of the time can be stable. The relative proportions that are stable are those that give the same average pay-offs to Hawks and Doves.

The variant on this which is based on ownership of a resource says 'Play Hawk if owner, play Dove if intruder'. Other things being equal, this is a stable strategy. No one can get a better average pay-off than they do by playing this rule. The strategy is known as 'Bourgeois'.

Inheritance

The second major way in which ownership and property make a difference is the opportunity they offer for the inheritance of wealth. We saw in the last chapter that inheritance made a major difference to the reproductive success of Krummhorn farmers and the Portuguese nobility.

The nature of the reproductive strategies that are favoured when material resources can be inherited has been explored in a model by Alan Rogers.[74] He starts by distinguishing reproductive from material motivations and assumes that if there is a strong correlation between an individual's *long-term* fitness and its number of surviving offspring then reproductive motivations will be very strong. Equally, if there is a strong correlation between *long-term* fitness and wealth there will be strong material motivations. If one of the correlations is stronger than the other, then that motivation will predominate. When wealth is not heritable, the correlation between long-term fitness and number of offspring is always stronger than the correlation between long-term fitness and wealth. The question that Rogers explores is whether this situation changes when wealth is heritable, assuming that inherited wealth makes it easier to earn wealth during an individual's lifetime. It emerges from his model that the number of offspring and wealth are both very strongly correlated with long-term fitness, so there is no reason to expect either kind of motivation to predominate.[75]

Rogers concludes that where wealth is heritable it has a value in addition to its effect on the number of an individual's offspring, because a rich person can increase the wealth of descendants several generations away by continuing to earn:

At evolutionary equilibrium, material and reproductive motivations should both be important. In such a world material motivations would be in no sense subordinate to reproductive ones. Resources should be valued even when they have no immediate effect on reproduction.[76]

Similar issues have been explored by Ruth Mace,[77] in a model that explored the relationship between birth scheduling and parental investment in relation to the inheritance of resources. She assumed, first, that parents invest in their offspring in such a way as to maximize their own reproductive success, a reasonable assumption in the light of what we have seen in previous chapters. Her second assumption was that the availability of inherited resources is crucial to a child's success in life. In these circumstances, if some offspring are unlikely to inherit, they are unlikely to contribute to their parents' fitness, and may even detract from it if investment of resources in them is detrimental to investment in those who will inherit. Indeed, this is precisely the situation we saw earlier in Eckart Voland's account of Krummhorn. Rich farmers invested resources in their one inheriting son who kept the farm. As a result of this, such farmers had a greater long-term reproductive success than other social groups. Other sons of rich farmers, on the other hand, were actually more susceptible to childhood mortality than those of other social groups; it was not worth investing so much in them.

The object of Mace's model was to establish what was the optimal allocation of wealth to children in the sense of producing the maximum number of grandchildren. Her model took into account environmental risk, mortality risk and the economic costs of raising children. She based it on a traditional African pastoralist system in which wealth is represented by livestock, and where those who have wealth find it easier to obtain more, while those with little are at risk of losing what they have. Families must pay a bride-price to the bride's family when a son marries, as well as providing a herd of livestock to support the new family; daughters receive a small dowry on marriage. As we saw earlier, the allocation of greater resources to sons rather than daughters is very common and arises because reproductive success is more closely related to wealth in males than in females. Mace's model focuses on decisions about investment in sons; daughters are essentially cost-neutral because the dowry given to a daughter and the bride-price received more or less cancel one another out.

Two important features emerged from the model. First, the relationship among the number of living sons and the amount of wealth required for people to decide to have another baby shows that, the higher the number of living sons, the greater the wealth required before people will take the decision to have another baby; in other words, wealth is correlated with fertility (fig. 40). The other key result in Mace's model concerns the relationship between the maximum number of sons to inherit and the wealth of the parents: the wealthier the parents, the more sons will inherit a herd, rather than smaller numbers of sons getting bigger herds. In other words, in contrast to Voland's Krummhorn example, in this case it does not pay to invest all the inherited resources in a single son. However, there is still a ceiling on the number of inheriting sons. If a family has more sons than it can give an adequate inheritance to, there will be no parental fitness advantage to be gained by giving them any inheritance at all. This prediction corresponds to Mace's empirical finding among the group that provided the basis for defining the model, that the more elder brothers a man has, the more disadvantaged he is in terms of inherited wealth and reproductive success.[78]

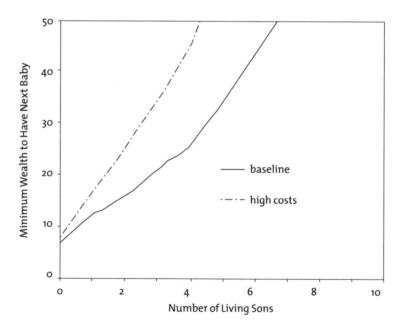

40 *The relationship in Mace's model between the number of living sons and the amount of wealth required for people to decide to have another baby. The solid line shows the relationship for the basic model and the dashed line that for when higher costs per son are assumed.*

Rogers' and Mace's studies make it clear that the possibility of inheriting resources represented a major new development in the strategies available for maximizing reproductive success and provided a basis for material motivations as much as directly reproductive ones to play an important role in achieving long-term fitness. In particular, when resources can be inherited, the value of each additional unit does not necessarily go down as more units are accumulated, it can remain constant or even increase, because it can be used to generate even more wealth in the future. Other processes relevant to owned resources will also enhance this effect. If a resource can be stored for long periods, extra units in excess of immediate consumption will continue to hold their utility. The development of market-type exchange systems, where excess units of one resource can be exchanged for another, will produce the same effect. In these circumstances the potential for inequality in resource control, and indeed in terms of reproductive success, may be virtually limitless.[79]

Clearly though, apart from the nature of the resources themselves and whether or not they lend themselves to being owned, ownership also implies a new kind of social institution. Modern hunter-gatherers are known to resist such ownership and to insist on sharing when group members try to establish private property rights. Nevertheless, the significant point here may be that some people try. One tactic is to leave the group and go somewhere that it is possible to establish such rights. Peyton Young's formulation of stochastically stable best pay-off game conventions that we saw earlier may be relevant here. Most people will play the current best strategy but there will always be some who do not do so some of the time and sometimes alternative strategies will take over, even as a result of purely chance events. The probability of this sort of thing happening is greater in smaller groups than larger ones. If it turns out to give better pay-offs, then it in turn may be stochastically stable and may even spread to other groups where similar conditions prevail. In the words of Sam Bowles,[80] a Rousseauian social equilibrium is replaced by a Bourgeois one.

THE ARCHAEOLOGY OF OWNERSHIP

As I have suggested already, private ownership is dependent on the nature of the resources. They must be divisible and excludable, as well as enduring. This provides us with a basis for predicting the possible existence of ownership in the prehistoric past by looking at the resources exploited.

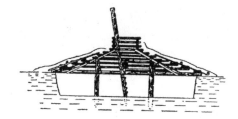

41 *Left, a schematic 19th-century illustration of an earth-covered pit house with a central ladder descending through the smoke hole. Below, the floor plan of Housepit 7 at the site of Keatley Creek. Stippling = hearths; outlines = storage pits; black dots = post-holes.*

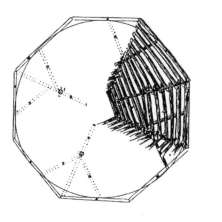

N

An interesting reconstruction and analysis of a situation where resources do seem to satisfy the criteria for ownership has recently been provided by Brian Hayden's[81] study of the site of Keatley Creek, near the Fraser River on the Canadian Northwest Plateau, dated to *c.* 2400–1100 years ago. The starting point for his study was an analysis of the spatial patterning in the archaeological residues found within the large circular pithouses at the site (see fig. 41), which contained a series of hearths forming a ring around the wall. Each hearth was associated with a range of debris consistent with domestic rather than specialized functions, suggesting that the hearths represented a series of domestic groups. However, there were differences in the patterns between the eastern and western halves of the house pits. All the large hearths were in the western half of the houses and the large storage pits were associated with them, even though both halves seem to have been occupied by domestic groups rather than used for different activities. Hayden concluded that the pattern existed because the large houses were occupied by high-status domestic groups in one half and dependent low-status groups in the other. Smaller and poorer houses were not differentiated in this way.

The question then arose as to why these large residential groups had come into existence, and why some groups seemed richer and more powerful than others. An analysis of the salmon remains which were the subsistence staple revealed that residents of smaller and poorer pit houses consumed only pink salmon, which are the easiest species to catch but the least desirable of those available. Residents of larger houses, on the other hand, were the exclusive consumers of larger sockeye and chinook salmon, varieties that keep further away from the river bank and can thus be caught only from rocks jutting out into the river or from specially constructed fishing platforms. In recent times such sites were largely owned by specific families, and Hayden infers from the bone distribution that only the residents of the larger houses had access to the best fishing locations. He concludes that the main reason for the formation of the large residential groups was control of the most productive fishing sites which, on the evidence of ethnographically recorded trade in dried salmon, would also have been the most lucrative. Elite members of the house groups would have had the rights to the production sites and poorer families without such rights would have attached themselves to them in exchange for the benefits they received from providing a source of labour. The resources and labour that elite members of such groups controlled are indicated by the presence of prestige burials, including such items as trade shells and whalebone from the coast.

Characterization analysis of the stone debitage from the large pit houses showed that each was associated with a distinctive combination of lithic materials.[82] In Hayden's view this not only confirmed that the large pit houses represented distinct economic entities, but also suggested that each group had exclusive access to the resources of a different mountain area containing the specific lithic resources used. In addition, the fact that the same distinctive types of materials were found in the earliest levels of the pit house middens as in the latest indicated a continuity of inherited rights to territory and resources associated with particular groups. In some cases this appears to have lasted for more than a thousand years. It also suggests that the large pit houses were in the possession of the same residential group for extremely long periods:

The persistence of the largest and most successful of these residential corporate groups as discrete, identifiable entities for over 1000 years is a remarkable testimony to the powerful effect that control over lucrative economic resources can

exert over the social structure of [what Hayden calls] transegalitarian communities, whether complex hunter-gatherers or agriculturalists.[83]

Once ownable and heritable resources come to play an important role in
affecting fitness, the nature of social competition for reproductive success
changes, because it will become increasingly focused around such resources.
Moreover, we can use our knowledge of the relationship between heritable
resources and reproductive success to make predictions about other aspects
of the societies involved. Thus, to take Hayden's example, given that the
number of good fishing sites must have been fixed, we would predict a
situation like that described by Voland, with one, or at most a very few,
individuals inheriting the resource, and less parental investment devoted to
those who will not inherit, because that is the most effective way of ensuring
long-term economic and therefore reproductive success. The long-term
existence of the same rich households would strongly suggest that this was
the case.

Of course, agriculture provides the most obvious basis for the creation
of reproductively advantageous heritable resources, but it is important to
realize that this will not always be the case. Just as some foraged resources
lend themselves to ownership and inheritance whereas others do not, the
same is true of agriculture. It is not a matter of foraging versus farming but
of resource permanence and potential for ownership in terms of
excludability and divisibility. Thus, the swidden clearings of shifting
horticulture are not a potentially heritable resource because they are
abandoned after a few years. Fixed fields, on the other hand, are much more
likely to be, as are stands of fruit trees and, of course, herds of animals, as
Mace's study showed.

The sorts of considerations just outlined may well be relevant to the
origins of Near Eastern agriculture, already discussed in earlier chapters in
relation to optimal foraging and intensification. One of the most striking
features of this process is the evidence for the rapid emergence of
significant social inequalities and of death rituals clearly reflecting a concern
with ancestry[84] (see fig. 42). Even before cereal cultivation began, stands of
wild cereals would have possessed the characteristics of excludability and
divisibility which lend themselves to ownership. At this early date such
resources might have been the object of between-group competition and
developing territoriality, rather than within-group differentiation. On the
other hand, the switch that took place rather later in the main animal

42 *A plastered skull found under the floor of a house at the Early Neolithic site of Jericho.*

resource, from hunted gazelle to herded sheep/goat, may well have been at least as important from the point of view of creating an owned and heritable resource where one did not exist before, as for any difference it made to subsistence and nutrition. Once such resources became the basis of subsistence, the nature of social competition for reproductive success would have changed, to emphasize material resources at least as much as directly reproductive ones. Furthermore, the difference between ownable and heritable foraging resources, such as Hayden's fishing locations, and those offered by certain forms of agriculture is that the former are essentially fixed, at least in the absence of technological innovations such as fish traps, whereas agricultural resources are readily open to intensification in many circumstances. But this should not be thought of as a one-way street of the kind we have seen in the unilinear schemes of social evolution described earlier. For example, a local population collapse might lead to a reversion from fixed fields to less intensive forms of shifting agriculture which no longer provided a basis for ownership.

CONCLUSION

At this point it is worth recapitulating the argument. Game theory provides a more satisfactory framework than long-standing 'social evolution' theory for conceptualizing social institutions. Robert Foley and Phyllis Lee's scheme suggests a possible initial framework for the kinds of social contract that existed in early human societies. The lack of material differentiation among many foragers and horticulturalists is not a result of Zen self-denial but of the nature of the resources around which competition for reproductive success is centred, which do not have the characteristics of enduring excludability and divisibility. By and large, resources lower down the optimal foraging hierarchy have these characteristics to a greater degree than those higher up, although technological innovations, such as methods for the mass capture of resources, may also push such resources up the ranking. Because such resources may be owned and inherited, and because inheritance affects long-term reproductive success, then material motivations become as important as directly reproductive ones and such resources become key foci of competition. In more abstract terms, the shape of the utility curve of additional units of resource changes. Far from them providing diminishing returns, additional units hold and even increase their value, as they are stored, exchanged and passed on for the benefit of future generations of inheritors; the rich can get richer. Such resource ownership would also have enhanced the possibilities of competition for prestige, following the handicap principle. These ideas generate many fruitful hypotheses for approaching the archaeological record and Hayden's analysis of Keatley Creek shows that such ideas can indeed be addressed successfully on the basis of data accessible to archaeologists.

There are many possibilities of different social institutions or game conventions and which ones are reached will depend on a group's history. On the other hand, if new conventions offer better pay-offs in new conditions they are likely to spread eventually. Nevertheless, the inertia in the existing conventions may be considerable and change may take a long time to occur, especially in large populations. How these processes work out in the context of between-group relations, and how we may investigate them archaeologically, will be the subject of the next chapter.

COMPETITION, COOPERATION AND WARFARE: THE ROLE OF GROUP SELECTION

NOW THAT WE HAVE SEEN the importance of starting at the individual level if we are to understand how social cooperation can arise and be maintained, the question is whether the group has any role to play in selection. This question remains hotly disputed within evolutionary biology in general, and in evolutionary studies of human society in particular. The view among many is that while group selection is possible in principle, the conditions under which it would work in practice are rare. Furthermore, the suggestion that group selection is required for cooperative solutions to coordination problems to be reached has been clearly demonstrated not to be the case by the work of Samuel Bowles and Herbert Gintis[1] and other game theorists described above. In this chapter we will look at the issues surrounding group selection and its relation to inter-group competition, before going on to present some case studies which demonstrate that archaeological data can be used to investigate patterns of group cooperation and competition over the long term. In fact, the case studies bring together a number of the different threads picked up in previous chapters.

GROUP SELECTION

Joseph Soltis and his colleagues[2] have shown that in certain circumstances cultural group selection, that is to say, selection on cultural traits characteristic of groups, where the groups are distinct from one another culturally rather than genetically, can be a significant process. There are three requirements for such cultural group selection to work. There have to be cultural differences between groups; those differences have to affect the persistence or proliferation of groups; and the differences have to be transmitted over time.[3] Nevertheless, even when these conditions exist, cultural group selection will still only occur if it is powerful enough to override other processes, especially selection acting at the individual level.

As we have seen already, common-type advantage – the advantage of following generally expected patterns of behaviour – as well as conformism, can both lead to differences being maintained between groups. If patterns of group uniform behaviour which are different between groups affect the rates at which groups grow and split to form new groups, and conversely the rates at which groups become extinct, then group selection can predominate over individual selection. Clearly, a favourable trait, such as high levels of cooperation, must first become common within a single cultural group, but the work of Brian Skyrms, and Bowles and Gintis, described in the previous chapter, provides mechanisms by which this can occur, to the benefit of individuals within the group. It follows from what has just been said that such group selection can only occur when new groups form by the splitting of existing advantaged groups. If they are formed by the fusion of individuals from a variety of different groups, with a variety of behaviours, then there will be no basis for group selection to operate. Equally, group extinction does not necessarily involve the death of all the group's members but simply their dispersal to other groups, so that the group's specific features as a group disappear.

These seem not implausible conditions to have arisen quite frequently in human history, not least in the light of the regional population fluctuations which are likely to have occurred, as we saw in Chapter 5. Joseph Soltis et al.[4] suggest that evidence for group formation and extinction rates from New Guinea provides support for the importance of group selection as an evolutionary mechanism in this case. They go on to estimate the maximum rate of cultural change that can be produced by selection between cultural groups, on the basis of known group extinction rates from New Guinea. This maximum rate will be reached if we assume that a single inherited between-group cultural difference is responsible for extinctions, and likewise for group proliferation. In these circumstances group selection could lead to the replacement of one cultural variant by another in the population of all the groups as a whole in a minimum of 500 years; real rates will obviously be lower. Soltis et al. conclude that cases of cultural change which occur more quickly than this cannot be accounted for by group selection.

Barbara Smuts[5] sees between-group selection as fundamentally about the benefits of cooperation. However, as we have seen, cooperation can emerge without the operation of group selection. Soltis et al.'s results suggest that the key process is inter-group competition. Indeed, it is worth making the point that while cooperation is generally seen as preferable to selfish individualism, it may simply be that cooperation at one level is a requirement for successful competition, including warfare, at the next level up. However, defence raises a specific issue in this respect. It represents a public good which is essentially indivisible and non-excludable, and a public good of a high-stakes kind. If defence is maintained then everyone in the group benefits, while the penalties for failure are likely to be extremely high. On the other hand, the risks to the individual of being involved in defence are also high, so there are potentially considerable benefits to a free rider who can enjoy the benefits of the defensive efforts of others without incurring the risks.[6] If a group is small, it may be very difficult to be a free rider since everyone may be needed for defence. John Patton[7] has explored this question for the community of Conambo, a group of 185 people without centralized leadership living in 23 households in the Ecuadorian Amazon. Levels of violence in this group have been high and Patton found that 15 out of the 30 immediate male ancestors whose cause of death he could establish had died from shotgun blasts. Although levels of violence have recently decreased, security remains the overwhelming concern among these people. Patton was able to show that willingness to fight in conflicts between different coalitions was based on a principle of reciprocal altruism in which willingness to take risks was repaid with social status and better warriors had higher social status than others. However, this is a very small group. Once groups get beyond a certain size, the potential for free-riding may be considerable. Centralized or corporate institutions may be more effective in preventing this.

In this connection, Soltis et al.[8] present the example of the Faiwolmin group in New Guinea, as described by Fredrik Barth.[9] Within the Faiwolmin area, the elaboration of ritual organization and specialization varies from east to west, with the western communities having more male age sets and more cult houses. Social organization varies spatially in a similar way, in that western Faiwolmin communities form nucleated villages centred on the cult houses while in the east populations are dispersed. Fredrik Barth's argument[10] is that the centralized communities have a military advantage and as a result have been able to expand towards the east, where the system of organization cannot organize as many people for defence. The centralization and more elaborate rituals were innovations introduced to the western Faiwolmin by groups to the west of them.

In fact, there has been a major re-assessment in recent years of the extent of violence in traditional societies, both states and non-states, which would tend to support the argument for the importance of inter-group competition and therefore potentially of group selection, as outlined by Soltis and his colleagues.[11] It is quite clear that the incidence of violence in particular areas is not constant over time and the question then arises as to the factors leading to violence as opposed to more cooperative forms of social relations.

Nevertheless, this still presupposes the existence of individual-level propensities to act with violence in certain circumstances and Richard Wrangham[12] has recently proposed what he calls the 'chimpanzee violence hypothesis', suggesting that selection has favoured a tendency among adult male chimpanzees to assess the costs and benefits of violence and to attack rivals when the probable net benefits are sufficiently high. He suggests that the same pattern is found in human males, pointing out the parallels between chimpanzee raiding of neighbouring groups and what is also found among small-scale human societies in contexts of inter-group hostility. The situation arises where a raiding group attacks isolated and vulnerable members of a neighbouring group. In these contexts, the likely cost of violence to any member of the raiding group is small, while the benefits arise from the increased probability of winning inter-community dominance contests and, as a result, gaining improved access to food and females, as well as increasing their own safety. All these lead to increased fitness. Both in humans and non-human primates, populations with male-bonded groups have a greater tendency for males to be aggressors. Wrangham[13] concludes that selection has favoured emotional dispositions in males that can lead to the early emergence of aggressive behaviour in certain circumstances.

Azar Gat[14] has recently come to what are in many respects similar conclusions, pointing out that the principle behind deadly violence is fighting only with highly favourable odds. Thus, among tribal societies, he suggests, confrontational events are about display, while serious attempts at killing are made when the victims of the attack can be caught relatively defenceless and incapable of harming their attackers. As soon as success has been achieved, such raiders are most likely to withdraw, because once the enemy is aware of what is going on, the odds in favour of the attackers, and therefore the benefit/cost ratio, are likely to decrease.

In the light of the fact that those who are raiders today are likely to be raided themselves tomorrow, Gat raises the interesting question of why they would want to raid in the first place. His proposed answer is the great advantage that goes to the side making the first strike. If you think that a neighbouring group may raid you, the only thing to be done is raid them first. Of course, we do not know the pay-offs which are obtained by successful raiding, although Napoleon Chagnon[15] showed that among the

Yanomami warriors were reproductively more successful than men who hadn't killed. Even less do we know how the pay-offs from raiding compare with those that might be achieved by a cooperative approach to inter-group relations. Nevertheless, Gat's suggestion that such groups are in a Prisoner's Dilemma in which the equilibrium is the deleterious one of both sides raiding each other seems plausible. Since neighbouring groups are not always raiding one another, his proposal also raises the question of what determines in a particular case whether a cooperative or a non-cooperative inter-group equilibrium will be achieved, and what makes the interaction pattern go from one state to another.

Archaeology is in a good position to answer these sorts of questions because of the long time perspective it provides on the history of particular regions and because archaeological indicators of the extent of violence are quite well established in such forms as traces of violence on skeletons, the presence of defences at sites and the incidence of weapons.[16]

Douglas Kennett and James Kennett[17] examined the social consequences of climatic instability in the Northern Channel Islands of southern California between AD 450 and 1300. They showed that the already uneven distribution of a variety of key resources was affected by climate variability at both shorter-term and longer-term time-scales, making the risk of shortfall in food supplies even greater than it was already. At least by AD 650 a settlement pattern was established of relatively large villages at roughly equal intervals along the coast, situated in positions with good views. Osteological evidence exists of violence among these communities. Cranial injuries were especially common between 550 BC and AD 650, with patterns of healing suggesting the existence of sublethal violence not unlike that seen in Yanomami club fighting. Patterns through time in the incidence of lethal violence could also be traced, by the presence of projectile points embedded in skeletons and other projectile wounds. The frequency was highest between AD 650 and 1300 and decreased significantly after AD 1300. The bow seems to have been introduced to the area around AD 500 and may have been connected with the increased violence, but up to AD 800 many wounds continued to be made by spear points. Growing violence occurred at the same time as evidence of the increasing importance of fishing, which was connected to a decline in terrestrial resources. The authors suggest that the increased violence might have been connected with competition for productive inshore fishing grounds. However, climate stress associated with persistent drought goes back before this time, leading to greater sedentism near perennial water sources and competition for these locations. After AD 1300 violence declined as environmental conditions became more stable and cooperative strategies based on trade came to dominate inter-group relations.

FROM COOPERATION TO CONFLICT AMONG EUROPE'S FIRST FARMERS

A second example of changing patterns of cooperation and competition that we can trace archaeologically concerns the history of the first farming communities in Central Europe which, after nearly 500 years, seems to have ended in conflict and collapse. We have already looked at these communities in a different connection in Chapter 5.

The introduction of agriculture into Central Europe seems to have resulted from colonization by the incoming farmers of the Linear Pottery Culture.[18] It occurred very quickly. The earliest settlements in Austria and Hungary date to *c.* 5700/5600 BC while the earliest ones in Belgium and the Netherlands, 1500 km to the west, are already there by 5400 BC. A great deal is known about these early farmers, because their settlements of long houses are archaeologically very obvious and have been the subject of extensive work. As we saw in Chapter 5, the large-scale excavation of an area along the valley of a small stream, the Merzbach, in advance of strip mining for brown coal, revealed a whole micro-region of early farming settlement, and detailed analysis of the finds and the stratigraphy has made it possible to characterize its history, which lasted from *c.* 5300 to 4800 BC.

Initially there was a single colonizing settlement. This initial settlement continued to be occupied for the full 500 years and continued to be the largest. However, other settlements were subsequently founded in the vicinity, the majority of which had a more intermittent occupation. A summary version of the settlement history is shown in fig. 44 (pages 248–249). It seems likely that most if not all of the settlements were descended, directly or indirectly, from the founding settlement.

Again as we saw in Chapter 5, it is possible to trace the number of houses in use at a particular time to obtain an idea of the population history of the area (see fig. 18). The number of houses gradually increased from the initial 3 to 16 after an estimated 200 years of occupation; it then fell back slightly to 10 before increasing again to 16 after another *c.* 120 years. Over the following 50–100 years the number of houses rapidly decreased until the area was abandoned altogether; in the final phases before abandonment ditched enclo-

sures existed. The fact that the area was actually abandoned is further confirmed by the results of pollen analysis, which show that agricultural
indicators disappeared and the area was reafforested. In the latest phases
there were two ditched enclosures in the area, the latest of which outlasted
the latest evidence for houses.[19]

Although the history of settlement is exceptionally well documented in
this specific micro-region, the pattern it reveals, including the existence of a
main founding settlement and a final phase with ditched enclosures, seems to
characterize many other settlement areas of these first farmers. There has
been considerable discussion of the function of the late enclosures, but the
idea that they were often defensive has been supported in recent years by the
finding of two massacre sites dating to this late phase (fig. 43). At the site of
Talheim in Germany a large pit contained the
remains of 34 individuals, from small children
to old people.[20] At least 18 people had unhealed
wounds to the skull; in most cases the shape
of these wounds matched the shape of the
stone axes used for everyday wood-working.

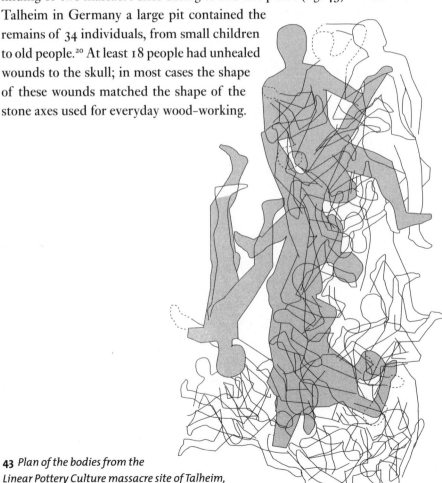

43 *Plan of the bodies from the
Linear Pottery Culture massacre site of Talheim,
Germany; men shaded, others are women and children.*

More recently, at the site of Asparn-Schletz in Austria, a similar find was made.[21] The site is an oval enclosure made up of two concentric ditches up to 4 m wide and 2 m deep. At the bottom of the outer ditch were human skeletons and parts of skeletons, making up at least 67 individuals. All the skull remains showed traces of violence and again in many cases the holes in the skulls showed the shape of various forms of axes. Numerous indirect fractures on the base of the skull suggested that wounded individuals on the ground were struck on the side of the head. Many of the skeletons were incomplete and traces of carnivore tooth marks on some of the bones suggest that the bodies lay exposed for some time. The site seems to have been abandoned after the massacre.

In summary, in the late phase of early farming occupation we have evidence of ditched enclosures and population decline as well as massacres. It has been suggested that conflict arose widely in Central Europe in this period, as a result of population pressure and/or soil exhaustion arising from 400–500 years of constant use of the same areas. It has also been suggested that climate change led to a drier period at this time, which would have led to lowering of groundwater levels; many later settlements show evidence of the digging of wells.

A further source of information on aspects of inter-group cooperation and conflict during this period comes from the study of exchange patterns.[22] Almost throughout the period, supplies of high-quality flint for tools were obtained from special sources and exchanged very widely. However, in the latest phase exchanged flint declined in frequency at settlement sites and increasing proportions of the lithic assemblages were made up of material from local sources of poorer quality. The same is true of the hard stone resources used to make stone axes. It appears then that at the end of the early farming period, for whatever reason, the exchange routes which gave access to key sources of raw material ceased to operate, after a period of perhaps 400 years, or 16 generations, when relations between settlements seem to have been essentially peaceful and cooperative.

One way of looking more closely at what was going on during this period is to examine the changes in the pottery in the Merzbach area mentioned above, where we have very detailed information, especially on the chronology.[23] Richard Wilkinson and I[24] carried out an analysis to test whether the diversity of the changing decorative patterns on the pottery of the two continuously occupied sites in the area could be modelled as a neutral drift process in which change is essentially random[25] or whether more directional forces were involved, which might provide information about patterns of selection and social relations.

We concluded that the transmission process in the case of the early farming pottery decoration did not correspond to the neutral model; or rather, while drift was occurring, other forces were also at work; specifically, in the later phases there was a bias in favour of using novel decorative motifs.

Christiane Frirdich, the author of the study whose data were the subject of our analysis, argued that the long-lasting uniformity in the use of a small number of traditional decorative band types which characterized the early phases of occupation was maintained by the imposition of strict social norms on band type choice, and that the rapid change that followed represented a relaxation of such norms.[26] Our results do not provide evidence for the imposition of strict norms in the early phases, but do suggest that the change which occurred during the later phases was an active preference for novelty, rather than a relaxation of previous constraints (see fig. 45, page 250).

Interestingly, the move towards a pro-novelty bias in the transmission of decoration types, which occurred in phase VIII, did not take place straight-forwardly in step with the developing colonization of the Merzbach micro-region. New sites were already being established in phase V and this process continued through phases VI and VII; between phases IV and VII the number of contemporary houses also went up, from 7 to 16, a number subsequently equalled but never exceeded. Phases VIII–IX, when the switch to pro-novelty or anti-conformist bias took place, were actually a time when the number of houses and occupied sites decreased, to 4 sites and 10 houses in phase VIII, with 4 sites and 12 houses in phase IX, although in the follow-ing phases it gradually increased to a maximum of 7 sites and 16 houses again in phase XII. The pro-novelty bias may reflect a concern to establish distinct local identities once the area had more or less filled up. It may be that the rise in the number of houses in the valley to its maximum of 16 led to some sort of local crisis, reflected in the drop to 10 houses in the following phase. It was precisely at this time that potters started actively selecting for novelty in their pottery decoration. The next time, a few generations later, that the number of houses in the area reached 16 it was followed by decline and final abandon-ment, after a phase in which the evidence for the building of enclosures suggests the possibility of violence.

The close initial links of common descent between communities, gener-ated by the speedy colonization process and the continuing close proximity of the settlements within particular micro-regions, would have provided

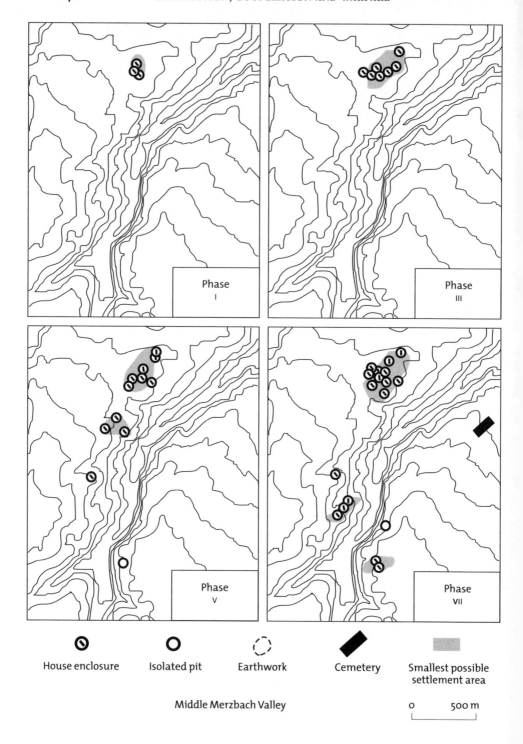

House enclosure   Isolated pit   Earthwork   Cemetery   Smallest possible settlement area

Middle Merzbach Valley

0   500 m

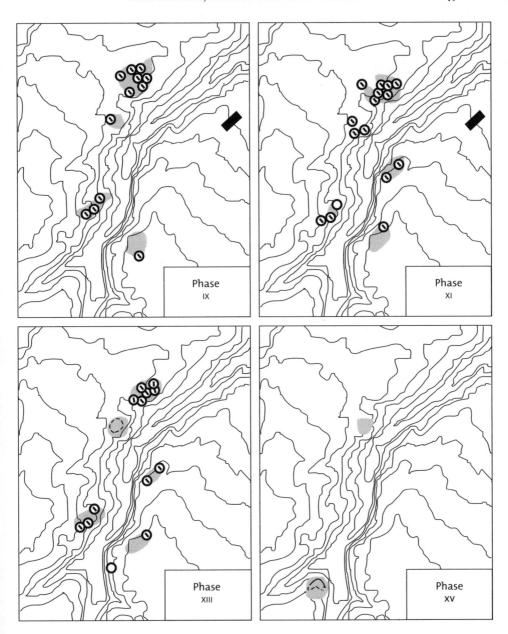

44 *Settlement plans for some of the successive phases of occupation by early farmers of the Linear Pottery Culture in the Merzbach valley. Shows the rise, stabilization and collapse of the populations over a 500-year period, including the appearance of earthworks at the end of the occupation.*

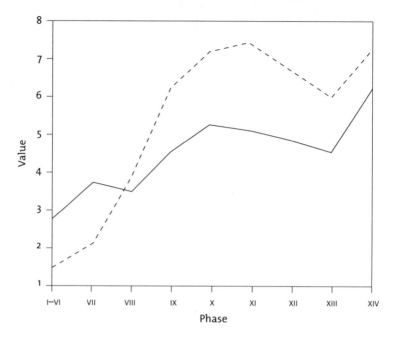

45 *Changing ceramic diversity patterns in the early farming Linear Pottery Culture settlements of the Merzbach valley, showing the marked divergence in the later phases between the real pattern (the dashed line) and the pattern predicted by a drift model (the solid line), with a bias in favour of novelty in the real pattern.*

ideal conditions for the emergence and maintenance of pro-social norms of interaction between people living in different settlements. Moreover, for the first couple of hundred years of this colonization process there need have been no conflict of interest between the individual and group levels: sufficient resources were available for everybody, hence the five-fold growth in population. The time when the growth in house numbers stopped and the number actually declined must be the point where density-dependent checks on population began to be effective and this is where we might expect conflicts to have started arising between group and individual interests, producing Prisoner's Dilemma situations. No effect is seen at the larger regional scale, since the free movement of lithic materials seems to have continued. Nevertheless, at a local level something seems to have happened. As we have seen, individual settlements began to show a pro-novelty bias in their pottery production. A cladistic analysis (see above, Chapter 4) of the pottery decoration from all the settlements in the Merzbach valley carried out by Mark Collard and myself[27] showed that in the later phases individual settlements mostly had their closest links with a single ancestral settlement phase, rather than with several, suggesting that interaction between nearby settlements was not being reflected in ceramic style choices. In these new circumstances though the number of houses in the Merzbach region gradually climbed once again to the previous maximum.

The subsequent decline in population and eventual regional abandonment could perhaps be seen as a 'tragedy of the commons' situation, in which individual households continued to try and secure their own subsistence interests at the expense of others, with agricultural failure for everybody as a consequence. Another possibility is that conflict was at a higher level. Precisely what level is unclear. As we have already seen, the decline in the use of high-quality lithic resources obtained from distant sources and their replacement by local resources of lower quality can be taken as an indication of the breakdown of exchange relations, but this could have resulted from conflict at any scale. The number of enclosures in a given micro-region may be a better guide. In the case of the Merzbach valley, the evidence is such that it is hard to say whether there were two enclosures, or only one, during the final phases. In other words, if they are indeed a reflection of conflict, as the massacre evidence elsewhere suggests, it is unclear whether there was conflict within the Merzbach micro-region or between the Merzbach community as a whole and others. If, for the moment, we assume the latter, then we can raise the question of whether cultural group selection could have been operating, with the different micro-regions as the groups competing with one another. The fact that the Merzbach valley was abandoned rather than re-occupied by a competing group from elsewhere with different cultural traditions suggests that this is unlikely. Some sort of internal conflict seems more probable. If the two enclosures were indeed contemporary they might represent alliances between different groups of households. At all events, the final outcome was the abandonment of the area, although in some areas of Central Europe successor communities with new cultural traditions did emerge and spread, probably by the sort of population mechanisms discussed in Chapter 5.

In summary, a group of communities descended from a common ancestor reached a local ceiling and members started changing their social strategies as reflected in pottery decoration, adopting novel decorative forms on a greater-than-expected scale in a process that was the opposite of conformist transmission. At the same time they tended not to be susceptible to the practices of their neighbours. This may reflect a shift away from an initial closeness based on their relation to the founding settlement. However, it was only much later that relations seem to have become hostile, apparently part of a much larger breakdown in social relations over a broad area reflected in the collapse of exchange relations and the widespread occurrence of enclosures, as a new and deleterious inter-group equilibrium became established, eventually leading to population decline and abandonment.

COSTLY SIGNALLING AND INTER-GROUP COMPETITION

Competition between groups need not always involve violence. Azar Gat,[28] like others before him, suggests that confrontational warfare between different groups was essentially a matter of bluff since normally very few people were killed. Rather, we may see such confrontations as a kind of honest signalling of the strength of the groups concerned to their enemies, as a basis for deterring attack. As we have seen, this is the Dove strategy in conflicts, making a threatening display to which an opponent may or may not respond with real violence. Fraser Neiman[29] has proposed that the calendrical monuments erected by the Classic Maya states of Mesoamerica may be seen in this light, since the wasteful investment of resources in monument building gives an indication of the competitive ability of the political entities which produced them. The starting point of Neiman's argument is that the monuments in the different centres and the violent scenes they depict were precisely what would be expected from political competitors advertising their quality to intimidate rivals. However, the costly signalling hypothesis gives more specific predictions than this. The amount of wasteful advertising in any competitive system should depend on the variation in the competitive ability of the entities involved, including the ability of the worst competitor, and the pay-offs for advertising, which depend on the audience that the conspicuous signal reaches: the larger the audience, the greater the pay-off. In this case, in other words, the monumental architecture should vary in scale and elaboration in relation to the range of political quality among the Maya states and the pay-offs to advertising. Neiman finds this prediction confirmed. This is the reason why Maya scholars have been right to see the end of monument building as an indication of Maya 'collapse'. It represented a decrease in the amount of wasteful advertising associated with a shrinkage in the range of competitive ability of Maya polities, as well as one in audience size, related to a decrease in population density and in the spatial range over which political competition occurred.

HIERARCHY AND GROUP SELECTION

In the last chapter, the neo-evolutionary anthropological schemes of authors such as Elman Service, with his sequence from bands to tribes to chiefdoms and states, were discussed and criticized, not least because of their implicit naïve group selectionism. We can now begin to see such schemes in a rather better light in terms of multi-level selection. For example, if a particular community or group of communities makes the innovation of having a chief and that innovation results in the group concerned competing more success-fully with other groups, killing or absorbing their members and fissioning into other similar successful communities, then we have an example of cul-tural group selection at work, since the traits characteristic of chiefdoms are the key to success and will proliferate as a result. There will not necessarily be a conflict here between the group and the individual level – individuals may gain greater reproductive success as members of the group than they would do otherwise, despite having to pay costs such as tribute. Nevertheless, they stand or fall together in success terms. If the group is defeated and ceases to exist, the conditions of defeat are likely to be such that individual reproductive success is affected for the worse, at least for males. The replica-tive success of their cultural traits is also likely to be adversely affected. To use the evolutionary philosopher David Hull's terms, the level of the key evolutionary 'interactors' has shifted: it is no longer individuals or households, but chiefdoms, while the 'replicators' whose propagation is affected will be genetic and cultural traits at the individual level, as well as group-level traits.

This sort of process may be what we see in the Central European Bronze Age, already discussed in Chapter 7. By the later Early Bronze Age around 1600 BC local site and social hierarchies had developed that were competing with one another.[30] Although prestige competition between males no doubt continued within the local polities, it was now the between-group competi-tion that defined the conditions of social and economic life. Those groups that had managed to attain greater power within a particular local area needed to maintain it through the accumulation of wealth and followers. As John Robb has proposed,[31] strategies for different men may have gradually diverged, in that well-situated groups could have used their success in exchange and/or subsistence production to attract followers, which would have led to further success. As such groups became more powerful, inde-pendent, peripherally situated men would have found increasing difficulties in gaining wealth and prestige and, as a result, in reproducing themselves, physically and socially:

They may have accepted second-class status in a powerful unit as a route to personal power more effective than life without powerful friends and relations. The result would have been the simultaneous enlargement of [some] units and differentiation within [and between] them.[32]

In addition, the emergent competition between these higher-level units would have made followers more vulnerable to the depredations of their leaders' competitors and thus yet more dependent on their own leaders. In this model, the growth of a differentiated warrior ideology by the end of the Early Bronze Age, seen, for example, in the wide distribution of similar prestige weapons (see fig. 46), would have been the outcome of a group selection process, since groups which did not adopt such innovations would have been broken up and absorbed. An intra-group corollary of this would have been the sort of reproductive stratification associated with the rise of male inequality discussed in Chapter 7.

However, we need to qualify slightly the account of group selection given so far. Once you have a situation where a higher level of entity is in existence, then the individuals or kin groups at their head can make decisions for the entity as a whole. In other words, the decision-making forces affecting what is culturally transmitted between individuals that were described in Chapter 3 still apply, but now at a higher level, with implications for the entity as a whole. In particular, the processes of direct and indirect bias can operate: comparing the outcome of your existing way of doing something with the way others do it and adopting their method if it seems to produce better results, or imitating those individuals that you hold in especially high regard. Furthermore, just as direct bias at the individual level can be seen as a kind of attempt (which may or may not be successful) to anticipate natural selection, so individuals such as chiefs are potentially in a position to make decisions that try, in effect, to anticipate the consequences of cultural group selection, and have implications for all the members of a given political entity. This seems to be at least one basis for explaining the fact that new forms of group-level trait sometimes spread far more quickly than they would if the process at work was a strict cultural-group selection model of the kind described by Joseph Soltis and his colleagues. As we saw above, given what we know about group extinction and proliferation rates, time spans of the order of 500–1,000 years are required for this sort of process to work.

In contrast, major social evolutionary changes occurred in Mesoamerica over only 300 years, between 1150 and 850 BC, that Kent Flannery and Joyce

Marcus ascribe to intense competition between large numbers of local chief-doms which were '(1) sufficiently isolated to find the best adaptations for their respective regions, yet (2) sufficiently in contact to borrow relevant innovations from other regions as they arose.'[33] This situation would have made it possible for groups over a large area to arrive at the best available adaptive peak in the shortest possible time (see fig. 47). The argument was first developed by the geneticist Sewall Wright,[34] but Flannery and Marcus argue that it is equally relevant to cultural evolution.[35]

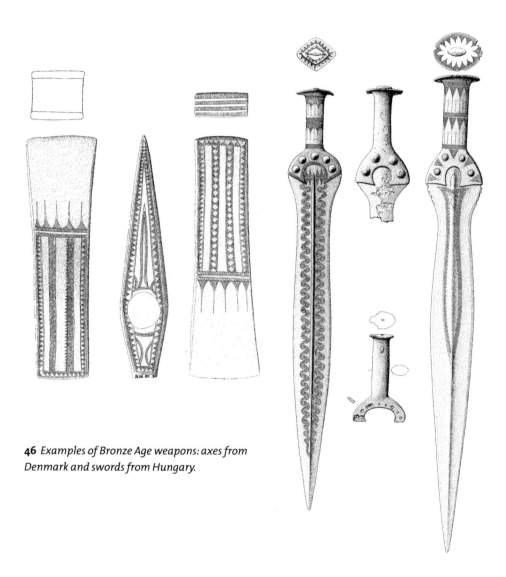

46 *Examples of Bronze Age weapons: axes from Denmark and swords from Hungary.*

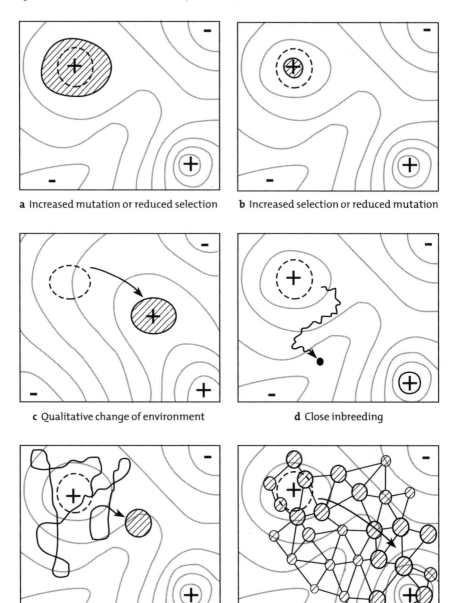

a Increased mutation or reduced selection

b Increased selection or reduced mutation

c Qualitative change of environment

d Close inbreeding

e Slight inbreeding

f Division into local races

47 *Six possible models for evolutionary change, redrawn from Sewall Wright (1939, fig. 9). Contour lines indicate a rugged adaptive landscape, with genetic combinations of high selective value shown as peaks. Model* **f** *has the greatest potential for rapid evolutionary advance.*

INTER-GROUP COOPERATION AND INDIVIDUAL LEVEL BENEFITS

Competition may not be the only reason for different groups to cooperate and, even if it is a cause of cooperation developing in the first place, this doesn't mean that once in place it does not offer collateral benefits. A good ethnographic example of a situation where such cooperation seems to hold is the traditional land and water management and ritual system on the rice terraces of Bali, which has recently attracted a lot of attention from theorists interested in the self-organization of complex systems.[36] Local groups of farmers (subaks) manage their own land and irrigation system, as well as the crop-planting schedule. However, their actions have effects on neighbouring subaks, both in terms of water management and the creation of conditions which make the spread of crop pests more or less likely. It turns out that over quite large areas rice planting is synchronized, even though there is no system of centralized control and farmers are only interested in doing what is best for them locally. Furthermore, simulations suggest that the patterns of synchronization produce near optimal results in terms of best use of the water and the minimization of pest damage.

On the basis of real data from the rice fields, Steven Lansing and his colleagues modelled each subak as an entity making decisions about whether or not to synchronize its planting with its neighbours and looked at the effects on water, pests and rice growth. After the first year of the simulation individual subaks would compare their harvest with that of their neighbours and, if any had done better than them, they would imitate their cropping pattern the following year. Over time, areas with identical cropping patterns emerged and the yields of individual subaks rose. The pattern of cooperation in the model that most closely resembled the real water temple network gave the best average yields, as well as low variance in yields from year to year. This lack of variance in yield also corresponds to reality. If changes in rainfall or pest virulence are modelled, changes in cropping pattern occur and a new beneficial equilibrium is quickly reached. The water temple ritual system facilitates cooperation but does not in itself account for the overall patterns of cooperation that emerge. Here then we do not have a 'tragedy of the commons' but a situation in which cooperation produces great benefits for all involved.

It is also possible to explore such issues with archaeological case studies.

Cooperation and self-interest in the North American Southwest

One of the most notable features of the archaeology of the American South-west is the so-called 'Chaco phenomenon', the florescence around Chaco Canyon of elaborate architecture, large-scale ritual, structures such as 'roads' and indications of long-distance exchange contacts, in the period between AD 900 and 1300.[37] Some have seen these features as evidence of developed social stratification and the existence of elites, while others have argued that they could have been produced by egalitarian societies of the kind known from the recent ethnography of the region. A number of years ago Greg Johnson[38] reviewed the evidence and argued for a distinctly limited degree of inequality and an organizational pattern which had a number of levels but was essentially non-hierarchical in nature. He concluded that the Chacoan phenomenon represented a fragile cooperative solution to problems posed by increasing population size and the associated increase in mutual interactions, a solution based on ritual institutions.

Although Chaco is exceptional in scale, such phenomena of aggregation together with evidence of communal ritual are a recurring feature of the American Southwest between the 9th and 14th centuries AD, and an explana-tory model to account for them has been developed by Timothy Kohler and Carla van West[39] from a basis in the self-interest of individual households. They begin by showing that pooling of food is most likely to develop in cir-cumstances of *high* mean productivity, high variability in productivity from year to year, and great spatial differences in productivity. This contrasts with the standard models of risk and its implications which have been used in archaeology, since these presuppose great variability in space/time but *low* mean productivity – in other words, where there appears to be most need of sharing. However, an analysis of likely consumption functions suggests that sharing is not likely to be in the best interest of individual households when little food is available, since greater utility is obtained, on average, by not sharing. In such circumstances, on the self-interest assumption, sharing will be likely to break down if it is present, and if it is not present it is unlikely to develop.

Kohler and van West obtained palaeo-productivity estimates for a 1500 sq. km region in southwest Colorado, covering the period AD 900–1300, taking into account soil depth and estimates of soil moisture derived from palaeoenvironmental studies. These were used to define periods of high and low average production. Measures of spatial and temporal variability were also calculated. Aspects of the archaeological record believed to be relevant as evidence for food sharing included community growth and aggregation, the existence of Great Kiva ritual structures, and the presence of reservoirs. The breakdown of sharing was taken to be evidenced by the dissolution of aggregated sites. In general terms, the patterning in the archaeological record follows that predicted by the model, in that aggregation episodes are associated with periods when expected cooperation is high; this is the case, for example, with the appearance of the Chacoan phenomenon. The break-up of this system and the final abandonment of the region both occur in periods when defection from sharing arrangements was the advantageous thing to do from the point of view of household self-interest. Evidence for cannibalism also occurs in periods when abandonment of sharing is predicted. However, the pattern is complicated by indications of high levels of cooperative behaviour at times when population is high. This is the opposite of what is anticipated by the model, since higher population would be expected to lead to lower levels of food per household. It appears that, while defection into an open landscape at times of low production was easy when population was low, this changed as population increased, because alternative resources to defect to were no longer available. When the region was abandoned towards AD 1300, climatic factors were cutting productivity – and thus the utility of sharing – at the same time that the increasingly full landscape was removing the option of defecting.

From this study it emerges that a model of behaviour based on the self-interest of the participants generates patterns in the settlement of the region which correspond closely to those actually found, in terms of the aggregation and dispersal of settlement. There is no trade-off here between individual and group interest: cooperation occurs when it is in individual interests and disappears when it is not. This appears to be in marked contrast to ethnographically known patterns of social organization in the Southwest, which place great emphasis on the group at the expense of the individual. However, there is also a contrast in settlement processes: while the period from AD 900 to 1300 was characterized by the cyclical aggregation and dispersal patterns we have seen, since that time aggregated village settlement in areas actually occupied has been uninterrupted. The reason for this, Kohler and van West suggest, is the emergence of new sharing rules, emphasizing village-level activities, combined with new sanctions against defection. In the societies which then emerged, egalitarianism and an emphasis on group values represented an active commitment to cooperation at the expense of maximizing individual pay-offs.

Hierarchy and risk reduction in prehistoric Hawai'i

The previous two case studies both represented examples where patterns of cooperation were achieved from the household level, without any overarching form of regional organization. The earlier discussion of hierarchy emphasized the importance of competition in the emergence of higher-level group entities and the shift to higher levels of selection. However, even if we accept that this is how they often originate, it should not be assumed that they do not offer any benefits at the individual or household level, once they are in existence.

Thegn Ladefoged and Michael Graves[40] demonstrated a shift in the scale of selection in the context of subsistence strategies in Polynesian Hawai'i. They analysed aspects of the size and distribution of fields, arguing that these evolved through time as a response to optimality and risk factors. During the first period of settlement, coastally based communities used dispersed fields focused on areas of higher rainfall and supplemented agriculture with marine resources. In the following phase less-dispersed field systems were constructed in upland areas which had higher and less variable rainfall. This entailed increased energy costs, because of the increasing distance of the agricultural areas from the coast. Costs were further increased by the construction of smaller fields than in the previous period. The field walls served as erosion inhibitors and as windbreaks, slowing evapo-transpiration from the sweet potato crops.[41] In the final period additional fields were created still further away from the coast and located in areas of lower rainfall. Ladefoged and Graves propose that this new development represented a shift in the scale of selection operating on agricultural production, because it arose as a result of the activities of the chiefly elite that had developed by this time. In other words, individual food-producing households and their decisions were no longer affected solely by the direct costs and benefits of their own agricultural investment but depended also on the political activities of chiefs. The chiefs actively instigated agricultural production in more marginal areas of the district, probably using some of the produce for ceremonies. Nevertheless, the larger organizational scale of the chiefly economies made this a viable possibility because they had the potential to make up for poor harvests in these areas in drier years by the use of distributional mechanisms. These buffered both chiefs and commoners from the occasional crop failures resulting from dry-farming in areas with marginal rainfall, but of course at the expense of yet further increased costs to the producers since some of the crop was reserved for chiefly use.

As Ladefoged and Graves are aware, their analysis takes us right back to the neo-evolutionary arguments of the 1960s and 1970s about the adaptive and exploitative aspects of chiefdoms, and in many respects supports Service's arguments about the importance of chiefly redistribution, although their theoretical foundations are different from his group functionalism. In fact, they do not provide the basis for evaluating whether cultural group selection was taking place, in the sense that groups organized in this way were expanding and absorbing those that were not, or that other groups were adopting the new organizational pattern to be able to compete, nor are they claiming that this was the reason these chiefdoms arose in the first place. To investigate these issues would need a further study. However, it seems reasonable to suppose that the reproductive success of chiefdom members and the replicative success of their cultural traits would be affected by the fortunes of the chiefdom as an entity, just as we suggested for the European Bronze Age example.

Peter Richerson and Robert Boyd[42] have suggested that complex societies such as chiefdoms, and especially states, are sufficiently integrated to be regarded as crude 'superorganisms', just like the colonies of the social insects. In other words, they have some of the properties that individual organisms have in terms of functional integration, a revival of the 19th-century organismic analogy for society. On the other hand, when the overhead costs of such systems become greater than the benefits they provide to the participants, they become vulnerable to collapse and fragmentation, as Joseph Tainter[43] proposed some years ago for the collapse of perhaps the most famous of all pre-modern complex societies, that of the Roman Empire.

-10-

HISTORY, ADAPTATION AND SELF-ORGANIZATION

I BEGAN THIS BOOK BY SUGGESTING that in many respects archaeology had lost its way in recent years and that its current concern with trying to write 'human interest' stories based on conveying supposed 'lived human experience' produced unconvincing results and assumed the existence of what the anthropologist Henrietta Moore[1] has called 'hyperactive individuals'. Moreover, it positively ignored archaeology's key strength in providing information about long-term patterning in the human past, much of which would have been only dimly apparent to people alive at the time and is only discernible to the archaeologist in retrospect. The proposal was that this situation could be changed if archaeology adopted a Darwinian evolutionary perspective. The subsequent chapters have tried to make good this claim by looking at the relevance of evolutionary theory to understanding a whole series of subjects which have been central to archaeological concerns for a long time. Indeed, there is a sense in which this book is a very 19th-century one in the issues it addresses. If that is so, it is because the 19th-century pioneers of anthropology asked most of the right questions.

It should be clear by now that the application of evolutionary ideas to the understanding of these issues does not involve the kind of simplistic genetic determinism which is the knee-jerk assumption of many archaeologists and anthropologists as soon as they hear the words 'Darwinian evolution' in connection with the study of human cultures and societies. The issues raised are often complex, both substantively and in terms of their philosophical implications. If the approach is reductionist (and proud to be so!), it is, in Dan Dennett's words,[2] a 'circumscribed' and not a 'greedy' reductionism.

Our starting point was behavioural ecology, which provides a powerful set of ideas for understanding animal behaviour through the development of specific predictions based on the principles of Darwinian evolution by natural selection. It was apparent that studying behaviour from this perspective raises complex issues concerned with identifying units and levels of selection. Behaviour can have consequences far beyond the body of the individual instigating it, in ways that have consequences for the individual concerned, and genetic 'interests' are dispersed through populations of related individuals. These complexities have led to the making of a distinction between 'replicators' (genes) and 'interactors', entities that interact as a whole with their environment in such a way that their differential survival has consequences for the differential replication of the replicators that produced them.[3] The situation is further complicated by the fact that behaviour is a long way from genes in terms of causal chains connecting the two, and animal behaviour is often very flexible. This has led behavioural ecologists to make use of the 'phenotypic gambit' as a basis for generating hypotheses, the assumption that the particular behaviour they are studying is under selection in some straightforward way. It should be clear from the examples given in earlier chapters that the framework is not self-verifying or circular and the strategy has been remarkably successful in producing convincing explanations of particular animal behaviours, despite, or perhaps because of, the simplicity of the assumptions.

Since humans too are a species that has evolved through natural selection, the same ideas can in principle be applied to them, in terms of using the phenotypic gambit to develop hypotheses about human behaviour based on predictions derived from the principles of natural selection. We have seen a lot of evidence to suggest that the same considerations are indeed relevant to humans. Life history theory, for example, provides a framework for understanding human reproductive decision-making and the trade-offs it involves in the light of external conditions, such as the hypothesis that those who have more resources will be more reproductively successful, a prediction borne out, as we have seen, by ethnographic and historical studies.[4] Similarly, optimal foraging theory, through the diet breadth, patch choice and related cost-benefit models, seems to account for many features of ethnographically observed resource exploitation patterns. Sexual selection theory also seems to be relevant. The fact that the variance in reproductive success is greater for human males than it is for females indicates that human males have a bias towards mating effort and females towards parenting effort, with the result that males tend to compete for females. One of the key means by which they do this is by offering resources and we have seen considerable evidence that males with more resources are more reproductively successful and that the same is largely true of the women who are married to them. Perhaps most remarkable in this context is the fact that the Trivers-Willard hypothesis seems to be confirmed in human societies. When the reproductive success of the next generation is predictable from that of the current generation, as it often is when it depends on wealth, then we find that those at the bottom end of the spectrum invest more heavily in female children and those at the top in males.

In addition, many interaction principles explicable in terms of evolutionary cost-benefit considerations are found in both human societies and those of other animals. Costly signalling has been mentioned. Prisoner's Dilemma is just as relevant to whether animals cooperate, through such strategies as reciprocal altruism, as it is for humans. The same goes for the Hawk-Dove Game in animal and human contexts, and its Bourgeois version when one of the competitors is a territory-holder. However, it is less clear that the same is true for the principles of larger-scale forms of human organization of the kind we have referred to as 'superorganisms'. The only analogies here are the societies of the social insects and these work on a very different basis.

Nevertheless, whether we are talking about humans or other animals, about life histories, foraging strategies, sexual selection, or other forms of social interaction, patterns of costs and benefits will depend on the structure of relevant aspects of the local environment (meant in the broadest sense) and behaviour can be very sensitive to these. Local environments have histories that include the impact of previous generations of the population being studied on that environment – sometimes referred to as *niche construction*[5] – and on other populations within it. The effects of predator and prey populations on one another, for example, and the cyclical fluctuations in numbers to which they often lead over time are very well known. We saw too in Chapter 7 that while the principles of sexual selection are always the same, the conditions under which it operates, and therefore the specific strategies that are successful, depend on broader social and economic patterns which take shape and change over time, and to which flexible behaviour can respond.

Culture makes a difference in the way evolution operates because it represents a second inheritance system, conveniently labelled memetic, additional to the genetic one, operating through the mechanism of social learning. There is increasing evidence that the importance of this mechanism for evolution in non-human species has been much underrated.[6] The fact that cultural transmission operates through social learning does not make it less Darwinian than genetic transmission. Both are specific instances, with their own properties, of a more general category of information transfer processes that lead to the production of heritable variation and its modification through time.

The existence of cultural traditions adds two new possibilities to the way evolutionary change can take place. Natural selection on people's survival and reproductive success can occur through selection on their cultural traditions, not simply on their genes via their genetically inherited dispositions. In addition, processes of cultural selection can also operate, so that frequencies of cultural attributes change as a result of conscious and unconscious decision-making based on a variety of criteria, not through natural selection on people's survival and reproductive success. Of course, in any individual the 'biological' and the 'cultural' are inextricably mixed. Indeed, the craft skills and much other cultural knowledge that individuals acquire as they grow up are truly 'embodied'. Nevertheless, this does not reduce the analytical importance of making a distinction between different attributes and the specific factors affecting them if we want to understand why they work the way they do and the effects they have. This is especially important because the routes of cultural transmission are different from those of genetic inheritance and the forces of cultural selection have no genetic parallel. For example, making a particular kind of stone tool may be an 'embodied' skill, but we will fail to understand it if we imagine that its continuity through time depends on genetic rather than cultural transmission.

Because so much of human life depends on socially acquired knowledge, the history of cultural descent is important. Recognition of this has led to renewed attention to long-standing problems concerned with establishing whether different societies show patterns of similarity because of contact and transmission or as a result of 'the psychic unity of humankind'. Cladistics-based comparative methods can help us to resolve these problems and to distinguish similarities based on descent from those based on convergent adaptation.

THE ROLE OF ARCHAEOLOGY

As we saw in Chapter 1, Eric Smith's three styles in the evolutionary analysis of human behaviour did not envisage any role for an archaeological contribution. Now that we have reached the end of the book, what can we identify in response? There is also another challenge from what might be described as the opposite direction. What explanatory work do evolutionary ideas do that is not already being done by other, more established, means?

Cultural traditions

A first contribution is tracing the history of socially learned traditions, and the forces acting on those traditions, through time. Obviously, this is most easily done for histories of artifact form, but that does not mean it cannot be achieved for the history of social norms of other kinds. The key to tracing traditions and understanding how they are maintained and why they change is to put the artifact (or other) traditions at the centre of our investigation, *not* people. It is the artifacts that are the 'interactors' in David Hull's terms, the entities that interact with the environment in such a way that their differential success at what they do has consequences for the differential perpetuation of the procedures and ideas behind them. It is people and their decision-making that represent the selective environment for these artifact and other traditions, altering the form and frequency of particular types. Understanding the selection processes involved is likely to require some sort of behavioural reconstruction. For example, we saw in Chapter 9 that in the later phases of occupation of the Merzbach valley, the Linear Pottery Culture farmers were showing a bias in favour of novelty in their use of decorative motifs which seemed to be connected with social tensions arising from the filling up of the local area.

Finding artifact or other traditions that are correlated with one another over time and therefore have similar histories provides us with a means of identifying and characterizing cultural packages whose changing patterns then have to be explained. The nationalistic assumption of cultural essentialism that initially motivated the culture historical framework in the late 19th century meant that traditional methods of identifying cultural traditions in specific spheres of life and the relationships between them were insufficiently rigorous. However, it should not be assumed that natural selection and the decision-making forces of cultural selection are the only factors affecting cultural traditions. Drift is also relevant. Indeed, assessing the extent to which cultural drift is the sole process at work on a tradition provides us with a basis for assessing the extent of selection, as the Merzbach pottery example also showed. Similarly, at the inter-site level, evaluating the extent to which similarities and differences in cultural traditions between sites are merely a function of the extent of interaction between them, as Fraser Neiman did with his Illinois-Woodland period pottery, provides a basis for inferring the likely degree of insulation of a particular tradition from outside influences, and therefore of the extent to which it is likely to be open to change as a result of blending.

Populations

Archaeology is also a key source of information on the history of populations. As we have seen, for example in the case of the sub-Alpine lake-villages, high-resolution archaeological evidence suggests that regional human populations fluctuated considerably over time, a pattern which there is good reason to expect on theoretical grounds. However, tracing the history of specific populations at a regional scale is still by no means easy. If we can show that particular artifact traditions, or features such as technological styles, are likely to have been largely vertically transmitted, then we may be able to use such traditions as proxies for tracing population histories. Population expansions are likely to be associated with selectively advantageous cultural innovations in some domain. On the other hand, a good proxy indicator of population history is likely to be one that is not under selection in its own right but is simply carried along with the population as a result of continuity in the transmission process. However, in the light of the long history in archaeology of unconvincing attempts to link 'pots and peoples', great care is needed, and preferably support from other lines of evidence. One such line of evidence is the use of isotope studies of the bones and teeth of ancient skeletons to identify migration patterns.[7] Another, as we have seen, is the use of present-day genetic evidence. Nevertheless, the level of chronological resolution of such evidence remains relatively poor: good enough to answer some questions, but not others. Furthermore, while people are now very much aware of the importance of distinguishing the date of origin of a genetic marker from the time of its spread as a result of population expansion, the methods available for dating expansions, such as the use of mismatch distributions,[8] also have a large degree of uncertainty on their dating estimates.

For the last 2,000–3,000 years in particular, historical linguistic patterns clearly have a major role to play in tracing population histories, as we saw, for example, in the case of Patrick Kirch and Roger Green's analysis of the colonization of Polynesia.[9] However, if we are going to try and make inferences the other way round, using archaeological evidence to infer past linguistic patterns, we need a much better understanding of the relationship between language change and material culture change, and indeed social processes in general, beyond the clear cases of population expansion and colonization of new areas. This requires much greater attention to sociolinguistic models than has been common among archaeologists and historical linguists in the past. Part of the way forward here has been outlined by Malcolm Ross in his exploration of the relationship between changes in social networks and processes of change in a community's language,[10] and indeed these ideas are used by Kirch and Green. One plausible suggestion might be that where we have evidence of close contact between people of very different origins that has led to change in areas of life, such as technological style, acquired over a long period of time in childhood then language change might also be expected. We saw instances of precisely such contact in Pierre Pétrequin's study of the late Neolithic of the French Jura, where groups from very different backgrounds in Central Europe and southern France seem to have come together, producing a new ceramic tradition.[11] However, even in those cases where we can clearly use language evidence to trace population histories, the only way we will ever understand the reasons for population expansions and contractions in the past is by analysing archaeological evidence.

Resource exploitation

As we have seen, only archaeology can tell us about the relation between human populations and resources over time. In contrast to the history of cultural traditions, this task is firmly 'people-centred', since it is concerned with the decisions people make about getting a living, the factors affecting those decisions, and the consequences they have. An historical and archaeological perspective is essential to understanding human resource use for several different reasons, all related to the fact that a snapshot, synchronic analysis has to accept certain things as given, for example the current resource distribution, when in fact they are open to change. First, it provides us with the time-scale to see the consequences of particular modes of resource exploitation. Second, human exploitation of the natural environment represents a process of niche construction for later generations which has an impact on their subsistence possibilities. Third, resource use depends on technology, and technological innovations and their diffusion are historical processes associated with cultural traditions, not automatically called into existence by the needs of particular adaptations. Finally, cultural traditions in other spheres of social life may have an impact on the way environments are exploited. We need to be able to trace the histories of these traditions, as we did in our examination of animal exploitation by circum-Alpine Neolithic communities, to find out.

Sexual selection

As we have seen, there are well-established archaeological methodologies for addressing questions about resource exploitation and it may seem that this is much less the case with the study of sexual selection. However, sexual selection takes place in a broader context of social institutions and patterns of resource distribution, and archaeology's track-record in providing information about past social practices and institutions is actually quite good. In other words, we have potentially quite a strong basis for generating hypotheses about likely patterns of sexual selection in particular contexts. This can enable us to make effective use of a variety of forms of evidence likely to be relevant to addressing sexual selection itself. Examples include stable isotope studies of human skeletons of the kind already mentioned in discussing population history, but in this case used to assess whether males or females were tending to move from their community of origin on marriage, since this has an impact on the relative status and power of males and females and also on the extent of female economic independence. Genetic evidence tends to suggest that a pattern of female movement is more general,[12] a pattern that was also indicated by the strontium isotope analysis of early farming Linear Pottery Culture skeletons from Central Europe.[13] We have also seen the potential offered by studies of grave goods and costume in the light of evolutionary theory, while the study of patterning in male and female activities on the basis of distributional evidence of artifacts at settlement sites also offers great possibilities, for example as an indicator of male attempts to control females.[14]

Social institutions and practices

The history of social institutions and practices is much more like the history of artifact traditions. They are phenomena that are in a sense external to people, who provide the selective environment for them. However, there is also a major difference between the processes affecting stability and change in the histories of artifacts, and many other cultural traditions, and those affecting social institutions. In the case of the latter, the key process is not social learning affected by various forms of weak selection, but the ongoing selection process represented by the game pay-offs which people get when they interact with one another using a current set of expectations, and which are open to change when people on a large scale defect from those expectations.

In fact, things are more complex than this because there is a relevant social learning element – the norms and social values that people acquire as they grow up, which will clearly be conditioned by previous generations' experiences of the kinds of social interaction behaviour that gain the best pay-offs. A further complexity is the fact that social institutions interact with such things as the properties of resources to produce other institutions, such as private ownership, which in turn create their own dynamic for further institutional changes, as we have seen.

No synchronic or short-term analysis can address these questions, because at such time-scales social institutions cannot be seen as anything other than constraints affecting individual actions. The reconstruction of past social institutions and practices has long been recognized as the province of archaeologists using the sort of social evolution perspective described in earlier chapters. What has been argued for here is a shift of perspective on these long-standing issues which to some extent requires the development of new methodologies. Nevertheless, we have seen that archaeological evidence can already be used to make convincing inferences about patterns of resource ownership and resulting inequalities, for example in Hayden's Keatley Creek study.[15] Fluctuations between patterns of cooperation, independent action and warfare over time are also archaeologically visible, as the patterns seen in the southwestern United States, on the American Pacific coast and in the history of the first farmers in Central Europe have demonstrated. Ladefoged and Graves' analysis of the development of Hawaiian field systems[16] also suggests that the appearance of higher levels of selection resulting in improved risk-buffering for individual farmers (albeit at a cost) is also archaeologically recognizable.

Making sense of complexity

It will be very apparent that the agenda for archaeology just outlined is a very complex one. It is, of course, not nearly complete. The interactions between cultural traditions, population histories, resource exploitation histories and the others that have been discussed have not been thoroughly explored and some topics extremely important from a Darwinian perspective have not received nearly the attention they deserve. One is the origin and diffusion of technological innovations and the way in which these processes are linked to other aspects of the cultural traditions within which they emerge. Similarly, although considerable attention has been paid to adaptation/selection

processes and to the importance of the histories of particular cultural lineages, far less attention has been paid to processes of self-organization or of
niche construction.

Some of the topics which have been discussed require a 'people-centred'
approach, others, centred on the history of traditions and institutions, do
not, although people obviously play a key role, as conscious and unconscious
agents of selection on those traditions and as evaluators of the pay-offs produced by particular game conventions. However, this is not about attempting
to empathize with people's lived experience. It is about retrospectively recognizing patterns in what people did, and therefore in the 'decisions' they
made, and postulating the factors that affected them and the consequences
they had, in the light of the principles of evolutionary theory.

It is these that provide the framework for making sense of the complexities of the archaeological record of past human behaviour and its
organization. It is important not to let ourselves be overwhelmed by that
complexity, a weakness to which archaeologists are constitutionally prone.
On the last page of *On the Origin of Species* Darwin famously asked his reader
'to contemplate an entangled bank, with birds singing in the bushes, with
various insects flitting about, and to reflect that these elaborately constructed
forms, so different from each other and dependent on each other in so
complex a manner, have all been produced by laws acting around us.'[17] It is
time for archaeologists to stop being beguiled by the complexities of their
own entangled banks and to start producing accounts of human history that
make use of the principles Darwin established.

Notes

Chapter 1 (pages 9–21)

1. This point has also been made, from a very different theoretical perspective, by Moore (2000).
2. Important in the sense that it is likely to be one of the best defences against the political abuses of archaeology which have been so extensively documented in recent years. See e.g. the papers in Kohl and Fawcett (1995).
3. See e.g. Shanks and Tilley (1987).
4. Bradley (1993).
5. The early history of these controversies has recently been described by Irons and Cronk (2000), who also point out some of the fallacies embodied in many of the attacks on sociobiology, especially those contained in Marshall Sahlins' influential book, *The Use and Abuse of Biology* (1976).
6. Mitochondria are small organs found in individual cells which have their own genetic material. Both males and females have them but during the process of sexual reproduction they are only passed on by the female. Thus they represent a female-only, mother-daughter, genetic line. The concept of 'mitochondrial Eve' has been widely misunderstood because it has been taken to mean that there must have been a point in time when there was only a single human female ancestor alive. In fact, all it means is that if we could trace all the female ancestors of the population in the world today the family tree would eventually coalesce, by definition, on a single ancestral female. Many other females would have been alive at the same time but at various times between then and the present their mitochondrial DNA lineages have died out because they either had no children at all or only sons. How far back in time you have to go to get back to the common ancestor depends on the size of the population in the intervening period. See e.g. Harpending (1997).
7. Krings *et al.* (1997).
8. Some are already addressed in Dawkins (1976, second revised edition 1989). Others are dealt with in Degler (1991), Dennett (1995), Ridley (1996, 1999), Hrdy (1999), Radcliffe-Richards (2000), Avital and Jablonka (2000).
9. For reviews of this topic, see Relethford (1995), Rogers and Jorde (1995). A more recent example is Quintana-Murci *et al.* (1999).

10. E.g. Hagelberg *et al.* (1999).
11. Ammerman and Cavalli-Sforza (1984) proposed that present-day gene distributions in European populations supported the view that farming spread into Europe from the Near East by a process of population expansion and gradual mixing with existing populations that they called 'demic diffusion'. More recently, analyses of modern mitochondrial DNA variation (e.g. Richards *et al.* 1996) have led to the conclusion that most of the female-descended mtDNA lineages in Europe go back earlier than this, suggesting that a Neolithic population influx from the Near East did not play a major role. Similar conclusions were reached by Semino *et al.* (2000) on the basis of an analysis of modern male-descended Y-chromosome data. More recently, however, it has been strongly argued that these interpretations are mistaken and that demic diffusion was actually the most important mechanism of Neolithic spread (e.g. Barbujani and Bertorelle 2001, Chikhi *et al.* n.d.). Some of the complex issues raised by the argument are discussed by Fix (1999, 168-182).
12. E.g. Sims-Williams (1998).
13. The Neanderthals survived until after 30,000 years ago in southern Iberia. See e.g. Gamble (1999, 384).
14. A recent work that carried through this agenda on a large scale is Gamble (1999).
15. Smith (2000).
16. Some proponents of this approach would argue that, even if you acknowledge the importance of culture in principle, it is a useful methodological gambit to ignore it and see how far you can get in explaining things without it: trying out the simplest explanation (in the sense of involving the minimum number of assumptions) first. This approach will be adopted in a number of places in the chapters that follow.
17. In Dawkins' version, as we saw earlier, these are conceived in terms of memes, but it will become apparent later that this is by no means the only possible view. It is worth adding that the uniqueness of culture to humans is being increasingly questioned. See Avital and Jablonka (2000).
18. E.g. Irons (1998), Flinn (1997).
19. E.g. Mace and Pagel (1994).

CHAPTER 2 (pages 22–34)

1. See e.g. Avital and Jablonka (2000, especially Chapter 2).

2. Krebs and Davies (1993, Chapter 1).

3. Of course, fixed genes, those that occur in the same version in all members of a species, may also influence behaviour, which will then be uniform for that specific behaviour, other things being equal. However, it is the variation in behaviour of the members of a species that is of interest here.

4. Grafen (1984); see also Smith and Winterhalder (1992, Chapter 2). The genetic constitution of an individual is known as its *genotype*. The form and behaviour of the individual that emerges as the result of growth and development affected by its local environment is its *phenotype*.

5. Jarman (1974); Krebs and Davies (1993, Chapter 2).

6. Smith and Winterhalder (1992, 51).

7. Smith and Winterhalder (1992, 50).

8. Krebs and Davies (1993, 48-53).

9. Kacelnik (1984).

10. Dawkins (1982).

11. Wynne-Edwards (1962).

12. Trivers (1971).

13. Wilkinson (1984); Krebs and Davies (1993, Chapter 11).

14. Hamilton (1964), but anticipated by Fisher (1930) and Haldane (1953).

15. See Krebs and Davies (1993, Chapter 13) for a clear account of this.

16. Nesse and Williams (1999).

17. Lloyd (in press).

18. Hull (1980, 318).

19. Sober and Wilson (1998).

20. Krebs and Davies (1993) provide many examples of these.

21. Kelly (1995, 51).

22. Smith and Winterhalder (1992, 54-55).

CHAPTER 3 (pages 34–65)

1. See Durham (1991) for a more extended discussion of this point.

2. A good example of this is Kuper (1999).

3. Avital and Jablonka (2000, 59); Jablonka (2000).

4. Avital and Jablonka (2000, 54).

5. Boyd and Richerson (1985, 33).

6. Binford (1962) and other papers gathered together in Binford (1972a).

7. Of course, both the social and the physical environment are likely to be modified by culturally-influenced human activity in a process of 'niche construction' (see e.g.

Odling-Smee *et al.* 1996), such as the clearance of forests or the building of cities.

8. Flinn (1997); Boone and Smith (1998).

9. Avital and Jablonka (2000).

10. Plotkin (1997, 195).

11. Russon (1997, 176).

12. The mechanisms of social learning among animals and the consequences they have in terms of the formation of animal traditions which are cumulative through time continue to be the subject of enormous debate. Some psychologists argue that the only thing which differentiates social from individual learning is the source of the information: in social learning the sources are other members of the same species but the mechanisms involved are the same processes of reinforcement and trial-and-error learning by which other information about the world is acquired. Thus social learning in birds and mammals is an inevitable consequence of the fact that individuals at least to some extent associate with other members of the same species (Avital and Jablonka 2000, 90-95). Others argue that, for some species at least, additional mechanisms are involved. The one which has been most discussed, and which is most controversial, is observational learning, or imitation, 'learning to do an act by seeing it done' (Russon 1997, 178). All are agreed that imitation is a very complex cognitive process because it involves the copying of an observed behaviour, a process which requires the translation of information received by one means, visual or aural, into an output produced by another, a pattern of action, which matches the original. It has proved extremely difficult to demonstrate the existence of 'real imitation' in non-human animals, because there is a great variety of mechanisms by which the behaviour of one individual animal can come to resemble that of another without involving the complexity of imitation; on the contrary, most of these mechanisms are relatively simple in cognitive terms (Whiten and Ham 1992). Much of the debate has revolved around primates, especially the great apes, and the extent to which they are capable of true imitation, but imitation itself has turned out to have many complex dimensions whose significance is disputed. Whiten (2000) gives an up-to-date review of the primate debates. Some authors (e.g. Boyd and Richerson 1996) maintain that only true imitation leads to the development of cumulative traditions, others that any form of social learning will do.

13. Avital and Jablonka (2000, 133-135). See also volumes of studies edited by Zentall and Galef (1988), Heyes and Galef (1996) and Box and Gibson (1999).

14. E.g.Whiten *et al.* (1999) and many examples in Avital and Jablonka (2000).

15. Kaplan (1996, 103).

16. Kaplan (1996, 105).

17. Boesch (1993).

18. Shennan and Steele (1999).

19. Hewlett and Cavalli-Sforza (1986).

20. Ruddle (1993).

21. See Shennan and Steele (1999).

22. Ruddle (1993, 20). Italics in original.

23. Boyd and Richerson (1985, 46-55).

24. Boyd and Richerson (1985, 55).

25. Boyd and Richerson (1985, 55).

26. Guglielmino *et al.* (1995).

27. Edgerton with Goldschmidt (1971), cited in Boyd and Richerson (1985, 57-59).

28. Avital and Jablonka (2000, 280).

29. Diamond (1987), cited in Avital and Jablonka (2000, 282-284).

30. Dawkins (1976; 1982, 109-112); see also Blackmore (1999) for a more extended analysis.

31. Dawkins (1982, 290).

32. *Cf.* Dennett (1995).

33. Dennett (1995); Cullen (1996); Gladwell (2000).

34. Cullen (1995, 1996).

35. Godin (2000).

36. Wood *et al.* (1976), cited in Whiten (1999).

37. E.g. Whiten (1999).

38. Sperber (1996, 100-118).

39. Lake (1998, 86).

40. Boyd and Richerson (2001).

41. Whitehouse (1996).

42. Edelman (1992).

43. Avital and Jablonka (2000, 95).

44. For an interesting discussion of the link between mitochondrial DNA transmission and the transmission of traditions in matrilineal groups of sperm whales, see Whitehead (1998).

45. Shennan and Steele (1999).

46. See again Ruddle (1993). Similar findings are reported by Maceachern (1998), Pinçon and Ngöie-Ngalla (1990), Gosselain (1992), O'Hear (1986), Delneuf (1991) and Arnold (1989).

47. Herbich (1987).

48. Mainberger (1998, 244).

49. Arbogast *et al.* (1997, 600).

50. Boyd and Richerson (1985); Cavalli-Sforza and Feldman (1981).

51. Barth (1987).

52. Boyd and Richerson (1985, chapter 4).

53. Avital and Jablonka (2000, 70-71).

54. Fitzhugh (2001).

55. See e.g. Diamond (1997), Crosby (1986).

56. Kirch and Green (2001, 73-74).

57. Kimura (1983).

58. Dunnell (1978).

59. Rivers (1926, 190-210).

60. Not the islands of the Torres Strait between New Guinea and Australia.

61. Rivers (1926, 200).

62. Rivers (1926, 204).

63. Ramenofsky (1998a, 1998b); Boone and Smith (1998).

64. Boyd and Richerson (1985, Chapter 5).

65. *Cf.* Pétrequin (1993).

66. Boyd and Richerson (1985, Chapter 8).

67. Boyd and Richerson (1985, 287). We'll see in Chapter 8 that this sort of process can also be seen from a different evolutionary perspective, that of expensive signalling.

68. See, for example, Cavalli-Sforza and Cavalli-Sforza (1995).

69. Boyd and Richerson (1985, Chapter 7).

70. Boyd and Richerson (1988a, 30).

71. Or even if an adaptation is initially acquired by social learning, the learned adaptation may provide the basis for the process of genetic assimilation, in which selection conditioned by the learned adaptation leads to a genetic basis for the behaviour. See Avital and Jablonka (2000, Chapter 9).

72. Boyd and Richerson (1988a, 43).

73. Boyd and Richerson (1996).

74. Local bird song traditions being one of the few exceptions to this. See e.g. Payne (1996).

75. Mithen (1999).

76. For a discussion of Pleistocene climate fluctuations, see Richerson *et al.* (2001).

77. Dennett (1995, 346).

78. Williams (1992, 15), cited in Dennett (1995, 361).

79. Cavalli-Sforza and Feldman (1981). See Boyd and Richerson (1985, 182-186) for a simple verbal and mathematical model that demonstrates this point.

80. Boyd and Richerson (1985, 190).

81. Shennan (2001).

82. Histories of particular genes and histories of human populations are not the same thing either. A given population, for example, will contain a variety of gene lineages, for example different varieties of mitochondrial DNA, which may have different origins. However,

when we are dealing with cultural traits transmitted non-genetically by a variety of routes, the gap between trait histories and population histories is potentially even greater.
83. Hull (1980, 318). See also O'Brien and Lyman (2000, 240-242).

CHAPTER 4 (pages 66–99)

1. See e.g. Trigger (1989), Lyman *et al.* (1997).
2. See Shennan (1989a), Jones (1997).
3. See e.g. Kohl and Fawcett (1995), Diaz-Andreu and Champion (1996), Kohl (1998).
4. Although American ethnographers also developed the so-called culture area approach, which involved creating distribution maps of the ethnographic present rather than the prehistoric past.
5. See e.g. O'Brien and Lyman (2000, 291-299). A rather different seriation technique was invented by the British archaeologist Sir Flinders Petrie, at the end of the 19th century. He traced the sequence of slightly changing forms of a series of pottery vessel types. He showed that the ordering of slightly changing forms could actually be used to put sites and assemblages in a chronological sequence even when there is no stratigraphic information available. He used this technique to put in chronological order the grave assemblages from Egyptian Pre-Dynastic cemeteries. O'Brien and Lyman (2000, 275-278) refer to this particular technique as *phyletic seriation*.
6. Lyman *et al.* (1997).
7. Lyman *et al.* (1997, 92).
8. Kroeber (1931, 151), cited in Lyman *et al.* (1997, 9). But note that Pitt-Rivers (1875) was already emphasizing the importance of arranging artifacts so that the order reflected not just their sequence but also the history of their transmission, i.e. the pattern of homologous relationships.
9. Brew (1946, 53), cited in Lyman *et al.* (1997, 101).
10. Lyman *et al.* (1997, 105).
11. E.g. Deetz (1965).
12. See e.g. the essays collected in Binford (1972a).
13. As Andrew Sherratt (pers. comm.) has pointed out to me, this represents a kind of equilibrium analysis like that used in classical economics, and assumes a more or less instant congruence of cultural adaptations with their current environment. As we saw in the previous chapter, the phylogenetic inertia inherent in inherited information means that this kind of instant response is most unlikely

in systems dependent on inherited information so it cannot be assumed that particular situations represent adaptive equilibria.
14. See e.g. Binford (1962) and compare with Dunnell's (1978) definition of style as neutral variation discussed above.
15. Strongly criticized by Binford (1972b) in Clarke's own edited book, *Models in Archaeology*.
16. However, although Clarke was not thinking in Darwinian terms, the parallels between the approach he developed in *Analytical Archaeology* and current Darwinian approaches to the analysis of cultural traditions are extremely close. See Shennan (1989b; in press) and O'Brien and Lyman (2000, 262-264) for accounts of Clarke's key ideas and their link to evolutionary approaches.
17. See e.g. Tschauner (1994). The various 'post-processual' approaches which came to dominate British archaeology in the 1980s and 1990s, saw artifact variation and change in terms of the creation and manipulation of social meanings, especially in the context of maintaining, asserting or resisting social power. Such questions are certainly important and archaeology has the capacity to explore them in prehistoric contexts where other sources of information are unavailable, as we will see in later chapters. Nevertheless, the view taken here is that such studies concern the role of material culture in internal political processes, and that until the advent of the first states no political units had either the scale or the power to have a major cultural impact over large areas or long spans of time. In other words, while these ideas and approaches are relevant at local spatial scales, applying them to patterns of change at regional and larger scales is mistaken.

This suggestion is strongly supported by the results of a recent analysis comparing the sizes of a large sample of ethnographically documented entities with those of a sample of European Neolithic 'cultures' (Wotzka 1997). It was shown that, with the exception of entities which were politically highly centralized, the scale of the ethnographic entities was much smaller than that of the archaeological ones. Furthermore, if one looked only at those ethnographic entities which could be said to represent individual political units or areas characterized by a conscious group identity, then the largest of them barely overlapped in size with the smallest archaeological entity. Accordingly, it seems unlikely that internal political processes hold the key to explaining the major changes in material cultural patterns which we see over time in the prehistoric archaeology of regions with non-state societies across the world. Similar conclusions are reached by Maceachern (1998) in his analysis of the factors affecting cultural variation in the Mandara region of West Africa.

18. O'Brien and Lyman (2000, Chapter 6).
19. O'Brien and Lyman (2000, 283-284).
20. O'Brien and Lyman (2000, 283-284).
21. This may be a genuine innovation made locally or an introduction from outside which is novel to the local area. In general, local innovations are more likely to arise from the latter process. See Neiman (1995).
22. Lipo *et al.* (1997); O'Brien and Lyman (2000, 287).
23. Neiman (1995).
24. Frirdich (1994); Stehli (1994).
25. Boyd *et al.* (1997).
26. *Cf.* David Clarke's discussion in *Analytical Archaeology* of archaeological entities as polythetic rather than monothetic sets.
27. See papers in Hodder (1978), including Shennan (1978).
28. Boyd *et al.* (1997, 371, 377).
29. Rushforth and Chisholm (1991).
30. Rushforth and Chisholm (1991, 78); also cited in Boyd *et al.* (1997, 374).
31. Rosenberg (1994).
32. Gould and Lewontin (1979).
33. Andrew Sherratt (pers. comm.) has reminded me that the Bauplan idea goes back to the 'natural morphology' of Cuvier and can be traced through Richard Owen in the 19th century to D'Arcy Thomson and then Brian Goodwin in the 20th century.
34. Rosenberg (1994, 320).
35. Ortman (2000).
36. The idea that pottery often imitates basketry is one of long standing and parallels between the two are found in many cultures all over the world. It was first suggested by the German archaeologist Schuchhardt in connection with the pottery of the so-called Nordic TRB culture of the European Neolithic (Sherratt pers. comm.). Items made of one material that imitate those of another are known as skeuomorphs in the jargon and it is usually the case that the skeuomorph can be considered a cheap substitute for the thing it is imitating. However, whatever the case in other

cultures where pottery skeuomorphs of baskets are found, Ortman is making a much stronger claim based on detailed comparative analysis involving a number of different cultural spheres.

37. Ortman (2000, 637).
38. Bettinger and Eerkens (1999).
39. Most recently documented by mitochondrial DNA evidence. See Kaestle and Smith (2001).
40. A good summary of the modern view of such linguistic processes and their relation to the histories of human communities is Ross (1997). See too Kirch and Green (2001, Chapter 2).
41. Durham (1990, 1992).
42. Kirch (1984). For an updated version of this thesis, see Kirch and Green (2001).
43. Goodenough (1957).
44. Moore (1994). This represents a revival of a debate that has roots in the 19th century. See Tylor (1888), cited in Kirch and Green (2001).
45. Strictly speaking, the word should be 'rhizomatic'.
46. Moore (1994, 925).
47. Terrell *et al.* (1997).
48. Lesser (1961).
49. Dennett (1995, 350-351).
50. Aunger (n.d.).
51. Pétrequin (1993).
52. Pétrequin (1993, 46).
53. Pétrequin (1993, 48).
54. Pétrequin (1993, 55).
55. Neiman (1995).
56. Neiman (1995, 27).
57. Rosenberg (1994, 330).
58. Dole (1993).
59. E.g. Renfrew (1987), Cavalli-Sforza and Cavalli-Sforza (1995), Renfrew and Boyle (2000), Kirch and Green (2001), Ehret (1998).
60. Kirch and Green (2001, 13).
61. Romney (1957, 36).
62. Kirch and Green (2001); Ehret (1998); Bellwood (1997).
63. Ross (1997) provides a strong justification for the importance of the phylogenetic model in linguistic change, albeit with modifications from earlier versions, and despite the role of other processes.
64. See e.g. Barbujani and Bertorelle (2001).
65. Although there are tools designed to use present-day genetic evidence to make inferences about the existence of population expansions and their estimated date through the use of genetic 'mismatch' distributions. See e.g. Sherry *et al.* (1994).

66. Hennig (1965). For a fascinating account of the development of cladistics told by a participant-observer philosopher from an evolutionary epistemology perspective, see Hull (1988).

67. This is a complex issue and there are various possible criteria, although the one most commonly used is maximum parsimony, the minimum set of branchings to fit the data. The number of possible trees for more than a very small number of species is astronomical and there may be many equally parsimonious ones.

68. Harvey and Pagel (1991).

69. Mace and Pagel (1994).

70. Gray and Jordan (2000).

71. The 'entangled bank' refers to a phrase on the last page of *On the Origin of Species* about the complexity of life on the one hand and the simplicity of the principles accounting for it on the other. John Terrell borrowed it and used it, rather against the point that Darwin was making, as a descriptive phrase for his model of Pacific cultural patterns, based on complex interactions over a long period.

72. Gray and Jordan (2000, 1054). However, it should be noted that although both the archaeology and the language relationships fit very well with this model of expansion from Taiwan, the genetic information is not so clear, suggesting that Polynesian populations include genetic features that must have originated in eastern Indonesia a long time ago (see Richards 2001).

73. Kirch and Green (2001, 97).

74. Wotzka (1997) and see note 17.

75. Gray and Jordan (2000, 1054).

CHAPTER 5 (pages 100–137)

1. Binford (1968).

2. Boserup (1965).

3. Renfrew (1976).

4. Carneiro (1970).

5. See e.g. Cowgill (1975).

6. E.g. Feinman and Neitzel (1984).

7. Fisher (1958), cited in Borgerhoff-Mulder (1992); Fisher (1930), cited in Hill and Hurtado (1996). Detailed reviews may be found in Charnov (1993) or Stearns (1992). A shorter overview may be found in Hill and Hurtado (1996, 18–39).

8. Lack (1947).

9. Kaplan (1996, 92).

10. Hill and Hurtado (1996, 13).

11. Brown (1991).

12. Kaplan (1996, 95).

13. Hill and Hurtado (1996).

14. Hill and Hurtado (1996, 356).

15. Voland (1998, 354).

16. Kaplan (1996, 109).

17. Kaplan (1996, 102).

18. Kaplan (1996, 103).

19. Hill and Kaplan (1999).

20. Key (2000, 335). The reason for the long lactation period is not entirely clear but it is possible that the considerable importance of paternal care in humans is relevant to their short inter-birth intervals.

21. Hill and Hurtado (1996, 471).

22. Hill and Hurtado (1996, 472).

23. Hill and Hurtado (1996, 475–476).

24. It is often claimed that in countries which have been through the 'demographic transition', the marked decrease in family size which first occurred in the industrializing societies of Western Europe and has gradually spread across the world, this is no longer the case, especially now that artificial means of birth control are widely available. However, this is very much open to debate. It is clear that modern populations are markedly stratified in terms of amounts of parental investment and the returns that are gained from it. Within a given social stratum there is a lot of evidence that the association between wealth and reproductive success continues to hold. See Kaplan (1996) and Mace (2000).

25. Hill and Hurtado (1996, 318).

26. Irons (1979).

27. Voland (1995).

28. Wrigley (1983).

29. Voland (1998, 356).

30. Voland (1998, 358).

31. Wiessner and Tumu (1998).

32. Wrigley (1983, 133).

33. Pennington (1996).

34. Sahlins (1972).

35. Hill and Hurtado (1996, 319-320).

36. It will become clearer in the next chapter how this last process works. Obviously, it involves pressure to start the use of the new resource but whether population growth ensues will depend on the capacity of the new resources to sustain larger numbers of people.

37. Bettinger (1998).

38. Voland (1998).

39. *Cf.* Wood (1998).

40. Basgall (1987) and see the next chapter for a more extended account of this case study.

41. Stiner *et al.* (2000).

42. Peltenburg *et al.* (2001).

43. See Chapter 1, note 11; also van Andel and Runnels (1995) and Zilhão (2000).

44. Sellen and Mace (1997), Boone (in press).
45. See again, Chapter 1, note 11.
46. Lüning and Stehli (1994).
47. Meiklejohn *et al.* (1997).
48. Jakes (1988).
49. Sattenspiel and Harpending (1983).
50. Buikstra *et al.* (1986).
51. Meiklejohn *et al.* (1997).
52. Price (1991).
53. Zvelebil (1996).
54. Boone (in press).
55. Richerson *et al.* (2001).
56. Boone (in press).
57. Belovsky (1988); Winterhalder *et al.* (1988); Boone (in press).
58. Keckler (1997).
59. Lahr and Foley (1998); Ambrose (1998).
60. Neel (1978).
61. See also Neves (1995).
62. Arbogast *et al.* (1996), Pétrequin (1997), and see below. For another French Neolithic example see now also Scarre (2001).
63. Kalis and Zimmermann (1997).
64. Matson *et al.* (1988).
65. Jones *et al.* (1999).
66. *cf.* Halstead and O'Shea (1989).
67. Richerson *et al.* (2001).
68. David and Lourandos (1998).
69. Hegmon *et al.* (2000).
70. Pétrequin and Pétrequin (1999).
71. Dixon (1997).
72. Neiman (1995).
73. Billamboz (1995).
74. Pétrequin (1997); Arbogast *et al.* (1996).
75. Gross-Klee and Maise (1997).
76. Magny (1993); Maise (1998).
77. Arbogast *et al.* (1996).
78. Maise (1998).
79. In fact, by the 18th century the broader food supply network that had been established meant that the impact of this sort of crisis was not as severe as it had been in earlier times. For a discussion of these sorts of issues in a historical context and their relation to price levels, see Fischer (1996).
80. Gross *et al.* (1990).
81. Wolf (pers. comm.).
82. Rosenberg (1994).
83. Again, the very exact date is made by possible by dendrochronological dating.
84. For a description of this sequence, see Wolf (1993).
85. Pétrequin *et al.* (1999).

CHAPTER 6 (pages 138–176)

1. See e.g. Steward (1936a, 1955). In Britain at around the same time a not dissimilar approach to the ecology of past human societies was being developed by Graham Clark (e.g. 1954).
2. Kelly (1995, 42-43).
3. Kelly (1995, 43).
4. Moore (1965), cited in Kelly (1995, 43).
5. For the potlatch seen in this way, see Suttles (1968). For 'social storage' in general, see Halstead and O'Shea (1989).
6. Rappaport (1968).
7. See Harner (1977) for cannibalism, Harris (1989) for warfare.
8. Binford (1968).
9. Renfrew (1972).
10. Service (1962).
11. See e.g. Kelly (1995, 45).
12. From the character Dr. Pangloss in Voltaire's *Candide*, who believed, despite all the evidence, that 'Everything works for the best in this best of all possible worlds'.
13. However, there is a variety of other possible alternative optimality criteria on which choices may be based. For example, minimizing the risk of starvation will not necessarily involve the same strategy as maximizing the energy input in a given period. See Krebs and Davies (1993) for some of the possibilities. The example of starlings carrying food back to the nest that we saw in Chapter 2 showed that they were maximizing their food delivery rate rather than their own energetic efficiency.
14. Krebs and Davies (1993, 68-69).
15. Krebs and Davies (1993, 70-72).
16. E.g. Hill and Hurtado (1996).
17. Kaplan and Hill (1992, 173-174).
18. Altman (1987).
19. Kelly (1995, 89); Alvard (1995).
20. Kelly (1995, 90).
21. Of course, the archaeological record brings in different complications, including deposition and decay processes, but these are not necessarily insuperable. See e.g. Rogers (2000).
22. Kelly (1995, 90-97); Kaplan and Hill (1992, 178-184).
23. Kelly (1995, 91).
24. O'Connell and Hawkes (1981), cited in Kaplan and Hill (1992, 183).
25. Mithen (1989).
26. Kaplan and Hill (1992, 175-176).
27. Kaplan and Hill (1992, 176).
28. Janetski (1997).
29. Of course, we have to use the well-

established methods of archaeological taphonomy – the study of destruction and decay processes – to ensure that the proportions of small and large animals are telling us something about the past, rather than about the state of preservation of our bone sample. For an example of the issues involved, in this case the inference that variation in the bone assemblages from a site in France relates to Palaeolithic diet breadth, see Grayson and Delpech (1998).

30. See again note 30.

31. Nagaoka (in press).

32. Basgall (1987).

33. Broughton (1997).

34. Butler (2000).

35. Steadman (1995). See also Broodbank (2000, 8).

36. Stiner et al. (2000); Mannino and Thomas (in press).

37. Stiner et al. (2000).

38. Alvard (1995, 1998).

39. Alvard (1998, 63).

40. Alvard (1998, 63).

41. Alvard (1998, 64).

42. Smith (1991, 256), cited in Alvard (1998, 66).

43. Kaplan and Hill (1985, 236), cited in Alvard (1998, 66).

44. Porcasi et al. (2000, 217).

45. Alvard (1998, 71).

46. Winterhalder and Goland (1993).

47. Winterhalder and Goland (1993, 715).

48. Bar-Yosef (1998).

49. Bar-Yosef (1998, 168).

50. Richerson et al. (2001). These authors also offer an answer to a question that the preceding account of the sorts of processes involved in the origins of agriculture has not addressed. Why did it take place at this time rather than 20,000 or 30,000 years earlier? Their suggestion is that the rapid climatic oscillations of the late Pleistocene period would have prevented the development of reliable plant-based adaptations.

51. Vita-Finzi and Higgs (1970).

52. Chisholm (1962).

53. Boserup (1965).

54. Stone and Downum (1999, 115).

55. Stone and Downum (1999).

56. Brockway (1993), cited in Ridley (1996).

57. Shennan (1999).

58. Rowlands (1979).

59. Warnier (1985).

60. Warnier (1985, 79).

61. Shennan (1998, 1999).

62. Iovanovic (1991); Hauptmann (1989).

63. Richerson et al. (2001).

64. As we saw there, Avital and Jablonka (2000) would emphasize the importance of such traditions in affecting animal behaviour as well.

65. See e.g. Binford (1983) for the importance of information-gathering among foragers.

66. Hunt (2000).

67. Bright et al. (in press).

68. Boyd and Richerson (1985).

69. Fitzhugh (2001).

70. Cf. Rosenberg's (1994) discussion of the processes involved in cultural origins which was outlined in Chapter 4. It is also worth pointing out that this is not so different from Boserup's view. She imagined that population pressure would lead to the generation of innovations which would then allow population to grow further.

71. See Fitzhugh's (2001) analysis of utility curves and their shapes.

72. Diamond (1997).

73. Macfarlane and Harrison (2000).

74. Macfarlane and Harrison (2000).

75. Young et al. (2000).

76. The relative proportions of wild and domestic animals don't tell us anything about the absolute numbers of animals actually killed and eaten. This is what the absolute bone densities give an indication of, so long as it can be shown that there are not major differences in bone preservation or rubbish disposal practices between the different phases, which is the case here. See Schibler et al. (1997).

77. Schibler et al. (1997). It is worth adding that the move away from cereal growing didn't lead to people forgetting how to do this, although it might have done if it had been more thorough-going and carried on longer.

78. Pétrequin et al. (1998).

CHAPTER 7 (pages 177–205)

1. Recent reviews include Gilchrist (1999), Sørensen (2000), Conkey and Gero (1997).

2. Although this is now beginning to change. See e.g. Knapp (1998).

3. Low (2000, 38). See also Krebs and Davies (1993, Chapters 8 and 9).

4. Krebs and Davies (1993, 176-177); Trivers (1972).

5. See e.g. Krebs and Davies (1993, 183-184).

6. See e.g. Krebs and Davies (1993, 184-186, 227-229), Birkhead and Møller (1992).

7. Krebs and Davies (1993, 187-188).

8. Krebs and Davies (1993, 195); Hamilton and Zuk (1982).

9. Krebs and Davies (1993, 201-202).
10. Krebs and Davies (1993, 210). In fact, the situation is more complex than this and part of the reason for bird monogamy may be lack of opportunities for polygamy. At all events there is now a lot of evidence that a significant proportion of the chicks produced are the result of extra-pair matings. See Krebs and Davies (1993, 225-230).
11. For a description of some of these variations, see Krebs and Davies (1993, 215-225).
12. Krebs and Davies (1993, 237-238).
13. This explanation for the sex ratio was first demonstrated by Sir Ronald Fisher (1930). In fact, the situation is slightly more complicated than I have described. See e.g. Krebs and Davies (1993, 177-182).
14. Trivers and Willard (1973).
15. Krebs and Davies (1993, 181-182).
16. This topic is dealt with in much greater detail by Buss (1989, 1994), Low (2000) and Betzig (1986).
17. Cited in Krebs and Davies (1993, 179).
18. Low (2000, 56).
19. See e.g. Buss (1989, 1994). However, this will not always be the case, for example where, as a result of local ecological considerations and social circumstances, males do not have much in the way of resources to offer.
20. Hill and Hurtado (1996).
21. Neel (1978, 406).
22. Neel (1978, 377).
23. Voland (1995).
24. Voland (1995, 144).
25. Voland (1995, 145).
26. Voland (1995, 146).
27. Borgerhoff-Mulder (1990, 1996).
28. See e.g. Betzig (1986).
29. Boone (1986).
30. Boone (1986, 866).
31. Cronk (2000).
32. As Cronk (2000, 215) emphasizes, this situation doesn't arise because dead baby boys are somehow adaptive for Mukogodo parents; they are a cost, not a benefit. However, their situation doesn't allow them the possibility of keeping more sons alive while keeping their daughters as healthy as they do. An increasing number of other cases are appearing that seem to fit the Trivers-Willard hypothesis. See e.g. Irons (2000) on Yomut pastoralists and other cases cited in the same paper.
33. Voland (1995).
34. For a review of the cross-cultural evidence on this, see Hewlett (1991).

35. Hill and Hurtado (1996, 194).
36. Hill and Hurtado (1996, 449).
37. Neel (1978).
38. Not dissimilar situations are found in those modern societies where women are successful in the employment market or where their economic independence is provided by state support.
39. Hartung (1985).
40. Mace and Holden (1999).
41. Gaulin and Boster (1990), cited in Cashdan (1996, 138).
42. Dickemann (1981), cited in Cashdan (1996, 138).
43. It should not be thought that such practices are unique to humans. A number of species practise mate-guarding at times when females are fertile. See e.g. Krebs and Davies (1993, 184).
44. Strassmann (2000).
45. Sellen et al. (2000).
46. This deleterious effect decreased when there was more than one co-wife, possibly as a result of cooperation between the wives. See again Sellen et al. (2000).
47. See e.g. Krebs and Davies (1993, 246-252).
48. Low (2000, 73).
49. Low (2000, 74).
50. Low (2000, 113-114).
51. Draper (1997).
52. Morelli (1997).
53. See e.g. Hawkes (1990). It has to be acknowledged that this is a hugely controversial subject among workers in the field of the evolutionary ecology of male-female relations. Hillard Kaplan and his colleagues (e.g. Kaplan et al. 2000) emphasize the important role of male provisioning of women and children in the course of human evolution, in an updated version of a long-standing model of the evolution of human pair-bonding which emphasizes the importance of meat in human subsistence. This is strongly contested by Kristen Hawkes and colleagues (e.g. Hawkes et al. 2000, Blurton-Jones et al. 2000), who emphasize the role of hunting as mating effort, both in terms of extra-marital affairs and also as a basis for stepfathering, which can be part of a bargain that gives a man sexual access to a woman. Here then we have a sexual selection model of men conforming to women's preferences. On this view the key to female provisioning is the investment of mothers and especially grandmothers. Male mate-guarding may be accepted as a means of avoiding disruption to

women's foraging by other importuning males, with a preference for males who are good guards.

Other explanations of the hunting of large game for wide sharing emphasize the dangers of injury and disease to individual hunters and the role of reciprocal altruism in solving such problems when they arise, which corresponds to more traditional assumptions about the role of sharing and reciprocity (e.g. Sugiyama and Chacon 2000).

It is important to emphasize that all these debates are taking place within the framework of evolutionary ecology, which is shared by all the protagonists.

54. Low (2000, 114); Murdock and Provost (1973).
55. Low (2000, 114).
56. Although it may be female interest *per se*, in that a woman may choose to behave that way in order to gain a husband, given the social circumstances. Of course, it is a highly constrained choice.
57. For activity and stress differences see e.g. Slaus (2000), Sofaer Derevenski (2000). For examples of recent archaeological work on male and female residence patterns, see Price *et al.* (2001), Schulting and Richards (2001).
58. Kohn and Mithen (1999).
59. See e.g. Thornhill and Møller (1998), Møller and Thornhill (1998).
60. Mithen (1990).
61. Hawkes (1990).
62. Engels (1972).
63. E.g. Childe (1958).
64. Neustupny (1967).
65. See e.g. Carol Palmer's (1998) discussion of traditional plough agriculture in Jordan, where she describes the male sexual symbolism of the plough.
66. See Sherratt (1981).
67. Bogucki (1993).
68. Mace and Holden (1999).
69. Pétrequin and Pétrequin (1988).
70. Robb (1994).
71. Gimbutas (1989). See also Mallory (1989).
72. Low (1979).
73. Giles (1999).
74. Sørensen (1997).
75. Sørensen (1997).
76. Giles (1999, 40).
77. Giles (1999, 40).
78. Treherne (1995).
79. Shennan (1975).
80. Rega (1997).
81. Low (1990).
82. Jockenhövel (1991).
83. Giles (1999, 43).

CHAPTER 8 (pages 206–238)

1. Childe (1958).
2. Lyman *et al.* (1997).
3. See e.g. Steward (1955).
4. White (1949).
5. Service (1962).
6. *Cf.* Shennan (1993a).
7. Renfrew (1974).
8. Giddens (1984).
9. E.g. Shennan (1977).
10. Trigger (1998).
11. Shennan (1993a).
12. Blanton (1998).
13. Foley and Lee (1989, 1996); Foley (1996).
14. Maynard Smith and Szathmary (1995).
15. E.g. Hodder (1984).
16. Bourdieu (1977).
17. Douglas (1978).
18. Eldredge and Gould (1972).
19. Sober and Wilson (1998).
20. Axelrod (1984).
21. Boyd and Richerson (1988b); Boone (1992, 308).
22. Boyd and Richerson (1992).
23. Boone (1992, 309).
24. Cox *et al.* (1999).
25. Skyrms (1996).
26. Skyrms (1996, 18-19).
27. Skyrms (1996, 61).
28. Bowles and Gintis (1998).
29. Bowles and Gintis (1998, 22).
30. Maynard Smith (1982).
31. Young (1998).
32. Young's approach amounts, in many respects, to a mathematical specification of the structuration and practice theory assumptions of the sociologists Anthony Giddens (eg. 1984) and Pierre Bourdieu (e.g. 1977) who have been very influential in archaeology.
33. Young (1998, 6).
34. Young (1998, 19).
35. Bowles (in press a).
36. Bowles and Hopfensitz (2000).
37. Kelly (1985).
38. Renfrew and Cherry (1986).
39. Trigger (1998, 120), citing Hallpike (1986, 75-76).
40. Service (1962).
41. Fried (1967).
42. Sahlins (1972).
43. See e.g. Wilmsen (1989), Wilmsen and Denbow (1990), Shott (1992), Kent (1993).

44. E.g. Foley and Lee (1989, 1996), Foley (1996).

45. The term 'hominin' has replaced the traditional term 'hominid' as part of an overhaul of taxonomic terms.

46. E.g. Aiello and Wheeler (1995), Ruff and Walker (1993).

47. Foley (1996, 106).

48. Kaplan et al. (2000).

49. Hames (2000).

50. Sugiyama and Chacon (2000).

51. Blurton-Jones (1984).

52. See e.g. Aldenderfer (1993).

53. Whitley (1994).

54. E.g. Steward (1936a, 1938).

55. Whitley (1994, 366-367).

56. Riches (1992).

57. Shennan (1996), and see again Aldenderfer (1993). Given the obliqueness of cultural transmission this raises the question of whether such competition could lead in a different direction from reproductive success, even if this does not seem to be the case for Whitley's study.

58. Boone and Kessler (1999, 270).

59. Boone and Kessler (1999, 271).

60. Boone and Kessler (1999, 262-265).

61. Boone and Kessler (1999, 270).

62. Zahavi (1975).

63. Sugiyama and Chacon (2000).

64. Sugiyama and Chacon (2000, 388).

65. Owens and Hayden (1997).

66. Transegalitarian foragers are often also referred to as complex hunter-gatherers. They are societies which are usually at least partly sedentary, where there is evidence of social differentiation, often based on the differential control of resources, intermediate between strictly egalitarian societies and politically stratified chiefdoms (Hayden 1998).

67. Owens and Hayden (1997, 153).

68. Of course this is not true of the carcasses themselves which are in principle ownable in this way. As we have seen though, they are a strictly short-term asset, with a diminishing usefulness for each extra unit beyond a certain point.

69. Boone (1992).

70. Boone (1992, 316).

71. Boone (1992, 317).

72. Cf. Mann (1986).

73. See e.g. Krebs and Davies (1993, 151-155).

74. Rogers (1995).

75. Rogers (1995, 92).

76. Rogers (1995, 94).

77. Mace (1997).

78. Mace (1997, 395).

79. See again Betzig (1986).

80. Bowles (in press b).

81. Hayden (1997).

82. Hayden et al. (1996).

83. Hayden (1997, 259).

84. See Bar-Yosef (1998).

CHAPTER 9 (pages 239–261)

1. Bowles and Gintis (1998).

2. Soltis et al. (1995).

3. Soltis et al. (1995, 474).

4. Soltis et al. (1995, 481).

5. Smuts (1999, 323).

6. Boone (1992, 329).

7. Patton (2000).

8. Soltis et al. (1995, 479-480).

9. Barth (1971).

10. Barth (1971, 186), cited in Soltis et al. (1995, 480).

11. See e.g. Keeley (1996), Martin and Frayer (1997), Maschner and Reedy-Maschner (1998), Petrasch (1999), Guilaine and Zammit (2001), Walker (2001).

12. Wrangham (1999).

13. Wrangham (1999, 22).

14. Gat (1999).

15. Chagnon (1988).

16. Although clearly the first of these represents the most direct source of evidence, and it should not be assumed automatically that the incidence of an iconography emphasizing weapons in the archaeological record and the incidence of violent injury automatically correlate with one another. Robb's (1997) study of the skeletal evidence for violence in prehistoric Italy suggested that it decreased during the Eneolithic, precisely the time when we see an increasing emphasis on the association between weapons and males in contemporary iconography and grave goods.

17. Kennett and Kennett (2000).

18. Debate about whether the spread of the Linear Pottery Culture (Linearbandkeramik) represents a colonization by expanding groups of farmers or the adoption of an agricultural way of life by local foragers continues. Compare, for example, Jochim (2000) with Bogucki (2000). In my view the evidence favours the colonization argument. Evidence of local foragers adopting pottery and interacting with the incoming farmers may be seen in the presence of sites with pottery of a style called La Hoguette, after the site in Normandy where it was first found, and the

existence of small quantities of La Hoguette pottery on early Linear Pottery sites in the western part of the Linear Pottery distribution. Most recently, stable isotope studies of human bones and teeth have suggested that a considerable proportion of the population of early Linear Pottery cemeteries in southern Germany must have migrated into the area from elsewhere (Price *et al.* 2001).

19. See again Lüning and Stehli (1994), Kalis and Zimmermann (1997).
20. Wahl and König (1987).
21. See Teschler-Nicola *et al.* (1999), Petrasch (1999).
22. Zimmermann (1995).
23. See Stehli (1994), Frirdich (1994).
24. Shennan and Wilkinson (2001).
25. See the discussion of this issue in Chapters 3 and 4.
26. Frirdich (1994, 355).
27. Collard and Shennan (2000).
28. Gat (1999).
29. Neiman (1997).
30. See e.g. Shennan (1993b).
31. Robb (1994).
32. Robb (1994).
33. Flannery and Marcus (2000, 30).
34. Wright (1939).
35. As Flannery and Marcus point out, the process they describe and the process they evoke to explain it correspond closely to Colin Renfrew's 'peer polity interaction' model. It was also noted in the previous chapter that this can also be seen to fit in well with Peyton Young's model of social institutions as game conventions giving best pay-offs, where conventions giving better pay-offs are likely to spread.
36. See e.g. Lansing (2000).

37. See e.g. Cameron and Toll (2001).
38. Johnson (1989).
39. Kohler and van West (1996).
40. Ladefoged and Graves (2000).
41. Ladefoged and Graves (2000, 427).
42. Richerson and Boyd (1999).
43. Tainter (1988).

CHAPTER 10 (pages 262–271)

1. Moore (2000).
2. Dennett (1995, 80-83). He also quotes Dawkins (1982, 113): 'Reductionism is a dirty word, and a kind of 'holistier than thou' self-righteousness has become fashionable.'
3. Hull (1980).
4. Again it is worth noting that the demographic transition has not necessarily changed this long-standing pattern, as the work of Kaplan (1996) and Mace (2000) discussed in Chapter 5 makes clear. The key issue is the scale of investment in offspring required for them to become successful adults, and the fact that the returns on such investment are not necessarily the same for different social groups.
5. Laland *et al.* (2000).
6. Avital and Jablonka (2000).
7. Price *et al.* (2001).
8. Sherry *et al.* (1994).
9. Kirch and Green (2001).
10. Ross (1997). See also now Mufwene (2001).
11. Pétrequin (1993); see also Pétrequin *et al.* (1999), Wolf (1993).
12. Seielstad *et al.* (1998).
13. See again Price *et al.* (2001); also Schulting and Richards (2001).
14. *Cf.* Hastorf (1991).
15. Hayden (1997).
16. Ladefoged and Graves (2000).
17. Darwin (1859 [1996, 395]).

BIBLIOGRAPHY

Aiello, L. and P. Wheeler 1995. The expensive
tissue hypothesis. *Current Anthropology* 36,
199-`222.

Aldenderfer, M. 1993. Ritual, hierarchy and
change in foraging societies. *Journal of
Anthropological Archaeology* 12, 1–40.

Altman, J. C. 1987. *Hunter Gatherers Today: An
Aboriginal Economy in North Australia*.
Canberra: Australian Institute of Aboriginal
Studies.

Alvard, M. 1995. Intraspecific prey choice by
Amazonian hunters. *Current Anthropology* 36,
789–818.

—— 1998. Evolutionary ecology and resource
conservation. *Evolutionary Anthropology* 7,
62–74.

Ambrose, S. 1998. Late Pleistocene human
population bottlenecks, volcanic winter, and
differentiation of modern humans. *Journal of
Human Evolution* 34, 623–651.

Ammerman, A. J. and L. L. Cavalli-Sforza
1984. *The Neolithic Transition and the Genetics
of Populations in Europe*. Princeton: Princeton
University Press.

Arbogast, R. M., V. Beugnier, N. Delattre, F.
Giligny, A. Maitre, A. M. Pétrequin, and P.
Pétrequin 1997. La répartition des témoins et
le fonctionnement de la cellule domestique. In
P. Pétrequin (ed.), *Les Sites Littoraux
Néolithiques de Clairvaux-Les-Lacs et de
Chalain (Jura) III. Chalain station 3,
3200–2900 av. J.-C.*, pp. 583–639. Paris:
Éditions de la Maison des Sciences de
l'Homme.

Arbogast, R. M., M. Magny, and P. Pétrequin
1996. Climat, cultures céréalières et densité
de population au néolithique: le cas des lacs
du Jura français de 3500 à 2500 av. J.-C.
Archäologisches Korrespondenzblatt 26,
121–144.

Arnold, D .E. 1989. Patterns of learning,
residence and descent among potters in Ticul,
Yucatan, Mexico. In S. J. Shennan (ed.),
Archaeological Approaches to Cultural Identity,
pp. 174–184. London: Unwin Hyman.

Aunger, R. n.d. Exposure versus susceptibility
in the epidemiology of 'everyday' beliefs.
Unpublished paper.

Avital, E. and E. Jablonka 2000. *Animal
Traditions: Behavioural Inheritance in
Evolution*. Cambridge: Cambridge University
Press.

Axelrod, R. 1984. *The Evolution of Cooperation*.
New York: Basic Books.

Barbujani, G. and G. Bertorelle 2001. Genetics
and the population history of Europe.
*Proceedings of the National Academy of Sciences
USA* 98, 22–25.

Barth, F. 1971. Tribes and intertribal relations
in the Fly headwaters. *Oceania* 41, 171–191.

—— 1987. *Cosmologies in the Making: A
Generative Approach to Cultural Variation in
Inner New Guinea*. Cambridge: Cambridge
University Press.

Bar-Yosef, O. 1998. The Natufian culture in the
Levant, threshold to the origins of
agriculture. *Evolutionary Anthropology* 6,
159–177.

Basgall, M. 1987. Resource intensification
among hunter-gatherers: acorn economies in
prehistoric California. *Research in Economic
Anthropology* 9, 21–52.

Bellwood, P. 1997. Prehistoric cultural
explanations for widespread language
families. In P. McConvell and N. Evans (eds.),
Archaeology and Linguistics, pp. 123–134.
Melbourne: Oxford University Press.

Belovsky, G. 1988. An optimal foraging–based
model of hunter–gatherer population
dynamics. *Journal of Anthropological
Archaeology* 7, 329–372.

Bettinger, R. L. 1998. Comment on M.
Rosenberg, Cheating at musical chairs:
territoriality and sedentism in an evolutionary
context. *Current Anthropology* 39, 665–666.

Bettinger, R. L. and J. Eerkens 1999. Point
typologies, cultural transmission, and the
spread of bow-and-arrow technology in the
prehistoric Great Basin. *American Antiquity*
64, 231–242.

Betzig, L. 1986. *Despotism and Differential
Reproduction: A Darwinian View of History*.
New York: Aldine.

Billamboz, A. 1995. Proxyséries
dendrochronologiques et occupation
néolithique des bords du lac de Constance.
Palynosciences 3, 69–81.

Binford, L. R. 1962. Archaeology as
anthropology. *American Antiquity* 28,
217–225.

—— 1968. Post-Pleistocene adaptations. In S.
R. and L. R. Binford (eds.), *New Perspectives
in Archaeology*, pp. 313–341. Chicago: Aldine.

—— 1972a. *An Archaeological Perspective*. New
York: Seminar Press.

—— 1972b. Contemporary model building:
paradigms and the current state of
Palaeolithic research. In D. L. Clarke (ed.),
Models in Archaeology, pp. 109–166. London:
Methuen.

—— 1983. *In Pursuit of the Past: Decoding the Archaeological Record*. London and New York: Thames and Hudson.

Birkhead, T. R. and A. P. Møller 1992. *Sperm Competition in Birds: Causes and Consequences*. London: Academic Press.

Blackmore, S. 1999. *The Meme Machine*. Oxford: Oxford University Press.

Blanton, R. E. 1998. Beyond centralization: steps toward a theory of egalitarian behavior in archaic states. In G.M Feinman and J. Marcus (eds.), *Archaic States*, pp. 135–172 Santa Fe, New Mexico: School of American Research Press.

Blurton-Jones, N. 1984. A selfish origin for human food sharing: tolerated theft. *Ethology and Sociobiology* 5, 1–3.

Blurton-Jones, N., F. W. Marlowe, K. Hawkes, and J. F. O'Connell 2000. Parental investment and hunter–gatherer divorce rates. In L. Cronk, N. Chagnon, and W. Irons (eds.), *Adaptation and Human Behavior*, pp. 69–90. New York: Aldine de Gruyter.

Boesch, C. 1993. Aspects of transmission of tool use in wild chimpanzees. In K. R. Gibson and T. Ingold (eds.), *Tools, Language and Cognition in Human Evolution*, pp. 171–183. Cambridge: Cambridge University Press.

Bogucki, P. 1993. Animal traction and household economies in Neolithic Europe. *Antiquity* 67, 492–503.

—— 2000. How agriculture came to north-central Europe. In T. D. Price (ed.), *Europe's First Farmers*, pp. 197–218. Cambridge: Cambridge University Press.

Boone, J. L. 1986. Parental investment and elite family structure in preindustrial states: a case study of late medieval-early modern Portuguese genealogies. *American Anthropologist* 88, 859–878.

—— 1992. Competition, conflict and development of social hierarchies. In E. A. Smith and B. Winterhalder (eds.), *Evolutionary Ecology and Human Behavior*, pp. 301–338. New York: Aldine de Gruyter.

—— in press. Subsistence strategies and early human population history: an evolutionary ecological perspective. *World Archaeology* 34.

Boone, J. L. and K. L. Kessler 1999. More status or more children? Social status, fertility reduction, and long-term fitness. *Evolution and Human Behaviour* 20, 257–277.

Boone, J. L. and E. A. Smith 1998. Is it evolution yet? A critique of evolutionary archaeology. *Current Anthropology* 39, S141–174.

Borgerhoff-Mulder, M. 1990. Kipsigis women's preferences for wealthy men: evidence for female choice in mammals. *Behavioral Ecology and Sociobiology* 27, 255–264.

—— 1992. Reproductive decisions. In E. A. Smith and B. Winterhalder (eds.), *Evolutionary Ecology and Human Behavior*, pp. 339–374. New York: Aldine de Gruyter.

—— 1996. Responses to environmental novelty: changes in men's marriage strategies in a rural Kenyan community. *Proceedings of the British Academy* 88, 203–222.

Boserup, E. 1965. *The Conditions of Agricultural Growth: The Economics of Agrarian Change under Population Pressure*. Chicago: Aldine.

Bourdieu, P. 1977. *Outline of a Theory of Practice*. Cambridge: Cambridge University Press.

Bowles, S. in press a. Individual interactions, group conflicts and the evolution of preferences. In S. Durlauf and P. Young (eds.), *Social Dynamics*. Cambridge, Mass: MIT Press.

—— in press b. *Ecomonic Behavior and Institutions: An Evolutionary Approach to Microeconomics*. Princeton: Princeton University Press.

Bowles, S. and H. Gintis 1998. The moral economy of community: structured populations and the evolution of pro-social norms. *Evolution and Human Behaviour* 19, 3–25.

Bowles, S. and A. Hopfensitz 2000. The co-evolution of individual behaviors and social institutions. *Santa Fe Institute Working Papers* 00–12–073.

Box, H. O. and K. R. Gibson (eds.) 1999. *Mammalian Social Learning. Comparative and Ecological Perspectives*. Cambridge: Cambridge University Press.

Boyd, R., M. Borgerhoff-Mulder, W. H. Durham, and P. J. Richerson 1997. Are cultural phylogenies possible? In P. Weingart, S. D. Mitchell, P. J. Richerson, and S. Maasen (eds.), *Human By Nature*, pp. 355–386. Mahwah, NJ: Lawrence Erlbaum.

Boyd, R. and P. J. Richerson 1985. *Culture and the Evolutionary Process*. Chicago: University of Chicago Press.

—— 1988a. An evolutionary model of social learning: the effects of spatial and temporal variation. In T .R. Zentall and B. G. Galef (eds.), *Social Learning: Psychological and Biological Perspectives*, pp. 29–48. Hillsdale NJ: Lawrence Erlbaum.

—— 1988b. The evolution of reciprocity in sizeable groups. *Journal of Theoretical Biology* 132, 337–356.

—— 1992. Punishment allows the evolution of cooperation (or anything else) in sizeable groups. *Ethology and Sociobiology* 13, 171–195.

—— 1996. Why culture is common but cultural evolution is rare. *Proceedings of the British Academy* 88, 77–93.

—— 2001. Memes: universal acid or a better mouse trap. In R. Aunger (ed.), *Darwinizing Culture: The Status of Memetics as a Science*, pp. 143–162. Oxford: Oxford University Press.

Bradley, R. 1993. Archaeology: the loss of nerve. In N. Yoffee and A. Sherratt (eds.), *Archaeological Theory: Who Sets the Agenda?*, pp. 131–133. Cambridge: Cambridge University Press.

Brew, J. O. 1946. Archaeology of Alkali Ridge, southeastern Utah. *Peabody Museum of American Archaeology and Ethnology, Papers* 21. Cambridge, Mass.

Bright, J. W., A. Ugan, and L. Hunsaker in press. Effect of handling time on subsistence technology. *World Archaeology* 34.

Brockway, G. P. 1993. *The End of Economic Man.* New York: Norton.

Broodbank, C. 2000. *An Island Archaeology of the Cyclades.* Cambridge: Cambridge University Press.

Broughton, J. M. 1997. Widening diet breadth, declining foraging efficiency, and prehistoric harvest pressure: ichthyofaunal evidence from the Emeryville Shellmound, California. *Antiquity* 71, 845–862.

Brown, D. E. 1991. *Human Universals.* New York: McGraw Hill.

Buikstra, J. M., L. W. Konigsberg, and J. Bullington 1986. Fertility and the development of agriculture in the prehistoric Midwest. *American Antiquity* 51, 528–546.

Buss, D. M. 1989. Sex differences in human mate preferences: evolutionary hypotheses tested in 37 cultures. *Behavioral and Brain Sciences* 12, 1–49.

—— 1994. *The Evolution of Desire: Strategies of Human Mating.* New York: Basic Books.

Butler, V. L. 2000. Resource depression on the northwest coast of North America. *Antiquity* 74, 649–661.

Cameron, C.M. and H.W. Toll 2001. Deciphering the organization of production in Chaco Canyon. *American Antiquity* 66, 5–13.

Carneiro, R. L. 1970. A theory of the origin of the state. *Science* 169, 733–738.

Cashdan, E. 1996. Women's mating strategies. *Evolutionary Anthropology* 5, 134–143.

Cauvin, J. 2000. *The Birth of the Gods and the Origins of Agriculture.* Cambridge: Cambridge University Press.

Cavalli-Sforza, L. L. and F. Cavalli-Sforza 1995. *The Great Human Diasporas: The History of Diversity and Evolution.* Reading, Mass: Addison-Wesley.

Cavalli-Sforza, L. L. and M. W. Feldman 1981. *Cultural Transmission and Evolution: A Quantitative Approach.* Princeton: Princeton University Press.

Chagnon, N. 1988. Life histories, blood revenge and warfare in a tribal population. *Science* 239, 985–992.

Charnov, E. L. 1993. *Life History Invariants.* Oxford: Oxford University Press.

Chikhi, L., R. A. Nichols, G. Barbujani, and M.A. Beaumont n.d. Y genetic data support the Neolithic Demic Diffusion Model. Unpublished paper.

Childe, V. G. 1958. *The Prehistory of European Society: How and Why the Prehistoric Barbarian Societies of Europe Behaved in a Distinctively European Way.* Harmondsworth, Middlesex: Penguin.

Chisholm, M. 1962. *Rural Settlement and Land Use: An Essay in Location.* London: Hutchinson.

Clark, J. G. D. 1954. *Excavations at Star Carr. An Early Mesolithic Site at Seamer near Scarborough, Yorkshire.* Cambridge: Cambridge University Press.

Clarke, D. L. 1968. *Analytical Archaeology.* London: Methuen.

Collard, M. and S. J. Shennan 2000. Processes of culture change in prehistory: a case study from the European Neolithic. In C. Renfrew and K. Boyle (eds.), *Archaeogenetics: DNA and the Population Prehistory of Europe*, pp. 89–97. Cambridge: McDonald Institute for Archaeological Research.

Conkey, M. W. and J. M. Gero 1997. Programme to practice: gender and feminism in archaeology. *Annual Review of Anthropology* 26, 411–437.

Cowgill, G. L. 1975. On the causes and consequences of ancient population change. *American Anthropologist.*

Cox, S. J., T. J. Sluckin, and J. Steele 1999. Group size, memory, and interaction rate in the evolution of cooperation. *Current Anthropology* 40, 369–376.

Cronk, L. 2000. Female-biased parental investment and growth performance among the Mukogodo. In L. Cronk, N. Chagnon, and W. Irons (eds.), *Adaptation and Human Behavior*, pp. 203–222. New York: Aldine de Gruyter.

Crosby, A. W. 1986. *Ecological Imperialism: The Biological Expansion of Europe, 900–1900.* Cambridge: Cambridge University Press.

Cullen, B. 1995. Living artefact, personal ecosystem, biocultural schizophrenia and post–processual thinking. *Proceedings of the Prehistoric Society* 63, 69–90.

—— 1996a. Social interaction and viral phenomena. In J. Steele and S. J. Shennan (eds.), *The Archaeology of Human Ancestry: Power, Sex and Tradition*, pp. 420–433. London: Routledge.

—— 1996. Cultural virus theory and the eusocial pottery assemblage. In H. Maschner (ed.), *Darwinian Archaeologies*, pp. 43–59. New York: Plenum.

Darwin, C. 1859 (1996). *The Origin of Species*. Oxford: Oxford University Press.

David, B. and H. Lourandos 1998. Rock art and socio-demography in northeastern Australian prehistory. *World Archaeology* 30, 193–219.

Dawkins, R. 1976. *The Selfish Gene*. Oxford: Oxford University Press.

—— 1982. *The Extended Phenotype*. Oxford: W.H. Freeman.

Deetz, J. 1965. *The Dynamics of Stylistic Change in Arikara Ceramics*. Urbana: University of Illinois Press.

Degler, C. 1991. *In Search of Human Nature*. Oxford: Oxford University Press.

Delneuf, M. 1991. Un champ particulier de l'experimentation en céramique: les ateliers de poterie traditionelle du Nord-Cameroun. In *25 Ans d'Études Technologiques en Préhistoire* (XI Rencontres Internationales d'Archéologie et d'Histoire Antibes), pp. 65–82. Juan-les-Pins: Éditions APDCA.

Dennett, D. 1995. *Darwin's Dangerous Idea*. London: Allen Lane, The Penguin Press.

Diamond, J. 1987. Bower building and decoration by the bowerbird *Amblyornis inornatus*. *Ethology* 74, 177–204.

Diamond, J. M. 1997. *Guns, Germs and Steel: A Short History of Everybody for the Last 13,000 Years*. London: Chatto and Windus.

Diaz-Andreu, M. and T. C. Champion (eds.) 1996. *Nationalism and Archaeology in Europe*. London: UCL Press.

Dickemann, M. 1981. Paternal confidence and dowry competition: a biocultural analysis of purdah. In R. D. Alexander and D. W. Tinkle (eds.), *Natural Selection and Social Behaviour*, pp. 417–438. New York: Chrion Press.

Dixon, R. M. W. 1997. *The Rise and Fall of Languages*. Cambridge: Cambridge University Press.

Dole, G. 1993. Homogeneidade e diversidade no Alto Xingu vistas a partir dos cuicuros. In V. Penteado Coelho (ed.), *Karl von dem Steinem: Un Século de Antropologia no Xingu*, pp. 377–403. São Paulo: Edusp.

Douglas, M. 1978. *Cultural Bias*. London: Royal Anthropological Institute.

Draper, P. 1997. Institutional, evolutionary and demographic contexts of gender roles: a case study of !Kung Bushmen. In M. E. Morbeck,

A. Galloway, and A. Zihlman (eds.), *The Evolving Female*, pp. 220–232. Princeton: Princeton University Press.

Dunnell, R. 1978. Style and function: a fundamental dichotomy. *American Antiquity* 43, 192–202.

Durham, W. H. 1990. Advances in evolutionary culture theory. *Annual Review of Anthropology* 19, 187–210.

—— 1991. *Coevolution: Genes, Culture and Human Diversity*. Stanford: Stanford University Press.

—— 1992. Applications of evolutionary culture theory. *Annual Review of Anthropology* 21, 331–355.

Edelman, G. M. 1992. *Bright Air, Brilliant Fire. On the Matter of the Mind*. London: Allen Lane.

Edgerton, R. B. with W. Goldschmidt 1971. *The Individual in Cultural Adaptation: a Study of Four East African Peoples*. Berkeley: University of California Press.

Ehret, C. 1998. *An African Classical Age: Eastern and Southern African World History, 1000 BC to AD 400*. Charlottesville: University Press of Virginia.

Eldredge, N. and S. J. Gould 1972. Punctuated equilibria: an alternative to phyletic gradualism. In T. M. J. Schopf (ed.), *Models in Paleobiology*, pp. 82–115. San Francisco: Freeman, Cooper.

Engels, F. 1972. *The Origin of the Family, Private Property and the State*. London: Lawrence and Wishart, 1972.

Feinman, G. and J. Neitzel 1984. Too many types: an overview of sedentary prestate societies in the Americas. In M. Schiffer (ed.), *Advances in Archaeological Method and Theory*, 7, pp. 39–102. New York: Academic Press.

Fischer, D. H. 1996. *The Great Wave: Price Revolutions and the Rhythm of History*. Oxford: Oxford University Press.

Fisher, R. A. 1930. *The Genetical Theory of Natural Selection*. Oxford: The Clarendon Press.

—— 1958. *The Genetical Theory of Natural Selection* (2nd edition). New York: Dover.

Fitzhugh, B. 2001. Risk and invention in human technological evolution. *Journal of Anthropological Archaeology* 20, 125–167.

Fix, A. G. 1999. *Migration and Colonization in Human Microevolution*. Cambridge: Cambridge University Press.

Flannery, K. V. and J. Marcus 2000. Formative Mexican chiefdoms and the myth of the 'Mother Culture'. *Journal of Anthropological Archaeology* 19, 1–37.

Flinn, M. 1997. Culture and the evolution of

social learning. *Evolution and Human Behaviour* 18, 23–67.

Foley, R. A. 1996. An evolutionary and chronological framework for human social behaviour. *Proceedings of the British Academy* 88, 95–117.

Foley, R. A. and P.C. Lee 1989. Finite social space, evolutionary pathways and reconstructing hominid behaviour. *Science* 243, 901–906.

—— 1996. Finite social space and the evolution of human social behaviour. In J. Steele and S. J. Shennan (eds.), *The Archaeology of Human Ancestry: Power, Sex and Tradition*, pp. 47–66. London: Routledge.

Fried, M. 1967. *The Evolution of Political Society*, New York: Random House.

Frirdich, C. 1994. Kulturgeschichtliche Betrachtungen zur Bandkeramik im Merzbachtal. In J. Lüning and P. Stehli (eds.), *Die Bandkeramik im Merzbachtal auf der Aldenhovener Platte*, pp. 207–394. Bonn: Habelt.

Gallay, A. and L. Chaix 1984. *Le Site Préhistorique du Petit Chasseur, Vol 5, Le Dolmen M XI*. Lausanne: Cahiers d'Archéologie Romande 31.

Gamble, C. 1999. *The Palaeolithic Societies of Europe*. Cambridge: Cambridge University Press.

Gat, A. 1999. The pattern of fighting in simple, small-scale, prestate societies. *Journal of Anthropological Research* 55, 563–583.

Gaulin, S. J. and J. S. Boster 1990. Dowry as female competition. *American Anthropologist* 93, 994–1005.

Giddens, A. 1984. *The Constitution of Society*. Cambridge: Polity Press.

Gilchrist, R. 1999. *Gender and Archaeology*. London: Routledge.

Giles, A. 1999. Gender dynamics in the past: insights from a Darwinian study of human ornamentation. Unpublished M. A. dissertation, Institute of Archaeology, University College London.

Gimbutas, M. 1989. *The Language of the Goddess*. London: Thames and Hudson.

Gladwell, M. 2000. *The Tipping Point*. Boston: Little, Brown.

Godin, S. 2000. *Unleashing the Idea Virus*. New York: Simon and Schuster.

Goodenough, W. H. 1957. Oceania and the problem of controls in the study of cultural and human evolution. *Journal of the Polynesian Society* 66, 146–155.

Gosselain, O. P. 1992. Technology and style: potters and pottery among Bafia of Cameroon. *Man* (N.S.) 27, 559–586.

Gould, S. J. and R. C. Lewontin 1979. The spandrels of San Marco and the Panglossian paradigm: a critique of the adaptationist programme. *Proceedings of the Royal Society of London*, Series B, 205, 581–598.

Grafen, A. 1984. Natural selection, kin selection and group selection. In J. R. Krebs and N. B. Davies (eds.), *Behavioural Ecology: An Evolutionary Approach* (2nd edition), pp. 62–84. Oxford: Blackwell.

Gray, R. D. and F. M. Jordan 2000. Language trees support the express-train sequence of Austronesian expansion. *Nature* 405, 1052–1055.

Grayson, D. K. and F. Delpech 1998. Changing diet breadth in the Early Upper Palaeolithic of southwestern France. *Journal of Archaeological Science* 25, 1119–1129.

Gross, E., S. T. Jacomet, and J. Schibler 1990. Stand und Ziele der wirtschaftsarchäologischen Forschung an neolithischen Ufer- und Inselsiedlungen im unteren Zürichseeraum (Kt. Zürich, Schweiz). In J. Schibler, J. Sedlmaier, and H. Spycher (eds.), *Beiträge zur Archäozoologie, Archäologie, Anthropologie, Geologie und Paläontologie. Festschrift Hans R. Stampfli*, pp. 77–100. Basle: Helbing and Lichtenhahn Verlag.

Gross-Klee, E. and C. Maise 1997. Sonne, Vulkane und Seeufersiedlungen. *Jahrbuch der Schweizerischen Gesellschaft für Ur- und Frühgeschichte* 80, 85–94.

Guglielmino, C.R., C. Viganotti, B. Hewlett, and L. L. Cavalli-Sforza 1995. Cultural variation in Africa: role of mechanisms of transmission and adaptation. *Proceedings of the National Academy of Sciences, USA* 92, 585–589.

Guilaine, J. and J. Zammit 2001. *Le Sentier de la Guerre: Visages de la Violence Préhistorique*. Paris: Seuil.

Gurven, M., K. Hill, H. Kaplan, *et al.* 2000. Food transfers among Hiwi foragers of Venezuela: tests of reciprocity. *Human Ecology* 28, 171–218.

Hagelberg, E., M. Kayser, M. Nagy, L. Roewer, H. Zimdahl, M. Krawczak, P. Lio, and W. Schiefenhövel 1999. Molecular genetic evidence for the human settlement of the Pacific: analysis of mitochondrial DNA, Y chromosome and HLA markers. *Philosophical Transactions of the Royal Society of London B* 354, 141–152.

Haldane, J. B. S. 1953. Animal populations and their regulation. *Penguin Modern Biology* 15, 9–24.

Hallpike, C. 1986. *Principles of Social Evolution*. Oxford: Oxford University Press.

Halstead, P. and J. O'Shea (eds.) 1989. *Bad Year*

Economics. Cambridge: Cambridge University Press.

Hames, R. 2000. Reciprocal altruism in Yanomamö food exchange. In L. Cronk, N. Chagnon, and W. Irons (eds.), *Adaptation and Human Behaviour*, pp. 397–416. New York: Aldine de Gruyter.

Hamilton, W. D. 1964. The genetical evolution of social behaviour. I, II. *Journal of Theoretical Biology* 7, 1–52.

Hamilton, W. D. and M. Zuk 1982. Heritable true fitness and bright birds: a role for parasites? *Science* 218, 384–387.

Harner, M. 1977. The ecological basis for Aztec sacrifice. *American Ethnologist* 4, 117–132.

Harpending, H. 1997. Living records of past population change. In R. R. Paine (ed.), *Integrating Archaeological Demography: Multidisciplinary Approaches to Prehistoric Population*, pp. 89–100. Carbondale: Center for Archaeological Investigations, Southern Illinois University at Carbondale.

Harris, M. 1989. *Cows, Pigs, Wars and Witches*. New York: Vintage.

Hartung, J. 1985. Matrilineal inheritance: new theory and analysis. *Behavioral and Brain Sciences* 8, 661–688.

Harvey, P. H. and M. D. Pagel 1991. *The Comparative Method in Evolutionary Biology*. Oxford: Oxford University Press.

Hastorf, C. 1991. Gender, space and food in prehistory. In J. Gero and M. Conkey (eds.), *Engendering Archaeology*, pp. 132–162. Oxford: Blackwell.

Hauptmann, A. 1989. The earliest periods of copper metallurgy in Feinan, Jordan. In A. Hauptmann, E. Pernicka, and G. A. Wagner (eds.), *Old World Archaeometallurgy*, pp. 119–135. Bochum: Deutsche Bergbau-Museum.

Hawkes, K. 1990. Why do men hunt? Some benefits for risky strategies. In E. Cashdan (ed.), *Risk and Uncertainty in Tribal and Peasant Economies*, pp. 145–166. Boulder, CO: Westview Press.

—— 1992. Sharing and collective action. In E. A. Smith and B. Winterhalder (eds.), *Evolutionary Ecology and Human Behavior*, pp. 269–300. New York: Aldine de Gruyter.

Hawkes, K., J. F. O'Connell, N. Blurton-Jones, H. Alvarez, and E. L. Charnov 2000. The grandmother hypothesis and human evolution. In L. Cronk, N. Chagnon, and W. Irons (eds.), *Adaptation and Human Behavior*, pp. 237–258.

Hayden, B. 1997. Observations on the prehistoric social and economic structure of the North American Plateau. *World Archaeology* 29, 242–261.

—— 1998. Practical and prestige technologies: the evolution of material systems. *Journal of Archaeological Method and Theory* 5, 1–55.

Hayden, B., E. Bakewell, and R. Gargett 1996. The world's longest–lived corporate group: Lithic analysis reveals prehistoric social organization near Lillooet, British Columbia. *American Antiquity* 61, 341–356.

Hegmon M., M. C. Nelson, and M. J. Ennes 2000. Corrugated pottery, technological style, and population movement in the Mimbres region of the American southwest. *Journal of Anthropological Research* 56, 217–240.

Hennig, W. 1965. Phylogenetic systematics. *Annual Review of Entomology* 10, 97–116.

Herbich, I. 1987. Learning patterns, potter interaction and ceramic style among the Luo of Kenya. *African Archaeological Review* 5, 193–204.

Hewlett, B. S. 1991. Demography and child-care in preindustrial societies. *Journal of Anthropological Research* 47, 1–37.

Hewlett, B. S. and L. L. Cavalli-Sforza 1986. Cultural transmission among Aka pygmies. *American Anthropologist* 88, 922–934.

Heyes, C. M. and B. G. Galef (eds.) 1996. *Social Learning in Animals: The Roots of Culture*. San Diego: Academic Press.

Hill, K. and A. M. Hurtado 1996. *Ache Life History: the Ecology and Demography of a Foraging People*. New York: Aldine de Gruyter.

Hill, K. and H. Kaplan 1999. Life history traits in humans: theory and empirical studies. *Annual Review of Anthropology* 28, 397–430.

Hodder, I. (ed.) 1978. *The Spatial Organisation of Culture*. London: Duckworth.

Hodder, I. 1984. Post-processual archaeology. In M. B. Schiffer (ed.), *Advances in Archaeological Method and Theory* 8, pp. 1–26. Orlando: Academic Press.

Hrdy, S. B. 1999. *Mother Nature: A History of Mothers, Infants and Natural Selection*. New York: Pantheon Books.

Hull, D. L. 1980. Individuality and selection. *Annual Review of Ecology and Systematics* 11, 311–332.

—— 1988. *Science as a Process: An Evolutionary Account of the Social and Conceptual Development of Science*. Chicago: University of Chicago Press.

Hunt, R. C. 2000. Labor productivity and agricultural development: Boserup revisited. *Human Ecology* 28, 251–277.

Iovanovic, B. 1991. La metallurgie énéolithique du cuivre dans les Balkans. In J. P. Mohen and C. Eluère (eds.), *Découverte du Metal*, pp. 93–102. Paris: Picard.

Irons, W. 1979. Cultural and biological success.

In N. Chagnon and W. Irons (eds.), *Evolutionary Biology and Human Social Behavior: An Anthropological Perspective*, pp. 284–302. North Scituate, Mass: Duxbury Press.

—— 1998. Adaptively relevant environments versus the Environment of Evolutionary Adaptedness. *Evolutionary Anthropology* 6, 194–204.

—— 2000. Why do the Yomut raise more sons than daughters? In L. Cronk, N. Chagnon, and W. Irons (eds.), *Adaptation and Human Behaviour*, pp. 223–236. New York: Aldine de Gruyter.

Irons, W. and L. Cronk 2000. Two decades of a new paradigm. In L. Cronk, N. Chagnon, and W. Irons (eds.), *Adaptation and Human Behaviour*, pp. 3–26. New York: Aldine de Gruyter.

Jablonka, E. 2000. Lamarckian inheritance systems in biology: a source of metaphors and models in technological evolution. In J. Ziman (ed.), *Technological Innovation as an Evolutionary Process*, pp. 27–40. Cambridge: Cambridge University Press.

Jakes, M. A. 1988. Demographic change at the Mesolithic-Neolithic transition: evidence from Portugal. *Rivista di Antropologia* 66 (supplement), 141–158.

Janetski, J. C. 1997. Fremont hunting and resource intensification in the eastern Great Basin. *Journal of Archaeological Science* 24, 1075–1088.

Jarman, P. J. 1974. The social organization of antelope in relation to their ecology. *Behaviour* 48, 215–267.

Jochim, M. 2000. The origins of agriculture in south–central Europe. In T. D. Price (ed.), *Europe's First Farmers*, pp. 183–196. Cambridge: Cambridge University Press.

Jockenhövel, A. 1991. Räumliche Mobilität von Personen in der mittleren Bronzezeit des westlichen Mitteleuropa. *Germania* 69, 49–62.

Johnson, G.A. 1989. Dynamics of southwestern prehistory: far outside – looking in. In L. S. Cordell and G. J. Gumerman (eds.), *Dynamics of Southwest Prehistory*, pp. 371–389. Washington DC: Smithsonian Institution.

Jones, S. 1997. *The Archaeology of Identity: Constructing Identities in the Past and Present*. London: Routledge.

Jones, T. L., G. M. Brown, L. M. Raab, J. L. McVickar, W. G. Spaulding, D. J. Kennett, A. York, and P. L. Walker 1999. Environmental imperatives reconsidered: demographic crises in western North America during the Medieval climatic anomaly. *Current Anthropology* 40, 137–170.

Kacelnik, A. 1984. Central place foraging in starlings (*Sturnus vulgaris*). I. Patch residence time. *Journal of Animal Ecology* 53, 283–299.

Kaestle, F. A. and D. G. Smith 2001. Ancient mitochondrial DNA evidence for prehistoric population movement: the Numic Expansion. *American Journal of Physical Anthropology* 115, 1–12.

Kalis, J. and A. Zimmermann 1997. Anthropogene Einflüsse auf die Umwelt – Eine kanonische Korrespondenzanalyse von prähistorischen Pollenspektren. In J. Müller and A. Zimmermann (eds.), *Archäologie und Korrespondenzanalyse: Beispiele, Fragen, Perspektiven*. Espelkamp: Verlag Marie Leidorf.

Kaplan, H. 1996. A theory of fertility and parental investment in traditional and modern human societies. *Yearbook of Physical Anthropology* 39, 91–135.

Kaplan, H. and K. Hill 1985. Food sharing among Ache foragers: tests of explanatory hypotheses. *Current Anthropology* 26, 223–246.

—— 1992. The evolutionary ecology of food acquisition. In E. A. Smith and B. Winterhalder (eds.), *Evolutionary Ecology and Human Behavior*, pp. 167–202. New York: Aldine de Gruyter.

Kaplan, H., K. Hill, J. Lancaster, and A. M. Hurtado 2000. A theory of human life history evolution: diet, intelligence and longevity. *Evolutionary Anthropology* 9, 156–184.

Keckler, C. 1997. Catastrophic mortality in simulations of forager age-at-death: where did all the humans go? In R. R. Paine (ed.), *Integrating Archaeological Demography: Multidisciplinary Approaches to Prehistoric Population*, pp. 311–326. Carbondale, Illinois: Center for Archaeological Investigations.

Keeley, L. 1996. *War Before Civilisation*. New York: Oxford University Press.

Kelly, R. C. 1985. *The Nuer Conquest*. Ann Arbor: University of Michigan Press.

Kelly, R. L. 1995. *The Foraging Spectrum: Diversity in Hunter-Gatherer Lifeways*. Washington DC: Smithsonian Institution Press.

Kemenczei, T. 1991. *Die Schwerter in Ungarn. II. Vollgriffschwerter*. Munich: C. H. Beck.

Kennett, D. J. and J. P. Kennett 2000. Competitive and cooperative responses to climatic instability in coastal southern California. *American Antiquity* 65, 379–395.

Kent, S. 1993. Sharing in an egalitarian Kalahari community. *Man* (N.S.) 28, 479–514.

Key, C. A. 2000. The evolution of human life history. *World Archaeology* 31, 329–350.

Kimura, M. 1983. *The Neutral Theory of Molecular Evolution*. Cambridge: Cambridge University Press.

Kirch, P. V. 1984. *The Evolution of the Polynesian Chiefdoms*. Cambridge: Cambridge University Press.

Kirch, P. V. and R. C. Green 2001. *Hawaiki, Ancestral Polynesia: An Essay in Historical Anthropology*. Cambridge: Cambridge University Press.

Knapp, A. B. 1998. Who's come a long way, baby? Masculinist approaches to a gendered archaeology. *Archaeological Dialogues* 5, 91–125.

Kohl, P. L. 1998. Nationalism and archaeology: on the constructions of nations and the reconstructions of the remote past. *Annual Review of Anthropology* 27, 223–246.

Kohl, P .L. and C. Fawcett (eds.) 1995. *Nationalism, Politics and the Practice of Archaeology*. Cambridge: Cambridge University Press.

Kohler, T. A. and C. R. van West 1996. The calculus of self–interest in the development of cooperation: sociopolitical development and risk among the northern Anasazi. In J. A. Tainter and B. B. Tainter (eds.), *Evolving Complexity and Environment: Risk in the Prehistoric Southwest*, pp. 169–196. Reading, Mass: Addison–Wesley.

Kohn, M. and S. Mithen 1999. Handaxes: products of sexual selection? *Antiquity* 73, 518–526.

Krebs, J. R. and N. B. Davies 1993. *An Introduction to Behavioural Ecology*. Oxford: Blackwell.

Krings, M., A. Stone, R. W. Schmitz, H. Krainitzki, M. Stoneking, and S. Paabo 1997. Neanderthal DNA sequences and the origin of modern humans. *Cell* 90, 19–30.

Kroeber, A. L. 1931. The culture–area and age–area concepts of Clark Wissler. In S.A. Rice (ed.), *Methods in Social Science*, pp. 248–265. Chicago: University of Chicago Press.

Kuper, A. 1999. *Culture: The Anthropologists' Account*. Cambridge, Mass: Harvard University Press.

Lack, D. 1947. The significance of clutch size. *Ibis* 89, 302–352.

Ladefoged, T. N. and M. W. Graves 2000. Evolutionary theory and the historical development of dry-land agriculture in north Kohala, Hawai'i. *American Antiquity* 65, 423–448.

Lahr, M. M. and R. A. Foley 1998. Towards a theory of modern human origins: geography, demography and diversity in recent human evolution. *Yearbook of Physical Anthropology* 41, 137–176.

Lake, M. 1998. Digging for memes: the role of material objects in cultural evolution. In C. Renfrew and C. Scarre (eds.), *Cognition and Material Culture: The Archaeology of Symbolic Storage*, pp. 77–88. Cambridge: McDonald Institute for Archaeological Research.

Laland, K. N., J. Odling-Smee and M. W. Feldman 2000. Niche construction, biological evolution, and cultural change. *Behavioral and Brain Sciences* 23, 131–145.

Lansing, J. S. 2000. Anti–chaos, common property, and the emergence of cooperation. In T. A. Kohler and G. J. Gumerman (eds.), *Dynamics in Human and Primate Societies: Agent-based Modelling of Social and Spatial Processes*, pp. 207–224. New York: Oxford University Press.

Lesser, A. 1961. Social fields and the evolution of society. *Southwestern Journal of Anthropology* 17, 40–48.

Lipo, C. P., M. E. Madsen, R. C. Dunnell, and T. Hunt 1997. Population structure, transmission and frequency seriation. *Journal of Anthropological Archaeology* 16, 301–334.

Lloyd, E. A. in press. Units and levels of selection: an anatomy of the units of selection debates. In R. Singh, C. Krimbas, D. Paul, and J. Beatty (eds.), *Thinking about Evolution: Historical, Philosophical and Political Perspectives*. Cambridge: Cambridge University Press.

Low, B. S. 1979. Sexual selection and human ornamentation. In N. A. Chagnon and W. Irons (eds.), *Evolutionary Biology and Social Behaviour: An Anthropological Perspective*, pp. 462–487. North Scituate, Mass: Duxbury Press.

—— 1990. Sex, power and resources: ecological and social correlates of sex differences. *International Journal of Contemporary Sociology* 27, 49–71.

—— 2000. *Why Sex Matters: A Darwinian Look at Human Behaviour*. Princeton: Princeton University Press.

Lüning, J. and P. Stehli 1994. *Die Bandkeramik im Merzbachtal auf der Aldenhovener Platte*. Bonn: Habelt.

Lyman, R. L., M. J. O'Brien, and R. C. Dunnell 1997. *The Rise and Fall of Culture History*. New York: Plenum.

Mace, R. 1997. The co-evolution of human fertility and wealth inheritance strategies. *Philosophical Transactions of the Royal Society (London)*, Series B, 353, 389–397.

—— 2000. An adaptive model of human reproductive rate where wealth is inherited: why people have small families. In L. Cronk, N. Chagnon, and W. Irons (eds.), *Adaptation and Human Behavior*, pp. 261–282. New York: Aldine de Gruyter.

Mace, R. and C. Holden 1999. Evolutionary ecology and cross-cultural comparison: the case of matrilineality in sub-Saharan Africa. In P.C. Lee (ed.), *Comparative Primate Socioecology*, pp. 387–405 Cambridge: Cambridge University Press.

Mace, R. and M. D. Pagel 1994. The comparative method in anthropology. *Current Anthropology* 35, 549–564.

Maceachern, S. 1998. Scale, style and cultural variation: technological traditions in the northern Mandara mountains. In M. Stark (ed.), *The Archaeology of Social Boundaries*, pp. 107–131. Washington: Smithsonian Institution Press.

Macfarlane, A. and S. Harrison 2000. Technological evolution and involution: a preliminary comparison of Europe and Japan. In J. Ziman (ed.), *Technological Innovation as an Evolutionary Process*, pp. 77–89. Cambridge: Cambridge University Press.

Magny, M. 1993. Holocene fluctuations of lake levels in the French Jura and sub-Alpine ranges, and their implications for past general circulation patterns. *The Holocene* 3, 306–313.

Mainberger, M. 1998. *Das Moordorf von Reute*. Staufen: Teraqua CAP.

Maise, C. 1998. Archäoklimatologie – vom Einfluss nacheiszeitlicher Klimavariabilität in der Ur- und Frühgeschichte. *Jahrbuch der Schweizerischen Gesellschaft für Ur- und Frühgeschichte* 81, 197–235.

Mallory, J. P. 1989. *In Search of the Indo-Europeans: Language, Archaeology and Myth*. London and New York: Thames & Hudson.

Mann, M. 1986. *The Sources of Social Power* (Vol. 1). Cambridge: Cambridge University Press.

Mannino, M. A. and K. D. Thomas in press. Intensive Mesolithic exploitation of coastal resources? Evidence from a shell deposit on the Isle of Portland (southern England) for the impact of human foraging on populations of inter-tidal rocky shore molluscs. *Journal of Archaeological Science*.

Martin, D. and D. Frayer (eds.) 1997. *Troubled Times: Violence and Warfare in the Past*. Toronto: Gordon and Breach.

Maschner, H. D. G. and K. L. Reedy-Maschner 1998. Raid, retreat, defend (repeat): the archaeology and ethnohistory of warfare on the North Pacific Rim. *Journal of Anthropological Archaeology* 17, 19–51.

Matson, R. G., W. D. Lipe and W. R. Haase IV 1988. Adaptational continuities and occupational discontinuities: the Cedar Mesa Anasazi. *Journal of Field Archaeology* 15, 245–264.

Maynard Smith, J. 1982. *Evolution and the Theory of Games*. Cambridge: Cambridge University Press.

Maynard Smith, J. and E. Szathmary 1995. *The Major Transitions in Evolution*. Oxford: W.H. Freeman.

Meiklejohn, C., J. M. Wyman, K. Jacobs, and M. K. Jackes 1997. Issues in the archaeological demography of the agricultural transition in Western and Northern Europe: a view from the Mesolithic. In R. R. Paine (ed.), *Integrating Archaeological Demography: Multidisciplinary Approaches to Prehistoric Population*, pp. 311–326. Carbondale, Illinois: Center for Archaeological Investigations.

Mithen, S. 1989. Evolutionary theory and post-processual archaeology. *Antiquity* 63, 483–494.

—— 1990. *Thoughtful Foragers*. Cambridge: Cambridge University Press.

—— 1996. *The Prehistory of the Mind*. London and New York: Thames & Hudson.

—— 1999. Imitation and cultural change: a view from the Stone Age, with specific reference to the manufacture of handaxes. In H. O. Box and K. R. Gibson (eds.), *Mammalian Social Learning: Comparative and Ecological Perspectives*, pp. 389–400. Cambridge: Cambridge University Press.

Møller, A. P. and R. Thornhill 1998. Bilateral symmetry and sexual selection: a meta-analysis. *American Naturalist* 151, 174–192.

Moore, H. 2000. Ethics and ontology: why agents and agency matter. In M. A. Dobres and J. Robb (eds.), *Agency and Archaeology*, pp. 259–263. London: Routledge.

Moore, J. H. 1994. Putting anthropology back together again: the ethnogenetic critique of cladistic theory. *American Anthropologist* 96, 925–948.

Moore, O. 1965. Divination – a new perspective. *American Anthropologist* 59, 69–74.

Morelli, G. 1997. Growing up female in a farmer community and a forager community. In M. E. Morbeck, A. Galloway, and A. Zihlman (eds.), *The Evolving Female*, pp. 209–219. Princeton: Princeton University Press.

Mufwene, S. S. 2001. *The Ecology of Language Evolution*. Cambridge: Cambridge University Press.

Murdock, G. P. and C. Provost 1973. Factors in the division of labor by sex. *Ethnology* 12, 203–225.

Nagaoka, L. in press. Explaining subsistence change in southern New Zealand using foraging theory models. *World Archaeology* 34.

Neel, J. V. 1978. The population structure of an Amerindian tribe, the Yanomama. *Annual Review of Genetics* 12, 365–413.

Neiman, F. D. 1995. Stylistic variation in evolutionary perspective: inferences from decorative diversity and inter–assemblage distance in Illinois Woodland ceramic assemblages. *American Antiquity* 60, 7–36.

—— 1997. Conspicuous consumption as wasteful advertising: a Darwinian perspective on spatial patterns in Classic Maya terminal monument dates. In C. M. Barton and G. A. Clark (eds.), *Rediscovering Darwin: Evolutionary Theory in Archaeological Explanation*, pp. 267–290. Arlington, Virginia: American Anthropological Association.

Nesse, R. M. and G. C. Williams 1996. *Evolution and Healing: The New Science of Darwinian Medicine*. London: Phoenix.

Neustupný, E. 1967. *The Beginnings of Patriarchy in Central Europe* (Czech). (Rozpravy Ceskoslovenské Akadémie Věd, Rada Společenskych Věd 77 [2]). Prague: Academia.

Neves, E.G. 1995. Village fissioning in Amazonia: a critique of monocausal determinism. *Revista do Museu de Arqueologia e Etnologia Sao Paulo* 5: 195–209.

Nicolis, F. 1998. Alla periferia dell' impero: il bicchiere campaniforme nell' Italia settentrionale. In F. Nicolis and E. Mottes (eds.), *Il Bicchiere Campaniforme e l'Italia Nella Preistoria Europea del III Millennio a.C*, pp. 46–68. Trento: Provincia Autonoma di Trento, Servizio Beni Culturali.

O'Brien, M. J. and R. L. Lyman 2000. *Applying Evolutionary Archaeology*. New York: Plenum.

O'Connell, J. and K. Hawkes 1981. Alyawara plant use and optimal foraging theory. In E. Smith and B. Winterhalder (eds.), *Hunter-Gatherer Foraging Strategies*, pp. 99–125. Chicago: University of Chicago Press.

Odling–Smee, J., K. N. Laland, and M.W. Feldman 1996. Niche construction. *American Naturalist* 147, 641–648.

O'Hear, A. 1986. Pottery making in Ilorin: a study of the decorated water cooler. *Africa* 56: 175–192.

Ortman, S. 2000. Conceptual metaphor in the archaeological record: methods and an example from the American Southwest. *American Antiquity* 65, 613–645.

Owens, D. and B. Hayden 1997. Prehistoric rites of passage: a comparative study of transegalitarian hunter-gatherers. *Journal of Anthropological Archaeology* 16, 121–161.

Palmer, C. 1998. 'Following the plough': the agricultural environment of northern Jordan. *Levant* 30, 129–165.

Patton, J. Q. 2000. Reciprocal altruism and warfare: a case from the Ecuadorian Amazon. In L. Cronk, N. Chagnon, and W. Irons (eds.), *Adaptation and Human Behavior*, pp. 417–436. New York: Aldine de Gruyter.

Payne, R. 1996. Song traditions in Indigo Buntings: origin, improvisation, dispersal and extinction in cultural evolution. In D.E. Kroodsma and E. H. Miller (eds.), *Ecology and Evolution of Acoustic Communication in Birds*, pp. 198–220. Ithaca: Cornell University Press.

Peltenburg, E., S. Colledge, P. Croft, A. Jackson, C. McCartney, and M. A. Murray 2001. Neolithic dispersals from the Levantine corridor: a Mediterranean perspective. *Levant* 33, 35–64.

Pennington, R. 1996. Causes of early human population growth. *American Journal of Physical Anthropology* 99, 259–274.

Petrasch, J. 1999. Mord und Krieg in der Bandkeramik. *Archäologisches Korrespondenzblatt* 29, 505–516.

Pétrequin, P. 1993. North wind, south wind: Neolithic technological choices in the Jura Mountains, 3700–2400 BC. In P. Lemonnier (ed.), *Technological Choices*, pp. 36–76. London: Routledge.

—— 1997. Management of architectural woods and variations in population density in the fourth and third millennia BC (Lakes Chalain and Clairvaux, Jura, France). *Journal of Anthropological Archaeology* 15, 1–19.

Pétrequin, P., R. M. Arbogast, C. Bourquin-Mignot, C. Lavier, and A. Viellet 1998. Demographic growth, environmental changes and technical adaptations: responses of an agricultural community from the 32nd to the 30th centuries BC. *World Archaeology* 30, 181–192.

Pétrequin, P. and A.M. Pétrequin 1988. *Le Néolithique des Lacs*. Paris: Errance.

—— 1999. La poterie en Nouvelle-Guinée: savoir-faire et transmission des techniques. *Journal de la Société des Océanistes* 108, 71–101.

Pétrequin, P., A. Viellet, and N. Illert 1999. Le Néolithique au nord-ouest des Alpes: rythmes lents de l'habitat, rythmes rapides des techniques et des styles? In F. Braemer, S. Cleuziou, and A. Coudart (eds.), *Habitat et Société* (XIXe Recontres Internationales d'Archéologie et d'Histoire d'Antibes), pp. 297–323. Antibes: Éditions APDCA.

Pinçon, B. and D. Ngöie-Ngalla 1990. L'unité culturelle Kongo à la fin du XIXe siècle. L'apport des études céramologiques. *Cahiers d'Études Africaines* 118, XXX–2: 157–178.

Pitt-Rivers, A. L.-F. 1875. On the principles of classification adopted in the arrangement of his anthropological collection, now exhibited in the Bethnal Green Museum. *Journal of the Anthropological Institute of Great Britain and Ireland* 4, 293–308.

Plotkin, H. 1997. *Evolution in Mind: An Introduction to Evolutionary Psychology*. London: Penguin.

Porcasi, J. F., T. L. Jones, and L. M. Raab 2000. Trans-Holocene marine mammal exploitation on San Clemente Island, California: a tragedy of the commons revisited. *Journal of Anthropological Archaeology* 19, 200–220.

Price, T. D. 1991. The Mesolithic of northern Europe. *Annual Review of Anthropology* 20, 211–233.

Price, T. D., R. A. Bentley, J. Lüning, D. Gronenborn, and J. Wahl 2001. Prehistoric human migration in the Linearbandkeramik of central Europe. *Antiquity* 75, 593–603.

Price, T. D., G. Grupe, and P. Schröter 1998. Migration in the Bell Beaker period of central Europe. *Antiquity* 72, 405–411.

Probst, E. 1991. *Deutschland in der Steinzeit*. Munich: Bertelsmann.

Quintana-Murci, L., O. Semino, H. J. Bandelt, G. Passarino, K. McElreavy, and A. S. Santachiara-Benerecetti 1999. Genetic evidence for an early exit of Homo sapiens sapiens from Africa through eastern Africa. *Nature Genetics* 23, 437–441.

Radcliffe-Richards, J. 2000. *Human Nature After Darwin*. London: Routledge.

Ramenofsky, A. 1998a. Evolutionary theory and the Native American record of artifact replacement. In J. G. Cusick (ed.), *Studies in Culture Contact: Interaction, Culture Change and Archaeology*, pp. 77–101. Carbondale, Illinois: Center for Archaeological Investigations, Southern Illinois University.

—— 1998b. Comment on, Is it evolution yet? A critique of evolutionary archaeology, by J. L. Boone and E. A. Smith. *Current Anthropology* 39, S164–165.

Rappaport, R. 1968. *Pigs for the Ancestors*. New Haven: Yale University Press.

Rega, E. 1997. Age, gender and biological reality in the Early Bronze Age cemetery at Mokrin. In J. Moore and E. Scott (eds.), *Invisible People and Processes: Writing Gender and Childhood into European Archaeology*, pp. 229–247. Leicester: Leicester University Press.

Relethford, J. H. 1995. Genetics and modern human origins. *Evolutionary Anthropology* 4, 53–63.

Renfrew, C. 1972. *The Emergence of Civilisation: The Cyclades and the Aegean in the Third Millennium BC*. London: Methuen.

—— 1974. Beyond a subsistence economy: the evolution of social organisation in prehistoric Europe. In C. B. Moore (ed.), *Reconstructing Complex Societies: An Archaeological Colloquium*, pp. 69–96. (Supplement to the Bulletin of the American Schools of Oriental Research No. 20). Chicago: American Schools of Oriental Research.

—— 1976. Megaliths, territories and populations. In S. J. De Laet (ed.), *Acculturation and Continuity in Atlantic Europe* (Dissertationes Archaeologicae Gandenses XVI), pp. 298–320. Brugge: De Tempel.

—— 1987. *Archaeology and Language: The Puzzle of Indo-European Origins*. London: Jonathan Cape.

Renfrew, C. and K. Boyle (eds.) 2000. *Archaeogenetics: DNA and the population history of Europe*, pp. 3–12. Cambridge: McDonald Institute for Archaeological Research.

Renfrew, C. and J. F. Cherry (eds.) 1986. *Peer Polity Interaction and Sociopolitical Change*. Cambridge: Cambridge University Press.

Richards, M. 2001. Comment on J. Terrell, *et al.*, Foregone conclusions? In search of 'Papuans' and 'Austronesians'. *Current Anthropology* 42, 117–118.

Richards, M., H. Corte-Real, P. Forster, V. Macaulay, H. Wilkinson-Herbots, A. Demaine, S. Papiha, R. Hedges, H. J. Bandelt, and B. Sykes 1996. Palaeolithic and Neolithic lineages in the European mitochondrial gene pool. *American Journal of Human Genetics* 59, 185–203.

Richerson, P. J. and R. Boyd 1999. The evolutionary dynamics of a crude super organism. *Human Nature* 10, 253–289.

Richerson, P. J., R. Boyd, and R. L. Bettinger 2001. Was agriculture impossible during the Pleistocene but mandatory during the Holocene? A climate change hypothesis. *American Antiquity* 66, 387–412.

Riches, D. 1992. Shamanism: the key to religion. *Man* (n.s.) 29, 381–405.

Ridley, M. 1996. *The Origins of Virtue: Human Instinctions and the Evolution of Cooperation*. London: Viking.

—— 1999. *Genome: The Autobiography of a Species*. London: Fourth Estate.

Rivers, W. H. R. 1926. *Psychology and Ethnology*. London: Kegan Paul, Trench, Trubner.

Robb, J. 1994. Gender contradictions, moral coalitions and inequality in prehistoric Italy. *Journal of European Archaeology* 2, 20–49.

—— 1997. Violence and gender in early Italy. In D. Martin and D. Frayer (eds.), *Troubled*

Times: Violence and Warfare in the Past, pp. 111–144. Toronto: Gordon and Breach.

Rogers, A. R. 1995. For love or money: the evolution of reproductive and material motivations. In R. Dunbar (ed.), *Human Reproductive Decisions*, pp. 76–95. London: Macmillan.

—— 2000. On equifinality in faunal analysis. *American Antiquity* 65, 709–723.

Rogers, A. R. and L. B. Jorde 1995. Genetic evidence on modern human origins. *Human Biology* 67, 1–36.

Romney, A. K. 1957. The genetic model and Uto-Aztecan time perspective. *Davidson Journal of Anthropology* 3, 35–41.

Rosenberg, M. 1994. Pattern, process and hierarchy in the evolution of culture. *Journal of Anthropological Archaeology* 13, 307–340.

Ross, M. 1997. Social networks and kinds of speech–community event. In R. Blench and M. Spriggs (eds.), *Archaeology and Language I: Theoretical and Methodological Orientations*, pp. 209–261. London: Routledge.

Rowlands, M. J. 1979. Local and long-distance trade and incipient state formation on the Bamenda Plateau in the late-19th century. *Paideuma* 25, 1–19.

Ruddle, K. 1993. The transmission of traditional ecological knowledge. In J. Inglis (ed.), *Traditional Ecological Knowledge: Concepts and Cases*, pp. 17–31. Canadian Museum of Nature.

Ruff, C. and A. C. Walker 1993. Body size and shape. In A. C. Walker and R. E. Leakey (eds.), *The Nariokotome Skeleton*, pp. 234–265. Cambridge, Mass: Harvard University Press.

Rushforth, S. and J. S. Chisholm 1991. *Cultural Persistence: Continuity in Meaning and Moral Responsibility among Bearlake Athabascans*. Tucson: University of Arizona Press.

Russon, A. E. 1997. Exploiting the expertise of others. In A. Whiten and R. W. Byrne (eds.), *Machiavellian Intelligence II*, pp. 174–206. Cambridge: Cambridge University Press.

Sahlins, M. 1972. *Stone Age Economics*. New York: Aldine.

—— 1976. *The Use and Abuse of Biology*. Ann Arbor: University of Michigan Press.

Sattenspiel, L. R. and H. C. Harpending 1983. Stable populations and skeletal age. *American Antiquity* 48, 489–498.

Scarre, C. 2001. Modeling prehistoric populations: the case of Neolithic Brittany. *Journal of Anthropological Archaeology* 20, 285–313.

Schibler, J., S. Jacomet, H. Hüster-Plogmann, and C. Brombacher 1997. Economic crash in the 37th and 36th centuries cal. BC in

Neolithic lake shore sites in Switzerland. *Anthropozoologica* 25–26, 553–570.

Schulting, R. J. and M. P. Richards 2001. Dating women and becoming farmers: new palaeodietary and AMS dating evidence from the Breton Mesolithic cemeteries of Téviec and Hoëdic. *Journal of Anthropological Archaeology* 20, 314–344.

Seielstad, M.T., E. Minch, and L. L. Cavalli-Sforza 1998. Genetic evidence for a higher female migration rate in humans. *Nature Genetics* 20, 278–280.

Sellen, D. W., M. Borgerhoff-Mulder, and D.F. Sieff 2000. Fertility, offspring quality, and wealth in Datoga pastoralists: testing evolutionary models of intersexual selection. In L. Cronk, N. Chagnon, and W. Irons (eds.), *Adaptation and Human Behavior*, pp. 91–114. New York: Aldine de Gruyter.

Sellen, D. W. and R. Mace 1997. Fertility and mode of subsistence: a phylogenetic analysis. *Current Anthropology* 38, 878–889.

Semino, O., G. Passarino, P. J. Oefner, A. A. Lin, S. Arbuzova, L. E. Beckman, G. De Benedictis, P. Francalacci, A. Kouvatsi, S. Limborska, M. Marcikiae, A. Mika, B. Mika, D. Primorac, A. S. Santachiara-Benerecetti, L. L. Cavalli-Sforza, and P. Underhill 2000. The genetic legacy of Palaeolithic Homo sapiens in extant Europeans: a Y chromosome perspective. *Science* 290, 1155–1159.

Service, E. R. 1962. *Primitive Social Organisation: An Evolutionary Perspective*. New York: Random House.

Shanks, M. and C. Tilley 1987. *Re-constructing Archaeology: Theory and Practice*. Cambridge: Cambridge University Press.

Shennan, S. E. 1975. The social organisation at Branč. *Antiquity* 49, 279–288.

Shennan, S. J. 1977. The appearance of the Bell Beaker assemblage in Central Europe. In R. Mercer (ed.), *Beakers in Britain and Europe*, pp. 51–70. Oxford: British Archaeological Reports.

—— 1978. Archaeological 'cultures': an empirical investigation. In I. Hodder (ed.), *The Spatial Organisation of Culture*, pp. 113–139. London: Duckworth.

—— 1989a. Introduction. In S. J. Shennan (ed.), *Archaeological Approaches to Cultural Identity*, pp. 1–32. London: Unwin Hyman.

—— 1989b. Archaeology as archaeology or anthropology? Clarke's Analytical Archaeology and the Binfords' New Perspectives in Archaeology 21 years on. *Antiquity* 63, 831–835.

—— 1993a. After social evolution: a new archaeological agenda? In N. Yoffee and A. G. Sherratt (eds.), *Archaeological Theory: Who*

Sets the Agenda? pp. 53–59. Cambridge:
Cambridge University Press.
—— 1993b. Settlement and society in Central
Europe 3500–1500 BC. *Journal of World
Prehistory* 7, 121–161.
—— 1996. Social inequality and the
transmission of cultural traditions in forager
societies. In J. Steele and S. J. Shennan (eds.),
*The Archaeology of Human Ancestry: Power,
Sex and Tradition*, pp. 365–379. London:
Routledge.
—— 1998. Producing copper in the eastern
Alps in the second millennium BC. In B.
Knapp, V. Pigott, and E. Herbert (eds.), *Social
Approaches to an Industrial Past*, pp. 191–204.
London: Routledge.
—— 1999. Cost, benefit and value in the
organization of early European copper
production. *Antiquity* 73, 352–363.
—— 2001. Demography and cultural
innovation: a model and some implications for
the emergence of modern human culture.
Cambridge Archaeological Journal 11.1, 5–16.
—— in press. Analytical Archaeology. In J.
Bintliff (ed.), *The Companion Encyclopaedia of
Archaeology*. Oxford: Blackwell.
Shennan, S. J. and J. Steele 1999. Cultural
learning in hominids: a behavioural ecological
approach. In H. O. Box and K. R. Gibson
(eds.), *Mammalian Social Learning:
Comparative and Ecological Perspectives*, pp.
367–388. Cambridge: Cambridge University
Press.
Shennan, S. J. and J. R. Wilkinson 2001.
Ceramic style change and neutral evolution: a
case study from Neolithic Europe. *American
Antiquity* 66, 577–593.
Sherratt, A. G. 1981. Plough and pastoralism:
aspects of the secondary products revolution.
In I. Hodder, G. Isaac, and N. Hammond
(eds.), *Pattern of the Past*, pp. 261–305.
Cambridge: Cambridge University Press.
Sherry, S. T., A. R. Rogers, H. C. Harpending,
H. Soodyall, T. Jenkins, and M. Stoneking
1994. Mismatch distributions of mtDNA
reveal recent human population expansions.
Human Biology 66, 761–75.
Shott, M. 1992. On recent trends in the
anthropology of foragers: Kalahari
revisionism and its archaeological
implications, *Man* (N.S.) 27, 843–871.
Sims-Williams, P. 1998. Genetics, linguistics
and prehistory: thinking big and thinking
straight. *Antiquity* 72, 505–527.
Skyrms, B. 1996. *Evolution of the Social
Contract*. Cambridge: Cambridge University
Press.
Slaus, M. 2000. Biocultural analysis of sex
differences in mortality profiles and stress

levels in the late medieval population from
Nova Raa, Croatia. *American Journal of
Physical Anthropology* 111, 193–209.
Smith, E.A. 1991. *Inujjuamiut Foraging
Strategies: Evolutionary Ecology of an Arctic
Hunting Economy*. New York: Aldine de
Gruyter.
—— 2000. Three styles in the evolutionary
analysis of human behaviour. In L. Cronk, N.
Chagnon, and W. Irons (eds.), *Adaptation and
Human Behaviour*, pp. 27–46. New York:
Aldine de Gruyter.
Smith, E.A. and B. Winterhalder 1992. Natural
selection and decision making: some
fundamental principles. In E. A. Smith and B.
Winterhalder (eds.), *Evolutionary Ecology and
Human Behavior*, pp. 25–60. New York:
Aldine de Gruyter.
Smuts, B. 1999. Multilevel selection,
cooperation, and altruism. *Human Nature* 10,
311–327.
Sober, E. and D. S. Wilson 1998. *Unto Others:
The Evolution and Psychology of Unselfish
Behavior*. Cambridge, Mass: Harvard
University Press.
Sofaer Derevenski, J. R. 2000. Sex differences in
activity-related osseous change in the spine
and the gendered division of labor at Ensay
and Wharram Percy, UK. *American Journal of
Physical Anthropology* 111, 333–354.
Soltis, J., R. Boyd, and P. Richerson 1995. Can
group-functional behaviours evolve by
cultural group selection? An empirical test.
Current Anthropology 36: 473–493.
Sørensen, M. L. S. 1997. Reading dress: the
construction of social categories and
identities in Bronze Age Europe. *Journal of
European Archaeology* 5, 93–114.
—— 2000. *Gender Archaeology*. Cambridge:
Polity Press.
Sperber, D. 1996. *Explaining Culture: A
Naturalistic Approach*. Oxford: Blackwell.
Steadman, D. 1995. Prehistoric extinctions of
Pacific island birds: biodiversity meets
zooarchaeology. *Science* 267, 1123–1131.
Stearns, S. 1992. *The Evolution of Life Histories*.
Oxford: Oxford University Press.
Stehli, P. 1994. Chronologie der Bandkeramik
im Merzbachtal. In J. Lüning and P. Stehli
(eds.), *Die Bandkeramik im Merzbachtal auf
der Aldenhovener Platte*, pp. 79–192. Bonn:
Habelt.
Steward, J. H. 1936a. The economic and social
basis of primitive bands. In R. H. Lowie (ed.),
*Essays in Anthropology Presented to Alfred
Louis Kroeber*, pp. 331–350. Berkeley:
University of California Press.
—— 1936b. Shoshoni polyandry. *American
Anthropologist* 38, 561–564.

—— 1938. *Basin Plateau Aboriginal Sociopolitical Groups*. Bureau of American Ethnology Bulletin 120. Washington DC.

—— 1955. *Theory of Culture Change*. Urbana: University of Illinois Press.

Stiner M. C., N. D. Munro, and T. A. Surovell 2000. The tortoise and the hare – small-game use, the broad-spectrum revolution, and paleolithic demography. *Current Anthropology* 41, 39–73.

Stone G. D. and C. E. Downum 1999. Non-Boserupian ecology and agricultural risk: ethnic politics and land control in the arid southwest. *American Anthropologist* 101, 113–128.

Strassmann, B. I. 2000. Polygyny, family structure and child mortality: a prospective study among the Dogon of Mali. In L. Cronk, N. Chagnon, and W. Irons (eds.), *Adaptation and Human Behavior*, pp. 49–68. New York: Aldine de Gruyter.

Sugiyama, L. S. and R. Chacon 2000. Effects of illness and injury on foraging among the Yora and Shiwiar. In L. Cronk, N. Chagnon, and W. Irons (eds.), *Adaptation and Human Behavior*, pp. 371–396. New York: Aldine de Gruyter.

Suttles, W. 1968. Coping with abundance: subsistence on the northwest coast. In R. B. Lee and I. DeVore (eds.), *Man the Hunter*, pp. 56–68. Chicago: Aldine.

Tainter, J. A. 1988. *The Collapse of Complex Societies*. Cambridge: Cambridge University Press.

Terrell, J. E., T. L. Hunt, and C. Gosden 1997. The dimensions of social life in the Pacific: human diversity and the myth of the primitive isolate. *Current Anthropology* 38, 155–196.

Teschler-Nicola, M., F. Gerold, M. Bujatti-Narbeshuber, T. Prohaska, Ch.Latkoczy, G. Stingeder, and M. Watkins 1999. Evidence of genocide 7000 BP – Neolithic paradigm and geo-climatic reality. *Coll. Antropol.* 23, 437–450.

Thornhill, R. and A. P. Møller 1998. The relative importance of size and asymmetry in sexual selection. *Behavioral Ecology* 9, 546–551.

Treherne, P. 1995. The warrior's beauty: the masculine body and self-identity in Bronze Age Europe. *Journal of European Archaeology* 3.1, 105–144.

Trigger, B. G. 1989. *A History of Archaeological Thought*. Cambridge: Cambridge University Press.

—— 1998. *Sociocultural Evolution*. Oxford: Blackwell.

Trivers, R. L. 1971. The evolution of reciprocal altruism. *Quarterly Review of Biology* 46, 35–57.

—— 1972. Parental investment and sexual selection. In B. Campbell (ed.), *Sexual Selection and the Descent of Man*, pp. 139–179. Chicago: Aldine.

Trivers, R. L. and D. E. Willard 1973. Natural selection of parental ability to vary the sex ratio. *Science* 179, 90–92.

Tschauner, H. 1994. Archaeological systematics and cultural evolution: retrieving the honour of culture history. *Man* 29, 77–93.

Tyldesley, J. 1986. *The Wolvercote Channel Handaxe Assemblage: A Comparative Study*. Oxford: BAR British Series 153.

Tylor, E. B. 1888. On a method of investigating the development of institutions, applied to laws of marriage and descent. *Journal of the Anthropological Institute* 18, 245–272.

Van Andel, T. H. and C. N. Runnels 1995. The earliest farmers in Europe. *Antiquity* 69, 481–500.

Vandkilde, H. 1996. *From Stone to Bronze: The Metalwork of the Late Neolithic and Earliest Bronze Age in Denmark*. Moesgard, Aarhus: Jutland Archaeological Society.

Vita-Finzi, C. and E.S. Higgs. 1970. Prehistoric economy in the Mount Carmel area of Palestine: site catchment analysis. *Proceedings of the Prehistoric Society* 36, 1–37.

Voland, E. 1995. Reproductive decisions viewed from an evolutionarily informed historical demography. In R. Dunbar (ed.), *Human Reproductive Decisions – Biological and Social Perspectives*, pp. 137–159. London: Macmillan.

—— 1998. Evolutionary ecology of human reproduction. *Annual Review of Anthropology* 27, 347–374.

Wahl, J. and H. G. König 1987. Anthropologisch–traumatologische Untersuchung der menschlichen Skelettreste aus dem bandkeramischen Massengrab bei Talheim, Kreis Heilbronn. *Fundberichte aus Baden-Württemberg* 12, 65–193.

Walker, P. L. 2001. A bioarchaeological perspective on the history of violence. *Annual Review of Anthropology* 30, 573–596.

Warnier, J. P. 1985. *Bamenda Précolonial*. Paris: Thèse de Doctorat d'État.

Wels-Weyrauch, U. 1978. *Die Anhänger und Halsringe in Südwestdeutschland und Nordbayern*. Munich: C. H. Beck.

—— 1991. *Die Anhänger in Südbayern*. Stuttgart: Franz Steiner.

White, L. A. 1949. *The Science of Culture: A Study of Man and Civilization*. New York: Farrar, Straus.

Whitehead, H. 1998. Cultural selection and

genetic diversity of matrilineal whales. *Science* 282, 1708–1711.

Whitehouse, H. 1996. Jungles and computers: neuronal group selection and the epidemiology of representations. *Journal of the Royal Anthropological Institute* 2, 99–116.

Whiten, A. 1999. Parental encouragement in Gorilla in comparative perspective: implications for social cognition and the evolution of teaching. In S. T. Parker, R. W. Mitchell, and H. L. Miles (eds.), *The Mentalities of Gorillas and Chimpanzees in Comparative Perspective*, pp. 342–366. Cambridge: Cambridge University Press.

—— 2000. Primate culture and social learning. *Cognitive Science* 24, 477–508.

Whiten, A., J. Goodall, W. C. McGrew, T. Nishida, V. Reynolds, Y. Sugiyama, C. E. G. Tutin, R. W. Wrangham, and C. Boesch 1999. Cultures in chimpanzees. *Nature* 399, 682–685.

Whiten, A. and R. Ham 1992. On the nature and evolution of imitation in the animal kingdom: reappraisal of a century of research. In P. J. B. Slater, J. S. Rosenblatt, C. Beer, and M. Milinski (eds.), *Advances in the Study of Behaviour*, pp. 239–283. San Diego: Academic Press.

Whitley, D. 1994. By the hunter, for the gatherer: art, social relations and subsistence change in the prehistoric Great Basin. *World Archaeology* 25, 356–373.

Wiessner, P. and A. Tumu 1998. *Historical Vines: Enga Networks of Exchange, Ritual and Warfare in Papua New Guinea*. Washington DC: Smithsonian Institution Press.

Wilkinson, G. S. 1984. Reciprocal food sharing in the vampire bat. *Nature* 308, 181–184.

Williams, G. C. 1992. *Natural Selection: Domains, Levels and Challenges*. Oxford: Oxford University Press.

Wilmsen, E. N. 1989. *Land Filled with Flies: A Political Economy of the Kalahari*. Chicago: University of Chicago Press.

Wilmsen, E. N. and J. R. Denbow 1990. Paradigmatic history of San-speaking peoples and current attempts at revision. *Current Anthropology* 31, 489–524.

Winterhalder, B. and C. Goland 1993. On population, foraging efficiency and plant domestication. *Current Anthropology* 34, 710–715.

Winterhalder, B., W. Baillargeon, and F. Cappelletto 1988. The population ecology of hunter-gathers and their prey. *Journal of Anthropological Archaeology* 7, 289–328.

Wolf, C. 1993. *Die Seeufersiedlung Yverdon Avenue des Sports. Eine kulturgeschichtliche und chronologische Studie zum Endneolithikum der Westschweiz und angrenzender Gebiete*. Lausanne: Cahiers d'Archéologie Romande.

Wood, D., J. S. Bruner, and G. Ross 1976. The role of tutoring in problem-solving. *Journal of Child Psychology and Psychiatry* 17, 89–100.

Wood, J. W. 1998. A theory of preindustrial population dynamics – demography, economy, and well-being in Malthusian systems. *Current Anthropology* 39, 99–135.

Wotzka, H. P. 1997. Maßstabsprobleme bei der ethnischen Deutung neolithischer 'Kulturen'. *Das Altertum* 43, 163–176.

Wrangham, R. W. 1999. Evolution of coalitionary killing. *Yearbook of Physical Anthropology* 42, 1–30.

Wright, S. 1939. Statistical genetics in relation to evolution. *Actualités Scientifiques et Industrielles* 802, 37–60. Paris: Hermann.

Wrigley, E. A. 1983. The growth of population in 18th-century England: a conundrum resolved. *Past and Present* 98, 121–150.

Wynne-Edwards, V. C. 1962. *Animal Dispersion in Relation to Social Behaviour*. Oxford: Blackwell.

Young, H. P. 1998. *Individual Strategy and Social Structure*. Princeton: Princeton University Press.

Young, R. L. 2000. A comparison of Kalasha and Kho subsistence patterns in Chitral NWFP, Pakistan. *South Asian Studies* 16, 133–142.

Zahavi, A. 1975. Mate selection – a selection for a handicap. *Journal of Theoretical Biology* 53, 205–214.

Zentall, T. R. and B. G. Galef (eds.) 1988. *Social Learning: Psychological and Biological Perspectives*. Hillsdale, New Jersey: Lawrence Erlbaum.

Zilhão, J. 2000. From the Mesolithic to the Neolithic in the Iberian peninsula. In T. D. Price (ed.), *Europe's First Farmers*, pp. 144–182. Cambridge: Cambridge University Press.

Zimmermann, A. 1995. *Austauschsysteme von Silexartefakten in der Bandkeramik Mitteleuropas*. Bonn: Habelt.

Zvelebil, M. 1996. The agricultural frontier and the transition to agriculture in the circum-Baltic region. In D. R. Harris (ed.), *The Origins and Spread of Agriculture and Pastoralism in Eurasia*, pp. 323–335. London: UCL Press.

ACKNOWLEDGMENTS

I must start by thanking Peter Ucko, Director of the Institute of Archaeology, University College London, for granting me the sabbatical year that made it possible to write this book, but also for his advice, help and support in all sorts of ways over many years. Cyprian Broodbank, Mark Collard, Gabrielle Delbarre, Amanda Giles, Kate Gregory, Clare Holden and Marek Kohn were kind enough to read the manuscript and make many helpful comments. Without their assistance the book would have been much worse than it is. The same is true for the comments provided by Andrew Sherratt and Chris Scarre, who read the manuscript for Thames & Hudson. James Steele has been a continuing source of stimulating evolutionary conversation. Sam Bowles dispelled some of my ignorance about institutional economics as well as pointing out some of the inconsistencies in my argument and inviting me to a workshop at the Santa Fe Institute where I learned a great deal. The British Academy provided the financial support which enabled me to collect the European Neolithic lake-village information which plays an important role at many points in the argument. I'm very grateful to Sue, Sophie and Henry Shennan for their indispensable help and encouragement over the many years of gestation of my evolutionary ideas. Lúcia Nagib provided critical comments and invaluable support.

In conclusion, I wish to acknowledge two sources of inspiration: Rob Boyd and Pete Richerson for their insights and achievements as well as their help and encouragement, and my Archaeology and Anthropology colleagues at UCL, especially the members of the AHRB Centre for the Evolutionary Analysis of Cultural Behaviour for the excitement of being able to work with them on evolutionary issues.

SOURCES OF ILLUSTRATIONS

The line illustrations listed below are redrawn from the following published sources.

1. Krebs and Davies 1993, fig. 3.2
2. Kaplan et al. 2000, fig. 3, reproduced by permission of Wiley-Liss, Inc., a subsidiary of John Wiley and Sons, Inc.
3. Ruddle 1993, table 1.
4. Hewlett and Cavalli-Sforza 1986, reproduced by permission of the American Anthropological Association from *American Anthropologist* 88(4).
5. Probst 1991.
6. Clarke 1968, figs. 38 and 46.
7. Neiman 1995, fig. 2.
8. Frirdich 1994, with permission of R. Habelt Publishers.
9. Ortman 2000, figs. 12 and 16.
10. Kroeber 1931.
11. Pétrequin 1993.
12. Pétrequin 1993.
13. Gray and Jordan 2000, fig. 1, reprinted by permission from *Nature* 405, 1052-1055 copyright 2000. Macmillan Publishers Ltd.
14. Gray and Jordan 2000, fig. 2.
15. Kaplan et al. 2000, fig. 10, reproduced by permission of Wiley-Liss, Inc., a subsidiary of John Wiley and Sons, Inc.
16. Kaplan et al. 2000, fig. 1

reproduced by permission of Wiley-Liss, Inc., a subsidiary of John Wiley and Sons, Inc.
19. Rogers 1992, figs. 12.3 and 12.5, reproduced with permission from E.A. Smith and B. Winterhalder. *Evolutionary Ecology and Human Behavior* (New York: Aldine de Gruyter). Copyright © 1992 Walter de Gruyter, Inc., New York.
20. Keckler 1997, fig. 11.1 and 11.2, redrawn with permission; copyright Board of Trustees, Southern Illinois University.
21. Kalis and Zimmermann 1997.
22. David and Lourandos 1998, fig. 2.
23. Pétrequin and Pétrequin 1999, fig. 17.
24. Neiman 1995, fig. 1.
25. Billamboz 1995.
26. Pétrequin 1996, fig. 11.
27. Pétrequin et al. 1999.
28. Pétrequin et al. 1999.
29. Kaplan and Hill 1992, figs. 6.1 and 6.2, reprinted with permission from E.A. Smith and B. Winterhalder. *Evolutionary Ecology and Human Behavior* (New York: Aldine de Gruyter). Copyright © 1992 Walter de Gruyter, Inc., New York.
30. Janetski 1997, fig. 3,

reproduced by permission of Academic Press.
31. Broughton 1997, reproduced by permission of J.M. Broughton and Antiquity Publications Ltd.
32. Schibler et al. 1997, with permission of Prof. J. Schibler.
33. Schibler et al. 1997, figs. 4 and 5, with permission of Prof. J. Schibler.
34. Pétrequin et al. 1998, fig. 5.
35. Cartoon by Anne Gibbons.
36. Tyldesley 1986, fig. 2.4.
37. Nicolis 1998, Gallay and Chaix 1984, foldouts 6, 7.
38. Wels-Weyrauch 1978, 1991.
39. Foley and Lee 1996, fig. 1.3.
40. Mace 1997, fig. 3, used with permission of The Royal Society and the author.
41. Hayden 1997, fig. 2.
42. Cauvin 2000, plate 7, by permission of Cambridge University Press.
43. Wahl and König 1987, with permission of Dr. J. Wahl.
44. Stehli 1994, with permission of R. Habelt Publishers.
45. Shennan and Wilkinson 2001, fig. 4.
46. Kemenczei 1991, Vandkilde 1996.
47. Flannery and Marcus 2000, fig. 22.

INDEX